The Scrapbook of
OLD TOM MORRIS

COMPILED *by* DAVID JOY

Sleeping Bear Press

Sleeping Bear Press
310 North Main Street
P.O. Box 20
Chelsea, MI 48118
www.sleepingbearpress.com

Printed and bound in Canada

10 9 8 7 6 5 4 3 2 1

Library of Congress Cataloging-in-Publication Data
Morris, Old Tom, 1821-1908.
The scrapbook of Old Tom Morris / [compiled] by David Joy.
p. cm.
ISBN 1-886947-45-7
Morris, Old Tom, 1821-1908. 2. Golfers—Scotland—Biography. I. Joy, David. II. Title.

GV964.M65 A3 2001
796.352'092—dc21
[B]
2001040090

INTRODUCTION

DURING THE WEEK of the 1990 Open Championship, the Byre Theatre in St. Andrews, Scotland, premiered David Joy's one-man show on the life of Tom Morris. Aged forty at the time, David played "Old Tom" at age 86 as he reflected on his life as the Grand Old Man of Golf. One of his preparations for the show was to put together a scrapbook just as Old Tom might have done it.

"Like a Bible to me, this book," 'Old Tom' told the audience during the show, "full of cuttings of all the early spring and autumn Meetings of the Royal and Ancient, the grand tournaments, the great matches...memories just flood back. I've played golf close on 80 years and that's more than most folks get to live! It's the one thing I have left for my future: time to be thinking about my past."

The original scrapbook that David used for the stage play was very much a theatre prop. But when Prince Andrew showed a keen interest in the scrapbook after attending the one-man performance, it gave David the idea to elaborate on it and compile a proper one that would be suitable for publication. Thanks to the encouragement of Wally Uhlein at the Acushnet Company (Titleist) and Sleeping Bear Press, this has been accomplished.

This scrapbook takes the reader through all of the dramatic changes that shaped the game, from the first mention of Old Tom in a local newspaper in 1842 to the national tributes and proposed memorials to him following his death in 1908. It also covers Tom's close association with Allan Robertson (the world's first golf professional), his four victories in the Open Championship, and the four Open wins and tragic death of his son "Young Tom." To be sure, golf fans and golf authorities alike will learn a great deal from *The Scrapbook of Old Tom Morris*.

The Scrapbook

TOM MORRIS
GOLF CLUB AND
BALL MANUFACTURER

Myself 1857

Tom Morris

ST MARY'S STUDIO
ST ANDREWS N.B

1

REGULATIONS

FOR THE

GAME of GOLF,

ADOPTED BY THE

ST. ANDREW'S SOCIETY OF GOLFERS,

At their Meeting, Friday 1st May, 1812.

I

The Balls must be teed not nearer the hole than two Club lengths nor further from it than four.

II

The Ball furthest from the hole must be played first.

III

The Ball struck from the tee must not be changed before the hole is played out, and if the parties are at a loss to know the one ball from the other, neither shall be lifted till both parties agree.

IV

STONES, Bones or any break-club within a Club-length of the Ball may be removed when the Ball lies on grass, but nothing can be removed if it lie on sand or in a bunker, if however it stick fast in the ground it may be removed.

V

If the Ball be in a Rabbit-scrape, the Player shall not be at liberty to take it out, but must play it as from any common hazard. If however it lie in one of the burrows, he may lift it, drop it behind the hazard and play with an iron without losing a stroke.

VI

If the Ball is half-covered or more with water, the Player may take it out, tee it and play from behind the hazard losing a stroke.

VII

If the Ball be in the supernumerary hole on the hole-across green, it may be dropped behind the hazard, and played with an Iron without losing a stroke.

VIII

When the Balls lie within six inches of one another, the Ball nearest the hole must be lifted till the other is played, but on the putting green it shall not be lifted, although within six inches unless it be directly between the other and the hole.

IX

Whatever happens to a Ball by accident must be reckoned a Rub of the green. If however the Player's Ball strike his adversary or his Cady, the adversary loses the hole: If it strike his own Cady, the Player loses the hole: If the Player strike his adversary's Ball with his club, the Player loses the hole.

X

If a Ball is lost, the stroke goes for nothing, the Player returns to the spot where the Ball was struck, tees it, and loses a stroke.

XI

If in striking, the club breaks, it is never-the-less to be accounted a stroke if the Player either strike the Ball or pass the Ball.

XII

In holing, you are not to place any mark to direct you to the hole. You are to play your Ball fairly and honestly for the hole and not on your adversary's Ball not lying in your way to the hole.

XIII

All loose impediments of whatever kind may be removed upon the putting green.

XIV

In all cases where a Ball is to be dropped, the party dropping shall front the hole to which he is playing and drop the Ball behind him over his head.

XV

When a Ball is completely covered with fog, bent, whin sic. as much thereof shall be set aside as that the player shall have a full view of his Ball before he plays.

XVI

When the Balls touch each other, one of them must be lifted till the other be played.

XVII

Any disputes respecting the play shall be determined by the Captain or the members present, and if none of the members are present, by the Captain and his annual council for the time.

The Royal and Ancient Golf Club
20th October, 1842

On Friday morning the inputs were played for by the caddies. These were gained by Tom Morris, junior, who holed the Links at 92 strokes; Thomas Morris, senior, at 99 and Alexander Herd at 103. Allan Robertson was prohibited by his brethern from competing for these stakes on account of his superior play, it being their impression that they would have no chance in any contest in which Allan took part.

← The first mention of my golf when still called Jnr! Allan and my father.

The old town crest

Left to right →
James Wilson. Willie Dunn. Bob Andrews
Willie Park Tom Morris Allan Robertson
"Daw" my caddie
and Bob Kirk

3

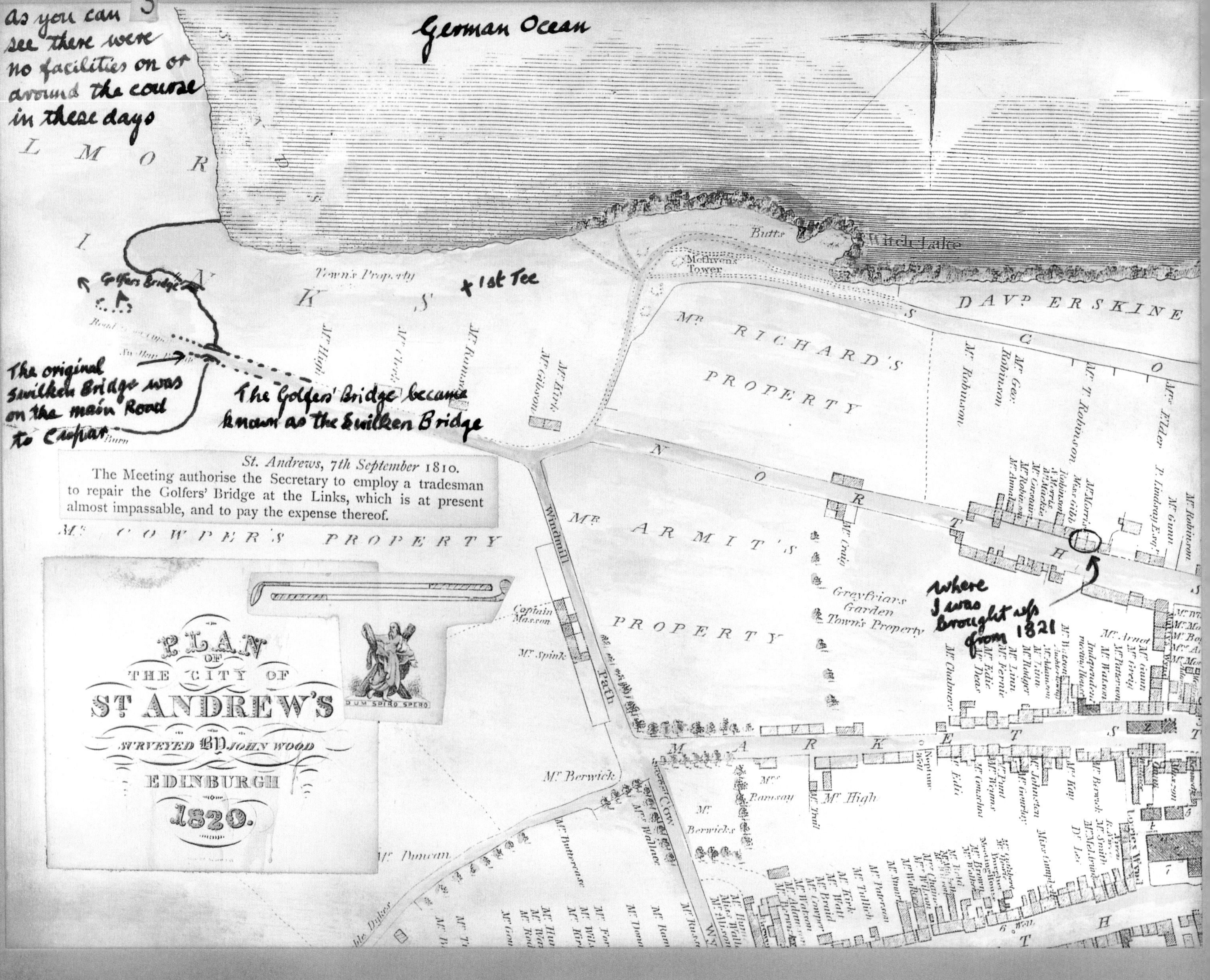
As you can see there were no facilities on or around the course in these days
German Ocean
Golfers Bridge
+ 1st Tee
The original Swilken Bridge was on the main Road to Cupar
The Golfers' Bridge became known as the Swilken Bridge
Where I was brought up from 1821
St. Andrews, 7th September 1810.
The Meeting authorise the Secretary to employ a tradesman to repair the Golfers' Bridge at the Links, which is at present almost impassable, and to pay the expense thereof.
Town's Property
Butts
Witch Lake
Methven's Tower
DAVD ERSKINE
MR RICHARD'S PROPERTY
MR ARMIT'S PROPERTY
MRS COWPER'S PROPERTY
Greyfriars Garden Town's Property
Windmill Path
N O R T H
M A R K E T
PLAN OF THE CITY OF ST ANDREW'S
SURVEYED BY JOHN WOOD
EDINBURGH
1820.
DUM SPIRO SPERO

St. Andrews, 4th May 1766.

We, the Noblemen and Gentlemen subscribing, Did this day agree to meet once every fortnight, by Eleven of the Clock, at the Golf House, and to play a round of the Links; to dine together at Bailie Glass', and to pay each a Shilling for his dinner,—the absent as well as the present.

The Club, taking into consideration that the Meetings have of late been thinly attended by the Members residing in town, in consequence of several Members giving parties on the ordinary days of meeting, and thereby preventing those who would otherwise give their presence at the Club from attending them,—Do Resolve that in future such Members as shall invite any of their friends, Members of this Club, to dinner on the days of meeting, shall forfeit to the Club a Magnum of Claret for himself, and one bottle for each Member so detained by them, for each offence, and the Captain and Council appoint this Resolution to be immediately communicated to General Campbell.

St. Andrews, 15*th September* 1786.

The Captain appoints the Silver Club to be played for on the 4th of October next. A Ball on Friday the 6th of October as usual.[1]

JOHN CHEAPE.

St. Andrews, 3*rd August* 1792.

It is proposed that a Fête Champêtre for the Ladies shall take place in the week of the October meeting. The Captain is instructed to give orders for the Room at Robertson's to be fitted up.

ALEX. DUNCAN, *Captain*.

St. Andrews, 3*rd October* 1806.

This day the Gold Medal was played for and gained by Walter Cook, Esq., Writer to the Signet, by holing the Links at 100 strokes.

St. Andrews, 3*rd September* 1796.

The Captain appoints the Silver Club to be played for on Wednesday the 5th day of October next. A Ball upon Friday as usual—the Secretary to obtain the Gows for the music if possible.

ALEX. ANDERSON.

Old St Andrews

St. Andrews, 3rd September 1767.

This day the Silver Club was played for, and gained by James Durham of Largo, Esq., by holing the Links at 94 strokes.[2]

WM. ST. CLAIR.

St. Andrews, 2nd October 1771.

This day a Gold Medal,[1] value Seven Guineas, given by the Society of Golfers, was played for by the gentlemen mentioned in the Book of Record of the Monthly Meetings, and gained by Mr. Beveridge by holing the Links at 101 strokes.

HENRY BETHUNE.

St. Andrews, 28th May 1773.

It is agreed that no person should be allowed to play for the Silver Cup to be given this year except members of either this or the Leith Society.

HENRY BETHUNE.

1856→

St. Andrews, 6th October 1773.

This day the Silver Cup (of Eight pounds value) was played for, and Mr. Arnot holed the Links at 105 strokes, but upon an objection made that he had transgressed the Rules by pulling back his ball, the Captain and Society appoint the Cup to be again played for on Friday next.

St. Andrews, 8th October 1773.

The Silver Cup[2] was this day played for and gained by Mr. Halket, by holing the Links at 114 strokes.

PAT. RIGG.

Course changed from 11 holes to 9 in 1764

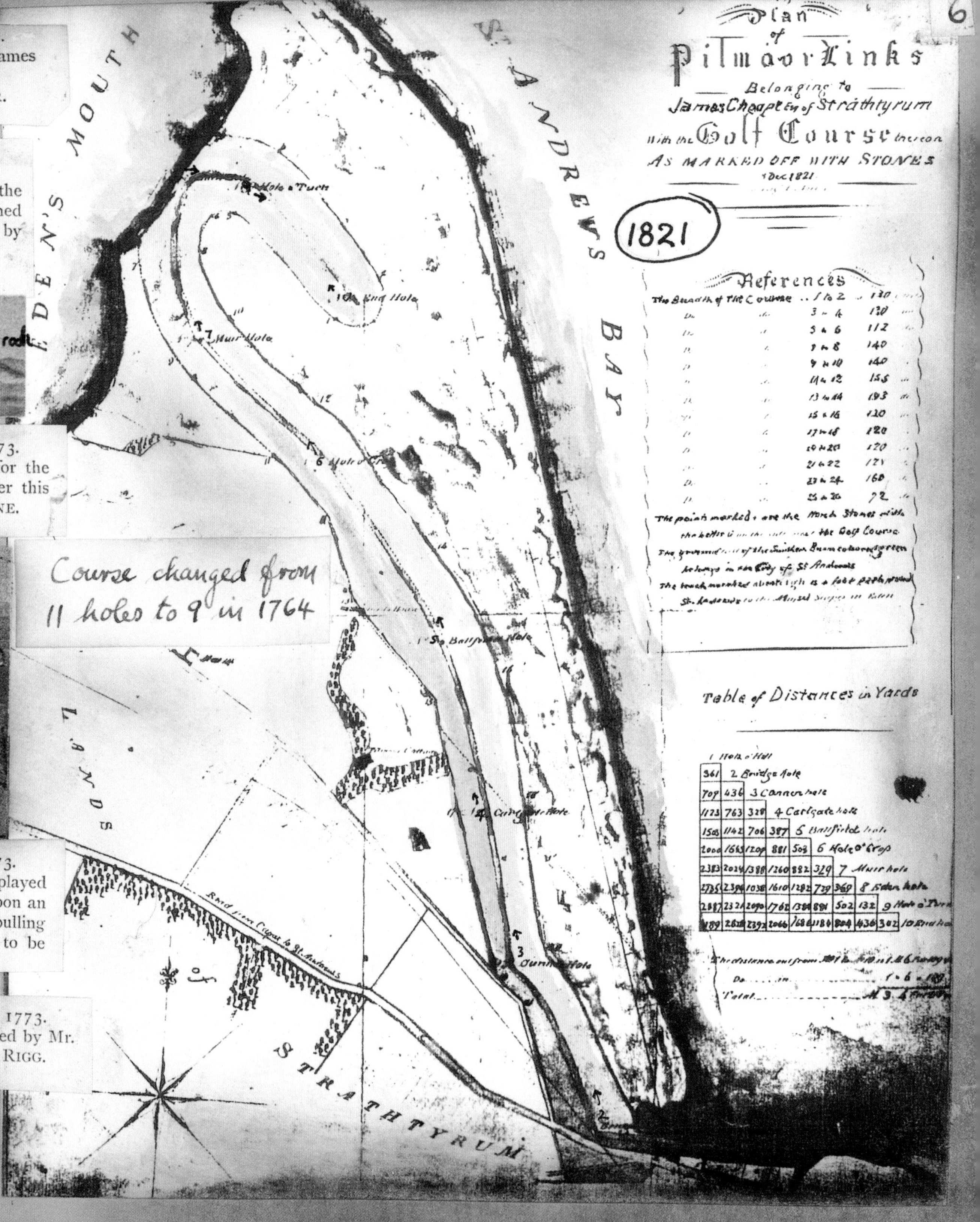

7

St. Andrews, 22nd October 1783.

Lord Balcarres, Mr. Durham, Mr. Anstruther, Mr. Sandilands, Mr. Cheape, and Captain Cheape, having engaged to dine here this day, and having neither come, nor sent, this meeting has decerned them to pay One Scotch Pint of Claret each at the first meeting they shall be present, under pains and penalties.

WM. MORISON, *Captain.*

St Andrews Links late 17th Century

1680s.

View from St Salvator's steeple
This photograph must have been taken when I was about 25 years old. →
As a wee boy - North Street was my Old Course! Gas lamps were the flags and with my first sawn-down cleek I'd whack chuckie stanes or wine corks down the road for hours on end.

SANCT ANDREWS.

St Andrews ! name unmeet for tuneful lay,
And all unapt the Bard for tuneful part—
Be his the task thy features to pourtray,
Thy every charm of nature and of art :
Thy bays, thy rocks, thy ruins that apart
Uplift their towers beneath the pale moon beam,
Thy Colleges that form the head and heart,
Professors, which those Colleges beseem,
Thy student, golfer-crew—a multifarious theme !

All here are golfers—strangers, natives, all
The sons of science, idleness, and war,
Who can or wield a club, or hit a ball,
Professor, soldier, student-lad, and tar,
And country laird, attracted from afar,
With some mischancy writer to engage ;
Whilst oft the rag, and spirit-chafing *jar*,
Provokes to sudden bet, and smothered rage,
Which twice another round will quietly assuage.

It is indeed a goodly sight to see
These red-coat champions marshalled for the fray,
Driving the ball o'er bunker, rut, and lea,
And clearing with imperious "fore," the way,
Enlivening still the game with laugh and say ;
Whilst trotting club-man follows fast behind,
Prepared with ready hand the "*tees*" to lay;
With nicest eye the devious ball to find,
And of the going game each player to remind.

It is in sooth a goodly sight to see,
By east and west, the Swilcan lasses clean,
Spreading their clothes upon the daised lea,
And skelping freely barefoot o'er the green,
With petticoats high kilted up I ween,
And note of jocund ribaldry most meet ;
From washing-tub their glowing limbs are seen
Veiled in an upward shower of dewy weet !
Oh ! 'tis enough to charge an anchorite with heat !

Galleons in the inner harbour 1848
This was a busy harbour in its day with horses and carts lined up.
Mostly with farm produce for short freighting runs – the trains have taken away a lot of that trade now.

St Salvators
North Street

Rock and Spindle
& Kinkell Braes

The School
Madras College

The Pends

West Port

Martyrs Monument

The Ladyhead fisher folk 1843

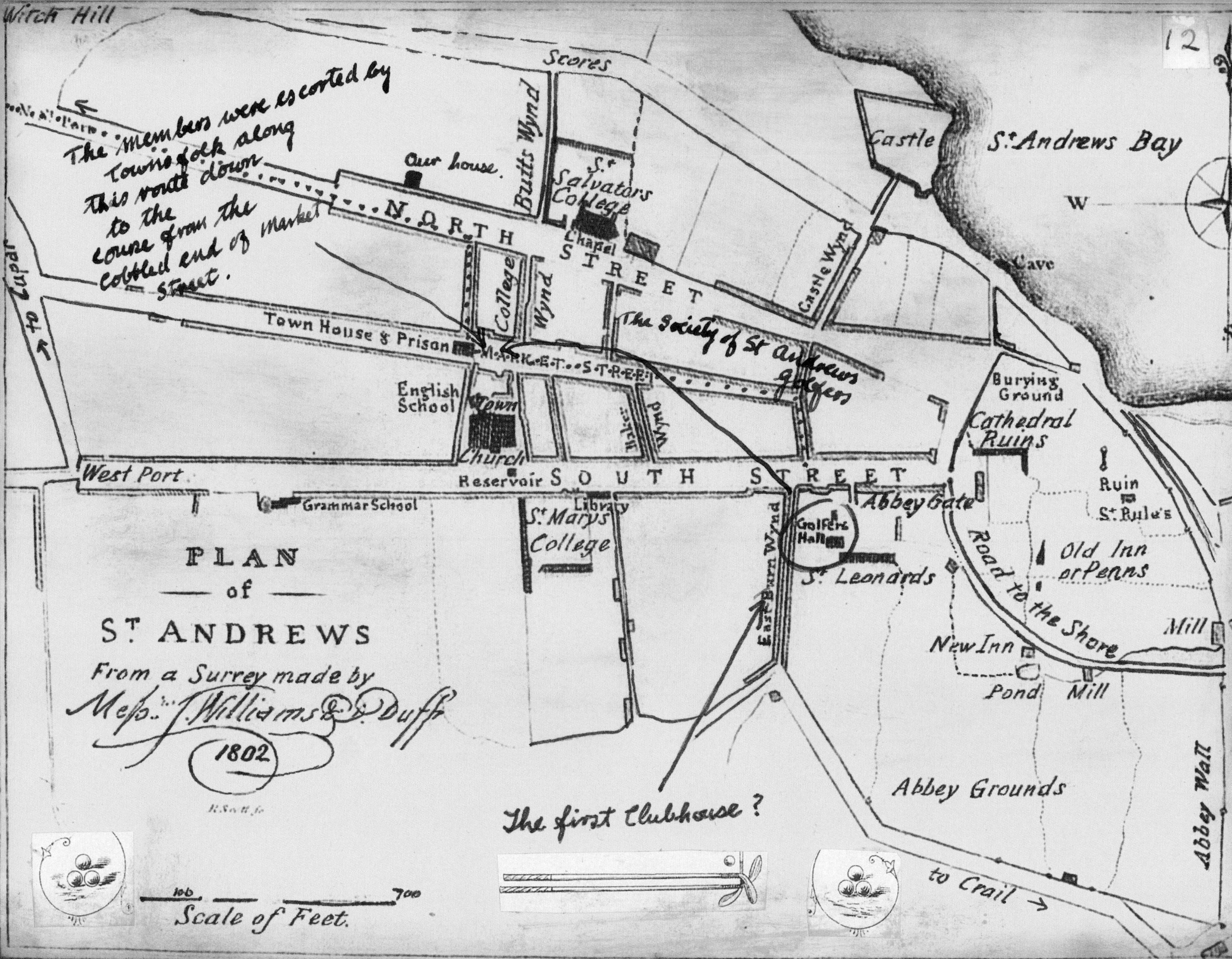
12
Witch Hill
Scores
Butts Wynd
Castle
St Andrews Bay
W
S
Our house.
St Salvators College
Chapel
NORTH STREET
College Wynd
Castle Wynd
Cave
Town House & Prison
MARKET STREET
English School
Town Church
Baker Wynd
Burying Ground
Cathedral Ruins
West Port
Reservoir
SOUTH STREET
Grammar School
Library
St Marys College
Abbey Gate
Golfers Hall
Ruin
St Rule's
Old Inn or Penns
St Leonards
East Burn Wynd
Road to the Shore
Mill
Quay
New Inn
Pond
Mill
Abbey Grounds
Abbey Wall
to Crail
PLAN of St ANDREWS
From a Surrey made by
Messrs. J. Williams & D. Duff
1802
100
700
Scale of Feet.
The members were escorted by townsfolk along this route down to the course from the cobbled end of Market Street.
The Society of St Andrews Golfers
The first Clubhouse ?

13

A Dutch print
Kolf – Kolven
– Was golf originally
from Holland?

MR. SAMUEL MESSIEUX,
(Who drove a ball 380 yards.)
with a feather ball

Here's Mr. Messieux, he's a noble player,
But something nervous, that's a bad affair;
He sadly spoils his putting when he's press'd,
But let him win, and he will beat the best.

Chambers' Journal DEC 1833 14

THE GAME OF GOLF.

In Scotland there prevail two sports for which there is hardly a parallel in the adjoining country: namely, golf and curling. The former is practised on commons, or any other kind of open grounds, it being only necessary that the grass should be very short. The chief implement is a club, called the golf, consisting of a long slender wand, and a loaded mass at the end, together with a small ball of leather, stuffed to great hardness with feathers, which is impelled by the above instrument, and to get which into a distant hole by the fewest strokes constitutes the game. The word *golf* is supposed to be derived from the German noun *kolbe*, a club. The game is very ancient, and has not been always confined to Scotland. In Strutt's "Sports and Pastimes of the People of England," it is mentioned, that "there are many games played with the ball, that require the assistance of a club or bat, and probably the most ancient among them is the pastime now distinguished by the name of goff. In the northern part of the kingdom, goff is much practised. It answers to a rustic pastime of the Romans, which they played with a ball of leather stuffed with feathers, called paganica, and the goff-ball is composed of the same materials to this day. In the reign of Edward the Third, the Latin name cambuca was applied to this pastime, and it derived the denomination, no doubt, from the crooked club or bat with which it was played."

It seems to be quite uncertain at what period the game of golf was introduced into Scotland; but it may be fairly presumed that this amusement, as well as football and archery, were practised to a considerable extent in the reign of our King James the First.

King Charles the First was much attached to the amusement of golfing, and, on his visit to Scotland in 1641, was engaged in it on Leith Links, when intimation was given him of the rebellion in Ireland; whereupon he threw down his club, and returned in great agitation to Holyroodhouse.

The Duke of York, afterwards James the Second, also delighted in the game. By joining publicly in it and other sports, he softened down among the Scottish nobility much of the prejudice excited by his unpopular principles; while his duchess equally pleased the ladies by treating them with *tea*, which had not till then been seen in the kingdom.

Many names might be added of illustrious individuals, who, in days gone by, as well as in more modern times, found relaxation and delight in practising the game; but none will create greater interest than that of Lord President Forbes. He is said to have been so keen a golfer as to play on the Sands at Leith, if the Links happened at any time to be covered with snow.

The mode of playing the game does not appear to be the same in all countries—at least the practice in Holland is different from that of England and Scotland. The method among us seems to resemble that of the Romans more than the Dutch. The game of the latter is particularly described in the following interesting communication, in the Statistical Account, by Dr Alexander Walker of Edinburgh, to Dr Carlyle of Inveresk:—

"The Dutch game called *kolf*, from which the word *golf* is derived, as both are probably from the Greek word *kolophos*, is played in an enclosed rectangular area of about sixty feet by twenty-five. The floor, which is a composition of sand, clay, and pitch, is made as level as a billiard-table; and the enclosing walls are for two feet above the floor, faced either with polished stone or sheet-lead, that they may cause the ball to rebound with accuracy. At about eight or ten feet from each end wall, a circular post of about five inches diameter is placed precisely in the middle of the area with regard to breadth, consequently opposite the one to the other, and at the distance of forty feet, or thereby. The balls used in the game are about the size of cricket-balls, made perfectly round and elastic, covered with soft leather, and sewed with fine wire. The clubs are from three to four feet long, with stiff shafts. The heads are of brass; and the face, with which the ball is struck, is perfectly smooth, having no inclination, such as might have a tendency to raise the ball from the ground. The angle which the head makes with the shaft, is nearly the same with that of the putting clubs used at golf. The game may be played by any number, either in parties against each other, or each person for himself; and the contest is, who shall hit the two posts in the fewest strokes, and make his ball retreat from the last one with such an accurate length, as that it shall lie nearest to the opposite end wall of the area. The first stroke is made from within a few inches of what is called the beginning post, and the player directs his ball as precisely as he can on the opposite one, that he may hit it if possible, computing at the same time the force of his stroke, so that, should he miss it (which from the distance may be supposed to be most frequently the case), his ball may rebound from the end wall, and lie within a moderate distance of the post, and before it; that is, between the two posts, rather than between the post and the end wall. The reason of preferring this situation of the ball will appear by reflecting how much easier it is, in that case, to send the ball, after striking the post, back again towards the other one. The skill of the game consists in striking the post in such a way, whether full or otherwise, as may send the ball towards the place where you wish it to rest. It combines the address required both in golf and in billiards. Five points make the game; and such is the difference between a capital and an ordinary player, that the former will give four points of the game, and frequently be the winner. This superiority of play I experienced myself at a *kolf baan* near the Hague, after I had considerable practice in the game, and was, in fact, no mean player. With the advantage of three points I was completely beaten; and even when I got four, I could hardly preserve any tolerable equality. There is generally a kind of apartment at one end of the *kolf baan*, two or three steps higher than the floor, where spectators may enjoy the sight of the game, as far as the clouds of tobacco smoke, with which they commonly fill it, will allow."

The game has been long known in India; and the following notice of the mode in which it is practised, is given from a letter addressed to the secretary of the Musselburgh club by one of its members, whose attainment in the knowledge of eastern languages is of a very high order:—

"The Indian, or rather the Persian, name of the game, is *govy* (strongly resembling the Scotch pronunciation of golf, viz. 'gouf'), meaning 'the ball;' and sometimes called 'chougan o govy,' or club and ball. The game is considered a royal one in the East, and is uniformly played on horseback. The club (according to the representation I have seen in pretty old Persian paintings of a party at play) is bent at the end, and somewhat like our own clubs. The handle, agreeable to the same drawing, seemed a good deal shorter, so as when a player was about to strike the ball, he was necessarily obliged to throw his body downward to the right side of his horse, with the chougan in his right hand, whilst he grasped the bridle, and guided his steed (usually at full gallop) with the left. The manuscript in which I saw the representation, was a highly celebrated work on the ancient history of Persia, by Ferdousi, esteemed one of the best Persian poets."

King Charles I
Leith Links 1642

The game of Palle Maille, or Pall Mall, which is mentioned in Strutt's book, as bearing a resemblance to golf, was played by striking a ball with a mallet through a high arch of iron, the merit consisting in doing so at the fewest number of strokes. Charles the Second and his courtiers practised this game in St James's Park, where there is a walk still called the Mall; the name being supposed to be derived from the mallet with which the game was played.

The question seems to have been once agitated, whether the game of golf was peculiar to England or Scotland. The importance of the inquiry is scarcely such as to command great investigation; but there is a tradition connected with it, which, if an ancient mode of determining disputed points be a correct one, must be considered as setting the matter for ever at rest. It is related as follows:—

"Two English noblemen, who, during their attendance at the Scottish court, had, among other fashionable amusements of the period, occasionally practised golf, were one day debating the question with his Highness the Duke of York, whether that amusement were peculiar to Scotland or England; and, having some difficulty in coming to an issue on the subject, it was proposed to decide the question by an appeal to the game itself; the Englishmen agreeing to rest the legitimacy of their national pretensions as golfers, together with a large sum of money, on the result of a match, to be played with his highness, and any Scotchman he could bring forward. The duke, whose great aim at that time was popularity, thinking this no bad opportunity both for asserting his claim to the character of a Scotchman, and for flattering a national prejudice, immediately accepted the challenge, and, in the meantime, caused diligent inquiry to made as to where the most efficient partner was to be found. The person recommended to him for this purpose was a poor man, named John Paterson, a shoemaker, who was not only reputed the best golf-player of his day, but whose ancestors had been equally celebrated from time immemorial.

On the matter being explained to him, Paterson was not quite satisfied as to how he should be able to acquit himself in such great company; but on the duke encouraging him, he said he would do his best.

The match was played, in which the duke was of course completely victorious; and the shoemaker was dismissed with a reward corresponding to the importance of his service, being an equal share of the stake played for.

With this money he immediately built himself a comfortable house in the Canongate, upon the wall of which the duke caused an escutcheon to be affixed, bearing the arms of the family of Paterson, surmounted by a crest, a dexter hand grasping a golf club—Motto, 'Far and sure.'

The house alluded to is situated on the north side of the Canongate, a little above Queensberry House."

The town of Musselburgh has been long famous for superior golfers, the beautiful and extensive links on both sides of the Esk being an incitement to the practice of the athletic exercise. A golf club was established there in the year 1774, and included among its members the most respectable gentlemen in the parish. To encourage the exercise of the game, they procured a handsome silver cup, which is played for annually, and a year's possession of it, and the honour of being captain of the club, are the gainer's trophies. He is bound to append a medal to the cup when he restores it.

The game also flourishes at Edinburgh and Leith, and still more remarkably, perhaps, at St Andrews, where very large stakes are sometimes played *for*, and where there is a regular manufactory of balls, both for home consumption and exportation.

15

Allan Robertson 113

CHAMBERS' EDINBURGH JOURNAL

CONDUCTED BY WILLIAM AND ROBERT CHAMBERS, EDITORS OF "CHAMBERS'S INFORMATION FOR THE PEOPLE," "CHAMBERS'S EDUCATIONAL COURSE," &c.

NUMBER 558. SATURDAY, OCTOBER 8, 1842. PRICE 1½d.

GOSSIP ABOUT GOLF.

It is curious to observe how even such a matter as sport is determined by local circumstances. *Cricket* may be said to be a natural result of the existence of the village greens of England. In like manner, *Golf* exists in Scotland by virtue of the previous existence of a certain peculiar kind of waste ground called *links*. Links are chiefly found along the shores of the Firth of Forth and the neighbouring coasts, being low undulating tracts composed of sand which has been blown up from the sea, and covered with a slight herbage, varied here and there by patches of broom and furze. They are generally common to the inhabitants of the nearest town, by whom they are devoted statedly to the feeding of a few sheep or geese, and occasionally to purposes of recreation and amusement. Thus there are links at Leith, Musselburgh, and Gullane, on the south side of the Firth, and at Kirkaldy, Dunbarnie, Crail, and St Andrews, on the north side—all of them, but especially the last, being fine open cheerful expanses of ground, albeit of little more than nominal value in the eye of the rural economist. On these prairies of the north, the game of golf, which is said to be of Dutch extraction, has been naturalised for hundreds of years, without spreading to other places, and this simply because in no other places is there ground adapted for the sport. A links (there is no distinct singular for the word) and golf go, it may be said, hand in hand together. Where there is no links there can properly be no golf; and where there is a links, there golf is as sure to be as a public-house by the side of a stable-lane, or the dandelion and groundsil where there is nothing else.

But what sort of game is this said golf? Why, to speak of it with a regard merely to its materialities, it is a game played with clubs of a peculiar form, and balls. Holes of a size fit to admit an ordinary-sized tumbler are made in the ground in a series, at the distance of from three to four hundred yards from each other. The player is furnished with a ball of about an inch and a half in diameter, formed of leather stuffed as hard as possible with feathers; and this he plays from hole to hole with his club, he and his opponent contending which shall get it *holed* by the smallest number of strokes. This is all that a man of no soul and *not a golfer* would see in the game, and all that he would say in description of it; but it would not be a more correct definition than that celebrated one of the sport of angling, "a stick and a string," &c. To appreciate golf fully, it must be studied in some such school as that of St Andrews, where its whole character is fully developed, in consequence at once of the admirably adapted ground, and the enthusiasm of the votaries.

This quiet venerable university town, where literary and philosophical society is agreeably mixed with miscellaneous persons in independent circumstances, happens to be skirted by a links of more than two miles in extent, a fine rolling field, as the Americans would describe it, bearing herbage and furze, and, as usual, open for the recreation of the inhabitants. St Andrews is confessedly the Melton of golf, for no other place presents ground nearly so well adapted for the amusement, or which is the haunt of so many players. The links is entirely composed of sand blown up from the sea, upon a spot where the waves must have once held sway, for the ancient sea-cliff is still distinctly traceable along the inland verge, although now softened down by time, and reduced to tillage, pasture, and pleasure-ground. With this fine slope on one side, and the German Ocean on the other, the striking outline of pinnacled St Andrews behind, and in front the distant hills of Perth and Forfar shires, extending from the central Grampians down to the Red Head near Arbroath, the whole scene is something more than beautiful; the very spaciousness of a view commanding objects much more than a hundred miles distant from each other, affects the beholder in an uncommon manner. At one end is what may be called the Golf Settlement, comprehending the Club-house with its flag-staff, houses for the makers of clubs and balls, and lodgings occupied by the more unfailing of the members. At that spot begins the series of holes, which extends curvingly outwards to the amount of nine from the starting one, along a tract which may be easily distinguished from the rest of the ground by its being comparatively feet-worn. Day after day, from a time beyond record, between the hours of eleven and five, have groups of golfers been seen pacing that course, in pursuit of their half-meditative game, equally regardless of summer's heat and winter's cold, of the scorching sunshine and the rain, if, indeed, it be not a fact which is usually spoken as a jest at St Andrews, "that it never rains on the links." Certainly, if it does ever rain there, the wet instantly disappears through the sandy ground, leaving the sward as firm and dry as before. I may here as well mention that the present Club—called Royal in consequence of the patronage of the late king, William IV., who bestowed a gold medal upon it—dates from 1754, and has at all times included the names of the most considerable men of the district, as also those of many of the best players of other places. Four times a-year, the members meet to contend for the various medals connected with the institution; after which there is always a festive meeting. The Club-house is used as a receptacle for the implements and dresses of the members, and connected with it there is a reading-room for such of these gentlemen as choose to subscribe to it.

It is about two o'clock of a fine August day, when, after a forenoon of useful avocations, I pop into the club-house to glance at the papers, and be in the way of any agreeable temptation that may arise. All is emptiness and silence within and without, for there are no visiting members, and many of even the resident ones are gone, some to grouse-shooting, some to watering-places, some here and some there. Most of the *cadies*, as the servants who carry clubs are called, have gone to work at the harvest, in pure despair of so much as one job per day, leaving only one or two to attend to the business of the green—who are to be seen leaning listlessly against the corners of distant houses, as if they thought employment a thing more to be wished for than expected. John Ness, porter to the club-house, and who is also a cady, seated on the low wall near the door, is heard through the open window remarking to a passing acquaintance, that things are most uncommon dull just now. An old gentleman is poring over the Standard; but he has for some years retired from sport, so that nothing is to be looked for from him. However, Colonel Elder has been practising for an hour or two on the green near the house, playing his balls to short distances, unable to get a partner, and, seeing me approach, he sends in to ask if I will come and play with him. This makes two, but a *foursome* is considered the preferable game, and we wait a few minutes longer in the hope of two more gentlemen appearing. As our good stars will have it, Captain Strong and another gentleman heave in sight, and the match is then made up. There are two skilful and experienced players, and two tyros, I being of the latter description. Each good player takes one of the other kind as his partner; and as one of the expert gentlemen is a little more expert than the other, a small odds is allowed to make up the inequality. The first thing to be done is to put on the light scarlet coat of the Club, a cap, and a pair of strongly nailed shoes, the last being necessary to give a firm footing on the green while playing the long strokes. Each man has his cady behind him carrying his clubs and balls. We take our station at the starting hole, and the first thing to be done is to *tee* the balls, of which each party or *side* has one. The cady of the gentleman who is to play the first stroke, takes the ball and puts it upon the top of a small lump of sand, merely to give it that prominence above the ground which will make it a fair object for the stroke. This is *teeing*. He then gives his master the play-club, which is the implement to be used when the ball lies unusually fair for a stroke. The club-part of this instrument is a piece of wood about four inches long, lined with horn below, and loaded with lead behind, having a straight face slightly sloping backwards. Its handle is a slender shaft of hard elastic wood (generally hiccory), thickening upwards to the part where it is grasped by the hands of the player, and where it is lined with strips of thin leather. The handle is of such a length, and it is attached to the club part at such an angle, that the player, having the ball about two feet in front of him, can easily strike it off, having first made the club swing back to his left side, so as to gain a purchase.

The first stroke is generally one which tells well in respect of distance, as the ball lies unusually fair, and the club used is that which strikes most powerfully. Some are so great in driving, or *swiping*, as this feat is variously called, as to make the ball go to a distance not easily credited. I have heard that, on one occasion, in frosty weather, a good player made his ball go two hundred and eighty yards. One of my own acquaintance assures me that he has played one to two hundred and sixty yards. Much of this effect is of course due to the nature of the ball, which, felt in the hand, seems as hard as a stone, but rebounds tremendously under a powerful appulsion.

Our game is for a trifle, as is the general practice at St Andrews. For reasons good, the two inexperienced players, who may be called Messrs Rawson and Greene, are appointed to strike off. Mr Greene makes a happy-looking stroke, and thinks he has been doing worthy service to his side; but lo! his ball lights upon a cart-track some hundred yards onwards, where a second stroke will probably be found no easy matter. This, you must understand, good reader, is one of the hazards of the game. A very expert player would fall short or go beyond; but Mr Greene is upon the road—"to ruin," as the St Andrews joke goeth. Well, but what is Mr Rawson about? Mr Rawson is a gentleman excessively anxious to do great things. He plays as an insane steam-engine would do. See how he musters strength, how he straddles for a posture, with what frenzied anxiety he eyes his ball! Gemini! what a *swipe* he takes—there he is down upon it—and, behold . . . . the ball runs some ten yards, and stops! The undisguisable fact is, that Mr Rawson has *topped* his ball; that is, he has hit it on the crown of its head, and his force has been mostly squandered in vain. Captain Strong, his partner, is too much a gentleman to make a single remark. He asks for his *long spoon*, which the cady hands to him. This is a club in all respects resembling the driver, excepting in its face being slightly curved, and more angular, so as to catch up a ball lying in grass. The captain is unerring and powerful, and his stroke almost repairs the disaster of his partner. He is said to have played *the odds*; that is, one stroke more than the stroke on the other side. The ball of this side being propelled farther than the point where the other is lying, it is now Colonel Elder's turn to play: he is said to play *the like*; that is, the stroke which makes the one side equal with the other. The ball being found deep in the loose earth of the cart-track, he calls for the *iron*; that is, a club with a comparatively short handle and a heavy spoon-like termination of iron, designed for exercising great force upon a ball lying in a difficult situation. The colonel uses the tool so dexterously, that the ball is sent a good way onward, and laid in a good place for Mr Greene's next effort. But ah! see a little in front, good reader, a treacherous trench zig-zagging across the green, the channel, to wit, of the Swilkin burn, or rivulet, which has chosen to make its exit into the sea in this most improper situation. The law of the links is, that when a ball is sent into the channel of this burn, it must be lifted out and laid on the rear bank, with the loss of a stroke in the reckoning. Mr Greene is most anxious to carry his ball over this difficulty, and for that purpose uses the long spoon, which is calculated to raise it well off the ground. It goes over . . . he breathes again . . . but who can calculate at golf! See! as it rolls onward along the grass, it meets a back-sweeping angle of the deceitful Swilkin, into which it disappears. Mr Greene is in despair, and the colonel looks grave. But there is no avoiding accidents, and one beautiful moral feature of golf is, that you never come by any misfortune without having tolerable hopes that an equally great one will befall your neighbour next minute. Mr Rawson, however, has been more fortunate this time, for he gets over the burn splendidly, and has laid his ball near the hole. When balls have advanced to this situation, a new kind of play, called *putting* (*u* being sounded as in *lull*), comes into requisition. It is performed with a short light club, with a straight and vertical face, and consists in slight careful strokes, designed to bring the ball close to the hole, or into it. Some men are good putters without being good drivers, while others are good drivers, but fail in putting, having perhaps more strength than nicety. It is a feat requiring great calculation of forces, and of the amount of friction which the nature of the ground to be passed over will occasion; and no man without good mechanical faculties can possibly excel in it. It is often amusing to see how a good player is disconcerted by a false step in putting, and how eager he is to find palliations for his failure. "That blade of grass turned me aside!" "I was disturbed by your moving." "Your shadow on the green put me out." Such are the excuses daily heard wrung from men who putt amiss. In fact, the exigency of the moment is, like oppression, sufficient to make a wise man mad. Well, the colonel and Mr Greene have as yet rather the worst of the hole. But the colonel is a capital putter, and a surprising hand at a *steal*; that is, a holing of the ball from a considerable distance. By one of these feats he makes up for the misadventure of the burn, and leaves the hole even with the antagonist party.

We tee again, and the colonel and captain play off for the next hole. There are no more cart-tracks, no more burns, but no want of difficulties for all that. All along the golfing course there is every here and there to be seen a yawning sand-pit, called in the technology of the links a *bunker*, which a stranger would suppose it a piece of gross negligence in the club to leave un-filled-up for a single day, but which is in reality valued as amongst the most important features of the ground, bunkers being hazards from which only skilful players may have any hope of escaping. Right in front of the teeing-place in this case, there is one gaping in the hither side of a knoll, which is sure to catch a ball not well raised, at once stopping short its career, and placing it in a situation from which it is difficult to strike it out. Our two players are over this; but Messrs Rawson and Greene, who have to play the next strokes, see others at convenient distances before them along the course. The bunkers are in fact a sad annoyance to the novice. The holes in some cases are planted in the midst of a set of them, calling for very peculiar skill in bringing up the balls. But to a true player they are the principal charm of the game. As a proof of this, it was lately mentioned in the Fife newspapers that a set of natives of the district, resident at Bombay, had begun to golf on the government esplanade, and enjoyed their sport greatly, although, it must be confessed, they found the ground very deficient in the proper irregularities—meaning, chiefly, *bunkers*. I may here mention that the Royal Golf Club has a lithographed plan of the course, in which all the bunkers, as well as other features of the ground, are laid down by name with all the care exercised in indicating sand-banks and sunk rocks in a mariner's chart. Here, too, of course, the holes are all duly noted, each having its appropriate name, as the Bridge Hole, the Heathery Hole, the Hole o' Cross, and the Hole o' Shell, while one, where an old woman sometimes waits to sell refreshments for bethirsted players, is called the Ginger Beer Hole. An exact knowledge of the topography of the links may well be supposed to be of the greatest consequence, where the ground is so various and in general so difficult.

Mr Rawson now plays, and makes so good a stroke, that the colonel remarks, in his dry way, that he promises ere long to be quite an artist. Mr Greene strikes next, and, eager to avoid a bunker right in the centre, sends his ball into the long deer's grass which skirts the course. The colonel plays it out with his iron at the odds, when, being still behind the position of the opposite party's ball, Mr Greene has to play it again, thus counting *two more*, or an excess of two over the strokes of the adversary. Captain Strong now, playing *one off two*, gives his ball one of those vigorous and well-managed strokes which distinguish him so much, and causes it, clear flying over all dangers, to alight about ten yards from the hole. Following up this advantage with good putting, the captain and Mr Rawson are triumphant. "Dat is one hole in my side, as the Pole said," remarks Captain Strong, referring to a foreigner who was a player at St Andrews some years ago. This is one of the established jokes of the links. On inquiry, I learned that, when his opponent jocularly asked him "which side?" the countryman of Kosciusko very smartly replied, "De right side, to be sure."

Tee again, and now it is Messrs Rawson and Greene's turn to strike off. Let them take care, for there are two small but dangerous bunkers exactly far enough off to receive a ball at the end of a moderate flight. Mr Greene escapes the peril for this time; his ball is seen lying clear on the sward at a very fair distance. Mr Rawson does his best. As there is a breeze at the time, he drives straight for the bunker, expecting that the wind will carry him the necessary distance aside. But the breeze lulls for a moment, and the ball takes a low course, where wind does not much affect it, and accordingly he proceeds in the line of danger. Some think he has gone in, some not, but we shall soon see. He *is* in—snug at the base of the little sand-cliff, where scarcely any club can reach. The cady of one of the opposite party is the first to ascertain the fact, and the gentlemen of that party give an "Ah, indeed!" with an air of concern as seeming sincere as could reasonably be expected. Strong takes his iron, and, making the best of a bad case, brings the ball spinning into the bottom of the pit, where it lies somewhat more fair. Rawson plays it out at *two more*, and at *three more* Strong gives it one of his famous strokes. The colonel now plays *one off three*, and even excels the last stroke. Things look rather bad for Strong and Rawson; but *nil desperandum*. And truly may this be said; for observe Mr Greene, in endeavouring with his short spoon to cant the ball over a bunker, so as to make it fall fair on the green beside the hole, has—oh! ye stars—gone in. Elder eyes the ball ruefully, but thinks he may repair the calamity. He takes his iron, and, striking deeply into the sand beneath, not only gets it out, but places it within a yard of the hole. That stroke was one off two. Captain Strong has now to play two more from a grassy place about ten yards off. For this he takes a short club not yet adverted to, called the *cleek*, the striking part of which consists of a thick slip of smooth iron, with its face inclined at an angle of forty-five degrees backward. It is useful for tilting a ball out of a rough place near the hole. He plays like an adept, and places his ball right between the other and the hole—in the language of the links, a *stymie*. It is now Mr Greene's duty to putt at one off two; but how to reach the hole, with a rival's ball directly in the way! The cadies stand round with suspended breath. Mr Greene scans the ground even to its slightest inclinations, and seems to mark every blade of grass. He goes behind, and, shutting one eye, carefully notes on which side of the interposed ball there is most room for a chance. With the putting club clenched spasmodically in his hands, he stands in a rigid pause of about a minute, and plays. His ball just grazes the other, and takes its place about six inches from the hole. Mr Rawson now putts at *the like*, and seems to have an easy task, as his ball is only eighteen inches from the hole. But the least over-exertion of strength baulks the simplest movements in golf; and, this being the case at present, behold his ball just wheels round the rim of the hole, and lies without. Colonel Elder is in at the odds, and so that hole is divided after all.

'Twere long to tell of every hole in the round; but yet, if this were done, there would be novel circumstances in each, for there is no space between any two holes exactly or even nearly like another, and consequently every step in the player's progress gives occasion to something peculiar in his play, and probably something new in his fortune. Sometimes he has to allow for the wind, sometimes for the dryness or wetness, as well as for the roughness or bareness, of the sward. Sometimes he must, in putting, allow for swelling or sloping ground, and approach the hole by a sort of sweep or curve, difficult to be calculated beforehand, and very difficult to be effected after it has been calculated. Sometimes, as we have seen, he tops his ball, which is not favourable to its progress; sometimes, hitting too low, he strikes what the wit of the links calls the greater ball (namely, the earth) without touching the lesser (namely, the golf-ball), or, at the best, raises the latter high in the air, without sending it on any considerable way. Then he may stand unfair, or he may *draw* his stroke, and thereby send the ball off the course, which is one of the most fatal of misfortunes. There is a space between holes containing ground of an unusually rough character, which bears a name not to be freely mentioned to ears polite. Some powerful players there are who can, in the words of a clever local poem, send a ball "smack over —— at one immortal go;" lighting upon a fine expanse beyond called the *Elysian Fields*. But the penalty of failure is so great, in consequence of the vast sand-pits lying below, that most players, even of good skill, are content to take a somewhat less rough by-course, which they generally pass over at two strokes, or three at most. There is another hole, from which the first stroke sends the ball over a hillock in front, with numerous pitfalls beyond, which are only to be escaped by mere favour of fortune. Then there are furzy places, where, when a man sends his ball, his antagonist asks if he designs to go a-hare-hunting . . . and, in fact, there is a tradition amongst the cadies, of an errant player having one day killed a hare with his ball. Too often, when a ball falls in such a place, it is never more seen. There are also rushy places most easy to be got into, but most consumedly difficult to get out of, the stalks of that herbage blunting the strokes of the heaviest clubs: here an antagonist, if too polite to fall a-laughing, is sure at least to whistle up the first bar or two of "Green grow the rashes O!" for a gentle joke is dearly loved at golf. There is one hole placed only at the distance of one full stroke from the other, but with tremendous bunkers between, into which inexperienced players can scarcely avoid falling. It is amongst the marvellous stories of the links that a deceased professor of the university once holed his ball here at one stroke, an event against which the chances must have been very great indeed; yet he, after all, lost the hole, as he could not find his ball till it was too late. A tolerably good player would be glad to do it at three, and a tyro, if unfortunate in the sand pits, would perhaps take so many as half a dozen. It may here be observed, that the whole round of the course—eighteen holes in all—is generally done by good players at from 100 to 105 strokes, though there are instances of its being done at so few as 90, and even, if cadies speak truth, at 87. I must, by the way, remark of cadies, that they are generally a faithful and zealous class of servants. They take the keenest interest in the play of their temporary master, carefully directing him if unskilful, gently counselling him if otherwise, and always feeling deeply both his successes and his failures. I have heard a cady sigh with genuine grief at a false stroke of his employer, and often observed that those against whose masters the game is going, walk along in as dispirited a condition as if the loss were their own. Some of them are extremely good players, having perhaps had the advantage of learning the game in their earliest boyhood. There is a ball-maker, Allan Robertson by name, who, besides having the highest character for his wares, is reputed to be the best player at St Andrews, and consequently in Scotland—I may as well add, in the world! This is an eminence which golfers must needs admire; and in the little world of the links, men of estate and title will be heard speaking of worthy Allan as if he were a kind of king amongst them.

I have here chanced to advert to a day when only one match is out; but often there may be seen five or six playing along after one another—occasioning such a pell-mell of balls, that quiet promenaders are fain to give the course a wide berth. Some men of leisure are out every day, and never make less than two rounds before dinner, often three, each round being a walk of four miles, to say nothing of the exercise of playing, so that it may well be supposed the golfers are a healthy people. Generally, they are quiet country gentlemen, or retired officers of the army or navy; but several of the professors also play. To judge from the perseverance of its votaries, the game is a most fascinating one:—only, perhaps, too much so, if it be true, which the non-golfing world allege, that genuine denizens of the links can converse during the evenings upon no other subject; but this I am inclined to think something of a calumny. They usually continue to enjoy it to an advanced age, the healthiness of the exercise being itself favourable to longevity; and there is at least one authentic instance of a gentleman playing till considerably past eighty. When unable any longer to play in the usual manner, they resort to what are called the *short holes*—a series placed in a small circle near the golf-house, where, of course, the play consists of *putting* alone. This breaks the fall from the high estate of the long-hole play; and one regards a couple of seniors at the short holes with something like the same mixture of melancholy and satisfaction with which he sees a set of good old hunters turned out into a comfortable park. They can also pop along the green for a hole or two after their juniors, and make remarks on the play of modern times in comparison with that of the great hands

← 1842

Allan

R & A's Gold Medal

← Silver Cross

WINNERS OF THE GOLD MEDAL

Given by the Club, from 1806 to 1836

During which period this Medal was the only one competed for

		Stro
1806	Walter Cook, Esq., W.S.	10
1807	Do.	10
1808	William Oliphant, Esq.	10
1809	Do.	10
1810	Dr. James Hunter, United College, St. Andrews	11
1811	Do. do.	11
1812	Robert Pattullo, Esq., of Balhouffie	10
1813	Do.	11
1814	Do.	11
1815	Dr. James Hunter, United College, St. Andrews	10
1816	David Moncrieffe, Esq., yr. of Moncrieffe	11
1817	Walter Cook, Esq., W.S.	11
1818	Captain H. L. Playfair	11
1819	Sir David Moncrieffe, Bart., of Moncrieffe	10
1820	Edward D'Oyley, Esq.	10
1821	Henry M. Low, Esq., W.S.	10
1822	Charles Shaw, Esq., Leith	10
1823	Henry M. Low, Esq., W.S.	12
1824	Do.	11
1825	Samuel Messieux, Esq.	10
1826	Robert Pattullo, Esq., junior	10
1827	Samuel Messieux, Esq.	11
1828	Robert Pattullo, Esq., junior	10
1829	Major Holcroft, R.A.	10
1830	Do.	11
1831	David Duncan, Esq., Rosemount	11
1832	John H. Wood, Esq., Leith	104
1833	Major Holcroft, R.A.	103
1834	Robert Oliphant, Esq., yr. of Rossie	97
1835	Do.	105
1836	Major William Wemyss	104

St. James' Palace, 6th Jan. 1837.

SIR—I have the honour to transmit, by the King's command, a Gold Medal, with Green Ribband, which His Majesty desires you will present in His name to "The Royal and Ancient Golf Club of St. Andrews," and which His Majesty wishes should be challenged and played for annually by that Society. The King orders me to add, that His Majesty has great satisfaction in availing himself of this opportunity to evince his approbation of that ancient Institution.—I have the honour to be, Sir, your most obedient servant, H. WHEATLEY.

Major Belshes then stated that as the Gold Medal was th only prize now given by the Club, and as there were numerou first-rate players who competed for it, he conceived that it woul tend to increase the interest in that game among these competito were an additional prize competed for yearly; and entertainin this opinion, he had great pleasure in now presenting to the Clu a "Silver Cross of St. Andrew." The Club unanimously accepte of the very handsome gift, and begged to record their sense o the deep interest which the Major has on all occasions manifeste for the prosperity of the Club. J. MURRAY BELSHES, *C.*

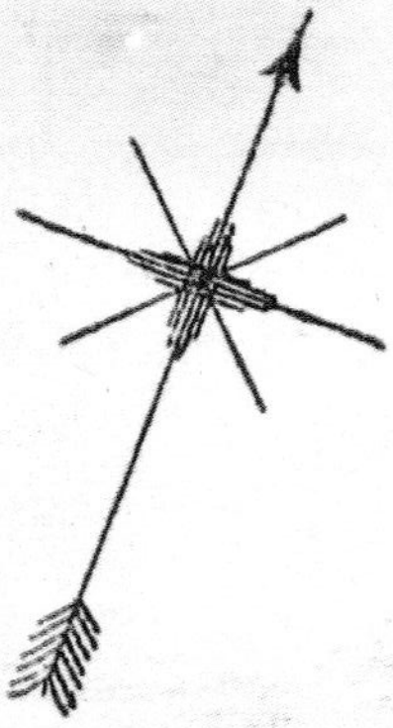

PLAN OF
THE GOLFING COURSE.
OVER THE LINKS OF
S^T ANDREWS.
1864

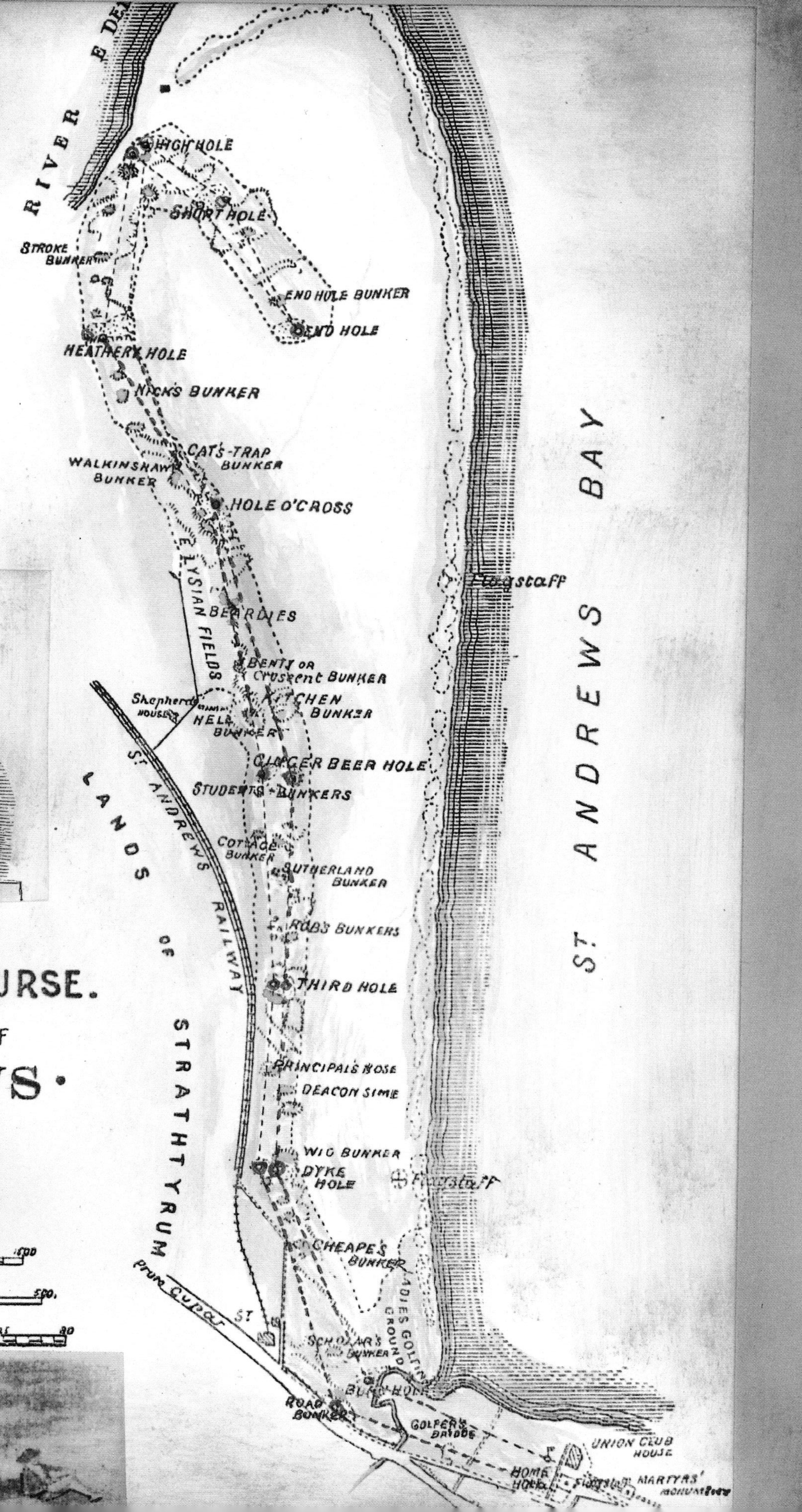

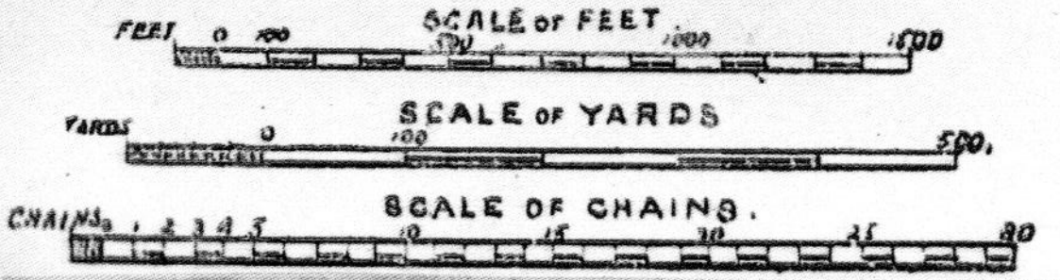

19

THE NINE HOLES OF THE LINKS OF ST. ANDREWS.

The First or Bridge Hole

R. C.

SACRED to hope and promise is the spot—
To Philp's and to the Union Parlour near,
To every Golfer, every caddie dear—
Where we strike off—oh, ne'er to be forgot,
Although in lands most distant we sojourn.
But not without its perils is the place;
Mark the opposing caddie's sly grimace,
Whispering: "He's on the road!" "He's in the burn!"
So is it often in the grander game
Of life, when, eager, hoping for the palm,
Breathing of honour, joy, and love and fame,
Conscious of nothing like a doubt or qualm,
We start, and cry: "Salute us, muse of fire!"
And the first footstep lands us in the mire.

Pages 116 to 118 describe the holes as they were

The Second or Cartgate Hole

R. C.

FEARFUL to Tyro is thy primal stroke,
O Cartgate! for behold the bunker opes
Right to the *teeing*-place its yawning chops,
Hope to engulf ere it is well awoke.
That passed, a Scylla in the form of rushes
Nods to Charybdis which in ruts appears:
He will be safe who in the middle steers;
One step aside, the ball destruction brushes.
Golf symbols thus again our painful life,
Dangers in front, and pitfalls on each hand:
But see, one glorious cleek-stroke from the sand
Sends Tyro home, and saves all further strife!
He's in at six—old Sandy views the lad
With new respect, remarking: "That's no bad!"

The Third Hole

R. C.

No rest in Golf—still perils in the path:
Here, playing a good ball, perhaps it goes
Gently into the *Principalian Nose*,
Or else *Tam's Coo*, which equally is death.

Perhaps the wind will catch it in mid-air,
And take it to *the Whins*—"Look out, look out!
Tom Morris, be, oh be, a faithful scout!"
But Tom, though *links-eyed*, finds not anywhere.
Such thy mishaps, O Merit: feeble balls
Meanwhile roll on, and lie upon the green;
'Tis well, my friends, if you, when this befalls,
Can spare yourselves the infamy of spleen.
It only shows the ancient proverb's force,
That you may further go and fare the worse.

The Fourth or Ginger-Beer Hole

P. P. A.

THOUGH thou hast lost this last unlucky hole,
I prythee, friend, betake thee not to swearing,
Or other form of speech too wildly daring,

Though some allege it tendeth to console.
Rather do thou thy swelling griefs control,
Sagacious that at hand a joy awaits thee
(Since out of doubt a glass of beer elates thee),
Without that frightful peril to thy soul.
A pot of beer! go dip thine angry beak in it,
And straight its rage shall melt to soft placidity,
That solace finding thou art wise to seek in it;
Ah! do not thou on that poor plea reject it,
That in thine inwards it may breed acidity—
One glass of Stewart's[1] brandy will correct it.

The Hell Hole

P. P. A.

WHAT daring genius first did name thee Hell?
What high, poetic, awe-struck grand old Golfer?
Misdeem him not, ye pious ones, a scoffer—
Whoe'er he was, the name befits thee well.
"All hope abandon, ye who enter here,"
Is written awful o'er thy sandy jaws,
Whose greedy threat may give the boldest pause,
And frequent from within come tones of fear—
Dread sound of cleeks, which ever smite in vain,[2]

The Heather Hole

P. P. A.

AH me! prodigious woes do still environ—
To quote *verbatim* from some grave old poet—
The man who needs must "meddle with his iron";
And here, if ever, thou art doomed to know it.
For now behold thee, doubtless for thy sins,
Tilling some bunker, as if on a lease of it,
And so, assiduous to make due increase of it;
Or wandering homeless through a world of whins!
And when,—these perils past,—thou seemest *dead*,

And hop'st a half—O woe! thy ball runs crooked,
Making thy foe just one more hole ahead,
Surely a consummation all too sad,
Without that sneering devilish "Niver lookit,"
The closing comment of the opposing cad.

The High or Eden Hole

R. C. JR.

THE shelly pit is cleared at one fell blow,
A stroke to be remembered in your dreams!
But here the Eden on your vision gleams,
Lovely, but treach'rous in its solemn flow.
The hole is perched aloft, too near the tide,
The green is small, and broken is the ground
Which doth that little charmed space surround!
Go not too far, and go not to a side;
Take the short spoon to do your second stroke;
Sandy entreats you will the wind take heed on,
For, oh, it would a very saint provoke,
If you should let your ball plump in the Eden.
You do your best, but who can fate control?
So here against you is another hole.

The Short Hole

R. C. JR.

BRIEF but not easy is the next adventure;
Legend avers it has been done in *one*,
Though such long *steals* are now but rarely done—

In *three* 'twere well that you the hole should enter.
Strangely original is this bit of ground,
For, while at hand the smooth and smiling green,
One bunker wide and bushy yawns between,
Where Tyro's gutta is too often found.
Nervous your rival strikes and heels his ball—
From that whin-bush at six he'll scarce extract it:
Yours, by no blunder this time counteracted,
Is with the grass-club lofted over all.
There goes a hole in your side—how you hug it!
Much as th' Australian digger does a nugget.

The End Hole

R. C. JR.

THE end, but not the end—the distance-post
That halves the game—a serious point to thee,
For if one more thou losest, 'twill be *three:*
Yet even in that case, think not all is lost.
Men four behind have been, on the return,
So favoured by Olympus, or by care,
That all their terrors vanished into air,
And caddies cried them *dormy* at the burn!
I could quote proverbs, did I speak at random:
Full many a broken ship comes into port,
Full many a cause is gained at last resort,
But Golf impresses most, *Nil desperandum.*
Turn, then, my son, with two against, nor dread
To gain the winning-post with one ahead.

POLICE BYE-LAWS

& REGULATIONS

MADE BY THE

PROVOST, MAGISTRATES,

AND TOWN COUNCIL

OF ST ANDREWS.

The Provost, Magistrates, and Town Council of St Andrews, by virtue of the powers conferred on them by the Acts 3 and 4, William IV., Cap. 46, and 10 and 11, Victoria, Cap. 39, do hereby enact and regulate as follows, viz:—

1. No Ashes, Filth, or refuse of any kind shall at any time be thrown from doors, windows, or stairs, upon the Streets or Lanes, but shall be kept in backets, and taken to the Scavengers' Carts or Barrows, which will pass every lawful day and twice on Saturdays.—Liquids may be poured into the gutters, but carefully, so as not to spread over the Streets, and shall on no account be thrown from doors, stairs, or windows.

2. All Slaughter-Houses and Fish Curers Premises shall be cleaned and the Dung and offal removed daily during the months from June to September inclusive, and shall be cleaned and removed once every three days during the rest of the year.—All other receptacles for Dung shall be cleaned out once a week during said period from June to September inclusive, and once a fortnight during the rest of the year;—and no person shall be allowed to accumulate more than one ton on his premises.—No Dung shall remain on the Streets more than one hour previous to removal; and from the 1st day of March to the 1st day of November, the whole shall be removed before 9 o'clock A.M., and during the rest of the year, before 10 o'clock A.M.—Failing removal within the

33. Keepers of tippling-houses, convicted of keeping houses resorted to by riotous or disorderly persons, or who supply spirituous liquors to persons under fourteen years of age, must find security, under the penalties specified in the 81st Section of said last mentioned Act.

34. Brokers and dealers in second-hand goods, except licensed pawn-brokers, must register their names with the Town Clerk.

35. No vagrancy or begging will be permitted within the bounds of Police.

36. Common Lodging-honse-keepers must, when required, report the names of their lodgers to the Town Officers, and give notice of the occurrence of any infectious disease in said Lodging Houses.

37. When the streets are required to be opened for the laying of water or gas pipes, or for any other purpose, application must be made to the Superintendant of the Streets, who will see that the Streets are repaired in a substantial manner, and upheld by the parties for twelve months.

38. No person shall cut turf on the Scores or Links, east from the Swilcan Burn, or injure the mounds at or near the Kirk-hill, or cut or injure the seats on the public walks, within the bounds of police, or the embankment at Danes-work.

39. No person shall ride on horseback on the public walks within the bounds of police.

40. In cases where offences are committed by children, from whom, or from whose Parents or Guardians, fines cannot be recovered, imprisonment will be awarded.

The PROVOST, MAGISTRATES, and TOWN COUNCIL hereby enact that penalties from One to Twenty Shillings shall be imposed for a breach of any of the foregoing Regulations, and of all Regulations expressly enjoined by the Statute 3 and William IV., Cap. 46, unless a special penalty be thereby affixed to the particular offence, which penalty will in that case be exacted.

In name and on behalf of the Provost, Magistrates, and Council,

ST ANDREWS, DEC. 1849.

H. L. PLAYFAIR, Provost.

Sir Hugh Lyon Playfair
The man who did so much for this town in the 1840s

The Old Union Parlour
The clubhouse behind the last green.

Sir Hugh getting a lift home!

The Tolbooth and Town Jail – cobbled end of Market Street
knocked down in 1857

The Right Hon. Earl of Elgin and Kincardine.
The Right Hon. James Earl of Wemyss.
The Hon. Thomas Leslie.
The Hon. James Leslie.
The Hon. Francis Charteris.
Sir James Wemyss, Baronet.
Sir Robert Henderson, Baronet.
Lieut.-General James St. Clair.
David Scot of Scotstarvet.
James Oswald of Dunnikier.
Mr. David Young, Professor of Philosophy.
James Lumsdain, Esq., Provost of St. Andrews.
James Wemyss of Weemysshall.
Walter Wemyss of Lathockar.
John Bethune of Blebo.
Henry Bethune of Clato.
Thomas Spens the Younger of Lathallan.
James Cheap of Sauchie.
Arthur Martin of Milntoun.
Maurice Trent of Pitcullo.
Robert Douglas, Esq.
Mr. John Young, Professor of Philosophy.

← The original members of the St Andrews Society of golfers 1754

Sketch for the Grand Match

The St Andrews Society of Golfers renamed the Royal and Ancient in 1834

St. Andrews, 4th May 1837.

Which day the Club had the honour of entertaining at a Public Dinner Lieut.-Col. M. Belshes, their present Captain, in testimony of their high respect and esteem for him, and to mark their sense of the deep interest he has uniformly taken not only in the prosperity of the Club, but also in, first, obtaining for it His Majesty's permission to assume the high and distinguished title of "The Royal and Ancient Golf Club of St. Andrews"; but, secondly, in successfully using his influence to procure for it from His Gracious Majesty the King the splendid Royal Medal presented to the Club yesterday. Lieut.-Gen. Sir John Oswald of Dunnikier, G.C.B., presided, and discharged the duties of the Chair in the most able, dignified, and efficient manner.

THE GOLFERS 1843.

Painted by CHARLES LEES, R.S.A.

A Grand Match played on St. Andrews Links by Sir David Baird, Bart., and Sir Ralph Anstruther, Bart., against Major Playfair and John Campbell, Esq., of Saddel.

Scene: The Ginger Beer Hole (15th), St. Andrews.

1. Sir John Muir Mackenzie, of Delvin, Bart.
2. Sir John Murray Macgregor, Bart.
3. O. Tyndall Bruce, Esq., of Falkland.
4. Sir Charles Shaw.
5. Col. Playfair, of St. Andrews.
6. The Earl of Eglinton.
7. Robert Lindsay, Esq., of Straiton.
8. James Hay, Esq., Leith.
9. Earl of Leven and Melville.
10. A. Robertson, Golf Ball Maker, St. Andrews.
11. Sheriff Gordon.
12. John Silgo of Carmyle.
13. Hamilton Anstruther, Esq.
14. John Whyte Melville, Esq,
15. Lord Beridale.
16. F. Blair, Esq., of Balkhoyock.
17. The Master of Strathallan.
19. J. Wolfe Murray, Esq., Cringlettie.
20. S. Ogilvie Fairlie, Esq., Goodham.
21. John Hay, Esq., of Morton.
22. Sir David Baird, Bart., of Newbyth.
23. Major Playfair, of St. Andrews.
24. Thomas Paton, Esq., of Glenalmond.
25. Sir Ralph Anstruther, Bart.
26. John Balfour, Esq., Balbirnie.
27. Hon. David Murray.
28. John Stirting, St. Andrews.
29. James Condie, Esq., Perth.
30. Col. Murray Belches, of Invermay.
31. James H. Dundas, Esq., W.S.
32. James Blackwood, Esq.
33. James Oliphant, Esq., W.S.
34. Charles Robertson, Esq.
35. Sir N. M. Lockhart, Bart., Carnwath.
37. Col. Moncrieff.
38. Lord Viscount Valentia.
39. John Campbell, Esq., of Glensaddel.
40. Henry Macfarlane, Esq., M.D., Perth.
41. W. Pirrie, a caddie.
42. Sir John Campbell, of Airds.
43. Hon. Henry Coventry.
44. George Cheape, Esq., of Wellfield.
45. W. Dunn, Golf Club Maker, Musselburgh.
46. Captain David Campbell.
47. W. Peddie, Esq., of Black Ruthven.
48. W. Wood, Esq., Leith.
49. G. Debster, Esq., of Skibo.
50. W. Goddard, Esq., Leith.
51. Robert Patullo, Esq., St. Andrews.
52. Sandie Pirrie.
53. Ginger Beer Girl.

Allan Robertson (2nd left) Tom Morris Mr Campbell of Saddell. Sandy Herd. Sir Thomas Moncrieffe Bart
Colonel Fairlie

R. Cathcart. Sir Hugh Lyon Playfair. Watty Alexander Gen Moncrieffe Sandy Herd George Whyte Melville.

Such is famed Bobson who in St Andrews thrives
And such the ball each vigorous hero drives
Who, with matchless art,
Shapes the firm hide, connecting every part.
Then in a socket, sets the well-stitched hide,
And through the eyelet drives the downy tide;
Packing and stuffing, the forceful brogue impels
The feathers harden and the leather swells
He grins and sweats, yet grins and urges more,
Till scarce the turgid globe contains its store.

↑
Ball maker in the 1770s
as was Allan's great grandfather

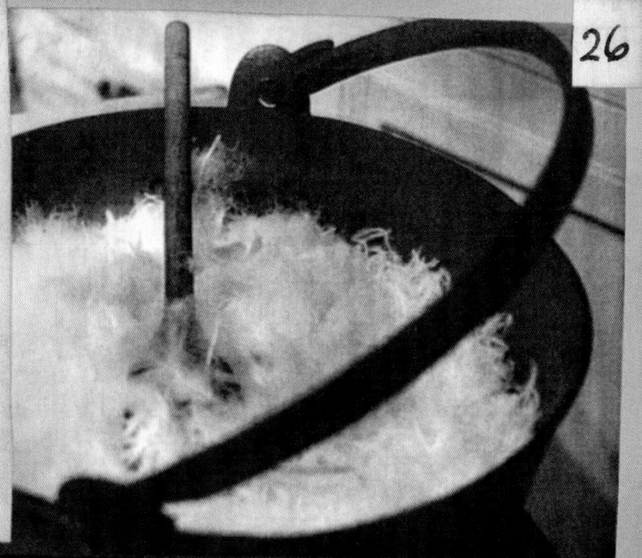

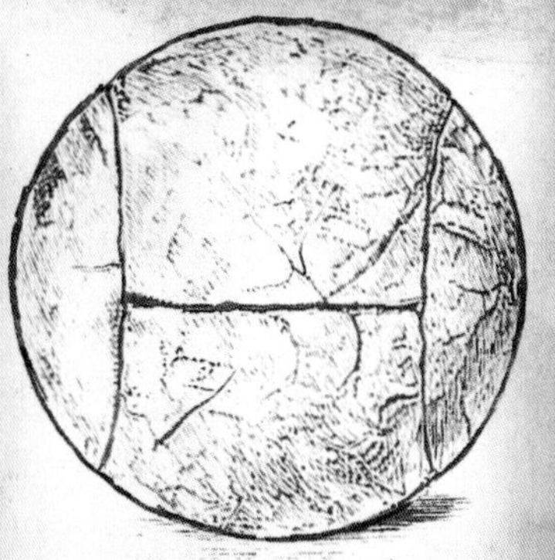
Very Old Feather Ball

Ball making equipment

Gutta-percha Balls were first introduced in 1848. Formerly the price of a ball, made of leather stuffed hard with feathers, was half-a-crown; now, however, the highest price is one shilling; and, unlike the old "ovals," those presently in use can be easily "made up" and do double duty at a very moderate rate per dozen.

James Allan Robertson

St. Andrews, 4th October 1764.

The Captain and Gentlemen Golfers present are of opinion that it would be for the improvement of the Links that the four first holes should be converted into two,[1]—They therefore have agreed that for the future they shall be played as two holes, in the same way as presently marked out. WM. ST. CLAIR.

yearly in time coming, the victor to be holder of the Silver Club, and to enjoy the dignity of Captain of the Society for the year. Annexed is a list of the names of those who have been Captains, from 1754 to the present day:—

1754. Baillie William Landale, St Andrews.
1755. Thomas Boswall, Esq., Writer, Edinburgh.
1756. Alexander Duncan, Esq., of Craigton, Advocate.
1757. No competition.
1758. Hugh Fraser, of Lovat, Esq.
1759. Sir James Carnegie, Bart., M.P.
1760. No competition.
1761. Alexander Duncan, Esq., of Craigton.
1762. Hugh Fraser, of Lovat, Esq.
1763. Sir Harry Seton, Bart.
1764. William St Clair, of Roslin, Esq.
1765. Hon. Francis Charteris, of Amisfield.
1766. William St Clair, of Roslin, Esq.
1767. James Durham, of Largo, Esq.
1768. William St Clair, of Roslin, Esq.
1769. Dr George Forrest, Professor of Civil History, United College, St Andrews.
1770. Henry Bethune, of Nydie, Esq.
1771. Ninian Imrie, Esq., of Denmuir.
1772. James Morison, Esq., of Naughton.
1773. Patrick Rigg, Esq., of Downfield.
1774. John Hay, Esq., of Leys.
1775. Right Hon. Alexander, Earl of Balcarres.
1776. Roger Aytoun, Esq., of Inchdairny.
1777. John Balfour, Esq., of Fairnie.
1778. Walter Boswell, Esq.
1779. James Morison, Esq., of Naughton.
1780. James Durham, Esq., of Largo.
1781. Alexander Duncan, Esq.
1782. Right Hon. Alexander, Earl of Balcarres.
1783. Major William Morison.
1784. Robert Low, Esq., of Clatto.
1785. Captain John Cheape.
1786. Colonel John Thomson, of Charlton,
1787. James Cheape, Esq., of Strathtyrum.
1788. Captain James Dalrymple.
1789. Captain William Nairne.
1790. Patrick Rigg, Esq.
1791. Alexander Duncan, Esq.
1792. Right Hon. the Earl of Crawford.
1793. John Patullo, Esq., of Balhouffie.
1794. Captain Alexander Aytone, of Kippo.
1795. Alexander Anderson, Esq., of Newbigging.
1796. James Morison, Esq., of Naughton.
1797. Thomas Erskine, Esq., of Cambo.
1798. Methven Erskine, Esq., of Airdry.
1799. John Dalyell, Esq., of Lingo.
1800. Robert Patullo, Esq.
1801. George Cheape, Esq., of Pusk.
1802. Hugh Cleghorn, Esq., of Stravithie.
1803. George Paterson, Esq.
1804. John Anstruther Thomson, Esq., of Charlton.
1805. Colonel David Dewar, of Gilston.
1806. William Dalgleish, Esq., of Scotscraig.
1807. General George Moncrieff.
1808. Alexander Guthrie, Esq., of Craigie.
1809. James Home Rigg, Esq., of Morton.
1810. John Maitland, Esq., of Kilmaron.
1811. Thomas Bruce, Esq., of Grangemuir.
1812. Robert G. Smyth, Esq., of Gibliston.
1813. General James Durham, of Largo.
1814. George Cheape, Esq., of Pusk.
1815. John Makgill, Esq., of Kemback.
1816. Sir John Anstruther, of Anstruther, Bart.
1817. David Moncrieff, Esq., yr. of Moncrieff.
1818. John Murray, Esq., of Lintrose.
1819. Robert Bruce, Esq., of Kennet.
1820. Right Hon. the Earl of Leven and Melville.
1821. Colonel Alexander Bethune, of Blebo.
1822. Alexander Binny, Esq., St Andrews.
1823. John Whyte Melville, Esq., of Strathkinness and Bennochy.

St Clair
121
on the
old 11 holes (22 holes)
1764

27

St. Andrews, 27th June 1771.

The Captain and Company agree and appoint that in time coming, the caddies who carry the clubs or run before the players, or are otherwise employed by the Gentlemen Golfers, are to get Fourpence sterling for going the length of the hole called the Hole of Cross, and if they go farther than that hole, they are to get Sixpence, and no more. Any of the gentlemen transgressing this rule are to pay two pint bottles of claret at the first meeting they shall attend.

HENRY BETHUNE.

St. Andrews, 4th September 1779.

It is enacted that whoever shall be Captain of the Golf, and does not attend all the meetings to be appointed throughout the year, shall pay Two Pints of Claret for each meeting he shall be absent at,—to be drunk at such meeting; but this regulation is not to take place if the Captain be not in Fife at the time.

WALTER BOSWELL.

Address to St Andrews

ST. ANDREWS! they say that thy glories are gone,
That thy streets are deserted, thy castles o'erthrown:
If thy glories *be* gone, they are only, methinks,
As it were, by enchantment, transferr'd to thy Links.
Though thy streets be not now, as of yore, full of prelates,
Of abbots and monks, and of hot-headed zealots,
Let none judge us rashly, or blame us as scoffers,
When we say that instead there are Links full of Golfers,
With more of good heart and good feeling among them
Than the abbots, the monks, and the zealots who sung them:
We have red coats and bonnets, we've putters and clubs;
The green has its bunkers, its hazards, and *rubs*;
At the long hole across we have biscuits and beer,
And the Hebes who sell it give zest to the cheer:
If this make not up for the pomp and the splendour
Of mitres, and murders, and mass—we'll surrender;
If Golfers and caddies be not better neighbours
Than abbots and soldiers, with crosses and sabres,
Let such fancies remain with the fool who so thinks,
While we toast old St Andrews, its Golfers and Links.

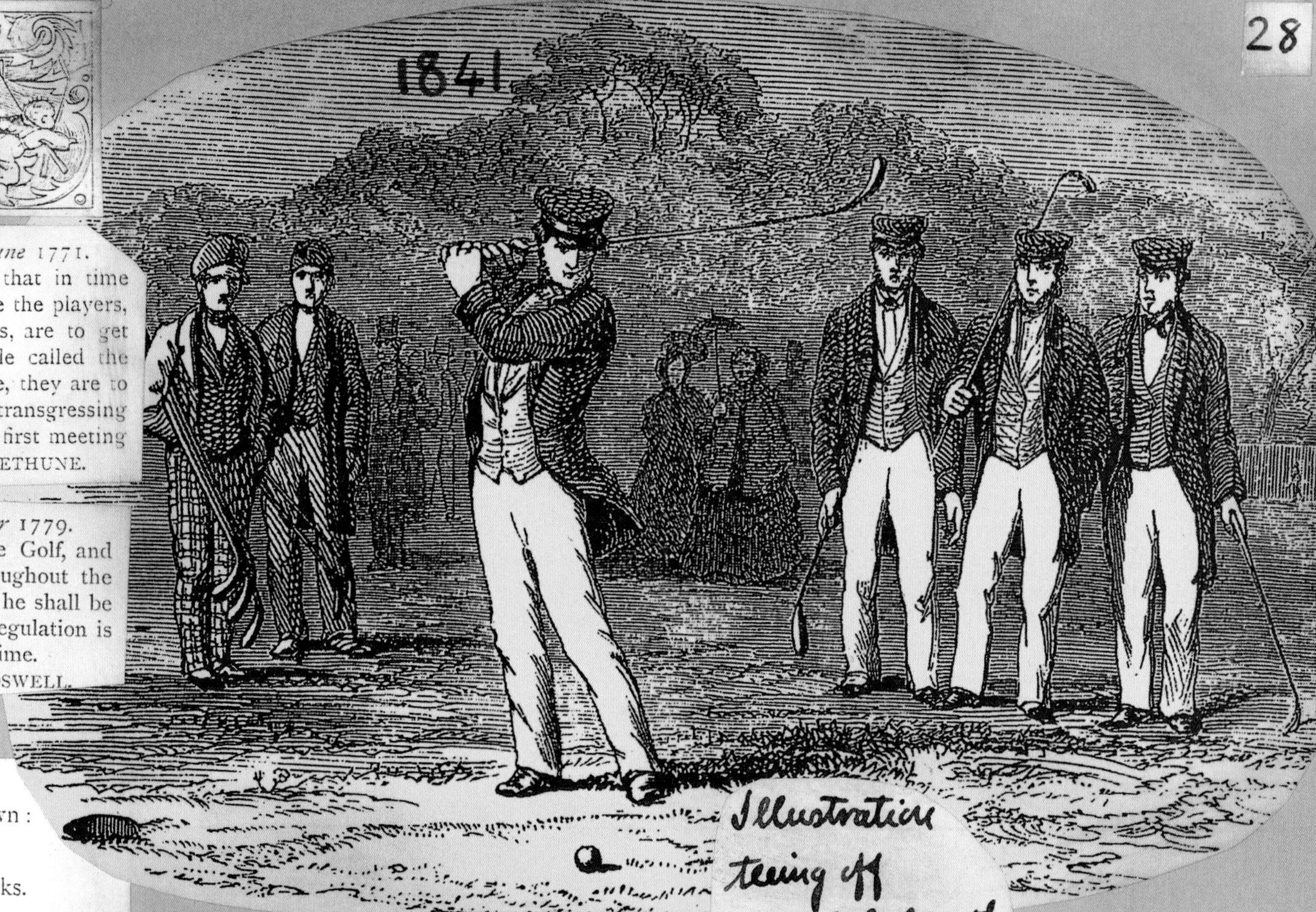

Illustration teeing off one club length from the hole

St. Andrews, 4th August 1780.

The Society took into their consideration that their Golfing Jackets are in bad condition,—Have agreed that they shall have new ones—viz. Red with yellow buttons. The undermentioned gentlemen have likewise agreed to have an Uniform Frock—viz. a Buff colour with a Red Cap. The Coat to be half lapelled, the Button white.

BALCARRES,
and Ten others.

Gourlay Feather Ball

St. Andrews, 6th March 1818.

The Secretary stated to the Club that from the subscriptions obtained from the Members he had paid the Club's subscription of One hundred Guineas for the privilege of the Town Hall and Supper Rooms above the same.

29

Articles & Laws in playing the Golf

viz

1 You Must Tee your Ball within a Club length of the Hole

2 Your Tee must be upon the Ground

3 You are not to Change the Ball which you Strike off the Tee.

4 You are not to Remove Stones, Bones or any Break Club for the Sake of playing your Ball Except upon the fair Green, and that only within a Club length of your Ball.

5 If your Ball come among Water, or any Watery filth, you are at liberty to take out your Ball, and ~~carrying~~ throw it behind the hazard six yards at least, you may play it with any Club and allow your Adversary a Stroke, for so getting out your Ball.

6. If your Balls be found any where touching one another, You are to lift the first Ball, till you play the last.

7. At Holing, you are to play your Ball Honestly for the Hole, and not to play upon your Adversary's Ball, not lying in your way to the Hole.

8 If you should lose your Ball, by its being taken up, or any other way you are to go back to the Spot, where you struck last, and drop another Ball, and Allow your Adversary a Stroke for the Misfortune

9. No Man at Holing his Ball, is to be Allowed to Mark his way to the Hole with his Club or any thing else.

10. The Ball be Stopd by any person, Horse, Dog, or any thing else, the Ball so stopd must be played where it lyes.

11. If you draw your Club in Order to Strike, and proceed so far in the Stroke as to be bringing down your Club; if then your Club shall break, in any way, it is to be Accounted a Stroke.

12. He, whose Ball lyes furthest from the Hole is Obliged to play first

13 Neither Trench, Ditch, or Dyke made for the preservation of the Links, Nor the Scholars holes or the Soldiers Lines shall be Accounted a Hazard. But the Ball is to be taken out, Teed and played with any Iron Club.

The 1st 13 Rules
1744

The Noblemen and Gentlemen above named being admirer[s] of the antient and healthfull Exercise of the Golf, and at th[e] sametime having the interest and prosperity of the Antient Cit[y] of St. Andrews at heart, being the ALMA MATER of the GOLF Did in the year of our Lord 1754 contribute for a SILVER CLUB weighing pounds ounces, and having a St. Andrew engraved on the head thereof, to be played for on the Links o[f] St. Andrews upon the 14th day of May said year, and yearly

St. Andrews, 14th May 1754.
The Silver Club was this day played for, in terms of the Regulations, and gained by Bailie William Landale, merchant in St. Andrews. JOHN SMART.

Parading the Captains' balls

St. Andrews, 16th Sept. 1825.

Which day the present Captain, having imposed on himself a fine of a Magnum of Claret for failure in public duty, imposed a similar fine on the old Captains present.

RALPH A. ANSTRUTHER.

St. Andrews, 17th Oct. 1827.

The Captain proposed that as the funds of the Club were at present inadequate to payment of their debt, the salary or allowance of Two Guineas now payable annually to the Leith Clubmaker for attending at the General Meeting should be discontinued.

J. CHEAPE, *C.*

That's how Hugh Philp got a start clubmaking.

St. Andrews, 25th Sept. 1833.

Previous to Captain Halkett Craigie resigning the chair, Captain Melville rose and stated, that on 3rd Nov. 1820, a Bet having been made by the late Sir David Moncrieffe, Bart., and himself, by which it was stipulated that the survivor should purchase and present to the Club A NEW SILVER PUTTER, with

Prophaning the Sabbath 15th Century

Photograph with Sir Hugh addressing the ball at Scotscraig (Tayport)

St. Andrews, 26th Sept. 1834.

Which day the Gold Medal was played for over the Links of St. Andrews, and gained by Robert Oliphant, Esq., younger of Rossie, by holing the course at 97 strokes.

ROBERT ANSTRUTHER, *C.*

St. Andrews, 4th May 1836.

It having been the anxious wish of a very great number of Members of the Royal and Ancient Golf Club of St. Andrews to convey to Charles Grace, Esq., their Secretary, some particular mark of the high and grateful sense they entertain of the very kind and handsome manner in which he has for a period of twenty-four years gratuitously devoted his time and attention to the management of their affairs, and at the same time bearing in mind that his late respected father contributed his valuable services in a similar manner for thirty years,—The Club, at a meeting held here this day, unanimously Resolve, That, in testimony of the regard and esteem in which Charles Grace, Esq., is held by the Members, and as a mark of the heartfelt gratitude they entertain towards him for the zealous and conscientious manner in which he has gratuitously discharged the duties of Secretary for twenty-four years,—PLATE, amounting in value to a sum of not less than One hundred Guineas, be presented to him by the Club; and that a Subscription, limited to One Sovereign each, be immediately entered into.

"At St Andrews the 29th September 1843 a number of young men met to consider what steps should be taken to form themselves into a Society, when it was proposed and agreed to that this Society should be considered as instituted on this day, and be called the St Andrews Mechanics' Golf Club, when it was proposed by A. Carstairs, cabinetmaker, and seconded and unanimously agreed to, that D. Todd, jun., painter, should be made Captain of the Club for the first year.

(Signed) "DAVID TODD.

"At St Andrews, the 30th September 1844 (the minutes read 31st September, but as there are only 30 days in September, I take it as a clerical error, and substitute 30th instead), the annual meeting of the Club, it was proposed by the retiring Chairman that Robert Wilson, blacksmith, should be Captain of the Club for the year, which was agreed to, upon which he begged leave to decline the honour, and made an amendment that the present Chairman be re-elected for another year, which, after considerable discussions and uproar was agreed to on the understanding that that rule should not be gone into for the future."

(Signed) "DAVID TODD.

Links, St Andrews,
Dec. 20th 1849.

"Sir,-According to my statement in last meeting, I move that no odds be given to the players for either medal or other prizes, but that all members of the Club should be classed into one, two, three, four, or five classes, also that a prize be given to each class and the medal open to all the members, this motion to take effect on and after January 1st 1850."- I am, Sir, yours truly,

"(Signed) ALLAN ROBERTSON

To the Members of the Mechanics Golf Club."

The members evidently had

FALLEN OUT WITH HANDICAPPING,

or more than likely, the good players objected to have to play with the indifferent in the medal competitions, hence the motion to separate into classes, and the motion was carried too by 15 votes to 2, while Allan Robertson and Tom Morris were appointed to meet with the Committee and to assist in this classification.

GREAT GOLFING MATCH FOR £200 ROBERTSON AND MORRIS v THE DUNNS

1849

The third and deciding game of this great match, for £100 a side, between Allan Robertson and T. Morris of St Andrews, and Messrs J. and W. Dunn of Musselburgh, took place on Wednesday the 8th instant, when the St Andrews players were successful. The match excited the utmost interest, and a large assemblage of spectators witnessed the concluding event of this important match. A special train from Edinburgh conveyed a large party to the Links at North Berwick, which presented a scene of great animation during the day. The play was of the most excellent description, and worthy of the reputation of the players; as may be seen from the result, the St Andrews party winning only by two at the last hole. We heard that, before commencing the last round, the Messrs Dunn were five – a – head, but in this round they lost every hole, which decided the match against them. Several heavy bets were dependent on the result; and a good many sums exchanged hands on the occasion

Home hole - Boys at play 1852
See page 145
for description
Station master's house
Railway
Station
Bleaching linen

THE HOME HOLE
AROUND 1849

THE EARLY DAYS OF THE ST ANDREWS GOLF CLUB.

HE MOST IMPORTANT MEETING OF ALL

he reconstitution of the Club. It was d in Mr Hastie's Inn on the 19th cember 1850. Hastie's Inn was situated en where the present Cross Keys Hotel is. Incidentally, it may be mentioned that at at time the total membership of the Club s only 37. At this meeting twenty-one embers were present. They were—Robert terson (captain), R. Lister, David Clark, mes M'Pherson, Alex. Galloway, William yton, jun., John Hastie, Adam M'Pherson, ndrew Rolland, John Linn, George Bruce, mes Howie, Walter Harris, Arch. Downie, hn Barker, Allan Robertson, Tom Morris vo famous names surely), Chas. Ritchie, hn Kiddie, George Morris, and John yne. The Secretary and Treasurer being sent, James Howie acted instead.

The following report on behalf of the Comttee appointed at last meeting was nded in for consideration:—"The Comttee unanimously agree to recommend the nexed draft of regulations for the adoption the Club—all fines to be abolished after ew Year's Day next; the Secretary and easurer to be instructed in future to record e results of all matches and competiti ayed.

1856

Hell Bunker. Mr Chambers ↑ Sir Hugh
Daw Anderson

MR BLAIR MR T. HAY MR J. BLACKWOOD MR T. CAMPBELL SIR THOMAS MONCRIEFFE SELF COL. FAIRLIE SANDY PIRIE BOB KIRK
MR OGILVIE KEEPER OF THE GREEN SANDY HERD

New Year's Day, 1851, duly came round, and with it the medal competition. We are told that twenty-three couples competed, and the result was that W. Ayton, jun., won the medal with a score of 94—one stroke less than the previous best. Geo. Morris gained the cross clubs with 96.

34

ALLAN ROBERTSON'S PUTTER

went to the medal winner, who, curiously enough, had contributed half of the cost of the putter—practically a case of winning your own prize.

James M'Pherson's play club was won by the Captain, Robert Paterson, with 101—5, 96, and the balls presented by Allan Robertson and Tom Morris were won by Geo. Morris, 96 scratch, and Alex. Grieve, 102—5, 97.

As I have a record of the scores of the others, I give them below in their order after deducting their handicaps. They may interest and amuse some readers:—

		H'cap.	
W. Ayton, sen., ...	127	26	101
Jas. M'Pherson, ...	107	5	102
Wm. Halkerson, ...	118	15	103
J. Linn, ...	110	5	105
John Bayne, ...	114	9	105
Chas. Ritchie, ...	117	12	105
David Clark, ...	124	12	112
Adam M'Pherson, ...	130	18	112
John Kiddie, ...	133	18	115
R. Lister.	131	15	116
Andrew King, ...	128	12	116
Archd. Downie, ...	130	12	118
John Bankier, ...	138	18	120
George Bruce, ...	130	9	121
Alex. Galloway, ...	143	12	131
James Herd, ...	132	Scratch	132
James Black, ...	157	20	137
Alex. Clyne, ...	153	7	146

Whatever was James Herd, a scratch player, doing to require 132 strokes to get round — actually 38 more than the medal winner? And what about Clyne? This is even a worse case. Here we have a player with a handicap of 7 running up a total of 153 strokes. There are other cases almost as bad, as a perusal of the returns show.

However, let us be charitable, and remember that it was the festive season—this surely can be the only possible explanation of these

FEARFUL AND WONDERFUL SCORES.

Otherwise the handicapping Committee must have been sadly at fault.

As usual the members dined together in Mr Hastie's Inn in the evening.

We come now to the month of March, 1851, when the quarterly meeting was held. The date, Friday 21st does not suggest that the members were at all superstitious. In fact, Friday appears to have been a pet day with the Mechanics' Club, for all its quarterly meetings took place on a Friday, and we have already observed that the June medal was always competed for on the third Friday of that month.

Sir Hugh organized the building of our own railway line to join up with the main line 3 miles away – we even bought our own train – and off I went to travel and join up with the Glasgow Ayr railway line – and to Prestwick with my wife and newly born son Tommy.

Many of the R&A Balls were held in the Cross Keys before the building of the Townhall.

The members used to be piped down from the cobbled end of Market Street down to the course for their meetings.

(Sir Hugh – centre (with his familiar top hat)

TOM LEAVES ST ANDREWS

1851

On the evening of Thursday last, a number of the friends of Mr Thomas Morris, a golf-ball maker, entertained him at supper in the Cross Keys Inn, to testify their personal esteem for him as an individual, as well as their sense of his merits as a golfer, previous to his leaving St Andrews for Prestwick, near Ayr, where a golfing club has recently been established, and to a situation in connection with which he has been appointed. Mr John Buddo occupied the chair, and the duties of croupiership were performed by Mr John Todd.

1st Captain of the St Andrews Mechanics Club in 1843

The Tolbooth and Town Jail

PRESTWICK 1851
NOT MUCH ROOM
FOR LAYING OUT A GREEN

The Royal and Ancient

St. Andrews, 16th Oct. 1850.

The Club Gold Medal having to-day been gained by Mr. George Condie, who holds the Silver Cross, and as, in conformity with the Rules of the Club, the Silver Cross falls to be surrendered to the Club and competed for to-morrow, the meeting accordingly directed that the Cross should be played for to-morrow morning at half-past nine o'clock. J. O. FAIRLIE.

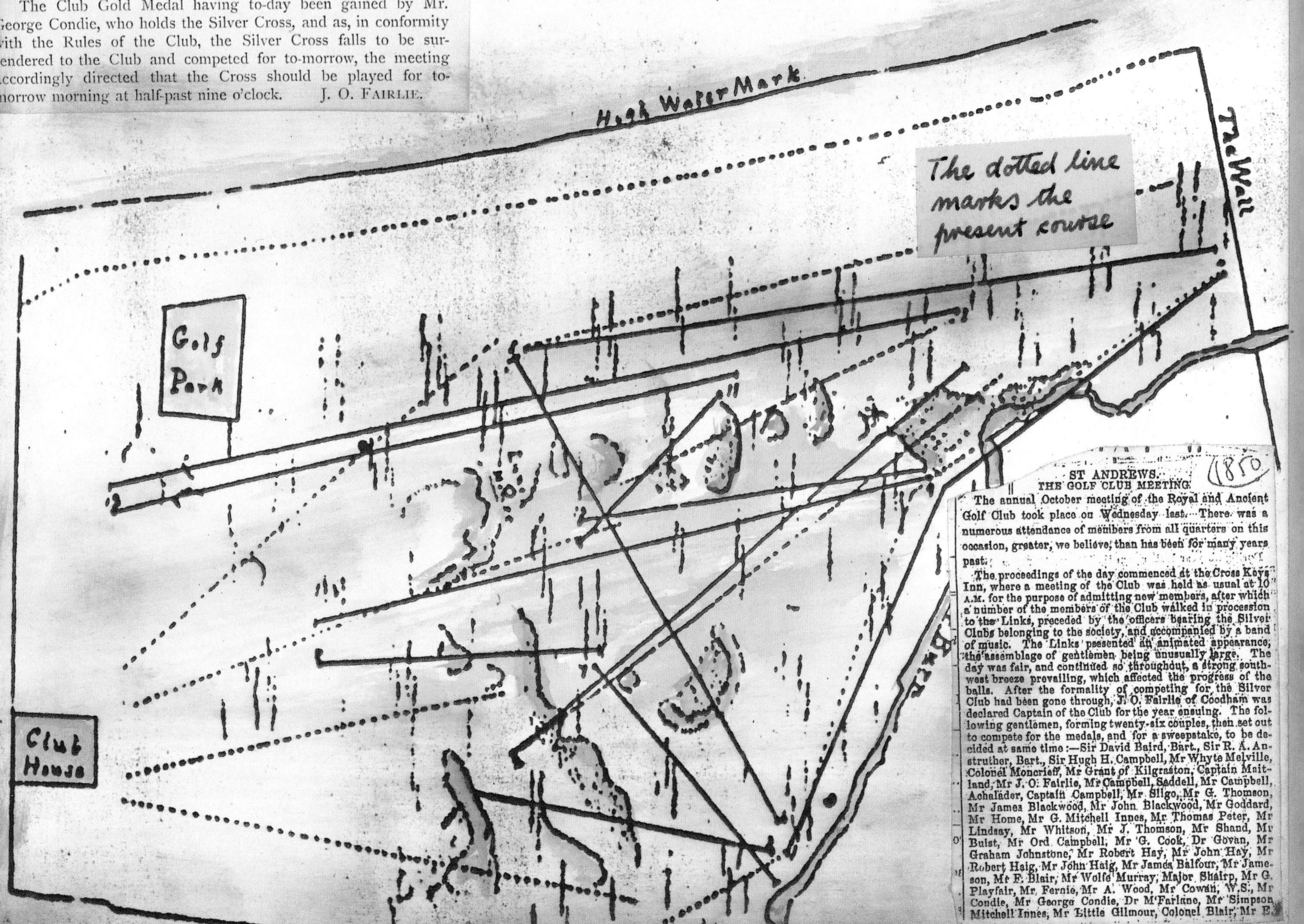

The dotted line marks the present course

(1850)

ST ANDREWS.

THE GOLF CLUB MEETING.

The annual October meeting of the Royal and Ancient Golf Club took place on Wednesday last. There was a numerous attendance of members from all quarters on this occasion, greater, we believe, than has been for many years past.

The proceedings of the day commenced at the Cross Keys Inn, where a meeting of the Club was held as usual at 10 A.M. for the purpose of admitting new members, after which a number of the members of the Club walked in procession to the Links, preceded by the officers bearing the Silver Clubs belonging to the society, and accompanied by a band of music. The Links pesented an animated appearance, the assemblage of gentlemen being unusually large. The day was fair, and continued so throughout, a strong south-west breeze prevailing, which affected the progress of the balls. After the formality of competing for the Silver Club had been gone through, J. O. Fairlie of Coodham was declared Captain of the Club for the year ensuing. The following gentlemen, forming twenty-six couples, then set out to compete for the medals, and for a sweepstake, to be decided at same time :—Sir David Baird, Bart., Sir R. A. Anstruther, Bart., Sir Hugh H. Campbell, Mr Whyte Melville, Colonel Moncrieff, Mr Grant of Kilgraston, Captain Maitland, Mr J. O. Fairlie, Mr Campbell, Saddell, Mr Campbell, Achalader, Captain Campbell, Mr Sligo, Mr G. Thomson, Mr James Blackwood, Mr John Blackwood, Mr Goddard, Mr Home, Mr G. Mitchell Innes, Mr Thomas Peter, Mr Lindsay, Mr Whitson, Mr J. Thomson, Mr Shand, Mr Buist, Mr Ord Campbell, Mr G. Cook, Dr Govan, Mr Graham Johnstone, Mr Robert Hay, Mr John Hay, Mr Robert Haig, Mr John Haig, Mr James Balfour, Mr Jameson, Mr F. Blair, Mr Wolfe Murray, Major Shairp, Mr G. Playfair, Mr Fernie, Mr A. Wood, Mr Cowan, W.S., Mr Condie, Mr George Condie, Dr M'Farlane, Mr Simpson Mitchell Innes, Mr Little Gilmour, Colonel Blair, Mr E.

The EARL of EGLINTON & WINTON
1851

Members of Prestwick Golf Club.

Entrance and subscription for 1851.

	Entrance	Subscription
Earl of Eglinton	1	1
W. M. Alexander Esq Ballochmyle	1.	1.
Lieut. Col. Hunter Blair Younger of Blairquhan	1	1
John T. Burnett Esq Gadgirth	1	1
James Kennedy Esq Dalreoch	1	1
L. Col. Campbell Esq. yr of Craigie	1	1
Thos. Smith Cunninghame Esq Caprington	1	1
The Honble Henry Coventry near Musselburgh	✓	
Norman M. Innes Esquire	1	1
Sampson M. Innes Esquire	1	1
Gilbert M. Innes Esquire not paid	✗	✗
Thomas M. Innes Esquire ~~not pd~~	1	1
Alexr M. Innes Esquire paid	1.	1
Robert Hay Esq New Club Edinburgh	1	1
Robert D. Fergusson Esq Cloncaird	1	1
John [illegible] Carry Forward £	13	13. =

Sto

Brought Forward £	13	13
John Dalrymple Esquire M.P.	1	1
John Campbell Esq of Glensaddell St Andrews	1	1
W. L. Gilmour Esq Inch Edinburgh	1	1
~~Sir D. Baird Bart Newbyth~~ dead		
Andw Gillon Esq Wallhouse	1	1
Alex: Oswald Esq M.P. Auchencruive	1	1
~~Col. Fairlie Holmes Kilmarnock~~		
The Revd Mr Pollock Glasgow	1	1
William Crawford Esq Grange	1	1
George Oswald Esquire	1	1
Arthur Campbell Junr Esq W.S.	1	1
C. D. Gairdner Esquire Auchans	1	1
Robert Gairdner Esq Banker Kilmarnock	1	1
Ord G. Campbell Esq Edinburgh	1	1
Dr Sloan Ayr	1	1
Adam Thomson Esquire Ayr	1	1
John Cuthbert Esq Ayr	1	1
Wm Kirkland Esq Ayr	1	1
J. O. Fairlie Esq Coodham	1	1
Regd Crawford Esq Younger of Crawfordland	1	1
Carry Forward £	31	31

31 - 31

Brought Forward £	31	31
Captain W. F. Hamilton Cairnhill	1	1
Capt. C. V. Hamilton Do	1	1
W. A. Hamilton Esq Do	1	1
~~Lord Archd Kennedy~~		
P. W. Kennedy Esq Drumellan	1	1
Charles Robertson Esq New Club Edinburgh		
~~Charles Campbell Esq~~ Ayr		
James Finnie Esq Newfield	1	1
Archd Finnie Esq Do	1	1
William Finnie Esq Do	1	1
Lord Charles Kerr		
A. D. Tait Esquire Millrig	1	1
Wm Dunlop Esq Annanhill	1	1
George Glennie Esq Glasgow	1	1
J. A. Riddell Esq East India House London	1	1
Lord Colville	1	1
F. C. Gross Esq Mitre Kilmarnock	1	1
George Thompson Esq Burnhouse	1	1
Samuel Hay Esq paid W.K.	1	1
£	45	55
Carried to page	45	45

45. 45.

39

St Andrews and District.

St Andrews Railway.—Passengers for week endi[redacted] 18th instant—1112.

Shipping.—Arrival.—The [redacted] Deen, in Norway, with timber.

Queen's Coronation.—Tues[redacted] of her Majesty's Coronation, will be a holiday in the banks here.

The Heriotters.—The annual excursion of the pupils, governors, &c., of George Heriot's Hospital, Edinburgh, takes place on Friday first, when they are to visit this city. They will arrive by the first train from the south. We understand that the boys will number about 180, and that they will breakfast in the City Hall, and dine in the quadrangle of the Old Castle, if the weather is favourable.

The Union Club-House.—'Coming events cast their shadows before.' We understand the brethren of the mystic tie have arrangements in progress for an imposing demonstration at the ceremony of laying the foundation-stone of this building on the 13th of next month. Deputations from all the Fife lodges will be asked to be present, and detachments from Edinburgh and Dundee are expected, in addition to the officials from the former place bringing the insignia of the fraternity, and the utensils employed on such occasions. The stone will be disposed by Mr Whyte-Melville, the Provincial Grand Master. The ceremony will likely be preceded by a procession through the city, accompanied by bands of music, and with all the intrinsic striking masonic characteristics. We hear it rumoured that it is in contemplation to have a three hours' cessation from business on that day to admit of shopkeepers and others joining in or viewing the spectacle. It is further reported that the succeeding day (Thursday) is proposed to be held as a total holiday in the town for the annual gathering for the games. Verily, highdays and holidays are becoming rife in these parts. Would not a boat race be a novel addition to the programme of the games? If the weather proved quiet, along the west sands would be a fine place for a pull. It could be in the evening, after the other day's doings are over. It is high water on the 14th July betwixt eight and nine P.M.

The Fascinations of Golfing and Salt Water are now in full influence here. The continued prevalence of easterly breezes hindered the bathing from early becoming general, and although the temperature of the water was very agreeable for immersion, it was chiefly confined to the stronger sex until the beginning of last week, when the weaker vessels were tempted to indulge, and after that period an extensive puddling and splashing was observable daily along the shore. The Madras boys come down and go through their ablutions, in herds composed of swimmers and tyros in the art, who set about kicking, spluttering, yelling, and leaping about like a lot of young savages, forming a somewhat lively scene. The change of the wind was accompanied with a change in the feeling of the water, which is much chillier than when Eurus was in power.—On the Links the fun grows fast and furious. Squadrons of gentlemen golfers, and caddies attendant, throng the course, inward or outward bound, until six o'clock, when they retire, and the working orders pour from the city, after their day's labour, and take the field in legions, roaming over the downs until darkness ends the sport. The members of the Mechanics' Golf Club are drilling and getting themselves in order for their half-yearly medal day, which falls on Friday. The former class re-appear in the evening and resort to playing at the short holes. A large collection of golfers from other places are located here at present. Among these are Lord Charles Keir, Sir Thomas Moncrieffe, Mr Grant of Kilgraston, Mr Ferguson Blair of Balthyack, Mr Peddie, Perth, Mr Thomas Patton, Perth, Mr George Gray, Perth, Mr Thomson of Burnhouse, Mr Skene of Pitlour, Mr Moncrieff, Skene, Mr Samuel Ferguson, &c.

FIFESHIRE JOU

of many who owe their present happiness (for health is the indispensable condition of enjoyment), perhaps their lives, to his skilful care. He carries with him the best wishes of all for his speedy recovery.

Another Golfers' Ball.—The golf-loving part of the community here have (to apply a popular phrase in a good sense) been 'on the ball' during the past fortnight. The Royal and Ancient Club led off, as registered last week, and on Friday night a fraternity of another class followed suit, viz., the St Andrews Golf Club, or as some still term it for the sake of distinction, or probably from a conservative spirit—averse to change, even in a name—the Mechanics' Golf Club. Again the Town-hall was attired in a befitting manner. The windows were bedecked around with wreaths of evergreens, interspersed with dahlias, the middle decorations being of holly, varied with bunches of rowan-tree berries. In front of this a *brilliant* idea of some cunning workman had been carried out in the formation of a royal crown in gas-lights. The gilt clubs, emblematic of the Society, had a prominent position within a circular garland of evergreens and dahlias. The front of the orchestra also in verdant garb, and the club flag hung over one corner, while another flag was displayed at the opposite side. The dames and their lords, as well as the damsels and gallants, began to arrive at nine o'clock; about forty couples were present, and before half-an-hour was gone, the dancing was opened by the new Captain, Mr Allan Robertson and partner to the accompaniment of the excellent music of Messrs M'Pherson, Sharp, and Liddle. Among others, 'Pop goes the Weasel' was put through its facings skilfully. About twelve the intervention of refreshment took place, after which the company resumed 'tripping it,' and continued right merrily - till 5 am!

The laying of the foundation stone for the Royal and Ancient Clubhouse

1852

ROYAL AND ANCIENT GOLF CLUB.

We last week noticed the competition of this Club upon the Wednesday, when the medal was gained by Mr Robert Hay, at 99 strokes; and the club medal by Mr Thomas Peter, do. The next in order of merit were—Colonel Grant, 103 strokes; Mr Patrick Alexander, 103 do.; Mr Hugh Alexander, 104 do.; Mr Whitson, 106 do.; Mr Balfour, W.S., 107 do.; Messrs Fairlie, Buist Skene, Home, Glennie, and Innes, came in at 108 respectively. The whole day's play was good, being a full average of previous years. It is perhaps only correct in us here to notice, that a week ago, an interesting match took place at North Berwick Links, betwixt J. O. Fairlie, Esq., and Tom Morris, against Robert Hay, Esq., and William Dunn, when the former were successful. So soon as the competition for the medal was completed, the same parties who played at North Berwick went the round of St Andrews Links, and the result was that the tables were turned—Messrs Hay & Dunn beating.

1854

PRESTWICK GOLF CLUB.

Wednesday, the 17th was the seventh meeting of this now justly celebrated club. Owing to our war with Russia, Parliamentary debates, and several other reasons, the muster was not so strong as usual; still, at twelve o'clock, a fair sprinkling of golfers assembled at Tom Morris' house, and Sir Thomas Moncrieff having been called to the chair, a ballot for new members was taken and the following gentlemen elected:—J. C. Stewart, Esq. of Fasnacloich; John Hamilton, Esq. Sundrum; Edward J. Jackson, Esq. of Strathtyrum; Capt. Jackson, Ayr; William Baird, Esq. of Rosemount; E. A. Hunter, Esq., Newark; Capt. Hutchison, Wemyss Hall; John Grant, Esq., of Kilgranston. The following pairs then drew and started for the medal:—Rev. William Pollock and Captain W. F. Hamilton; J. Burnett, Esq., and J. Cuthbert, Esq.; Col. Fairlie, and Sir Thomas Moncrieff; G. Glennie, Esq., and J. C. Stewart, Esq.; F. Blair, Esq., and J. Hamilton, Esq.; Dr Scott and and Charles Campbell, Esq. Capt. Fairlie in the first round looked all over the winner, though closely run up to by Sir Thomas Moncrieff, but luck was against him the second round, and a new member, after beating the present holder, Mr Glennie, transferred the medal once more to a *maiden*. Mr Stewart held the rounds in 121, the smallest number it has ever been won in. Capt. Fairlie was second at 125, and Sir Thomas Moncrieff third at 130. Mr Stewart, by his good play, also carried off the sweepstakes. Several capital matches have been played during the week. Allan Robertson, from St. Andrews, came to see something of the "West Countrie," and pitted against Tom Morris with Prestwick golfers to make up the four, showed some first-rate play, and gave those who had never seen the city of our patron saint some idea how the northern players handle their clubs. All who met at this the seventh meeting at Prestwick left delighted, and only hoped that the Lord Advocate, an old friend to golf, has taken care that the new Valuation Bill, which provides for new boundaries of burghs, will in nowise interfere with the links of Prestwick, which at present stands A 1.—*Corres.*

Better copy of this report on next page. →

AUTUMN MEETING OF THE ROYAL AND ANCIENT GOLF CLUB.

The game of golf, unlike most other games, although very ancient, somehow or other never shows any symptoms of becoming antiquated. Year after year, its lovers "walk the course" with their cadies in their rear, without evincing the slightest appearance of diminished *gout* for their favourite sport. Indeed, the game has so much to recommend it, that, with all who have a practical acquaintance with it, it is a prime favourite. Unlike other outside sports, you may take the exercise it affords in the measure that best suits your ability or inclination. While abundant scope is afforded by it for the display of skill and activity, the frame is not taxed by severe exertion at one time, and a total cessation of it at another, but the exercise afforded is, throughout, of that equable and exhilerating character which is proved to be most conducive to health. If a gentleman be light and active, why, he may run after his ball if he has a mind; if on the contrary, he is of that particular build, which makes his "pair" averse to rapid locomotion, he may waddle after it as he best can. Possessed of such recommendations it is not surprising that when the game was comparatively a new one, perhaps three centuries ago, the passion of gentlemen for it, had to be regulated by the legislature. Forming as it did so formidable a rival to the sport of archery as to leave that sport in a very neglected condition, the law had to step in to compel attention to the latter—in the then state of society, the more useful art. But, indeed, the game of golf has been an object of attention to those in high places during almost the whole period of its existence. The unfortunate Charles I., while, it might be said, the axe was already hanging over his head, and his sovereignty was melting in his grasp before the rising power of the stern puritans, still found leisure to play at golf, of which he was passionately fond. His scarcely less unfortunate son James II., was also very partial to the game, and more recently still, the gruff good-natured William IV. took so much interest in it as to send down a medal to be competed for by the Ancient Golf Club of St Andrews. St Andrews, indeed, has been for centuries, the headquarters of the ancient game, its golf course being by far the finest in Scotland, and the meetings of veteran golfers on it are frequent, and the play generally very spirited.

Yesterday, the autumn meeting of the Royal and Ancient Golf Club took place. The day was beautiful, indeed as fine as could be wished, with the exception of a rather strong breeze from the westward, which made the play much more difficult than it would otherwise have been. At an early hour, the members of the Club met at the Cross-Keys Hotel for the despatch of business, and afterwards proceeded to the course. The discharge of a piece of ordnance gave notice of the commencement of the match, which accordingly began at a little past eleven o'clock, an extraordinary number of players taking part in the competition. (33 couples)

1850

Four of the most skilful gentlemen-golfers in the country engaged in a foursome over two rounds—Mr Hay and Captain Maitland Dougall, encountered by Messrs Fairlie and Goddard. The betters were alike in their risks, but the result was different from what was anticipated. Messrs Fairlie and Goddard had no chance with the younger gentlemen, who, at the end of the first round, had five holes to spare, and in the second round discomfited the opposite couple at the Hole o' Cross, having got six holes before them and five to play. Messrs Hay and Dougall are two whom it would be eminently difficult to overcome. Both stand high in the art. Mr Hay has been calling forth extreme admiration here during his visit by his extraordinary skill. His driving amply deserves the term 'long and sure.' He smites his balls with tremendous force.

'Now comes the day, the great, important day, big with the fate of *Allan* and of *Tom*,' as was parodied on the occasion by a humorous member of the Royal and Ancient. Saturday was the choicest day of the six. The atmosphere was clear and sharp, and a slight breeze [illegible] of the west. The rain during the night had sapped the ground well, but this was in noways detrimental, as will be seen. The afternoon was looked forward to with great anxiety, being the time for a struggle replete [illegible] between Mr Hay, the lion of [illegible]eck, in conjunction with William Dunn, against the pride of St Andrews—the invincible firm of Allan & Tom. The betting was extreme—the latter party giving two to one, some of their backers five to one; but the general odds were, we are informed, four to three. We propose being somewhat specific in recounting this important piece of golfing warfare, and hope that lovers of the game will appreciate the details:—

Half-past twelve was the hour of cause, when the set-off from the first hole took place, and then and there had collected an exceedingly numerous company to escort the actors, and view the proceedings in this all-absorbing trial of dexterity betwixt St Andrews and Musselburgh. The game was almost totally abandoned for the afternoon by the other players, and the course presented a fair field and no favour. Besides stranger and resident golfing gentlemen, in themselves a host, the match was witnessed by doctors, lawyers, and divines (young ones at least of the latter profession), professors, bankers, railway directors, merchants' clerks, tradesmen, workmen, Madras boys and other youngsters, as well as a goodly sprinkling of general idlers. All the attention of the city was concentered [illegible] crowd followed the players closely, observing with great excitement the effect of each stroke. The putting greens especially were places where the utmost concern was displayed as each and all looked on in breathless suspense. Mr Lees' picture of 'The Golfers' can best convey [illegible] of the sight.

Mr Hay and his partner began the battle [illegible] prestige of success, capturing the first two holes [illegible] in with the match at the Hole o' Cross, travelling inward the first round. At that time the star of St Andrews appeared to be in the descendant. The state of the poll was that the Musselburgh men had a majority of four holes. They had played an almost unexampled game in the outward half of the round. Mr Hay was reported to have been driving tremendously long balls, and with the most unerring precision, and Dunnie shewing himself a worthy mate; both also holing their balls at all distances in the green. This was too grand to last long. On the other hand, Allan and Tom had been doing well—gone out in forty-six. Allan had shown his wonted first-rate steady play, but Tom, it was insinuated, was at his old trade of 'funking'. The St Andrews folks at this juncture were desponding a little, and some quaking for the renown of their men. But the Hole o' Cross was the crisis in the conflict; Allan and Tom's good time was fast coming—neither of their right hands had forgot its cunning. Their never-failing pluck and characteristic uniformity under the adverse game began to tell, for they immediately commenced to apply the process of subtraction to their adversaries, by taking the Ginger Beer hole at six to the other's seven; ditto with the next, by five to six. Driving off at the succeeding one, Dunnie bunkered in the Principal's nose. Allan drove a wide ball the second shot, which Tom skilfully redeemed, but after all Dunnie seized half the hole by a wonderful put at two more, Allan failing to put in his at one off two. The Hay party still two holes a-head, but they lost the next by seven to five. The home hole was divided—Allan narrowly missing taking it all, which would have placed them on an equality. After a brief interval the battle was renewed, the players having as many if not more followers than before, and the excitement [illegible] Hay and Co. [illegible] will be noted were a hole a-head, but Dunnie, aiming at over the burn the second stroke, set his ball to water, while Tom cautiously drew short on the east side of the hazard, and accounts were immediately squared. Next hole did not alter matters, but at the third Allan plumped his ball into the Principal's beak; Tom scooped it out, but it rolled into a sheep track, and Hay and Co. got for the last time a-head. Allan and Tom retrieved at the fourth hole, and now that the tug of war was come, they began to assert their supremacy. They took the fifth hole at five, and the sixth at four. The high hole was next, which was then played admirably. A long tee ball of Allan's shot far a-head of Mr Hay's corresponding one; indeed, one could hardly conceive how Allan's little body could propel a ball so far. At second strokes Tom swiped past the hole, and Dunnie's was caught in a bunker, which Mr Hay did not eject, Dunnie doing it in his turn, while the other ball was at its destination in four to seven. Hole eight was halved. Hole of return went to Allan and Tom, but they owed it to a stimie. Homeward bound now, with four in favour of St Andrews men, to which was added one next hole, cancelled at high hole by Hay and Co., the second only they had won in eleven. The hole of Shell ran Allan's side up to five once more. Playing off here Mr Hay sent his ball astray, and Dun could not make much of it, but Mr Hay made a splendid swipe next, landing in the green at three, the same as the opposite one, but not so near the desired point by some yards. Allan made the decisive put—tumbling the ball in at a long distance—and instantly a spontaneous cheer signalized the success of Allan and Tom, by six a-head and five to play. The remaining holes were contested for a minor bet, we believe, but these need not be particularized. It was supposed that Allan and Tom in going over these—their success being declared—intentionally gave advantages by driving wide and being careless, but we don't think this was the case; suffice it to say, that at the thirty-sixth hole Allan and Tom's side was four holes in advance. In the progress inward, some boys removed the flags for guiding to the holes from their positions, and held them aloft in the procession, giving it the appearance of a triumphal entry. Such a scene has not been on the Links for many years; the last of a similar kind was, if we rightly remember, in the summer of 1848, when the two Dunnies tried to pluck the laurels from the brows of Allan and Tom. The combined prowess of the firm still endures, and they remain the cocks o' the green. Long may they hold that honourable elevation. St Andrews for ever!

The score of each party in this great match was as under-stated:—

40

ALLAN AND TOM.

1st round—5, 7, 4, 5, 8, 5, 5, 3, [illegible], outward 46
" 4, 3, 6, 5, 6, 5, 5, 5, 5, inward 44
— 90—total 1st round.
2d round—5, 6, 7, 4, 5, 5, 4, 4, 5, outward 45
" 4, 4, 6, 5, 7, 5, 6, 6, [illegible], inward 47
— 92—total 2d round.
Grand total—both rounds.........182 182

MR HAY AND DUNNIE.

1st round—4, 5, 4, [illegible], 7, [illegible], 4, 3, 2, outward 41
" 6, 3, 3, 5, 7, [illegible], 5, 7, 5, inward 47
— 88—total 1st round.
2d round—[illegible] outward [illegible]
" [illegible] inward 47
— [illegible]—total 2d round.
Grand total—both rounds.........18[illegible] 18[illegible]

41 **ROYAL AND ANCIENT GOLF CLUB**

St Andrews forever! 1852

....On Wednesday afternoon, Mr J.O. Fairlie and Tom Morris entered into a match with Mr Hay and William Dunn for one round – 18 holes. The latter were victorious by 2 holes, though the difference in the gross amount of strokes was only one. Mr Hay and Dunnie finishing in 92 and the opposing pair in 93. As a set-off against this, we have to state that on the preceding Thursday the same foursome was played over North Berwick Links in a match taken up for three rounds – 21holes – when Mr Fairlie and Tom shut up their opponents at the end of the second round, being eight holes in advance with seven to play. On the day previous Mr Hay had challenged the world with Dunn as his coadjutor...

'Now comes the day, the great, important day, big with the fate of *Allan* and *Tom*',

as was parodied on the occasion by a humorous member of the Royal and Ancient. Saturday was the choicest day of the six. The atmosphere was clear and sharp, and a slight breeze out of the west. The rain during the night had sapped the ground well, but this was in noways detrimental, as will be seen. The afternoon was looked forward to with great anxiety, being the time for a struggle, replete with interest in many ways, between Mr Hay, the lion of the week, in conjunction with William Dunn, against the pride of St Andrews – the invincible firm of Allan and Tom. The betting was extreme – the latter party giving two to one, some of their backers five to one; but the general odds were, we are informed, four to three. We propose being somewhat specific in recounting this important piece of golfing warfare, and hope that lovers of the game will appreciate the details: -

Half-past twelve was the hour of cause, when the set-off from the first hole took place, and then and there had collected an exceedingly numerous company to escort the actors, and view the proceedings in this all-absorbing trial of dexterity betwixt St Andrews and Musselburgh. The game was almost totally abandoned for the afternoon by the other players, and the course presented a fair field and no favour. Besides stranger and resident golfing gentlemen, in themselves a host, the match was witnessed by doctors, lawyers, and divines (young ones at least of the latter profession), professors, bankers, railway directors, merchants' clerks, tradesmen, workmen, Madras boys and youngsters, as well as a goodly sprinkling of general idlers. All attention of the city was concentered

'In the focus of the downs'

The crowd followed the players closely, observing with great excitement the effect of each stroke. The putting greens especially were places where the utmost concern was displayed as each and all looked on in breathless suspense. Mr Lees' picture of 'The Golfers' can best convey an idea of the sight.

Mr Hay and his partner began the battle with a great prestige of success, capturing the first two holes. We fell in with the match at the Hole O' Cross, travelling inward the first round. At that time the star of St Andrews seemed to be in the descendant. The state of the poll was that the Musselburgh men had a majority of four holes. They had played an almost unexampled game in the outward half of the round. Mr Hay was reported to have been driving tremendously long balls, and with the most unerring precision, and Dunnie showing himself to be a worthy mate; both also holing their balls at all distances in the green. This was too grand to last long. On the other hand, Allan and Tom had been doing well – gone out in forty-six. Allan had shown his wonted first-rate play but Tom, it was insinuated, was at his old trade of 'funking'. The St Andrews folks at this juncture were desponding a little, and some quaking for the renown of their men. But the Hole o' Cross was the crisis in the conflict: Allan and Tom's good time was fast coming – neither of their right hands had forgot its cunning. Their never – failing pluck and characteristic uniformity under the adverse game began to tell, for they immediately commenced to apply the process of subtraction to their adversaries, by taking the Ginger Beer hole at six to the other's seven; ditto with the next, by five to six. Driving off at the succeeding one, Dunnie bunkered in the Principal's nose. Allan drove a wide ball the second shot, which Tom skilfully redeemed, but after all Dunnie seized half the hole by a wonderful putt at two more, Allan failing to putt in his at one off two. The Hay party still two holes ahead, but they lost the next by seven to five. The home hole was divided – Allan narrowly missing taking it all, which would have placed them on an equality. After a brief interval the battle was renewed, the players having as many, if not more followers than before, and the excitement augmented. Hay and Co., it will be noted, were a hole ahead, but Dunnie, aiming at over the burn the second stroke, set his ball to water, while Tom cautiously drew short on the east side of the hazard and accounts were immediately squared. Nex[t] hole did not alter matters, but at the third Allan plumped hi[s] ball into the Principal's beak. Tom scooped it out, but i[t] rolled into a sheep track, and Hay and Co. got for the las[t] time ahead. Allan and Tom retrieved at the fourth hole, an[d] now that the tug of war has come, they began to assert thei[r] supremacy. They took the fifth hole at five, and the sixth a[t] four. The high hole was next, which was then playe[d] admirably. A long teeball of Allan's shot far ahead of M[r] Hay's corresponding one; indeed, one could hardly conceive how Allan's little body could propel a ball so far. At second strokes Tom swiped past the hole, and Dunnie's was caught in a bunker, which Mr Hay did not eject, Dunnie doing it in his turn, while the other ball was at its destination in four to seven. Hole eight was halved. Hole of return went to Allan and Tom, but they owed it to a stymie. Homeward bound now, with four in favour of St Andrews men, to which was added one next hole, cancelled at high hole by Hay and Co., the second only they had won in eleven. The hole of Shell ran Allan's side up to a five once more. Playing off here Mr Hay sent his ball astray, and Dunn could not make much of it, but Mr Hay made a splendid swipe next, landing in the green at three, the same as the opposite one, but not so near the desired point by some yards. Allan made the decisive putt – tumbling the ball in at a long distance – and instantly a spontaneous cheer signalised the success of Allan and Tom by six ahead and five to play. The remaining holes were contested for a minor bet, we believe, but these need not be particularized. It was supposed that Allan and Tom in going over these – their successes being declared – intentionally gave advantages by driving wide and being careless, but we don't think this was the case, suffice it to say, that at the thirty-sixth hole Allan and Tom's side was four holes in advance. In the progress inward, some boys removed the flags for guiding to the holes from their positions, and held them aloft in the procession, giving it the appearance of a triumphal entry. Such a scene has not been on the links for many years; the last of a similar kind was, if we rightly remember, in the summer of 1848, when the two Dunnies tried to pluck the laurels from the brows of Allan and Tom. The combined prowess of the firm still endures, and they remain the cocks o' the green. Long may they hold that honourable elevation. St Andrews for ever!

The Fairlies at home
at Coodham

William J.O.F. Isabella Henry E.L.F. Ogilvy Peggy
Alice Ruth Esther

June 1853

PRESTWICK GOLF CLUB.

The May meeting took place yesterday, the 25th, when John Campbell, Esq. of Glensaddell, having been called to the chair, the following gentlemen were added to the list of members:—Captain Boland; Sir Thomas Moncrieff, Bart.; Charles Gairdner, Esq.; —— Horne, Esq., Glasgow; William Briggs, Esq., H.E.I.C.S.; Chas. Campbell, Esq., Ayr; Thos. F. Hamilton, Esq.; Charles Shaw, Esq. On the links we observed Mrs Fairlie of Coodham, the Misses Hamilton, Belleisle, and a large party of spectators eagerly watching the keen contest for the medal. The members who competed started in pairs, in an order according to lot, and made the following numbers in two rounds:—Mr Fairlie, 1st round, 71; 2d do., 64—135. Mr Briggs, 1st round, 80; 2d do., 66—146. Mr W. A. Hamilton, 1st round, 67; 2d do., 68—135. Mr Gillon, 1st round, 80; 2d do., 75—155. Mr Campbell, Glensaddell, 1st round, 70; 2d do., 72—142. Mr Fergusson Blair, 1st round, 71; 2d do., 69—140. The Rev. Mr Pollock, 1st round, 71; 2d do., 77—148. Mr Glennie, 1st round, 71; 2d do., 61—132. Mr Reid, 1st round, 84; 2d do., 75—159. Mr Alexander, 1st round, 78; 2d do., 70—148. Captain C. V. Campbell, 1st round, 93; 2d do., 118—211. Mr Cuthbert, 1st round, 87; 2d do., 94—181. Mr Glennie, therefore, carried the Club gold medal for this year by completing the two rounds in 132 strokes. Mr Fairlie held the medal during the past year, and relinquishes it to a west country brother Golfer. This medal has only been twice played for and has never left the west, whilst the Eglinton gold medal has twice been taken by east country players. The links are in beautiful order and have been much played on for some time. The Earl of Eglinton and several parties had good matches last week. To-day, Mr Joseph Hume and Mr Gillon have engaged Mr Thomas Morris to play a match, the terms of which we have not heard, but the odds must be long, as Tom is "the king of Scotland," and reflects the highest credit on Prestwick. Mr Hunter's (of the Red Lion) luncheon was in his usual good style.

ACROSS THE GREEN.

"Hope springs eternal in the human breast.
It never is but always *to be* blest."

43

GOLF—THE LATE GRAND MATCH

1852

(To the Editor of the Fife Journal.)

SIR,—I recently had the pleasure of perusing your Correspondent's report of the play at the autumn meeting of golfers at St Andrews, and while I cheerfully accord to him the credit of having rendered a full and fair and interesting account of the various matches played, yet it was with regret that I observed he had been led—unwittingly I have no doubt—to use an expression in reference to the play of Tom Morris of Prestwick (but claimed by St Andrews as her *twin* champion), which, I am satisfied, none who watched his play attentively would say he merited. In describing the match, Allan and Tom against Mr Hay and Dunnie, your correspondent says that at one stage of it he was afraid Tom was at his '*old trade of funking*'—that is, showing a want of *nerve.* Now, with great deference to your correspondent, that is an imputation which I have informed myself, in the best quarter, could at no period of Tom's career be with truth attributed to him; and most certainly it seemed to be the general impression on the occasion referred to, that he played his part with the most consumate self-possession and skill. I am also assured, that he seldom, if ever, felt so confident in his play as on that occasion. Indeed, so confident was he that he gave the large odds of 5 to 1 on his play. But fortunately your correspondent has in his own report afforded a most satisfactory refutation of the charge, in his subsequent allusion to the '*never failing* pluck' of Tom and Allan as they turned the tide of the game, and to the fact that *they have come off conquerors in every match in which they have played together.* This circumstance alone, I think, ought to dissipate every doubt—should any really exist—as to Tom's *pluck.*

I have been induced to offer these remarks (for which I hope you will kindly assign a niche in your columns) as an act of justice to a deserving individual, of whom St. Andrews and Prestwick may well be prond; and to counteract the injurious tendency of the imputation complained of, as while it remained unchallenged, the effect of it undoubtedly would be to engender a want of confidence in his play on the part of his backers and friends, especially those of them who may not have been acquainted with him for any considerable period of time.—I remain, sir, your very obedient servant,

A GOLFER.

23d November, 1852.

A LETTER APPEARED IN LAST WEEK'S *Journal*, from 'A Golfer,' relative to a phrase applied to the play of Tom Morris, in the account of the great contest at the late autumn meeting, betwixt Allan Robertson and Tom against Mr Robert Hay and William Dunn. ~~Our correspondent has to remark~~, that when he joined the crowd accompanying the players, an individual, who announced to him the then state of matters, made the derogatory observation in regard to Tom, and hence it was employed in the report, probably without due consideration. Our correspondent just gave the expression as he got it. The words used were, 'Tom, *it was insinuated*, was at his old trade of funking.' The charge of funking appeared to be corroborated by the relation in which the antagonists stood to each other at the time—Allan and Tom being four holes behind. It will be seen that the accusation is not a direct one, and our correspondent afterwards regretted having adopted the expression complained of, being convinced that it was uncalled for, but, like human nature in general, he did not like to confess the impropriety. He feels obliged by the courteous tone assumed by 'A Golfer,' in putting Tom right. Though our correspondent could not judge personally of the nature of the play antecedent to the period mentioned, he can affirm that immediately after that, and throughout the course of the 23 holes which formed the rest of the match, and over which he surveyed the play, Tom amply sustained his fame by the dexterity he displayed in handling his golfing weapons. Our correspondent never witnessed the smallest departure on Tom's part from that enviable serenity which is the distinguishing feature of Allan and him, and is the more remarkable considering the pecuniary risks upon their prowess in the notable strifes which they undertake. The pair can always be implicitly depended upon in such circumstances to come off with flying colours. They can confidently bid defiance to all comers. They fear neither Dunnes nor *Brownies*, but will do them brown as fast as they like.

AUTUMN MEETING OF THE ROYAL AND ANCIENT GOLF CLUB.

The game of golf, unlike most other games, although very ancient, somehow or other never shows any symptoms of becoming antiquated. Year after year, its lovers "walk the course" with their cadies in their rear, without evincing the slightest appearance of diminished *gout* for their favourite sport. Indeed, the game has so much to recommend it, that, with all who have a practical acquaintance with it, it is a prime favourite. Unlike other outside sports, you may take the exercise it affords in the measure that best suits your ability or inclination. While abundant scope is afforded by it for the display of skill and activity, the frame is not taxed by severe exertion at one time, and a total cessation of it at another, but the exercise afforded is, throughout, of that equable and exhilerating character which is proved to be most conducive to health. If a gentleman be light and active, why, he may run after his ball if he has a mind; if on the contrary, he is of that particular build, which makes his "pair" averse to rapid locomotion, he may waddle after it as he best can. Possessed of such recommendations it is not surprising that when the game was comparatively a new one, perhaps three centuries ago, the passion of gentlemen for it had to be regulated by the legislature. Forming as it did so formidable a rival to the sport of archery as to leave that sport in a very neglected condition, the law had to step in to compel attention to the latter—in the then state of society, the more useful art. But, indeed, the game of golf has been an object of attention to those in high places during almost the whole period of its existence. The unfortunate Charles I., while, it might be said, the axe was already hanging over his head, and his sovereignty was melting in his grasp before the rising power of the stern puritans, still found leisure to play at golf, of which he was passionately fond. His scarcely less unfortunate son James II., was also very partial to the game, and more recently still, the gruff good-natured William IV. took so much interest in it as to send down a medal to be competed for by the Ancient Golf Club of St Andrews. St Andrews, indeed, has been for centuries, the headquarters of the ancient game, its golf course being by far the finest in Scotland, and the meetings of veteran golfers on it are frequent, and the play generally very spirited.

Yesterday, the autumn meeting of the Royal and Ancient Golf Club took place. The day was beautiful, indeed as fine as could be wished, with the exception of a rather strong breeze from the westward, which made the play much more difficult than it would otherwise have been. At an early hour, the members of the Club met at the Cross-Keys Hotel for the despatch of business, and afterwards proceeded to the course. The discharge of a piece of ordnance gave notice of the commencement of the match, which accordingly began at a little past eleven o'clock, an extraordinary number of players taking part in the competition.

The following were the gentlemen—33 couples—who appeared on the ground as competitors for the honours of the day. They were paired in the order stated:—Mr Ord G. Campbell, Mr Redham Home; Mr Alex. Duncan, Mr Robert Lindesay; Mr Joseph Hume, Mr R. Hebden; Mr John Blackwood, Mr Mason; Mr J. D. B. Hay, Mr Cruickshank; Mr Stoddart, Mr Glennie; Mr Grant Oswald, Mr Whyte Melville; Mr Balfour Ogilvy, Mr Skene; Mr Richard Cowan, Mr Allan Briggs; Mr F. Lindesay, Mr W. Lindesay; Mr A. Scott, Mr Hoddar; Mr Marjoribank, Mr Hunter, of Burnside; Mr Whitson, Mr J. C. Lindsay; Mr G. F. Buist, Mr H. Peter; Capt. Farquhar Campbell, Mr Bethune, of Blebo; Mr Fairlie, Mr Robert Hay; Mr Campbell, of Saddle, Captain Campbell; Mr Hunter, of Blackmen, Mr Fitzmaurice Scott; Captain Hutchison, Mr Skene; Mr R. Ferguson, Mr R. Cowan; Captain White Melville, Mr E. J. Jackson; Captain Murray, Mr W. A. Campbell; Mr Wolfe Murray, Mr Samuel Ferguson; Mr G. M. Innes, Mr G. Thomson; Viscount Dupplin, Sir T. Moncrieff; Mr Turnbull, Captain Campbell, Auchalader; Colonel Grant, Mr Balfour, W.S.; Mr Hugh Alexander.

The whole of the couples had finished the holing of the course by a quarter to four o'clock, when it was found that William the Fourth's Medal had been won by Mr Robert Hay, at 99 strokes; and the Club Gold Medal, by Mr Thomas Peter, at 101 strokes. The first sweepstakes was won by Mr John Hay, at 95 strokes; and the second by Messrs Grant and Skene, at 96 strokes.

The ground was in excellent order, firm and dry, and if it had not been for the strong wind the play would have been excellent; as it was, it was very spirited and fully maintained the character of the Ancient and Honourable Society.

Several matches are talked of as likely to take place soon; one for the heavy stake of £100 a-side, is expected to come off to-day, and will likely attract considerable attention.

1852

ROYAL GOLF BALL.

This annual re-union took place on Thursday evening, and was held as usual in the Town-hall, which had undergone suitable preparations for the purpose. The east end was ornamented with tasteful drapery, and at the west end the floral and evergreen decorations were exceedingly beautiful. Before ten o'clock the carriages had begun to arrive and deliver their elegantly arrayed occupants, and ere long the ball-room was thronged with a graceful and brilliant assemblage of beauty and fashion, such as this festive meeting always brings together. About 130 ladies and gentlemen appeared, among whom were those whose names are subjoined:—

Ladies—The Lady Catherine Whyte Melville; the Right Hon. Lady Bateman and the Hon. Misses Hanbury; the Hon. Mrs Geo. Whyte Melville; the Right Hon. Lady Abinger; Lady M'Neill; Lady Feilden; Mrs Jackson, Strathtyrum; Mrs Campbell of Saddel; Mrs Colonel Moncrieff; Mrs Lindsay of Straiton; Miss Lindsay; Miss Duncan and Miss Jelf Sharp; Mrs Oswald of Dunnikier; Mrs Anstruther of Tillicoultry and Miss Anstruther; Mrs Wolfe Murray of Cringletie; Mrs Jones of Pantglass; Mrs Major Playfair; Misses Playfair and Miss Jane Cook; Mrs Balfour Ogilvy of Tannadice and Mrs Balfour; Mrs Purvis of Kinaldie; Mrs Black of Clayton; Mrs Lyon Campbell; Mrs Professor Ferrier and Miss M'Neill; Mrs Colonel Weston; Mrs and Misses Thomson; Mrs Thoms of Seaview and Miss Wyse; Mrs Grahame, Abbey Park; Mrs Hebden; Mrs S. Ferguson; Mrs Dewar; Mrs and Miss Blackett; Misses Berry of Tayfield; Miss Inglis of Crammond; Misses Lindsay Carnegie; Miss Thomson, Kilmany Cottage; Miss Leith Hay; Misses Blair of Lunan; Miss Reeve of Edenpark; Miss Hosier; Miss A. Playfair, Misses Broughton, Misses Black, &c. &c.

Gentlemen—The Captains, Mr E. J. Jackson, Strathtyrum; Lord Charles Kerr; Sir Coutts Lindsay; Sir James Walker Drummond, of Hawthorn Den; Sir W. H. Feilden of Feniscawles; Vicomte de Labrosse; Mr Whyte Melville of Mount Melville; Mr George Whyte Melville, yr. of Mount Melville; Mr Oswald of Dunnikier; Mr Lindsay of Straiton; Mr James Anstruther of Tillicoultry; Mr R. S. Aytoun of Inchdairnie; Mr C. H. C. Inglis of Crammond; Mr Jones of Pantglas, M.P.; Mr Cunningham of Caprington; Mr Fairlie of Coodham; Mr Wolfe Murray of Cringletie; Mr Purvis of Kinaldie; Mr Paterson of Cunnoquhie; Mr Black of Clayton; Mr Balfour Ogilvy of Tannadice; Mr Hunter of Blackness; Mr Cruickshank of Langlay Park; Mr W. A. Campbell of Ormsary; Mr Blair of Lunan; Mr Robert Hay (winner of the Royal Medal); Professor Ferrier; Colonel Moncrieff, [illegible] Fusilier Guards; Major Playfair; Captain Broughton; Captain Tattnall, R.N.; Captain Wilkinson, 42d Highlanders; Captain Murray, [illegible]th Regiment; Captain Cox, Bengal Army; Capt. Butt, [illegible]th Highlanders; Lieutenant B[illegible], H.E.I.C.S., Bengal; Mr Alexander Duncan; Mr Samuel Ferguson; Mr R. J. Hebden; Mr Joseph Hume; Mr George Campbell [illegible]edenwood; Mr [illegible] of Tayfield; Mr George [illegible] Advocate; Mr Norman [illegible]

separate Return,

The Club dinner came off in the hall of the Cross Keys Hotel on Wednesday evening, about 50 members being present, Mr George Whyte Melville, captain for the past year, presiding. After removal of the cloth, the usual loyal, patriotic, and golfing toasts were given, and duly honoured. The captain then left the chair, and the new captain, E. J. Jackson, Esq., of Strathtyrum, took his place, amid the plaudits of the meeting. The captain then proposed the health of his predecessor, which was responded to with all the honours. The healths of the medal holders, and numerous others followed, and the evening was spent in an agreeable manner.

THURSDAY.—The proceedings of this day commenced by a celebrated and long talked of match, of two rounds or 36 holes of the Links, betwixt Robert Hay, Esq., and Wm. Goddard, Esq.—the former was successful by two holes. This match occasioned considerable interest; this will be seen when we mention that the first bets were £100 a-side. A great number of spectators went both the rounds.

The Ball came off in the evening in our Town Hall, [illegible] very tastefully decorated for the occasion. The greater number of the competitors and distinguished personages who appeared on the green were present, the whole numbering nearly 140, being the greatest number at any similar ball for years past. The arrangements and refreshments were provided by Mr Hastie, of the Cross Keys; [illegible] refreshment tables were laden with every delicacy which art or nature could produce for the season.

FRIDAY.—An interesting foursome took place to-day betwixt J. O. Fairlie, Esq., and W. Goddard, Esq., against Robert Hay, Esq., and Captain Maitland Dougal, when the latter were successful. Several other interesting matches took place, but no others on Friday created any noise.

SATURDAY.—The great match of this day, and, indeed, of the present meeting, was a foursome betwixt Mr Robert Hay and William Dunn, against our own Allan Robertson, and Tom Morris, consisting of two rounds of our links, or 36 holes. The first heats being £100 to £50 in favour of Allan and Tom. To persons out of St Andrews, or unacquainted with the game of golf, we could not give any proper idea of the amount of interest felt by all in the success of this match; the general feeling seemed to be that the honour of St Andrews was at stake. It is quite true that Tom Morris is not now amongst us, but still we claim him as a St Andrews champion, for there was he born and bred—bred a golfer—there has he fought side by side with Allan, and in every match hitherto have they been successful. Long before the hour of starting, numbers of the citizens were down at the Links, and a very large number of gentlemen went the round of the Links with the players. By the second round, the spectators had swelled to a crowd of many hundreds, composed of members of the Royal and Ancient Golf Club, magistrates, tradesmen, and shopkeepers, all feeling the deepest interest in the whole affair, and who had left their various employments to watch the proceedings. The following details may be read with some interest:—The first round was gone by Mr Hay and partner at 87 strokes, and the second round 97. The first round was gone by Allan and Tom at 90, and the second at 92. At the conclusion of the first round Messrs Hay and Dunn were one hole a-head. It is a curious circumstance, that at the hole-a-cross, or fourth hole coming in, Messrs Hay and Dunn were four holes a-head, with five holes to play. Fortune here seemed to favour her sons, for the tables then turned, so that the odds were reduced to one hole against Allan and Tom when at the close of the round. On starting for the second round, it will be seen that Tom and Allan were one hole behind, but they seemed to improve in their play, while their antagonists fell off. At the hole-a-cross the match was gained by Allan and Tom, with six holes and five to play. A short match was played for the remaining five holes, which Messrs Hay and Dunn won by two holes, thus, upon the whole, two rounds of the Links Allan and Tom won by four holes. The only expression of feeling that was vented was a cheer when the match was decided; in every other respect, no expression was made of sympathy with one or another.

Communication to the Editor.

PRESTWICK GOLF CLUB—THE 'CHAMPIONSHIP.'

Prestwick, near Ayr, 21st June 1853.

SIR—I perceive that you have had the kindness to insert in your paper of the 9th inst. a report of the exploits of our Prestwickian golfers at their last May meeting. This was well and good. But your St Andrews correspondent has, I also perceive, favoured your readers with an addenda to the report, in which he takes exception to part of it, and thus virtually ignores certain honours to which we have a perfect right. In the first place, he claims Mr Glennie as more an east than a west country player, because of his having learned the art of golf in St Andrews when a boy. True, Mr G., when a boy, served his apprenticeship (as it were) in St Andrews; but it is not to be denied that when he afterwards became a journeyman, and then a master (as he now truly is) in the art, he was much indebted to the influence of the west country practice for his many successes. And, moreover, Mr G. is now, and has been for some years, domiciled in the west, so that we Prestwickians cannot consent to relinquish the honour of claiming him as one of 'our own' paissant *corps*. In the second place, your correspondent, despite the fact of 'Tom' having by his skill and prowess vanquished 'Allan' in their *last* encounter, still maintains—but without favouring your readers with his grounds for doing so—that 'the real King of Scotland in regard to golfing reigns in St Andrews, and is well known as Allan Robertson—all others taking that dignity being guilty of high treason,' &c. It might have been painful to your correspondent's feelings to think of the palm of victory, which has so long reposed in quiescence in the sombre shade of old St Rule, gracefully waving, as it now does, in the 'westlin'' breezes by the shore of Kyle; and no doubt in his grief the ancient adage, '*Veritas nihil veretur nisi abscondi*' might have escaped his memory. But now that the healing influences of time and reflection must have come to his aid, it is to be hoped that he will gracefully concede to 'Tom' the honour claimed for him as 'King of Scotland' *quoad golfing*. And truly it does not seem to me that he can do otherwise in the face of his *own* report of the encounter alluded to, which appeared in your paper of the 9th of last month in the following terms:—'Allan and Tom encountered each other in single combat with the clubs and balls—a rare occurrence. Some little cash depended on the issue, which Allan—strange to say—lost, Tom surpassing him by 3 holes on the round.' But in case your correspondent should still refuse to own the 'soft impeachment,' and to set the question of supremacy *again* at rest, I have the imperial [illegible]

"PROCLAMATION OF WAR!"

'We, Tom, King of Clubs throughout Scotland, by right of conquest most indisputable, in a convocation of our most loyal golfing subjects, holden within our Royal Lodge at Prestwick, shire of Kyle, taking into our royal consideration that certain treasonable discourses or writings hath appeared and been promulgated in and through a printed paper styled '*The Fifeshire Journal*,' and that said discourses or writings appear to have been devised through or on behalf of our trusty and well-beloved cousin Allan, chief or governor of our golfing province of St Andrews in the east, and that the indulgence in such treasonable discourses or writings, if not speedily prohibited, may tend to stir up in the breasts of our loyal subjects a spirit of insubordination, and lead to the formation of plots to deprive, depose, or suspend us from the style, honour, and royal name we at present enjoy of 'King of Clubs:' And further, taking into our royal consideration that our said trusty and well-beloved cousin Allan would moreover, and notwithstanding our last royal combat with him, in which we were victorious, still seem to claim (at least said discourses and writings claim for him) jurisdiction, power, superiority, pre-eminence, and authority over us, by taking upon himself the style and title of 'the real, legitimate, and indisputable King of Clubs,' We, in our wisdom and clemency [illegible] have resolved again to satisfy our doubting subjects in our province of the east, that in us exclusively pertains the style and title of '*King* of Clubs;' and for that purpose, and to secure at sametime the peace and wellbeing of our ancient Kingdom of Clubs, do hereby, by and with the consent of our loyal Prestwickian subjects, announce to our doubting subjects in the east aforesaid, that we are prepared to peril our right to the kingly honours and dignities we now enjoy in a contest (in friendly mood) with our said well-beloved cousin Allan, and that by the ancient and chivalric ordeal of single combat (but with clubs and balls); and have accordingly commanded our faithful knights, squires, and caddies to hold themselves prepared to consider, arrange, and conclude such a cartel of combat as may befit our imperial dignity—we reserving only the power of fixing the single proviso in said cartel, that in the event of our being right royally 'floored' in said contest, the imperial and pleasing duty be accorded unto us of transferring the wreath of victory from our own royal brows to those of our said well-beloved cousin Allan, forasmuch as, in the performance of said duty, we shall simply feel that we are crowning our *other royal* self. Save the King!"

Hoping that you may find it convenient to give a place in your next issue to matter so important as the above, I remain, &c.,

A LOYAL PRESTWICKIAN.

(1852)

St Andrews and District.

ROYAL AND ANCIENT GOLF CLUB.

In last week's paper we gave an account of the proceedings of Wednesday. It may be well, however, to repeat the changes which then took place for the year in the posts of honour in the club, viz.:—

Edward James Jackson, Esq., Strathtyrum, havin been chosen Captain, received the Silver Club.

Robert Hay, Esq., Edinburgh, carried off King William the Fourth's Medal as dux in the competition, having holed the entire round at 99 strokes.

Thomas Peter, Esq., Kirkland, gained the Club Gold Medal, having scored 101 strokes.

At a meeting of the Club held on Wednesday forenoon twelve new members were ballotted for and admitted.

We may state, by the way, that the Royal Medal has only once before been won at 99 strokes since it became one of the prizes of the society. It was presented, by his Majesty's special command, by Lieut.-Colonel Murray Belshes, the then Captain, 3d May 1837. Annexed is a list of the successive gainers of this Medal since that period:—

1837—James Stewart Oliphant, jun., Esq., at	104	strokes
1838—Capt. (now Col.) J. Hope Grant, 9th Lancers	100	...
1839—John H. Wood, Esq., Leith	99	...
1840—Major H. L. Playfair	105	...
1841—Sir David Baird, Bart	100	...
1842—James Condie, Esq., Perth	103	...
1843—William M. Goddard, Esq., Leith	103	...
1844—James Hamilton Dundas, Esq	111	...
1845—James Calvert, Esq., Montrose	100	...
1846—James Calvert, Esq	111	...
1847—N. J. Ferguson Blair, Esq	108	...
1848—George Condie, Esq., Perth	104	...
1849—Wm. M. Goddard, Esq	105	...
1850—Sir David Baird, Bart.	100	...
1851—O'Brien B. Peter, Esq	103	...
1852—Robert Hay, Esq	99	...

On Wednesday afternoon, Mr J. O. Fairlie and Tom Morris entered into a match with Mr Hay and William Dunn for one round—18 holes. The latter were victorious by 2 holes, though the difference in the gross amount of strokes was only one, Mr Hay and Dunnie finishing in 92 and the opposing pair in 93. As a set-off against this, we have to state that on the preceding Thursday the same four[illegible] was played over North Berwick Links in a match [illegible] up for three rounds—21 holes—when Mr Fairlie and [illegible] but up their opponents at the end of the second round,

ROYAL AND ANCIENT GOLF CLUB.

We last week noticed the competition of this Club upon the Wednesday, when the medal was gained by Mr Robert Hay, at 99 strokes; and the club medal by Mr Thomas Peter, do. The next in order of merit were—Colonel Grant, 103 strokes; Mr Patrick Alexander, 103 do.; Mr Hugh Alexander, 104 do.; Mr Whitson, 106 do.; Mr Balfour, W.S., 107 do.; Messrs Fairlie, Buist Skene, Home, Glennie, and Innes, came in at 108 respectively. The whole day's play was good, being a full average of previous years. It is perhaps only correct in us here to notice, that a week ago, an interesting match took place at North Berwick Links, betwixt J. O. Fairlie, Esq., and Tom Morris, against Robert Hay, Esq., and William Dunn, when the former were successful. So soon as the competition for the medal was completed, the same parties who played at North Berwick went the round of St Andrews Links, and the result was that the tables were turned—Messrs Hay & Dunn beating.

45 Past Captains of the R & A since 1754 To the Earl of Eglinton

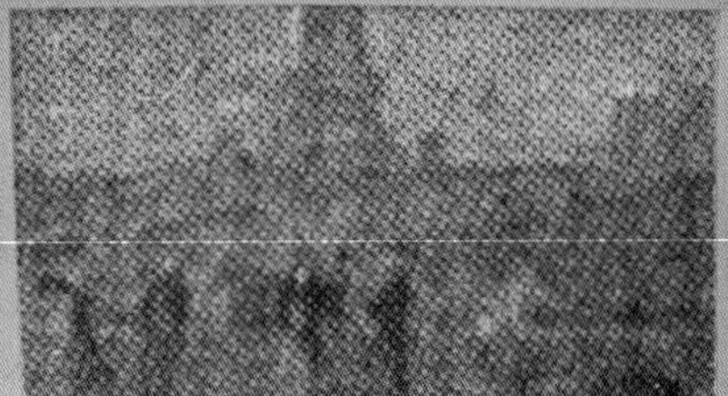

yearly in time coming, the victor to be holder of the Silver Club, and to enjoy the dignity of Captain of the Society for the year. Annexed is a list of the names of those who have been Captains, from 1754 to the present day:—

1754. Bailie William Landale, St Andrews.
1755. Thomas Boswall, Esq., Writer, Edinburgh.
1756. Alexander Duncan, Esq., of Craigton, Advocate.
1757. No competition.
1758. Hugh Fraser, of Lovat, Esq.
1759. Sir James Carnegie, Bart., M.P.
1760. No competition.
1761. Alexander Duncan, Esq., of Craigton.
1762. Hugh Fraser, of Lovat, Esq.
1763. Sir Harry Seton, Bart.
1764. William St Clair, of Roslin, Esq.
1765. Hon. Francis Charteris, of Amisfield.
1766. William St Clair, of Roslin, Esq.
1767. James Durham, of Largo, Esq.
1768. William St Clair, of Roslin, Esq.
1769. Dr George Forrest, Professor of Civil History, United College, St Andrews.
1770. Henry Bethune, of Nydie, Esq.
1771. Ninian Imrie, Esq., of Denmuir.
1772. James Morison, Esq., of Naughton.
1773. Patrick Rigg, Esq., of Downfield.
1774. John Hay, Esq., of Leys.
1775. Right Hon. Alexander, Earl of Balcarres.
1776. Roger Aytoun, Esq., of Inchdairny.
1777. John Balfour, Esq., of Fairnie.
1778. Walter Boswell, Esq.
1779. James Morison, Esq., of Naughton.
1780. James Durham, Esq., of Largo.
1781. Alexander Duncan, Esq.
1782. Right Hon. Alexander, Earl of Balcarres.
1783. Major William Morison.
1784. Robert Low, Esq., of Clatto.
1785. Captain John Cheape.
1786. Colonel John Thomson, of Charlton.
1787. James Cheape, Esq., of Strathtyrum.
1788. Captain James Dalrymple.
1789. Captain William Nairne.
1790. Patrick Rigg, Esq.
1791. Alexander Duncan, Esq.
1792. Right Hon. the Earl of Crawford.
1793. John Patullo, Esq., of Balhouffie.
1794. Captain Alexander Aytone, of Kippo.
1795. Alexander Anderson, Esq., of Newbigging.
1796. James Morison, Esq., of Naughton.
1797. Thomas Erskine, Esq., of Cambo.
1798. Methven Erskine, Esq., of Airdry.
1799. John Dalyell, Esq., of Lingo.
1800. Robert Patullo, Esq.
1801. George Cheape, Esq., of Pusk.
1802. Hugh Cleghorn, Esq., of Stravithie.
1803. George Paterson, Esq.
1804. John Anstruther Thomson, Esq., of Charlton.
1805. Colonel David Dewar, of Gilston.
1806. William Dalgleish, Esq., of Scotscraig.
1807. General George Moncrieff.
1808. Alexander Guthrie, Esq., of Craigie.
1809. James Home Rigg, Esq., of Morton.
1810. John Maitland, Esq., of Kilmaron.
1811. Thomas Bruce, Esq., of Grangemuir.
1812. Robert G. Smyth, Esq., of Gibliston.
1813. General James Durham, of Largo.
1814. George Cheape, Esq., of Pusk.
1815. John Makgill, Esq., of Kemback.
1816. Sir John Anstruther, of Anstruther, Bart.
1817. David Moncrieff, Esq., yr. of Moncrieff.
1818. John Murray, Esq., of Lintrose.
1819. Robert Bruce, Esq., of Kennet.
1820. Right Hon. the Earl of Leven and Melville.
1821. Colonel Alexander Bethune, of Blebo.
1822. Alexander Binny, Esq., St Andrews.
1823. John Whyte Melville, Esq., of Strathkinness and Bennochy.
1824. Lieut. Col. James Lindsay, yr. of Balcarres.
1825. Sir Ralph A. Anstruther, Bart., of Balcaskie.
1826. Charles Maitland Christie, Esq., of Durie.
1827. Capt. James Cheape, of Balgove, R.N.
1828. John Dalyell, Esq., of Lingo.
1829. Sir David Erskine, of Cambo, Bart.
1830. Francis Balfour, Esq., of Fernie.
1831. James Stewart Oliphant, Esq., of Rossie.
1832. Charles Craigie Halket, Esq., of Dumbarnie.
1833. Major Robert Anstruther, of Caiplie and Thirdpart.
1834. Sir John Oswald, of Dunnikier, K.G.C.B.
1835. Major John Murray Belshes, of Buttergask.
1836. Do. Do.
1837. Capt. George Moncrieff, of Balcurvie, Scots Fusilier Guards
1838. O. T. Bruce, Esq., of Falkland.
1839. John Grant, Esq., of Kilgraston.
1840. Henry Stewart, Esq., of St Fort.
1841. David Gillespie, Esq., of Mountquhanie.
1842. John Balfour, Esq., of Balbirnie.
1843. Sir David Baird, of Newbyth, Bart.
1844. Sir Thomas Moncrieffe, of Moncrieffe, Bart.
1845. George Makgill, Esq., of Kemback.
1846. Robert Lindsay, Esq., of Straiton.
1847. Frederick L. S. Wedderburn, Esq., of Wedderburn.
1848. James Wolfe Murray, Esq., of Cringletie.
1849. J. T. Oswald, Esq., of Dunnikier.
1850. James Ogilvie Fairlie, Esq., of Coodham.
1851. George Whyte Melville, Esq., yr. of Mount Melville.
1852. Edward James Jackson, Esq., Strathtyrum.
1853. The Right Hon. the Earl of Eglinton and Winton, K.T. Who is, therefore, reigning Captain.

PITTENWEEM.

THE CROPS.—Last week ...

ROYAL AND ANCIENT GOLFERS' BALL.

The Assembly attendant on this autumn meeting, and which forms perhaps the most extensively interesting event among its feats and festivities, was held on Thursday night in the Town Hall, the embellishments of which for the occasion evinced taste of the highest order. Along the walls were hung garlands of artificial flowers; and shields were suspended around the room. These shields are a new feature in the decorations, and imparted a novel and striking aspect to the old hall, causing it to appear quite magnificent. At the east end the Silver Clubs and Balls were surmounted with a shield bearing the initials of the noble Captain's title, with '1853' above, and 'welcome' below. Two shields on either side displayed the ensigns armorial of the new Captain and his immediate predecessor 'Gardez Bien' and 'Jamais Arriere' respectively. The north and south sides of the room contained each four shields. One of them had the Scottish and another the Irish national heraldic representations with the mottos. Another had a crown and horn emblazoned, and 'Otterburn Esperance' as an escutcheon pertaining to the Eglinton family, being commemorative of the noble Earl's ancestor, Sir John Montgomerie, who took a distinguished part in the battle of Otterburn, anno 1388, wherein James Earl of Douglas was slain, and in that conflict made prisoner of Henry Percy, the renowned Hotspur, for whose ransom he compelled Lord Percy to build the castle of Punnoon, in the Lordship of Eaglesham. The county motto '*virtute et opera*' with its Knight in Mail, and St Andrew and his Cross, also figured on shields, besides designs emblematic of the Society in Golf Clubs and balls, the most appropriate of which seemed to be that with the motto 'Frappe Fort,' which we understand to mean 'strike hard.' Mr Paterson, painter, of the city, has been entrusted with the delineation of the devices, which were most skilfully executed.

By [illegible] began the hurrying to and fro of carriages, and in due time had gathered the beauty and the chivalry to the number of about 120. Dancing was entered upon about half-past ten o'clock, the orchestra being occupied by the famous M'Kenzie performers.

At half-past twelve the supper room up stairs was resorted to, where a repast was served in all respects worthy of the company, and which, for the elaborate art and attention which had obviously been applied in its preparation, entitles Mr Hastie of the Cross Keys to the highest praise, and it afforded consequently to the guests infinite satisfaction and pleasure.

After supper, the noble EARL gave successively the usual loyal toasts; and thereafter proposed 'Mr Jackson, the Captain of the noble game of golf.'

MR JACKSON returned thanks; and was glad that, as noble Captain's predecessor, he had been favoured with such a good pupil. If he could teach golf he would do so; but, in comparison with his Lordship, he ought rather to be the pupil than the tutor.

MR JACKSON proposed 'Our new worthy and noble Captain, with all the honours.'

Lord EGLINTON replied; and referring to what Mr Jackson had said of his golfing abilities, he did not think it was in the power of the best golfer to teach him. It was the only game he could make no hand of, and he was only fitted to occupy the bottom of the worst bunker on the Links; but was happy at finding so great pleasure in his healthy walking every day, and pleasant companions, and at dinner he had equal pleasure.

MR WHYTE-MELVILLE was sure they all regretted the absence of one individual; and would therefore all join in drinking the 'Health of Lady Eglinton,' whose presence would have added so much to the beauty of the ball-room, and the happiness of that evening; and he expressed the wishes of all present in wishing her Ladyship a speedy recovery.

Lord EGLINTON returned thanks. He was certain that her Ladyship's inability to be present that night would cause her more pain than her illness would, and that had she been well she would have appeared both at the ball and on the Links.

Lord EGLINTON craved a large bumper—addressing himself particularly to the gentlemen—and proposed 'The Ladies.' He alluded humourously to a primitive sort of females that golfers occasionally met at the other end of the Links, who could hardly be classed among the fair sex, and whom he could hardly call ladies. They had now an opportunity of seeing the sex as they ought to be seen, and in the presence they now were they found themselves forgetting the misfortunes of bunkers and missed tee strokes.

At half-past one the assemblage again repaired to the ball-room, where—

'On went the dance, and joy was unconfined'—

until after four o'clock, when the company departed; and thus concluded the latest and one of the most delightful

1853

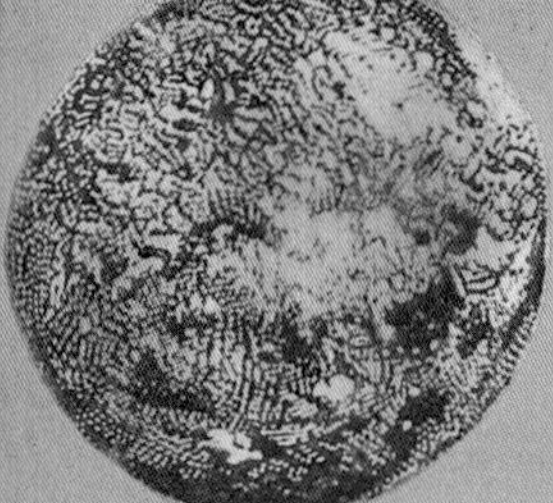

Smooth gutta | Early Park gutta | Hand Hammered Dunn.

St Andrews and District.

5 Sept 1854

Madras College.—At a meeting of the trustees of this Institution, held on 29th ult., M. Leopold Müller, teacher of Modern Languages, Montrose Academy, was appointed from among eighteen candidates to the situation of Master of French and German, vacant by the resignation of Mr Messieux.

St Andrews Golf Club.—The September meeting of this Club took place on Friday, when the members enjoyed a choice autumn afternoon for going the round. Mr George Morris came in dux, and got the medal, his score being 95. The prizes were won as under, viz.—Putter and two balls, the gift of a member of the Royal and Ancient Golf Club—Mr James M'Pherson, at 92

Driving Club, given by Allan Robertson—Mr John Flynn, &c. 93

Driving Club, given by Tom Morris—Mr George Morris, at 95

Two Balls—Mr Wm. Ayton, jun., at 100

One Ball—Mr Robert Paterson, at 101

Do. —Mr Alex. Clyne, at 106

The prize-winners, with the exception of George Morris, got previously settled odds, as is customary to equalize their chances with him as a first-class player. The scores indicate good play—above the ordinary run, we believe, on such occasions. The members afterwards met and dined in the Cross Keys Hotel, under the efficient chairmanship of the Captain—Mr Allan Robertson. The spread of good things was in keeping with the notable character of that place of entertainment, and the company passed the evening in the best of social harmony and hilarity.

The War.—When the news reached this on Monday of the battle gained by the allies over the Russians in the neighbourhood of Sebastopol, the bells in the city rang a merry peal in token of the victory, bringing back reminiscences of like doings and like rejoicings during the course of the long struggle which ended in 1815.

Burgh Court.—Catherine Carmichael, on 29th ult., was brought up before this court, charged with the theft of five stockings. An agent appeared on her behalf, and entered into a lengthened cross-examination of the prosecutor's witnesses, but she was found guilty and sent to Cupar jail for eight days. Also William Smith, *alias* Henry Maxwell, tinsmith, presently residing in St Andrews, charged with theft and assault, the latter aggravated by having been committed on an officer, while in discharge of his duty. He was found guilty, and sent to Cupar jail for eight days.

Council Meeting.—The Town Council met yesterday at ten o'clock A.M. The Provost occupied the Chair. The minute by the committee appointed to consider the proposal for a new road near the Butts, was read and approved of by the meeting. The committee were re-appointed. A petition against the erection of a lock-up-house was deferred until another meeting, the Provost suggesting that, in place of proceeding with the lock-up, a suitable building should be erected to contain the fire engine and the city chair. The meeting was informed that the Madras trustees had agreed to the appropriation of £150 from the Bell fund towards the expenses of the new market. Thereafter the recent Act of Parliament, for the Valuation of Lands and Heritages in Scotland, was laid before the Council. Mr Woodcock, writer, was appointed assessor under the new Act. Stent masters were appointed for the year, also committees to examine the clerk's and treasurer's accounts for the last year. A communication was then read from David Harley resigning his appointments of town-officer and crier, and it was remitted to the magistrates to look out for a competent person to fill the vacancy.

PRESTWICK GOLF CLUB.

June 1853 — June

The May meeting took place yesterday, the 25th, when John Campbell, Esq. of Glensaddell, having been called to the chair, the following gentlemen were added to the list of members:—Captain Boland; Sir Thomas Moncrieff, Bart.; Charles Gairdner, Esq.; —— Horne, Esq., Glasgow; William Briggs, Esq., H.E.I.C.S.; Chas. Campbell, Esq., Ayr; Thos. F. Hamilton, Esq.; Charles Shaw, Esq. On the links we observed Mrs Fairlie of Coodham, the Misses Hamilton, Belleisle, and a large party of spectators eagerly watching the keen contest for the medal. The members who competed started in pairs, in an order according to lot, and made the following numbers in two rounds:—Mr Fairlie, 1st round, 71; 2d do., 64—135. Mr Briggs, 1st round, 80; 2d do., 66—146. Mr W. A. Hamilton, 1st round, 67; 2d do., 68—135. Mr Gillon, 1st round, 80; 2d do., 75—155. Mr Campbell, Glensaddell, 1st round, 70; 2d do., 72—142. Mr Fergusson Blair, 1st round, 71; 2d do., 69—140. The Rev. Mr Pollock, 1st round, 71; 2d do., 77—148. Mr Glennie, 1st round, 71; 2d do., 61—132. Mr Reid, 1st round, 84; 2d do., 75—159. Mr Alexander, 1st round, 78; 2d do., 70—148. Captain C. V. Campbell, 1st round, 93; 2d do., 118—211. Mr Cuthbert, 1st round, 87; 2d do., 94—181. Mr Glennie, therefore, carried the Club gold medal for this year by completing the two rounds in 132 strokes. Mr Fairlie held the medal during the past year, and relinquishes it to a west country brother Golfer. This medal has only been twice played for and has never left the west, whilst the Eglinton gold medal has twice been taken by east country players. The links are in beautiful order and have been much played on for some time. The Earl of Eglinton and several parties had good matches last week. To-day, Mr Joseph Hume and Mr Gillon have engaged Mr Thomas Morris to play a match, the terms of which we have not heard, but the odds must be long, as Tom is "the king of Scotland," and reflects the highest credit on Prestwick. Mr Hunter's (of the Red Lion) luncheon was in his usual good style.

Boy teeing up the ball for his gentleman

A Golf Song

46

AIR—"*The Maiden of Fifty-Three*"

THERE never was a game like the old Scottish game,
That's play'd 'twixt the hole and the tee;
You may roam the world o'er, but the game at your door
Is the very best game you'll see.

So I'll sing you a song, 'twill be hearty and not long,
If kindly you'll listen to me,
Of tees, holes, and clubs—of hazards and of rubs—
And whatever else in golf may be.

Of the tee, first of all—nor to*tum* nor to*tal*,
Nor that o'er which old wives agree—
Of earth, clay, or sand, whatever is at hand,
Come, quickly, and make us our tee.

We get tee from the caddie—not a box but a laddie—
What though ragged and roguish he be,
The club's face he wipes, we go in for swipes,
And off fly the balls from the tee.

Grand Golf Match—William Park *v.* Tom Morris—£100 A-Side.—We are enabled to state that a match at golf has now been arranged between the above named professionals, for £100 a-side, the best of 144 holes, over the links, at St Andrews, Musselburgh, North Berwick, and Prestwick, 36 holes to be played on each green. The stakes fall to be lodged with Stuart Grace, Esq., honorary secretary, Royal and Ancient Golf Club, on or before the 30th September. Morris's money is already posted. Park's is yet forthcoming. If it is not lodged to-night, however, the match is off. The call will be opened here on Friday 8th October, and resumed at Musselburgh on 15th, North Berwick 22d, and Prestwick 29th October, for a finish.

Swallow killed on course!

ST ANDREWS.

1855

Holiday.—Wednesday first, the 28th instant, will be held as a holiday by the different banking establishments in the city, that day being the anniversary of the coronation of her Majesty the Queen.

Degree.—The Senatus Academicus of St Andrews have conferred the degree of A.M. upon Mr Fraser of the Madras College here, after a pretty severe examination, in terms of their resolutions of last year.

Swallow Killed by a Golf Ball.—On Tuesday, the 14th current, while engaged in a match at golf, Captain Cheape's ball struck a swallow on the wing and killed it at once. We never heard of a similar incident; the ball has been painted, and the swallow stuffed and set upon it.

Our Links are again clad with golfers, and bathing is again fairly started. We see the bathing coaches out for the season. An influx of strangers are also fairly on the flow, a considerable number being already forward, and a good demand for houses still. We have all the appearance of a gay season.

Gymnastic Games.—It is now resolved that the games ... after our market. We may

St Andrews and District.

ST ANDREWS ROYAL AND ANCIENT GOLF CLUB.

THE OCTOBER MEETING.

If the Derby and St Leger Days are great events amongst those who take an interest in racing, the October meeting of the 'Royal and Ancient' has an equal hold on the admirers of the noble and manly game of Golf. Reckoning it to be the principal meeting of the first Golfing Society in Scotland, it has always brought together a large number of gentlemen fond of the game. Now that the railway communication has made St Andrews so easily accessible from all parts of the kingdom, the October meeting has year by year increased in importance, and is now one of the principal sport meetings of the country.

The arrivals both on Monday and Tuesday by the different trains were very numerous. On Tuesday especially, the links presented a most animated appearance. No sooner had the one party struck off at the home hole than another was ready to commence. The lot just left had barely time to play their second stroke when those in waiting at the second hole struck off, eager for the fray, and anxious, doubtless, to get their hand in before the competition for the honours awarded yesterday. Caddies appeared to be at a premium, all sorts and sizes being pressed into the service, some of them so very juvenile that they were scarcely able to trudge the round under the weight of clubs tucked under their arms. The weather was most propitious for the prosecuting of the game, Old Sol being kindly with his beams, a clear bracing atmosphere with happily no wind to disturb the flight of the guttas in their upward and onward course.

Amongst others on the Links on Tuesday, we noticed Lord Eglinton, Lord Loughborough, (the captain elect), Sir Thomas Moncrieff, Sir Hugh Hume Campbell, Hon. Mr Drummond, Hon. Henry Coventry, Hon. George E. Lascelles, James Blackwood, Esq., John Blackwood, Esq., O. G. Campbell, Esq., A. Sutherland, Esq., William Playfair, Esq., Eliot Playfair, Esq., James Briggs, Esq., George Glennie, Esq., N. F. Blair, Esq., Captain Broughton, E. J. Jackson, Esq., Captain Hume, James Wolfe Murray, Esq., J. L. Campbell, Esq., Captain Lyon, Colonel Moncrieff, Colonel Frazer, W. L. Gilmour, Esq., William Peddie, Esq., A. Scott, John Whyte Melville, Esq., J. H. E. Wemyss, Esq., (the retiring captain), Captain Oswald, Major Hutchison, John Bruce, Esq., Hugh Alexander, Esq., David Hunter, Esq., John Farnie, Esq., Patrick Alexander, Esq., Robert Cathcart, Esq., Moncrieff Skene, Esq., J. O. Fairlie, Esq., David Greenhill, Esq., Doctor Govan.

The professionals were represented by Dun of Blackheath, Gourlay of Musselburgh, Tom Morris and

[THUR]SDAY, OCTOBER 18, 1855.

his brother George. Park was also on the Links. His challenge to play any man in the world for a cool hundred, which first appeared in Bell's Life, and was therefrom copied into many of the provincial papers, still remains unanswered. Since it has been in print, he has suffered a defeat from his old opponent Tom Morris, who, we understand, thrashed him on his own green. We hope before this meeting is over a match may be got up betwixt them, or failing that, with Dun, whose proficiency must surely be equal to the task.

Wednesday, (yesterday) which is reckoned the principal day of the meeting, was as favourable in a weather point of view as the most fastidious could desire. Many intending players arrived by the 9.50 A.M. train from the south and by the 10.40 train from the north. Amongst others we may mention William Hamilton, Esq.; Mr Cunningham of Craigend; A. Hastie, Esq. M.P.; Messrs Condie; Captain F. Campbell; John Balfour, Esq. of Balbirnie; T. F. Noble, Esq.; Messrs Thomson, Broughty Ferry; Robert Haig, Esq.; James Lindesay, Esq.; Lieutenant Haig; Sir James G. Baird, Bart.; Mr Honey; Col. Wm. Low; Mr Maberly; Alex. Miln, Esq.; Mr Thomson, Balgowan; Messrs Dalyell; Major Douglas; Geo. Gray, Esq.; J. H. Black, Esq.; Wm. Crosthwaithe, Esq.; Sir William Feilden.

The business meeting of the Club took place, as usual, in Hastie's Hotel, at 10 o'clock on the morning of Wednesday—the Captain being in the chair. At this meeting five new members were balloted for and admitted—viz., the Right Hon. the Earl of Rothes; Thomas A. Hog, Esq., younger of Newliston; Lieutenant James Briggs, 96th Regiment; and the Hon. Francis Drummond. Immediately thereafter the members adjourned to the Links to prepare for the coming struggle.

The honours at this meeting, we may here mention, are the Silver Club and Royal Adelaide Medal, which fall to the Captain for the year, Lord Loughborough. The Royal Medal, presented by his late Majesty King William the Fourth, and the Society's Medal—these remain for open competition.

Preliminaries having been adjusted, and everything made ready for a start, by the indefatigable secretary Mr Grace, and the warning gun having been fired, shortly after 11 o'clock Mr Whyte Melville and Mr Jackson, Strathtyrum, 'toed the scratch' as the first competing couple. They were followed in rapid succession by Mr J. O. Fairley and Mr George Condie; Colonel George Moncrieff and Mr Campbell, Achalader; Captain Lyon and Mr Archibald Scott; Mr John Bruce and Mr James Blackwood; Mr William Haig and Mr S. T. Thomson; Mr Cathcart and Captain Farquhar Campbell; Mr Elliot M. Playfair and Mr Hugh Alexander; Mr Greenhill and Captain Broughton; Lord Eglinton and Mr Gilmour; Mr W. A. Hamilton and Mr Cunningham; Sir James Baird and Mr Milne; Mr Robert Haig and Mr W. C. Thomson; Mr Bethune and Mr Sligo; Mr Hay Wemyss and Mr Hastie, M.P.; Lieutenant James Briggs and Mr William Playfair; Mr George Glennie and Mr Patrick Alexander; Mr J. C. Lindsay and Mr Fernie; Mr William Condie and Mr Robert Playfair; Captain Oswald and Major Hutchison; Mr John Blackwood and Mr Ferguson Blair; Mr James Condie and Mr Ord Campbell; Mr Noble and Dr Govan; Mr Wolfe Murray and Sir Hugh Hume Campbell; Hon. George E. Lascelles and Mr Peddie; and last, though not least, Hon. H. Coventry and Sir Thomas Moncrieff—making in all twenty-six couples.

A number of ladies were congregated at the first hole to see the start. We observed, among others, Hon. Mrs Coventry and Miss Coventry; Lady Feilden and Miss Feilden; Mrs Jiles; Mrs Fairlie; Mrs Wolfe Murray; Miss Thomson, Charlton; Mrs Dalyell, Lingo; Mrs Dean; Mrs Colonel Moncrieff; Mrs Broughton and the Misses Broughton; Mrs Briggs, Strathairly, and the Misses Briggs; Mrs Grant; Mrs Grace; Miss Paton, &c., &c.

It was nearly three o'clock ere the last couple made the round, and the cards of each player having been summed, it was found that the King William medal had been gained by

George Glennie, Esq. at 88 strokes.

The Society's medal was gained by

Wm. Thomson, Esq., Broughty Ferry, at 93.

The following were the next in order:—

Mr William Condie	95
Mr O. G. Campbell	97
Mr J. O. Fairlie	98
Mr George Condie	100
Sir Thomas Moncrieff	104
Mr Hugh Alexander	105
Mr W. Hamilton	106
Mr Patrick Alexander	106
Mr William Playfair	106

A sweepstake of £5 each, contributed by the competitors, and amounting to £10, 15s., was, as usual, played for. For this Mr Glennie, the winner of the King William Medal by his score of 88, came in first; Mr William Playfair and Mr Noble being equal, the remainder was therefore divided betwixt them.

It will be observed that the play, as noted above, is remarkably fine—Mr Glennie's score of 88 being the lowest in the annals of the Society. The same medal was gained two years ago at 90 by John Campbell Stewart, Esq., 72d Highlanders. Mr Thomson, the winner of the Society's Gold Medal, is also the holder of several medals belonging to the Forfarshire societies, and promises to become a crack player.

We believe there are some capital matches on the tapis, the particulars of which we will, if possible, give in our next.

St Andrews and District. 1855

ROYAL AND ANCIENT GOLF CLUB.

THE MAY MEETING.

In speculating about this meeting of the Royal and Ancient, it was generally thought that the muster of golfers would be small. The war has had an adverse influence on golfing fixtures as well as on meetings of a more weighty nature, while the general embodiment of the militia throughout the country detains many who but for military duties would be present. We have seen the Links more crowded on the day previous to a meeting than on Tuesday. Still, there was an average sprinkling of keen and well-known lovers of the game. The weather was favourable enough for golfing, but cold beyond precedent for the first day of summer. On the morning of Tuesday both rain and sleet fell, and those of our citizens who ventured forth on early morn for May dew must have got the same considerably diluted.

The Links have been in far better condition than at present, the long tack of dry weather having told on them severely. Mostly all the putting greens are innocent of grass, the little there is being wholly covered with sand, thus rendering the short game a matter of more difficulty.

Over the course in general, a plentiful supply of sand has been strewn during the strong westerly gales which we had for nearly the whole of last month. The Elysian fields especially have received a due share, some portions of that classic locality being nearly an inch deep.

In the professional ranks there is Prestwick Tom, as he is now called, who came direct from the Blackheath Meeting. Park, the Musselburgh don, has also arrived, and is in excellent play.

Yesterday (Wednesday) was as lovely a May day as could be desired for out-door exercises. The bitter east wind had decamped during the night, leaving in his stead a mild and genial substitute from the west. Old Sol shone brilliantly forth undimmed by cloud or speck. The business meeting of the Club took place in the Cross Keys, as usual, at half-past ten o'clock A.M. In the absence of the Captain for the year, Hay Erskine Wemyss, Esq. of Wemyss, Mr Whyte Melville occupied the Chair. Two new members were admitted, viz.:—Robt. Cathcart, Esq. yr. of Pitcairly, 74th Highlanders, and Lieut. William Haig, Fife Artillery Militia.

Thereafter the members proceeded to the Links to compete for the Silver Cross and Bombay Medal, which are the honours for award at this meeting. Fifteen couples started in the following order, being one couple more than last year:—

Captain Maitland, and Mr Campbell of Achalader; Mr Peddie and Mr A. Duncan; Captain Broughton and Mr Whyte Melville; Mr P. Alexander and Mr W. Playfair; Captain Oswald of Dunnikier, and Mr J. Fernie of Balfarg; Sir T. Moncrieffe and Mr Condie, Perth; Dr Govan and Mr Milton; R. Haig, Seggie, and Mr J. C. Lindsay, Dundee; Captain Lyon and Mr Robt. Hay, Duddingstone; Sir J. Baird and Captain Miles Riddell; Major Hutchinson and Mr Bethune of Blebo; Mr Gray, Perth, and Captain D. Campbell; Mr S. Thomson, Dundee, and Mr W. Haig; Mr H. Glass and G. Govan, jun.; Mr James Milne, and Mr Cathcart.

The round having been made, and the returns of the different competitors marked, the following stood at the head of the list:—

	Strokes.
Captain Maitland Dougal	98
Mr Condie, Perth	98

Those coming nearest to the above were:—

Mr Campbell, Achalader	99
Mr Patrick Alexander	99
Major Hutchinson	99
Mr J. Fernie, Balfarg	102
Mr Duncan	103
Mr H. Glass	103
Sir Thomas Moncrieffe	105
Mr George Govan, jun	105
Mr James C. Lindsay	106

Captain Maitland Dougal and Mr Condie being thus equal, they went another round to decide as to who should be the holder of the Silver Cross, when Captain Maitland Dougal was the victor at 94 strokes, the Bombay Medal of course falling to Mr Condie.

As usual there was a sweepstakes of five shillings a-head amongst the competitors, which amounted to upwards of £3. As Mr Campbell of Achalader and Major Hutchinson both came in at 99, the sweepstakes was divided betwixt them.

Several good matches started after the medal competition, some of which we may notice in our next.

Pleasure Excursion.—Since St Andrews was connected with the populous towns of Fifeshire and adjacent counties by railway, excursions during summer are becoming more and more frequent every year to visit this ancient metropolis of Scotland. The first of these for the season, consisting of a number of the letterpress printers of Edinburgh, and the workmen employed in Mr Carmichael's Foundry, Dundee, took place on Saturday last. The latter trip was accompanied by the Dundee instrumental brass band, and being in excellent tune, contributed in no small degree by its cheerful strains to add to the pleasure of the excursion.

Fertility of the Parton or Eatable Crab (Cancer Pagurus).—Strolling among our west rocks on Friday evening, I was fortunate enough to fall in with a full-grown female crab 'in pea,' or spawned. Curious to know what number the animal might produce, I took it home with me, and, with the kind assistance of Mr Govan, druggist, weighed the whole of the spawn, which was equal to 2941 grains, or about 7 oz. avord. I then weighed one grain, and, with the assistance of a pocket microscope and fine needle, was able to count that it contained 1120 eggs. This quantity multiplied by the number of grains—2941—gave the astounding total of 3,293,920; or, if every pea had formed an animal, there would have been produced from the single spawning of this single individual, *a parten to every man, woman, and child in all Scotland and about half-a-million over!!!*—*Correspondent.*

Golfing Notabilia.—On Wednesday the 27th ultimo while a match was being played at golf on our links, a ball, hit by the honourable F. Drummond, one of the players, struck a lark at the Beardy Bunker-hole o'cross Hole, and killed it on the spot. It is a strange coincidence that Captain Chiene killed a swallow in the same month, and a tradesman in town another of the feathered tribe in July of last year in the same manner, as noticed in our columns at the time. This is now the fourth bird which has been laid low on our Links by the same instrumentality.

Golfing.—As the game of golf now occupies a deservedly prominent place among the healthful recreations and popular pastimes of the age, and more especially in this city, we now present our readers with a complete list of the Golfing Clubs in the United Kingdom, with the dates of institution, in so far as is now known to exist, or to have existed. From this list it will be seen that there are at present twenty-two Golfing Clubs in Great Britain, and that eight, or more than one-third of these are in this county. It will also be observed that, although St Andrews cannot claim the honour of giving birth to the first Golfing Club, it is in point of number of Golfing institutions, as in every other respect, the Golfing metropolis of the United Kingdom:—

		Instituted.
The Edinburgh Burgess Golf Club		1735
The Blackheath Golf Club, London		1744
The Edinburgh Company of Golfers		1744
The Leith Golf Club		1744
The St Andrews Royal and Ancient Golf Club	14th May	1754
The Bruntsfield Links Golf Club, Edinburgh		1761
The Musselburgh Golf Club		1774
The Aberdeen Golf Club		1780
The Crail Golf Club, Fifeshire (defunct)		1786
The Burntisland Golf Club		1798
The Ancient Golf Club of Montrose, re-established in 1810, and designation changed in 1845 to Royal Albert Golf Club		Date not known.
Kingsbarns Golf Club, Fifeshire (defunct)		1815
The Scotscraig Golf Club, Fifeshire (defunct)		1817
The Thistle Golf Club, St Andrews (defunct)	Sept.	1817
The Innerleven Golf Club, Fifeshire		1820
The Perth Golf Club	5th April	1824
The North Berwick Golf Club	about	1830
The Hercules Golf Club, Fifeshire, 1835 / The Elie Golf Club	united	1830
The St Andrews Golf Club (late Mechanics)	29th Sep.	1843
The Monifieth Golf Club, Forfarshire		1845
The Leven Golf Club, Fifeshire		1847
The Carnoustie Golf Club, Forfarshire		1848
The Operative Golf Club, St Andrews	5th Feby.	1849
The Prestwick Golf Club, Ayrshire		1851
The Prestwick Mechanics' Golf Club		1851
The St Andrews Students' Golf Club		1855

James Ogilvie Fairlie in action!

GOLFIANA. Oct 1855

The principal golfing theme on Thursday was a foursome match of one round of eighteen holes between Allan Robertson, with Tom Morris of Prestwick for a partner, against James Dunn of Blackheath, and William Park, who has challenged any person in the world to play him at golf for £100 to £200 a-side. We believe that £500 in bets by various gentlemen hung on the issue of the match, at the conclusion of which Allan and Tom were victorious by 2 holes—they having holed the course in 94 strokes; while their opponents took 96.

Another good match was also played on Thursday between Mr Farquhar Campbell and Allan against Mr Cathcart and George Morris, upon which bets were also pending. Mr Cathcart and partner proved too much for their opponents by 2 holes on the round. Another match by the same parties was intended to come off on Friday, but, owing to other engagements by the parties, it did not take place. We understand, however, that it is still in anticipation.

On Friday a set-to was announced between Mr George Glennie (the medal-holder) and Mr Patrick Alexander, against Mr Hugh Alexander and Tom Morris. At the conclusion of the first match of 18 holes, Tom and Co. thrashed the medal-holder and partner by 5 holes. In a second match, however, Mr Glennie and partner turned tables on their opponents beating them by 1 hole; but, at the conclusion of a third match of 3 holes, Morris and Co. finally maintained their superiority, gaining the match by 1 hole. On the same day a nice interesting match took place between Allan and Mr Wemyss, against Mr Sutherland and Strath, a young professional of great promise, at the conclusion of which it was found that the two former had gained by 1 hole.

On Saturday a capital foursome started, and, as will be seen from the result of the day's play, consisting of Sir Thomas Moncrieff and Allan, against Mr Fairlie and Tom Morris. On the party holing out the Hole o' Cross, on their return the two latter were found to be 6 holes a-head out of the 13 played, and as there were only 5 holes to play, Mr Fairlie and Tom were victorious. Another match of 18 holes was then commenced from the Hole o' Cross towards the Home Hole. On arriving at the Short Hole, another was out again. This match was found to be vested in Sir Thomas Moncrieff and Allan, they having, in this match, turned tables on their opponents by 7 holes and 5 to play. A third and concluding match then ensued. Mr Fairlie and Tom Morris took the first 4 holes in a canter, but on arriving at the Burn Hole both parties were found to be equal, and the Home Hole was subsequently halved. Both sides were therefore equal on the day's play in so far as regards matches; but a stipulation having been made before starting that in the event of the matches being divided the number of holes was to overrule, Sir Thomas and Allan were successful by 1 hole. A heavy match also took place on Saturday between Mr Wemyss and Allan against Mr Archibald Hastie, M.P., and Park, which Mr Wemyss and Allan gained by 1 hole.

* Park's challenge to play any man in the world for £100 or £200 a-side is, we understand, not to remain much longer unanswered, as the following acceptance is to appear in *Bell's Life* of Saturday next, the paper in which the challenge originally appeared.—'Golf.—Thomas Morris, ball-maker, of Prestwick, is ready to play Mr Park of Musselburgh at golf for £100 a-side. The match to consist of 108 holes, thirty-six to be played on each of the following greens:—St Andrews, Prestwick, and Musselburgh. To toss for the choice of the green on which the match is to commence. Any communication addressed to Thomas Morris, as above will be attended to.' The match will cause not a little excitement in golfing circles, as the parties to be pitted against each other are certainly crack players.

The most exciting match of the season came off on Thursday between four of the best professional golfers of the day,—viz., Tom Morris of Prestwick, and Andrew Strath, St Andrews, against the brothers William and David Park, Musselburgh. The match was got up by several gentlemen at the May meeting, and heavy bets were staked on both sides—the favourites being Morris and Strath, as much as six to four, and in some instances three to one, being offered and taken.

Shortly after eleven o'clock they struck off, and on going the first round Morris and Strath came in two holes ahead, both parties having gone the round in 88 and 89 strokes—Tom and Strath going out in 46 and coming in at 42; the Parks going out in 47 and in at 42. After a short refreshment, they again struck off. Morris and partner took the burn hole, making them three ahead; the next hole was halved; they also gained another hole upon the next two, which made them four holes ahead; but, at the hole across, their propitious stars began to wane—Tom chanced to miss a short putt, and the hole was lost. From this point the Parks shot rapidly ahead—taking the next eight holes running!—and on coming in were dormy at the fourth hole. Morris and Strath took the next hole, but the Parks took the one following—thus winning the match by four. At the corner of the dyke hole, they played in the two remaining holes—the brothers gaining these also—thus making them victors by six holes on the two rounds of 36 holes.

We understand that the same match is to be played on Saturday. It may be remarked that the day was beautiful, and the green in excellent condition, with no wind to interfere with the play. A large concourse of spectators followed the players both rounds. The scores of the second round were —For the Parks, 45 out and 40 in—total, 85; Tom and Strath, 46 out and 49 in—total, 95.

Golf Club Meeting.—The Autumn meeting of the St Andrews Golf Club (late Mechanics) came off on Friday last, when 14 members of the society entered the list for the honours of the day. The results of the day's play are as follows:—The Society's medal gained by William Aytoun, jun., at 96 strokes; the Society's Silver Cross Clubs by John Sym, at 103 strokes. Odds were allowed to inferior players in competing for the following prizes:—1st, The choice of the two clubs presented by the Leven Golf Club, William Aytoun, jun.; 2d, the remaining club, Elias Jones; 3d, two balls, presented by Allan Robertson, John Sym; 4th, two balls, presented by Thomas Morris, William Aytoun, sen.; 5th, two balls presented by the Club, George Bruce; 6th and 7th, two balls, presented by the Club, Thomas Howie and Robert Tattison; 8th, a bunch of grapes, presented by Mr Grimmond, James M'Pherson. The weather, although not everything that could have been desired, was considered a good field day, and the play was upon the whole above the average. The annual ball took place in the Town Hall in the evening, and was pretty well attended. The hall was most tastefully decorated with evergreens, flowers, and flags, while the insignia of the Club occupied a prominent place. Dancing commenced shortly after nine o'clock, and was kept up with great spirit until half-past eleven, when the party retired to the Upper Hall to supper—Mr George Bruce, Captain of the Club, presided. Several appropriate toasts having been given and heartily responded to, the company reassembled in the Lower Hall, where dancing was resumed, and carried on until 5 o'clock.

GREAT GOLF MATCH. 1856

It may be in the recollection of our readers that a few months since a challenge appeared in our paper from Wm. Park of Musselburgh to play any man a match at golf, for £100 or £200 a-side. For some time it remained unnoticed, and Park's admirers feared his ambition for fame would not be gratified. At length an admirer and staunch friend of Tom Morris of Prestwick (formerly of St Andrews) accepted the challenge on his behalf. The stake was fixed at £100 a-side, and instead of two out of three matches on different links deciding the victory, it was stipulated that the men should play on four different links, 36 holes in each ground. This new feature in the terms of such matches was generally approved by the lovers of the game, and considered the fairest test of superiority. On Tuesday the first of the 36 holes was played over Musselburgh links. To complete this number they had to play four and a half rounds. The day was very unfavourable, more than half the time the rain fell heavily, accompanied by a cold north-east wind; still a large number of the admirers of this game walked the course and watched keenly the moves of the play. There are eight holes in the round. First round, Park holed the eight holes in forty strokes, Morris in 41; second, Park 39 strokes, Morris 42; third, Park 35 strokes, Morris 41; fourth, Park 39, Morris 38; four odd holes, Park 20, Morris 26. Park's figures stood 173 strokes, Morris 188. These figures are nearly, if not perfectly correct. The result of the play was that Park was eight holes ahead. His play, considering it was an unfavourable day for his style, was much admired. Morris fell off very much in the second and third rounds, the wind and rain being very severe then, and appeared to affect him very much. There are still 108 holes to play, and Morris's admirers, knowing by past experience his good play and nerve, believe he will be victorious.—*Bell's Life.*

GOLF MATCHES ON PRESTWICK LINKS.

The past week has been a very exciting one on Prestwick Links. The interest commenced on Wednesday, on which day the various golfing celebrities from a distance arrived by the train, to be in readiness for the medal play on Thursday. The two most important single matches on that day were Mr Glennie against Tom Morris, and Mr Ord Campbell against the justly celebrated Park. On Thursday the club medal was competed for, and from the number of first-class players present, was more keenly contested than on any previous occasion. On the two rounds being completed, it was found that Mr Glennie and Lieut. W. Hamilton, R.A.R., were equal at 127. These two immediately started for a third and decisive round, in which Lieut. Hamilton proved victor. This gentleman holds both the Prestwick Club Medals, and Mr Glennie holds that of the St. Andrew's Club. The day finished with a dinner in the King's Arms, Ayr,—Major Hamilton, R. A. R., Captain-General of the Club, in the chair. Among other topics, interesting to the golfing world, then discussed, was a suggestion to have a golfing tournament, wherein all clubs might have an opportunity of trying their respective powers.

On Friday, the second part of the grand match between Tom Morris and W. Park of Musselburgh came off. This match, consists of 36 holes, to be played on each of the following links—Musselburgh, Prestwick, North Berwick, and St. Andrews, for £100 a-side. At Musselburgh Park gained 8 holes, and at Prestwick 5. It must be said for Tom that he is not quite in the same tip-top condition he was six months ago; but, at the same time, it is difficult to conceive anything finer than Park's play, and professionals in all quarters will require to look to their laurels.

The meeting terminated on Saturday with a number of pri-

2nd May 1856 – Best of 36 Holes being 2nd of 4 Links match of 144 holes. Links

PRESTWICK GOLF ~~CLUB~~

Mr Tho. Morris — Park

~~1st~~ Round	1st	2nd	3rd	~~2d~~ Round	1st	2nd	3rd
1st	7	7	5	1st	7	6	6
2d	7	6	5	2d	5	5	5
3d	4	3	4	3d	5	3	3
4th	6	7	6	4th	6	8	5
5th	4	5	6	5th	5	5	5
6th	4	5	4	6th	4	4	5
7th	4	4	3	7th	3	3	3
8th	3	4	4	8th	4	4	4
9th	5	5	6	9th	7	5	5
10th	4	5	4	10th	3	3	4
11th	3	2	4	11th	3	2	4
12th	5	6	6	12th	6	6	5
	56	59	57		58	54	54
Sum				Sum			

	Morris	Park
1st Round—Sum	56	58
2nd Round – Sum	59	54
3d Round—Sum	57	54
Total	172	166

Hand-hammered Gutta

"In my prime!"
1856 →
Studio
Portrait
Prestwick.

St. Andrews, 21st Sept. 1855.

As David Anderson, the present keeper of the Golf course, has resigned his office, the meeting resolve to appoint Walter Alexander and Alexander Herd, caddies, in his place, at a salary of Six pounds betwixt them.

50

MR GEORGE GLENNIE

GEORGE WHYTE MELVILLE — CAPT MAITLAND DOUGALL — MR GEORGE GLENNIE — J. O. FAIRLIE — SANDY PIRIE

Winners of the Gold Medal
Presented by his late Majesty

1845	James Calvert, Esq., Montrose	100
1846	Do.	111
1847	N. J. Ferguson Blair, Esq.	105
1848	George Condie, Esq., Perth	104
1849	W. M. Goddard, Esq., Leith	105
1850	Sir David Baird, Bart.	100
1851	O'Brian B. Peter, Esq., Kirkland	105
1852	Robert Hay, Esq.	99
1853	John C. Stewart, Esq., 72nd Highlanders	90
1854	William Archibald Hamilton, Esq.	97
1855	GEORGE GLENNIE, Esq.	88

THE GOLD MEDAL

THE ROYAL AND ANCIENT GOLF CLUB.

THE MAY MEETING. 1856

Seldom have the Links presented so deserted an appearance on the days immediately preceding the medal day at this meeting as on Monday and Tuesday last. Excepting one or two strangers, and the usual quota contributed by the city and neighbourhood, there was nothing to indicate a mustering amongst the lovers of the noble and manly game. This paucity of players can be accounted for, however, from the fact of Park and Morris's third day's encounter taking place at North Berwick on Tuesday. Nearly all the gentlemen who attended the meeting there that day would therefore remain to see how the match went.

With regard to the great match, it would be noticed in last week's *Journal* that at the conclusion of the first day's play over Musselburgh Links, Park had come in a winner by 8 holes. Their second meeting was at Prestwick on Saturday last, when Park again had the better of his opponent by 5 holes. On intelligence reaching this of these reverses, the friends of Tom Morris were much chagrined, for it is but natural to suppose him the favourite with the denizens of the golfing metropolis.

Considerable anxiety was manifested here on Tuesday evening to hear the result of that day's play; and when it became current that Tom had had managed to beat his adversary by the narrow majority of two holes, thus reducing the balance against him to 11 holes, the *Morrisonians* were loud in their regrets that he had not been able to secure a heavier advantage on the day, so as to give him some heartening for the work of Saturday.

51

Whereas Charles Campbell Esqr. Ayr, as Treasurer of the Prestwick Golf Club

having paid to the **Scottish Union Insurance Company** the Sum of One Pound and sixpence above stated as the PRESENT PAYMENT, being the Premium and Duty on the Sum insured by this Policy from the Twentieth day of March 1856 to Whitsunday 1857, and agreed to pay the sum of Fifteen shillings also above stated, as the FUTURE ANNUAL PAYMENT, at the Term above mentioned, during the continuance of this Policy, for INSURANCE AGAINST LOSS OR DAMAGE BY FIRE, on

Building of house situated in the Village of Prestwick near Ayr occupied by Thomas Morris as Dwelling House and in which he manufactures Golf Clubs & Balls One Hundred and Twenty Pounds

On Household Goods and Furniture. Bed and Table Linen. Wearing Apparel. Printed Books. Plate Wine and Liquors in private and including Golf Clubs. Boxes Tools and such like therein Eighty Pounds

Time and Stated

Insurance for my house, workshop and possessions at Prestwick.

ROYAL AND ANCIENT GOLF CLUB BALL.

The Royal and Ancient Golf Club Ball came off on Thursday evening, and was a most brilliant affair; seldom, indeed, has such an assembly of youth beauty, and fashion, graced the halls of St Rule. Dancing commenced about 10 o'clock. Supper was served up in splendid style by Mr Hastie about 1 o'clock; after which dancing was resumed, and kept up till an early hour. Lord Loughborough makes a capital captain; and the ball of 1855, under his auspices, will long be remembered as one among the most pleasant and successful assemblies. Among those present were—

Ladies.—Hon. Mrs Coventry and Miss Coventry; Lady Arbuthnot and Miss Arbuthnot; Lady Feilden and Miss Feilden; Mrs Giles; Mrs Wolfe Murray; Mrs Colonel Moncrieff; Mrs Oswald of Dunnikeir; Mrs Stewart of St Fort; Mrs Dalyell of Lingo; Mrs Briggs of Strathairlie, and Miss Briggs; Mrs Grant, Cupar; Mrs Jackson, Strathtyrum; Mr Pitcairn of Pitcullo; Mrs Walker, Pitcairn; Mrs Hunter; Mrs W. Pitcairn; Mrs Meshem and Miss Meshem; Mrs Milton; Mrs and Miss Siborne; Mrs Stuart Grace; Mrs J. Blackwood; Mrs and Misses Ferrier; Miss Neaves; Miss Thomson, Charlton; Miss Leith Hay; Miss Cathcart, Pitcairly; Miss Chalmers, Larbert House; Miss Fraser; Miss B. J. Reeve, Eden Park; Miss Alexander; Misses Scott, Dalgairn; Miss C. Broughton; Miss A. L. Grace; Miss M. Lindesay, Balmungo; Miss M. Grace, Cupar; Miss Wade; Miss Watson Wemyss, Denbrae; Miss Farnie; Miss Murray; Miss Pearson; Miss Carstairs, Ferrybank; &c., &c.

Gentlemen.—The Captain, Lord Loughbourgh; Mr Hay Erskine Wemyss of Wemyss; Hon. Francis Drummond; Hon. G. G. Lascelles; Sir Wm. Feilden, Bart.; Mr Hastie, M.P.; Captain Oswald of Dunnikier; Col. Moncrieff, Scots Fusilier Guards; Mr Whyte Melville; Mr Wolfe Murray of Cringletie; Mr Balfour of Balbirnie; Sir James G. Baird, Bart.; Mr Thomson Gordon, Sheriff of Edinburgh; Mr Anstruther Thomson of Charlton; Provost Playfair; Mr Purvis of Kinaldy; Mr Ord of Howtell; Mr Sligo of Carmyle; Hon. Mr Campbell; Major Hutchinson; Mr Pitcairn of Pitcullo; Sheriff Grant; Mr Jackson of Strathtyrum; Mr Miln, yr. of Murie; Mr Moncrieff Skene, yr. of Pitlour; Mr Greenhill; Mr W. F. Webb; Hon. John Rollo; Mr Hunter, Blackness; Mr Berry of Tayfield; Capt. Patterson of Cunnoquhie; Mr G. S. Simpson, yr. of Pitcorthie; Dr Pitcairn; Mr Ord Campbell; Mr Cathcart, yr. of Pitcairly; Mr Cunningham of Craigend; Professor Ferrier; Mr James Blackwood; Mr John Blackwood; Captain Broughton; Mr Williamson Ramsay of Lixmount; Mr John Bruce; Mr R. Anstruther Dalyell; Mr Ralph Dalyell; Colonel Stuart, 14th Light Dragoons; Lieut. Jas. Briggs, 96th Regiment; Mr Chas. Campbell, Edenwood; Mr W. S. Milton; Mr John Campbell, H.E.I.C.S.; Lieut. E. M Playfair, Madras Artillery; Mr W. Playfair, Bengal Army; Mr Patrick Alexander; Mr Stamford Lumsdaine, Lathallan; Mr Marjoribanks; Mr A. Clerk Rattray; Mr H. D. Aytoun; Mr W. S. Playfair; Mr Cunningham; Mr Frederick Pitman; Mr Wilson of Dalmarnock; Mr W. Graham Sandford, Royal Perthshire Rifles; Mr Stuart Grace; Offi-

Hugh Philp died 1856 just as Allan kent how to swing a club Hugh kent how to make them

breed exhibited, but were not entered for prizes.

1856

GREAT GOLF MATCH.

This interesting match was brought to a conclusion on the 10th instant, at St Andrews. It will be remembered that Park was eight holes a-head at Musselburgh, five holes at Prestwich, in all 13. At North Berwick Morris won by two holes, still leaving his opponent 11 holes a head, with 30 to play. On Saturday last they met to play the match off; two rounds of the links were necessary, and a great number of gentlemen from a distance, as also the resident players, followed the men. Betting in favour of Park winning the match, but bets made that Morris would be victorious on that day's play. The play was very fine on both sides, and the struggle severe; at length when 29 holes had been played, Morris was three holes a head, leaving his opponent eight holes a head, with seven to play. Park was declared the winner, and heartily congratulated on the result. In order to decide the bets pending on that day's play, they played out the remaining seven holes, when Morris won two more, making him the victor on the day by five holes, and on the 144 played, six behind Park. It is stated that Morris has not been very well during part of the time occupied in the match, certainly he was not well on the first day. His backer challenged Park to another trial, for the same sum, seven links to be an additional course, but as that ground was quite unknown to Park, the offer has in the meantime, been declined.

We learn that W. Dunn of Blackheath has been backed against Park, for the same sum, to play in October, near Musselburgh, Prestwich, and St Andrews. This match will be as interesting as the one now concluded. Park has conducted himself in a very unassuming manner; his fine, easy style of play was much admired. Morris, though defeated, has a host of friends, and will not want backers for a match in which he has a fair chance.

Great Golf Match ↑ – Wasn't well during this one with Willie.

Mr Gilmour with Sandy Pirie Keeper of the Green caddying for him.

St Andrews and District.

THE ROYAL AND ANCIENT GOLF CLUB.

THE MAY MEETING. 1856

Seldom have the Links presented so deserted an appearance on the days immediately preceding the medal day at this meeting as on Monday and Tuesday last. Excepting one or two strangers, and the usual quota contributed by the city and neighbourhood, there was nothing to indicate a mustering amongst the lovers of the noble and manly game. This paucity of players can be accounted for, however, from the fact of Park and Morris's third day's encounter taking place at North Berwick on Tuesday. Nearly all the gentlemen who attended the meeting there that day would therefore remain to see how the match went.

With regard to the great match, it would be noticed in last week's *Journal* that at the conclusion of the first day's play over Musselburgh Links, Park had come in a winner by 8 holes. Their second meeting was at Prestwick on Saturday last, when Park again had the better of his opponent by 5 holes. On intelligence reaching this of these reverses, the friends of Tom Morris were much chagrined, for it is but natural to suppose him the favourite with the denizens of the golfing metropolis.

Considerable anxiety was manifested here on Tuesday evening to hear the result of that day's play; and when it became current that Tom had had managed to beat his adversary by the narrow majority of two holes, thus reducing the balance against him to 11 holes, the *Morrisonians* were loud in their regrets that he had not been able to secure a heavier advantage on the day, so as to give him some heartening for the work of Saturday.

The match now stands thus:—36 holes to play; Park 11 a-head—too great a majority, it is generally thought, for Tom to clear off. Of course the betting is all in Park's favour.

Fifeshire Journal: —"Mr Chambers, jun., against Mr Wallace. An immense crowd was in waiting at the Home Hole on Saturday forenoon, to witness the game of the gentlemen above named, between whom lay the tournament. A start was effected shortly after eleven o'clock. The game out was a series of give and take. At the Return Hole we find Mr Wallace one a-head. Hole about the order of the day, with a likelihood that the match would result as before in a tie. Great excitement on the part of the audience. At the Fourth Hole coming home, all even is yet the state of the poll. Mr Chambers won the next, whereby he became one a-head, with two to play. A mistake would now be fatal to either. On the green at the Burn Hole, at a like number, Mr Chambers fell to play the odds, and a lovely ball he played, lying 'dead' at the hole, amid the suppressed admiration of the onlookers. Wallace evidently did not like the nearness of his adversary's ball. He knelt to study the putt, looking at it in every way—played at last—did not hole, but 'stimied' his adversary. It was now Mr Chambers' turn to look aghast. Hole the ball he could not, although he very skilfully lifted the ball over his adversary's, striking the very edge of the hole. All square once more, and a hole to play. In striking off from the Burn Hole, Chambers drove wild towards the lifeboat house. 'That turns the match,' said a keen hand, who had been round with the combatants. Chambers, however, made a beautiful swipe, although he lay bad amongst long grass, and managed to get on the green at the same number of strokes as his wide-awake opponent. The odds was played by Chambers, and a dexterous odd it was, considering the locality. He laid his ball 'dead' with his iron within a few inches of the hole. Wallace's ball was a few yards from the hole. If he holed, the proud position for which so many had for nearly a week been striving, would be his. A halved match at least he could again make it. But no! His ball when played lies several feet short of the little round hole, and wandered away into a leap. But of this he failed to hole, so the match, by a *single stroke*, fell to his opponent. Mr R. Chambers, jun., Bruntsfield Club, Edinburgh, was thereafter declared to be winner of the Tournament."

Mr Chambers winning the Grand Tournament

← Dr Robert Chambers - prominent member
founder of Chambers Journal which Allan and I both read regularly

ROYAL AND ANCIENT GOLF CLUB.—THE OCTOBER MEETING.

The autumn meeting of the Royal and Ancient is this year a week later than usual, and has, we presume, been arranged so that it might not interfere with the meetings at Musselburgh, Prestwick, and Carnoustie, nor with Perth Races, which occupied two days of last week.

A desire to attend one or other of the sporting fixtures noted above prevented many from arriving here earlier. The links, during the week immediately preceding that of the meeting, were generally well frequented by golfers, but this year, saving and excepting the usual quota furnished by the city and district, there was nothing to indicate the approach of the crack October. Caddies were heard to complain of the times, like Othello, imagining their occupation gone—several of the fraternity betaking themselves to another calling to keep life in.

By Tuesday, however, there were lots of golfers up from all quarters. Amongst others who arrived and

The weather on Wednesday was favourable for the medal competitions. The druggy, misty, atmosphere which prevailed on the two days previously, creating fears amongst many that on the medal day we would have rain, had entirely disappeared, and old Sol, whose face had not been seen for days, shone forth brilliantly from out the blue serene. There was little or no wind to disturb the guttas in their transit through the air.

The proceedings on Wednesday commenced with the business meeting of the Society, which was held within the Club House at 10 o'clock, A.M. The following gentlemen were then and there admitted members of the Society, viz.:—Lieutenant Henry Playfair; Captain Wm. Ross King; Lieutenant Henry D. Dempster; Mr George Gordon; Mr Robert S. Pattison; Captain May, 72d Highlanders; Mr John Alston; and Admiral Drinkwater Bethune of Balfour. It was also resolved to hold the May meeting, as at present, on the first Wednesday of May, and the autumn meeting on the Wednesday nearest the first day of October.

At eleven o'clock those who were to compete for the Royal William and Club Gold Medals having been balloted for the order in which they should start, it fell to Mr Grant and Sir Ralph Anstruther to lead off, who were followed in succession by others. Having made the round of the Links, the following was the result:—Sir Hugh Lyon Playfair, Captain for the year, gained the Silver Clubs; Captain Maitland Dougall, Scotscraig, Royal William Medal, having holed the course at 92 strokes; Captain Boothby, Club Medal, 94.

The scores next to these were as under:—

Mr Hamilton at	97 strokes.
Mr Andrew Nicoll	98 ...
Mr Patrick Alexander	99 ...
Mr R. Mitchell	101 ...
Sir Thomas Moncrieff	103 ...
Mr George Glennie	103 ...
Mr Thomas R. Blair	104 ...
Mr J. D. B. Hay	105 ...
Mr S. Thomson	105 ...
Mr Fairlie	106 ...
Mr Ord Campbell ...	106 ...

The sweepstakes of 5s a-head, contributed by the medal competitors was then disposed of—Captain Boothby (the club medal-holder) gained the first prize; Captain Anstruther, yr. of Balcaskie, gained the second prize; and a third of the proceeds fell to Mr Andrew Nicoll, and Mr Robert Mitchell.

Park and Dunn's match will be played on Friday instead of Saturday, as mentioned in the *Journal* of last week.

RAFFIC—PASSEN

STATION

1857

St Andrews and District.

ROYAL AND ANCIENT GOLF CLUB.

THE MAY MEETING.

St Andrews Links were never in better condition for golfing purposes than now. Since the meeting in October, the Club has spent some twenty pounds in the repair of the course in straightening the walls of most of the bunkers, which had become much breached by frequent visitations, and in filling up other little holes and corners. The putting greens have had a thorough over-haul, re-turfed, and otherwise improved. On each green, with the exception of the first and return, two holes have been placed; the one is played to by parties going outwards, the other in the in-coming. To prevent mistakes, the out-going hole is supplied with a white flag, and its neighbour sports a red one, that being the colour for all the return holes. This is a decided improvement on the old system, preventing confusion and the delays which often had to be put up with, on medal days especially, when a party going out encountered another winding their way homewards on the same green, and there being only a hole betwixt them, the one party had to look on until the other had played out and got under weigh again.

The arrivals were by no means numerous. In fact, on the days previous to the medal day (yesterday), we never saw the links so devoid of red coats. This paucity of players has been found to form no criterion to the success of a meeting. St Andrews being now so easily got at from all parts by railway, the bulk of the players do not enter appearance until the morning of the medal day.

Amongst others on the Links on Tuesday—a day remarkably favourable for golf—we noticed Mr Grant of Kilgraston; Mr Cathcart; Captain Riddell; Captain Jones; Captain King; Mr Campbell, Achalader; Mr J. D. Buchanan Hay; Lord Charles Kerr; Mr Greenhill; Mr Thomson, Broughty; Mr Oswald, Dunnikier.

The professionals present were Tom Morris, his brother George, and Park the younger. Tom Morris arrived here from Musselburgh on Monday; he had encountered his old opponent, Park, in a foursome, which was played on Musselburgh course on Thursday last week—the match was between Mr Ord Campbell with Tom, against Mr Mitchell Innes and Park. The latter had the worst of it on the day's play. A good match will be played over St Andrews Links one day during the meeting week, made up of Allan with young Strath against Tom and Park, junior, who promises to turn out a don. This will test St Andrews, as against Prestwick and Musselbro'. Wednesday was as favourable for the doings of the day as could be wished—no high wind as is usual at this meeting—the air keen enough to brace one thoroughly in the enjoyment of the manly game.

£20 spent on refacing bunkers

Boy caddies

THURSDAY, MAY 7, 1857.

and Mr Nicol; Mr G. M. Govan and Mr Hamilton; Mr Fairlie and Mr Thomas Peter.

The gentlemen, above named, having all got off, there was a lull in the proceedings until their return. The first couple arrived at the home hole again shortly after two o'clock, the rest in rapid succession thereafter. Cards of players having been handed in, it was found that Captain Dougall made the round in the fewest strokes, his card showing 94; Mr William Thomson was 96. The Captain, however, holds the Royal Medal at present, and, by rule, he cannot at same time have the Cross. He was obliged to give up that to Mr Thomson, the next in point of numbers for the day, and fall back on the Bombay Medal.

The cards nearest to the two winners above named were—

Mr Henry M'Kechnie	99 strokes.
... Govan	100 ...
... Hamilton	101 ...
... Robert Mitchell	102 ...
... Robert Philp	104 ...
... O'Brien Peter	104 ...
Captain J. D. B. Hay	106 ...
Mr Crosthwaite	106 ...
... S. C. Thomson	107 ...
... Nicoll	108 ...
... James Lindesay	108 ..
... Sutherland	109 ...
... Robert Haig	109 ...
... J. Peter	109 ...

The usual sweepstakes of 5s from each competing member fell to Lieutenant Henry Playfair and Mr Robert Mitchell.

After the Medal competition, several good matches were arranged. A foursome, comprising Captain Dougall and Allan against Mr Hamilton and Tom Morris, resulted in the defeat of the former by two holes. The strokes were 88 and 92.

There were several others, particulars of which we must defer till next week.

57

James Wilson clubmaker

Bob Kirk Ballmaker

LAYING FOUNDATION STONE OF NEW TOWN HALL, ST ANDREWS, 1858.

The foundation stone of the Town Hall of St Andrews was laid on 2nd June 1858 with Masonic honours. On that day Masonic Lodge St Andrew, No. 25, assisted at the opening of the Provincial Grand Lodge of Fife in the large hall of the Madras College. Thereafter the Brethren, with deputations from twelve sister Lodges, were, along with the various public bodies, marshalled in procession, and accompanied by four instrumental bands of music proceeded through the principal streets of the city to the site of the new Town Hall. After an impressive prayer had been offered up by the P.G. Chaplain, Brother Cochrane, the foundation stone of the building was laid with all due Masonic form by Brother John Whyte-Melville, Provincial Grand Master. The ceremony was favoured with fine weather. The procession was a very large one, and everything passed off most successfully. After the ceremony the Masonic brethren returned to the Madras College, where about 250 sat down to dinner.

The New Town Hall.—The foundation-stone of this building is to be laid with masonic honours on Wednesday the 2d day of June, by John Whyte Melville, Esq., of Mount Melville, Dep. Grand Master for Scotland, and Provincial Grand Master for Fife.

In anticipation of the above event a number of gentlemen have been admitted members of the Mason Lodge here. The houses in the New Street are to be occupied at Whitsunday first, but unless some little activity is shewn in the formation of the Street, we fear the tenants will be put to much inconvenience.

Public Reading Room and Library.—The St Andrews Public Reading Room and Library is shortly to be removed from the rooms in Crail's Lane, to those more accessible and commodious premises in South Street, lately occupied by Mr Fletcher, bookseller.

... the Sutlej.—For the last few days ...

Spring 1858

ROYAL AND ANCIENT GOLF CLUB.

The Spring or May meeting of this celebrated golfing institution was held yesterday, under circumstances of a very auspicious kind, whether as regards the muster of members, the weather, the state of the green, or the play. There was certainly a stiff breeze blowing from the west, and the Links, in some parts, were rather "keen;" but on the whole, the May meeting of 1858 holds "high its head" among its many predecessors.

Among the gentl.men on the green we observed the following, all of more or less note in golfing circles:—Lord Charles Kerr; Hon. John Rollo; Sirs Ralph A. Anstruther, Thomas Moncreiff, Hugh Lyon Playfair, and Charles Ochterlonie; Colonels Cheape, Shortreed, and Low; Majors Dreghorn, Cheine, and Douglas; Captains Guthrie, Dougall, Hume, Broughton, and Montgomerie; Dr Govan; Messieurs J. H. E. Wemyss, Wolfe Murray, John Grant, J. O. Fairlie, J. Whyte Melville, John Balfour, J. T. Oswald, A. Bethune, D. Greenhill, W. A. Campbell, John Peter, A. Kinloch, Ralph A. Dalzell, Robert Hay, R. Philp, R. Haig, W. Thomson, Thomas Blair, R. F. Cathcart, W. Playfair, Robert Taylor, Fox Noble, G. Taylor, Robert Mitchell, J. Walkenshaw, J. and D. Blackwood, J. Watson, P. Graham, O. G. Campbell, J. Mason, James Skelton, Stein, Fell, W. Crossthwaite, D. Lindsay, J. Bruce Gardyne, W. Haig, S. Thomson, A. Nicol, R. Milne, A. Ferrie, A. Turnbull, J. Lindsay, D. Arklay, John Norrie, Lamb, F. Ogilvie, W. Horsbrugh, W. Pitcairn, Alexander Denman, Murray, &c., &c.

The Links were, as usual, also graced with the presence of a great number of ladies during the day.

There was not such a great turn out of "professional" golfers on the present occasion as we have seen. Besides "Allan, the King," we observed Tom and George Morris, Strath, &c. The "Parks" and "Dunns" were absent.

Precisely at eleven o'clock twenty couples started, in succession, to compete for the Silver Cross and Bombay Medal, in the following order:—Messrs Murray and Lamb; Lindsay and Ferrie; Noble and Black; Major Cheine and R. Mitchell; Wemyss and Campbell; S. Thomson and R. Haig; W. Thomson and A. Nicoll; Cathcart and Captain Hume; Bethune and Greenhill; Sir Thomas Moncrieff and Fairlie; Colonel Low and J. Peter; Crossthwaite and Blair; Dr Govan and Walkenshaw; Col. Cheape and R. Taylor; Captain Dougall and Robert Hay; Wolfe Murray and W. Playfair: W. Haig and R. Philp. Melville and Grant; R. Milne and Turnbull; Dalyell and Kinloch.

It was about three o'clock when the last couple returned to the first hole, when, on comparing cards, it was found that the members who had gone the round at fewest strokes were—Sir Thomas Moncrieff, 95; A. Bethune, Esq., 99; Captain Hume, 99. The first was of course at once declared winner of the first prize, or Silver Cross. It being "a tie" between the latter two gentlemen, they had to play another round, which they proceeded to do, and returned at half-past four o'clock, when Mr Bethune was declared winner by five strokes, who is therefore the holder of the Bombay Medal for the ensuing year.

The members of the club dined in the Union Club House at six o'clock.

The only very important matches after the settlement of the medals up to the hour of our despatch resulted as follows:—Mr Erskine Wemyss with Allan, gained a very close contest, his opponent being Mr Cathcart with Bob Kirk, by one hole; and Mr Whyte Melville and Robert Hay defeated Mr Grant of Kilgraston and Captain Maitland Dougall, also a closely contested match.

We understand that several excellent ones are on the tapis for the next three days, which we shall have pleasure in noticing next week.

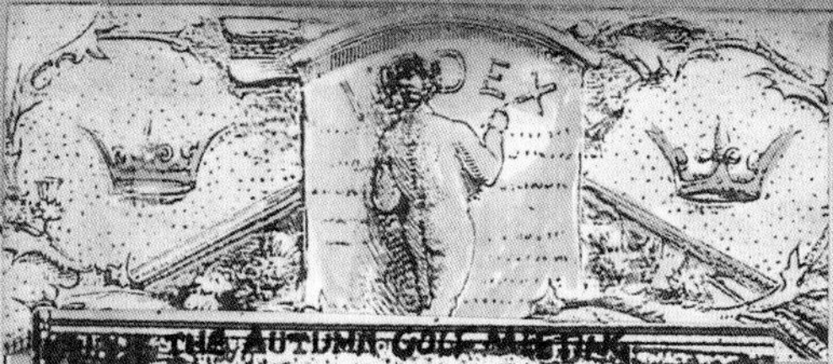

THE AUTUMN GOLF MEETING.

Monday, the opening day of the long-expected medal week, which forms a brilliant wind-up to the season, broke inauspiciously over the links. The wind was almost beyond precedent, boisterous, and by its frequent and tornado-like bursts, effectually baffled anything like good or accurate play. Tuesday, however, showed great improvement; the wind had lulled, and, in all other respects, the weather was propitious for play.

Yesterday, Wednesday, intending competitors for the medals were charmed to witness a magnificent autumn day—cold enough, to be bracing, and almost as still and quiet as midsummer.

The green throughout was in excellent order, to which, we have no doubt, the recent excellent innovation of the double putting greens have greatly contributed. An alteration was made in the morning of the medal, to secure a complete change of greens. This was effected by shifting the white flags (*i.e.*, going out) to the *left* of the course, and the red to the right.

The Meet, this season, was pretty well attended. Amongst the assemblage in front of the Union Club were.:—Captain Maitland Dougall; Messrs Patrick and Hugh Alexander; Major Dreghorn; Captain Fairly of Coodham; Messrs Robert Mitchell; More (Edinburgh); Moncrieff Skene of Pitlour; Hay E. Wemyss of Wemyss; Cowan (Edinburgh); Balfour; Cathcart of Pitcairlie; Brown Douglas; Heriot of Ramornie; Turnbull of Bellwood; R. Anstruther; Colonel Shortreed; Sir R. Anstruther; Hon. John Rollo; Stuart Grace, Esq.; General Moncrieff; Messrs Blackwood; F. Campbell, Esq.; Messrs Thomson of Burnhouse; Thomson of Charleton; Wm. Skene; A. G. Sutherland, Preston; Major Jocelyne: Messrs H. Fielding; H. Abel Smith; Captain Kinloch; Walkingshaw; Lamb; Bethune of Blebo; Major Chiene; Sir Hugh Playfair; Captain Lyon; Mr Watt; Captain Broughton; Neil F. Blair, Esq.; J. T. Oswald of Dunnikier; Captain Dalgleish; Messrs Taylor (Arbroath); Sir Charles Auchterlonie; Sir James Baird; Captain Hume; Messrs Mill of Murie; Thom; W. Haig, jun.; Thomson (Broughty); W. F. Ireland; Lord Loughborough; H. B. Farnie; W. Horsbrugh; Marquis of Bute; Colonel Low; Sir Thomas Moncreiffe; Lord Leven, &c., &c.

The Links were also graced, on this occasion, by the presence of several ladies, amongst whom were—the Marchioness of Bute and party; the Hon. Mrs Cheape and party; Lady Playfair; Mrs Methven and party, &c., &c.

A general meeting of the Royal and Ancient Golf Club was held at half-past ten A.M.; and before twelve the signal-gun was fired, and the competitors started away in the following series of couples, viz.:—

1 Captain Dougal and Captain Fairly.
2 Mr P. Alexander and Mr Blackwood.
3 Mr A. Turnbull and Mr Greenhill.
4 Mr J. T. Oswald and Major Chiene.
5 Mr Skelton and Mr Campbell.
6 Mr R. Mitchell and Mr H. Alexander.
7 Mr A. G. Sutherland and Captain Lyon.
8 Mr J. Peter and Mr Jameson.
9 Sir James Baird and Mr A. Miln.
10 Mr Bethune and Mr F. M. Heriot.
11 Mr W. Haig and Mr Nicol.
12 Captain Kinloch and Captain R. Anstruther.
13 Mr W. Skene and Mr F. Campbell.
14 Mr J. Balfour and Mr B. Douglas.
15 Mr Cathcart and Mr Thomson of Burnhouse.
16 Mr H. E. Wemyss and General Moncrieff.
17 Mr Cowan and Mr More.
18 Mr Skene and Sir Thomas Moncreiffe.
19 Mr Thom and Mr Arkley.
20 Mr Bromly and Mr T. Blair.

1 Mr Patrick Alexander, winner of the medal at 96 strokes, 48 out and 48 in.
2 Mr R. Mitchell, winner of the medal at 98 strokes.

After these gentlemen, the number were:—Mr Moore, 99; Captain Dougall and Mr Balfour, each 100; Mr Hugh Alexander, 101; Mr Skelton, 106: Mr J. T. Oswald and Mr T. Blair, 108; Mr H. E. Wemyss, 111; Mr J. Peter and Captain Fairlie, each 112; General Moncreiff and Mr Thompson, Burnhouse, 113.

The sweepstakes were won as follows:—1st, Mr Wemyss (with odds), 89; and 2d (equal), Mr More and Sir James Baird (with odds), at 92.

The play throughout was not so good as had been expected. Captain Dougall was not at all playing up to the mark, missing short puts on the green, and not drawing so far as usual. Captain Fairlie was most unlucky going out, being in nearly every bunker he could manage to come across. This player, however, played what was perhaps the prettiest shot of the day. In playing to the high hole coming in, Captain Fairlie went into the Eden, and lay soft at no great distance from the precipitous bank. By a beautiful slicing iron shot, however, he lofted his ball sheer on to the putting green, laying it some five yards from the hole. To any one that knows the difficulty of that particular stroke, its beauty will be apparent. The winners of the medals are both St Andrews met, and it is much to the credit of the Links that her own sons are asserting her supremacy.

We regret to state that Mr Neil Ferguson Blair was unable to attend this meeting, in consequence of an accident he received on Tuesday afternoon when out playing. A full swipe from a party in front, a little drawn, caught Mr Blair in the back of the head, and knocked him down, inflicting a severe cut. He was subsequently able to walk home, and it is expected he will soon be out again.

The Captain for the ensuing year is Mr Thomson of Charleton.

During the past week, and after the medal-play, a variety of singles and double matches have been played; but none are sufficiently interesting to necessitate detail.

A noticeable event in the annals of golfing, however, occurred on the 15th inst., when Allan—the champion—in a round with Mr Bethune of Blebo, holed the Links at 79, which has never been done before, and will not likely be soon done again. We subjoin the holes and strokes for the information of our readers:—

Going out — 1=4; 2=4; 3=4; 4=5; 5=5; 6=6; 7=4; 8=4; 9=4; in all, 40.

Coming in — 1=4; 2=3; 3=5; 4=6; 5=4; 6=5; 7=5; 8=4; 9=3; in all, 39.

In a round immediately previous, with the same opponent, Allan holed at 87, which is likewise beautiful play. About the middle of August, the following pretty round was played between Andrew Strath and Robert Andrew (professionals):—Strath out at 42, in at 43, in all, 85; and Andrew, out at 51, in at 39, in all, 90.

The long-talked-of match between Tom Morris and Park is to begin on Friday week, on the St Andrews links, and will be played on successive Fridays, at Musselburgh, North Berwick, and Prestwick. Backers on both sides are pretty confident of their men.

A mixed foursome was played in the afternoon between Sir Thomas Moncreiffe and Allan, against Captain Fairly and Tom Morris. The Baronet was a little off his play, and the latter couple won the round by 4 holes, and a shot match in by 2, holing the round at 89.

THE GOLFING AT ST ANDREWS.—In addition to the interest created by the national competition terminated on Saturday, much excitement was caused by the Parks brothers, of Musselburgh, playing a match of two rounds, or thirty-six holes, against Tom and George Morris, the former now of Prestwick, and the latter of Monifieth, but both natives of St Andrews. This was a most interesting match, as was evidenced by the bets freely offered and taken, and the crowd which accompanied the combatants. The result was the Morrises gaining by one hole. Tom Morris has challenged the elder Park (William) to play again for £200 a-side, a former match (in which Park was the victor) of thirty-six holes, on each of the four Links of St Andrews, Musselburgh, North Berwick, and Prestwick, which has been accepted, and will come off as soon as preliminaries are arranged.

58

St Andrews and District.

1858

ROYAL AND ANCIENT GOLF CLUB.

THE AUTUMN MEETING.

The strong and unexampled muster of golfers at the recent tournament arranged under the auspices of this influential Society, which came off so successful in the end of July last, would, it was thought, affect the attendance at this meeting. Any fears of a minimum gathering from that cause which might have been awakened have to all appearance been groundless. The arrivals on Monday, Tuesday, and even up to yesterday morning, of known practitioners at the noble game, were at least of an average with former years. The fact is, the game of golf has now obtained such a hold upon the gentry of Scotland, that if the inducement of good sport is held out by a club possessing a goodly muster roll of members, no fears need be entertained of a paucity of players, even were the statutory meetings added to during the course of the year, as has been done on two occasions now by the Royal and Ancient.

In former days the autumn meeting was held in the first or second week in October. It was found, however, that this arrangement often interfered with the Caledonian Hunt meeting, Ayr Races, or golfing fixtures of other clubs, and thereby prevented many gentlemen from appearing here. Two years ago this Society resolved to change their autumn gathering to the last Wednesday of September as more suitable for the members in general; and doubtless had this change not proved beneficial, it would ere now have been noticed.

The honours for award at this the principal meeting of the Royal and Ancient are the Silver Club. King William the Fourth's Medal, the Royal Adelaide Medal, and the Gold Medal of the Society. Although these are all set down for competition, strictly speaking there are but two eligible for competing members—in the Royal William Medal (the blue ribbon of the Society), and the Society's Medal. The Silver Club is held by the Captain of the year, constituting his insignia of office, whereon he puts a silver ball, with the name and designation in full, and date of his having held office. The Adelaide Medal is also worn by him on the festive occasions of the Society.

The winner of any of the medals belonging to the Society held such only for a year, and in addition had his name inscribed in the records, with the date and number of strokes by which the honour was gained. Some time ago, however, a change was made in this arrangement; feature, we doubt not, most agreeable to those having skill and proficiency enough in the game to carry off a prize. A winner now gets a beautiful model in gold or silver, as the case may be, of the particular medal he has won, to which a ribbon is attached for suspending to the button-hole of a coat, and it is expected that the neat little model will be worn by a *Medaller* at the Club's dinners, the annual Ball, and other festive seasons. The small fac similes of the valuable gold and silver medals of the Society have been made by Mackay, Cunningham, & Co., of Edinburgh, and as pieces of workmanship reflect great credit on that firm. Decorations for last year's holders of the King William, the Gold, and other honours won at the May meeting of the present year, were distributed to each at yesterday's meeting.

The captain for the year is appointed by the Council, who are the old captains, and the medal holders for the time being. The name of the captain is generally known sometime before the autumn meeting, but he is only proposed at the business meeting held on the day

54 Allan's death

ALLAN ROBERTSON THE CHAMPION GOLFER.

ALLAN ROBERTSON, the greatest golf-player that ever lived, of whom alone in the annals of the pastime it can be said that he never was beaten, was born at St Andrews on the 11th September 1815. He came of a golfing race. His grandfather, PETER ROBERTSON, who died in 1803, was a ball-maker and professional golfer. His father, too, DAVID ROBERTSON, who lived till 1836, followed the same trade, and was moreover a good player in his day—nay, few were better on the golfing green. As might be expected from such a generation of golfers, ALLAN took naturally to the Links. It is a fact that his very playthings as a child were golf clubs. As he grew up, this natural tendency joined to a natural desire of his father that his son should continue the business of ball-maker, decided ALLAN's profession, and in due course of time he likewise took up the awl and the feathers to learn the manufacture of golf balls.

At that period golfing was quite another thing from what it is now, or at least its accessories were. Gutta percha was unknown, and golf balls were composed of stout leather cases stuffed hard with boiled feathers. Their manufacture indeed was both a difficult and an arduous matter; and their expense when finished was such as to restrict the practice of the game, as a rule, to the more wealthy of the community. The Links of St Andrews, in consequence, were less frequented than now; the course was rougher; the sport had an aristocratic and portly mien; and the matches of professionals were as pregnant with interest as any public event. It is not so now; the St Andrews Links are crowded with careless multitudes luxuriating in the pastime cheapened to them by the discovery of gutta percha; and the game is popularized at the expense of its stately traditions.

ALLAN, however, commenced his golfing career in what, despite the dearness of leather, and the paucity of players, we must still call the palmy days of golf. His entire nature was bent on being a golfer. It is yet told on the Links, how ALLAN would rise betimes, and with shirt sleeves rolled up for better muscular play, start alone for practice across the deserted Links still wet with early dew. His success was abundant. ALLAN has improved in his day on the old theories of golf, and to him are owing many of the improved methods and styles of the present game. Some of these we will afterwards more particularly allude to.

In the spring of 1848, Mr CAMPBELL, of Saddell (we believe), brought a few experimental gutta percha balls from London to St Andrews. They were not very first-rate, to be sure; were not hammered, and flew heavily! Still the material was unquestionably good and adaptable; and consternation stood on every face, ALLAN's included. And no wonder. The leather ball trade was the only one St Andrews could boast, and it was considerable, extending to exports to the colonies as well as home consumption. In ALLAN's shop alone, there were made, for example, in 1840, 1021 balls; in 1841, 1392; in 1844, 2456; and so on. The introduction of gutta percha, which anybody could mould into a sphere, was a dreadful prospect for ALLAN and his brethren, and dire was their alarm. It is even related that ALLAN would gladly buy up all the gutta percha balls found among the whins, &c., and actually attempted to destroy the obnoxious interlopers with fire!

However, the influx was too great for this system to be pursued any longer, and about 1850 ALLAN entered regularly into golf ball making from gutta percha; and we are glad to know that his labour, whilst it was easier to himself, was not a whit less rewarded than in the old monopoly days of feathers.

The life of a professional golfer like ALLAN, is so c... omposed of continuous matches and a certain recurr... ing sameness of incident, that we have found it impos... sible to trace in anything like a consecutive story the ... incidents of ALLAN's life. All we can do is to re... all a few memories here and there, and give a selecti... on in chronological order of his more important ma... tches and feats.

Who will eve... r forget ALLAN, having once seen him? What Sir ... HUGH LYON PLAYFAIR has been to the city proper, ... has ALLAN been to the Links of St Andrews. ... They have unwittingly been in close partnershi... p. Sir HUGH renovated a rough, ruined street— ... ALLAN had an eye the while to the improvement of ... the Links; Sir HUGH attracted citizens, ALLA... N, golfers; ah! it was a magnificent partnership. ... and has done wonders. The analogy holds good bet... ween the two in other respects also. Who could ... do the honours of the

R 8, 1859.

Links like ALLAN? He was as perfectly at home with a descendant of WILLIAM the Conqueror as with one of the caddies. Without the least tinge of servility, ALLAN could accommodate himself to everybody, and arranged everything on the golfing links with the politeness of a BRUMMELL and the policy of a TALLEYRAND.

We have asked, Who that has once seen the champion golfer can ever forget him? Let us try to help the picture which every player will oft in fancy draw. Our scene is the St Andrews Links, on a genial summer's day. ALLAN's house crowns the summit of the slope; down towards the sea, the blue, beautiful sea, lies the white Club House, with its gravelled terrace. It is not yet eleven, that great hour of cause on the Links. Groups of caddies are prowling about; a clash and rattle of clubs are heard as you pass the club-maker's shops. One or two golfers are putting idly at the starting hole with their burnished cleeks, trying some impossible *putt*, which, if they had only done but yesterday, would have put a very different finish on to a certain match. Suddenly, a golfer appears at the Club House door; he looks about for somebody who is evidently lacking: "Where's Allan?"—the cry is repeated by telegraphic caddies right up to the champion's little garden. A minute elapses, and down comes the champion in hot haste to the Club House. He is, you will recollect, oh! golfer, not of much stature, compact, rather robust, indeed, with a short stoop, and shortnecked. His face is pleasant to look at—rather Hibernian, indeed, with its habitual expression of drollery, which has almost given the stalwart golfer one or two dimples. He is dressed, as you must well remember, in his favourite red jacket, and carries a cleek (a pet weapon) in his hand. But now the match is arranged. ALLAN has evidently got to nurse an elementary golfer. It is a foursome; ALLAN and his *protégé* against two rather good hands. Remark how pleasant the little man is; no miss of his partner causes a shade to his habitual good nature, and, ten to one, when the match comes in from their round, but the new player swears by ALLAN, and gives in his adhesion to golf for once and all.

But it was in a grand match that the figure of ALLAN should live in the memory of all. Who shall describe his elegant and beautifully correct style of play? The champion was remarkable for his *easy* style, depending on a long cool swing, and never on sheer strength. His clubs were of the *toy* description, as the slang of the links hath it, possessing no weight or mis-proportion of wood. Indeed, in a word, ALLAN's game throughout was pure unadulterated science. No man, perhaps, so well united in his play all the hits of the game. Pretty driver as he was, we still stake our belief on ALLAN's short game, especially in quarter shots. And this was an important point in ALLAN's practice. He it was that introduced the deadly use of the cleek in playing up to the hole. Previous to about 1848 or 1849, short wooden clubs, the baffing, or short spoons, were used for this important stroke,—both difficult, and frequently inaccurate. But ALLAN employed the cleek to jerk up his ball; however badly it might lie, it was all the same; and this killing game, destructive to a certain extent to the green, is now all but universal.

To return to ALLAN's great matches. His coolness was unique, and almost miraculous. He was never known to *funk*, or indeed change his off-hand manner in the least. He was never beaten—proud epitaph. It is something to be the best in anything, of all the world, and ALLAN stood confessed the model player. But it is not only as a golfer that ALLAN is to be deeply deplored. He was possessed of the best heart and kindliest feelings in the world. In the intricate dealings of the Links, in the formation and playing of great matches, ALLAN was honourable, just, and gentlemanly, from first to last.

ALLAN did much for golfing both in and out of St Andrews. He has laid out capital Links in various districts, and played thereon himself to the incitement of beginners. Traces of his labour and skill are to be seen at Wemyss Castle, Delvin, Mountquhanie, and many other places, seats of nobles and gentles.

A new era is about to dawn on the golfing links; the old stars are paling, when will others arise? HUGH PHILP, who knew how to make a club, is gone; gone too, fine ALLAN, who knew how to handle one.

Up to the spring of the present year, ALLAN was a hale, stout, little man, with scarcely the memory of an hour's illness. Temperate too, in an uncommon degree, regular in his habits, and enjoying daily exercise on the links, no one could reasonably foretell the rapid change that has taken him from us. In the spring, ALLAN had an attack of jaundice, proceeding, we believe, from an abnormal state of the liver. He never rallied; and after six months' weakness, he gradually sunk and died on the 1st of September. God rest him,

We have already noticed how impossible it is, especially with imperfect means of information, to give a consecutive or full account of the champion's feats, but we subjoin a few, in hopes that this meagre outline may testify, in some small way, to the merit, as a man and a golfer, of ALLAN ROBERTSON.

I. [1838] Allan holed the short hole going out at one stroke; and again in 1846.

II. [1839] Allan drove a teed ball from the corner of dyke hole going out, over all the three ditches—250 yards. His longest shot.

III. [1840] Allan played a grand match with Tom Alexander, ballmaker, Musselburgh, over the St Andrews Links, in October, and beat him by 4 holes, doing the round at 95.

IV. [1842] Allan and Sandy Herd, played in a double, against Tom Morris and Jamie Herd, beating them by 2 holes. Strokes 91 and 94.

V. [1842] Allan played a match with only a driver and cleek against Robert Chambers, Esq., Edinburgh, and holed the round at 96.

VI. [1842] Allan played a match in December with Tom Morris, beating him by 2 holes, and holing the Links at 93.

VII. [1843] Allan played during the month of June over the St Andrews Links, a great match of 20 rounds, two each day, against William Dunn of Musselburgh. Allan gained on the tenth, or last day, by two rounds and one to play. As Mr Carnegie sweetly sung on the occasion—

> Ten days they were fighting, ten days, ten days,
> Complete at their weapons, always, always,
> With club, cleek, and putter, my Muse cannot utter,
> A millioneth part of their praise, their praise!

VIII. [1843] Allan played a round at St Andrews in October, with James Calvert, Esq., Montrose, and holed the round at 88.

IX. [1843] Allan played a great match of 36 holes with Wm. Dunn of Musselburgh, beating him by 8 holes, and holing the second round at 88 strokes.

X. [1843] In a round with Robert Lindsay, Esq. of Straiton, Allan holed the 1st hole, going out in 4, and the 2d in 3: the whole round was done at 90.

XI. [1844] Allan played a match with William Dunn, over three links: 1st, on Musselburgh Links, where Dunn gained; 2d, at North Berwick Links, where Allan was victorious; and 3d, at St Andrews, where he also won, thus gaining the match also.

XII. Allan played a round with Captain David Campbell of Schehallion, and holed the Links at 87.

XIII. [1846] In April, Allan played another of his matches with W. Dunn: 1st, at Musselburgh, where Dunn beat Allan by 7 a-head and 5 to play; 2d, at St Andrews, where Allan won by 5 and 3, and 3d, at Leven, where he also was victor by 6 and 4 to play, thus winning the match.

XIV. [1846] Allan played with a single driving club against Captain Broughton, and holed the round of the St Andrews Links at 95.

XV. [1848] Allan drove, in two successive rounds, on the same day, a teed ball from the end hole to the foot of the short hole green. This was in September.

XVI. [1848] Allan played a threesome with Wm. Dunn and Tom Morris, over Dubbieside Links. Allan holed 18 holes (two rounds), at 80; Thomas Morris, at 89; and Dunn, at 91 strokes.

XVII. [1849] A great match for £400 was played in the summer between Allan and Tom Morris against the two Dunns of Musselburgh, on three links, Musselburgh, St Andrews, and North Berwick. At Musselburgh the Dunns won at a canter, winning by 13 holes and 12 to play. At St Andrews, however, Allan and Tom won their rounds, and retrieved some two or three holes. North Berwick was the deciding place, and at the commencement of the *last round of all*, the Dunns had four holes a-head, and only eight to play. However, Allan and Tom, by a magnificent game, gained the first hole, then the second, halved the third, gained the fourth, halved the fifth, and gained the sixth, thus making the poll *all even!* and two to play. These two holes Allan and Tom also won, thus obtaining the match, one of the most brilliant and extraordinary in the whole annals of golfing.

XVIII. [1850] In October Allan and Tom Morris played a foursome against the two Dunns for £50 a-side. Allan and his partner finished at the burn hole, by two and one to play, holing at 88.

XIX. [1852] In October, over the St Andrews Links, Allan and Tom Morris played a great match of 36 holes with Robert Hay, Esq., and William Dun, Blackheath, for £100 a-side. Allan and his partner won by six holes a-head, and five to play.

XX. [1853] In October, Allan played a round with Captain John Campbell Stewart, 72d Highlanders, winner at that meeting of the St Andrews Club, of the Royal Medal. This round was halved, though Allan was 3 a-head and 4 to play, and dormy at the Burn.

At this time also, Sir Thomas Moncrieffe and Allan played Tom Morris and Captain Fairlie The first round was won by Allan and his partner, at 3 and 1 to play; and the second by their adversaries at 4 and 3 to play. This foursome was played repeatedly, and on the whole play it may be said to have formed one of the closest matches on record.

XXI. [1857] Allan and Andrew Strath, in May, over the St Andrews Links, played a round against Tom Morris and Park, junior, winning by six holes. Strokes, 84 and 90.

XXII. [1858] On the 15th September, Allan, in round with Mr Bethune of Blebo, accomplished the round of the St Andrews Links at 79 strokes, a number altogether unparallelled, and likely to remain so. The following are the particulars of this superb score:—Going out—1 in 4; 2 in 4; 3 in 4; 4 in 5; 5 in 5; 6 in 6: 7 in 4; 8 in 4; 9 in 4. Total, going out, 40. Coming in—10 in 4; 11 in 3; 12 in 5; 13 in 6; 14 in 4; 15 in 5; 16 in 5; 17 in 4; 18 in 3. Total, toming in, 39.

XXIII. At various times Allan has holed the St Andrews Links at the following numbers, selecting his best holes:—Going out—1 in 3 strokes; 2 in 3; 3 in 3; 4 in 3; 5 in 4; 6 in 4; 7 in 5; 8 in 1; 9 in 3. Total, 27. Coming in—10 in [illegible] in 2; 12 in 3; 13 in 4; 14 in 4; 15 in 3, 16 in 3; 17 in 4; 18 in 3. Total, 29. Number of strokes to this selected round, 56.

[In comparing the above scores, it must be recollected that the St Andrews Links are now not nearly so difficult to play as they were 15 and 20 years ago.]

Allan

61

PRESTWICK GOLF CLUB.

Mr. J. O. Fairlie

HOLES.		STROKES.
1 First Hole,	12345678910	10
2 Alps,	12345678	8
3 Tunnel, (Red)	12345	5
4 Wall,	1234567	7
5 Sea Headrig,	123	3
6 Tunnel, (White)	123456	6
7 Green Hollow,	123	3
8 Station,	123	3
9 Burn,	1234567	7
10 Lunch House,	1234	4
11 Short Hole,	123456	6
12 Start Hole,	12345	5
13 First Hole,	12345678	8
14 Alps,	12345	5
15 Tunnel, (Red)	123	3
16 Wall,	12345678	8
17 Sea Headrig,	123456	6
18 Home,	1234	4
	TOTAL,	105

DATE,

BAD START FROM J.O.F.

1858

MY TESTIMONIAL

GRAND NATIONAL GOLF TOURNAMENT.

The following are the regulations of the approaching golf tournament:—

1. The Tournament shall consist of two classes of players. The championship of both shall be decided by a series of single matches of 18 holes—the play being reckoned by holes, and not by strokes.

In the First Class no odds shall be given. In the Second Class (which shall consist only of those who would receive odds from the first class), the players shall be handicapped against each other.

2. The Tournament shall take place at St Andrews, on the last Wednesday of July 1859, and following days. It shall be open to all gentlemen players, members of any established golf-club. Entry money, one guinea—half forfeit. Names to be entered with Stuart Grace, Esq., honorary secretary to the Union Club, St Andrews, not later than eleven o'clock A.M., of the last Wednesday of July, when the entry money must be paid.

A meeting of the competitors will be held at the Union Club, at eleven o'clock, on the last Wednesday of July; when opponents and the order of playing shall be drawn by lot, and the play shall commence immediately thereafter.

TESTIMONIAL.—It will be with heartfelt interest and satisfaction that our St Andrews friends will read the following, which we copy from the *Ayrshire Express*:—"TESTIMONIAL TO TOM MORRIS.—Immediately after the competition of the Prestwick St Nicholas Golf Club for three special prizes, Tom Morris was entertained at dinner in the Hall of the Red Lion—Mr W. Prain, Captain of the Club in the chair, &c. After the usual loyal toasts, &c. were proposed and drunk, the chairman called for a special bumper for the toast of the evening. In the course of an able speech he took occasion to remark that they all knew the claims which their worthy guest possessed to their respect and gratitude—his many good qualities as a man, and his famous powers as a golfer. Ever affable and obliging, Tom was the same to all frequenters of the Links, from the peer to the artizan, and unless specially engaged, his services were ungrudgingly placed at their disposal whenever they wished his co-operation or his counsel. That the St Nicholas Club appreciated all this care and attention to their interests individually and collectively, this festive entertainment was a strong proof, and that their gratitude should not be confined to words of empty compliment, they had recently subscribed for a testimonial, which he had now the pleasure in their name to put into the hands of their worthy guest. He (the chairman) begged the recipient to understand that this tangible token of esteem was not meant as a requital for his services, but only as a recognition of the obligations under which the Club had so long been laid. The chairman having presented the guest with an elegant gold watch, concluded by proposing the health, long life, and prosperity to Tom Morris, which we need scarcely add was pledged most enthusiastically."

Prestwick Alps 2ND.

NATIONAL GOLF TOURNAMENT AT ST ANDREWS. 1859

The third of these contests for the championship in this national game commenced at St Andrews yesterday. The morning sun broke through a nearly cloudless sky, but the heat was tempered by a good smart breeze from the west, not so great, however, as to interfere with the comfortable playing of the game. Subsequently the sky became cloudy, and rendered the day thoroughly agreeable. The Links were all that could be desired, the slight shower of the previous evening having improved them considerably.

The first grand tournament was played club against club, the second was man against man, but all playing even-handed, consequently first-class players only could make an attempt, and thus the numbers were much limited. This year it was again to be man against man, but there were two classes of players—first, those playing even-handed; second, handicapped, or, in golfing language, receiving odds.

By ten o'clock the links were the scene of attraction. Amongst those on the ground were—The Hon. Miss Cheape; Mr and Mrs Morris, India; Colonel and Mrs Henderson and Miss Henderson, India; General and Mrs Cannon; Mrs Captain Lyon and Miss Lyon; Mrs Purvis; Mrs Maitland Dougall; Miss Foulie; Miss Arbuthnot; Mrs General Moncrieff; Mr Blackwell; Mr Campbell Smith, advocate; Principal Tulloch; Sir Hugh Lyon Playfair; Captain Kinloch; Captain Hay; Sir Thomas Erskine, &c. &c. Many old professionals were also on the turf—William and David Park, Tom and George Morris, James Dunn; but Allan was missing, being ill.

The Tournament Committee consisted of the following well-known names:—Sir Hugh Lyon Playfair, John Whyte Melville, Sir Thomas Moncreiffe, Captain Maitland Dougall, Dr Greenhill, James Balfour, W.S., Robert Cathcart, Robert Haig, Francis Brown Douglas, F. L. M'Herriot, and J. O. Fairlie.

Before starting, the following bye-law was agreed upon as to the handicap playing:—"The odds to be taken in the usual manner, but where one-third or less is given, not to be taken in the first hole. In the event of a halved match, first blood decides, the odds to be taken in the same routine as before. *P.S.*—The players will be drawn in two classes as above; if there is a bye in each class, the two play together."

The balloting and odds arranging took a little less time than was anticipated, so that the first couple were ready to start at half-past eleven A.M.

The first-class players started as follow:—1st, Mr Glennie and Mr Robert Mitchell; 2d, Mr Ord Campbell and Mr J. O. Fairlie; 3d, Mr Robert Hay and Mr James Williamson; 4th, Mr Hay of Belton and Mr William Thomson; 5th, Captain Maitland Dougall and Mr Hamilton; 6th, Mr Hugh Alexander and Mr Clark, Edinburgh; 7th, Mr W. Playfair and Mr Condie; 8th, Mr M'Cuaig, jun., and Mr Bethune.

The second-class players started immediately thereafter in the following order:—First-Class Handicap—1st, Mr Cowan against Mr Scott; 2d, Mr Anderson against Mr Macarthur; 3d, Mr Alexander Duncan against Mr Colin M'Cuaig; 4th, Captain Thomson against Mr Whigham; 5th, Mr Sutherland against Mr Romanes; 6th, Mr Sibbald against Mr John Blackwood. Mr James Lindsay had a bye.—Second-Class Handicap—1st, Lord Duplin against Captain Lyon; 2d, Mr John Grant against Mr Wolfe Murray; 3d, Mr W. A. Campbell against Mr Mann; 4th, General Moncrieff against Mr Turnbull; 5th, Mr Whyte Melville against Captain Oswald; 6th, Mr William M'Donald against Mr Burn; 7th, Mr Curwen against Mr H. Inglis; 8th, Mr Everard against Mr Kinloch.

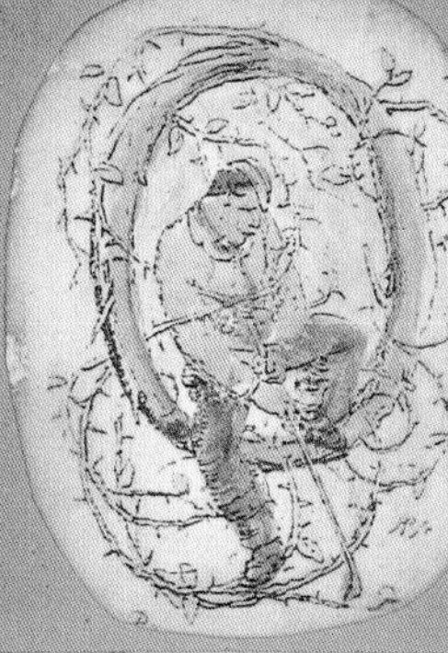

The odds were allocated as follows:—Messrs Sibbald, Lindsay, M'Cuaig, Macarthur, Anderson, and Cowan—[illegible]; Messrs Thomson, Romanes, Duncan, Whigham, Sutherland, Blackwood, and Scott—¼, or 4 strokes; Messrs Lyon, Oswald, M'Donald Everard, Wolfe Murray, and Lord Duplin—½, or 9 strokes; Messrs Whyte Melville, Moncrieff, Burn, Kinloch, Inglis, Mann and W. A. Campbell—⅔, or 12 strokes; Messrs John Grant, A. Turnbull, and Curwen—1, or 18 strokes in the round.

In the first round—1, Mr Glennie beat Mr Mitchell by 8 holes; 2, Mr Fairlie beat Mr Ord Campbell by 8 holes and 7 to play; 3, Mr Robert Hay beat Mr Williamson by 2 holes and 1 to play; 4, Mr Wm. Thomson beat Mr Hay by 2 holes and 1 to play; 5, Captain Maitland beat Mr Hamilton by [illegible] holes; 6, Mr Clark beat Mr Alexander by 8 holes; [illegible] Mr Condie beat Mr Playfair by 4 holes; 8, Mr [illegible]ig, jun., beat Mr Bethune by 1 hole.

The successful competitors [illegible] ballotted, [illegible]ted in their second round [illegible]ws:—1, Mr Clark against Mr Glennie; 2, M[illegible] against Mr Fairlie; 3, Mr Thomson against Mr Hay; 4, Captain Maitland Dougall against Mr M'Cuaig.

The return was as follows:—1, Mr Clark beat Mr Glennie by 5 holes; 2, Mr Condie beat Mr Fairlie by 6 holes; 3, Mr Robert Hay beat Mr William Thomson by 2 holes; 4, Captain Maitland Dougall gained the match by a stimy on Mr M'Cuaig. Messrs Clark, Condie, Hay, and Maitland Dougall are now the only first-classes left.

The Handicap players arrived as under:—1, Mr Cowan beat Mr Scott by 8 holes; 2, Mr M'Ar[illegible] Mr Anderson by 5 holes; 3, Mr Colin M'Cuaig beat Mr Alex. Duncan by 2 holes; 4, Mr Whigham beat Capt. Thomson by 1 hole; 5, Mr Romanes [illegible]t Mr Sutherland by 2 holes; 6, Mr J. Blackwood beat Mr Sibbald by 5 holes. 2d Class—1, Captain Lyon beat Lord Duplin by 2 holes; 2, Mr Wolfe Murray beat Mr Grant by 3 holes and 1 to play; 3, Mr Mann beat Mr W. A. Campbell by 1 hole; 4, General Moncrieff and Mr Turnbull had a tie, the only one that occurred; a short match decided in favour of General Moncrieff; 5, Captain Oswald beat Mr Whyte Melville by 2 holes; 6, Mr Burn beat Mr William M'Donald by 5 holes; 7, Mr Henry Inglis beat Mr Curwen by 6 holes; 8, Mr Everard beat Mr Kinloch by 1 hole.

Parties being again balloted, they once more started to try their skill, and in the following order:—First-Class Handicap—1, Mr Lindsay against Mr Romanes; 2, Mr Whigham against Mr M'Cuaig; 3, Mr Blackwood against Mr M'Arther.—Second-Class Handicap—1, Mr Wolfe Murray against Captain Oswald; 2, Mr Henry Inglis against General Moncrieff; 3, Mr Burn against Captain Lyon; 4, Mr Everard against Mr Mann; Mr Cowan a bye.

ST ANDREWS. E

Ladies' Sale.—The proceeds of the sale in aid of the Strathkinness Endowment Scheme amounted, we understand, to £320, after all expenses were paid, a sum greatly exceeding the expectations of the most sanguine friends of the cause. In addition, there was undisposed of, work to the amount of about £150—a good nest egg for the friends of the Town-hall to hatch

Influx of Strangers.—It is so far fortunate for many parties here that just at the very period of the vacations at the Madras College and other educational institutions, the season of the year is the most attractive for drawing to St Andrews, a vast number of visitors for a temporary period to enjoy the leisure, rest, change of air, &c., for which the locality has become so famed, and we are glad to understand that almost every house and lodging is let for the season. Let us hope none of the strangers will leave disappointed in the objects sought for.

Purchase of Property.—The Abbey Park, including mansion-house and grounds, so long the property of, and possessed by the late Colonel Glass, and which was a few years ago purchased by the Hon. T. Leslie Melville, has again changed hands, the new proprietor being Mr Smeaton, the celebrated and enterprising master of the very extensive boarding and educational establishment in this city. The price paid for the property on this occasion we understand is £3500; and it is believed that Mr Smeaton intends removing his entire establishment to the park as soon as the necessary arrangements are completed.

Encouraging.—It is highly satisfactory to learn that notwithstanding the comparatively large number of houses in St Andrews for receiving boarders of both sexes, and instructing them in all the varied branches of a classical, useful, and fashionable education, all of them are not only fully encouraged, but there is a demand for more of a similar kind. Several new establishments are to be opened immediately after the vacation, among which we may notice that of Messrs Cleghorn, one of whom has so admirably filled a leading position in Mr Smeaton's institution. Messrs Cleghorn have for this purpose rented the large house on the north side of South Street so long occupied as the Bank of Scotland's office, and we are sure all who know them will wish them every success in their arduous undertaking.

The Prince of Wales.—It having been rumoured that his Royal Highness intended visiting the ancient city during the tournament week, Messrs Cook & Son, booksellers, prepared a copy of the "Handy-Book of St Andrews," lately published, and of the "Golfer's Manual," published last year, for presentation to H.R.H. The two books were very handsomely bound together in morocco, the one containing a very beautiful calotype portrait of Provost Sir H. L. Playfair, by Mr Rodger; and the other an excellent lithographed portrait of "Allan." Messrs Cook forwarded the book to Holyrood Palace, and Colonel Bruce's letter, of which the subjoined is a copy, shows that his Royal Highness has been graciously pleased to accept of the offering.—"Holyrood Palace, 5th August 1859.—Gentlemen,—I am directed to state, in reply to your letter of the 1st instant, that his Royal Highness has been graciously pleased to accept of the volume which you have published on the city of St Andrews and the Game of Golf. I have the honour to be, &c., R. Bruce, Col.—Messrs J. Cook & Son."

GRAND GOLF TOURNAMENT AT ST ANDREWS. July 1859

WEDNESDAY.

The annual Golf Tournament at St Andrews commenced yesterday, under favourable auspices. The weather was bright, but windy, and the Links was all that could be desired; the course throughout in good order, and the putting greens well selected. The holes were placed to the left hand, out and in. A number of spectators were present to witness the start at noon, in spite of the gusty wind. Amongst others were—Mrs Moncreiff and party, Miss Lyon, Mrs Yorke and party, Mrs Skene, Mrs Condie, Miss Playfair, Mrs Buist, Miss Dillon, Miss Webster, &c. &c.; Sir Thomas Erskine, Colonel Mackay, Professor M'Donald, Mr Moncreiff Skene, Mr Macgregor, Major Dreghorn, Mr Skene, Colonel Yorke, R.E., Mr Farnie, Sir Hugh Playfair, Mr J. Paton, Mr Haig, Rev. Mr Cunningham, Mr Horsbrugh, Mr Lamb, Mr James Graham, Mr Purvis of Kinaldy, Mr Grace, Lieut. Lumsdaine, Mr Ireland, Mr Tullis of Auchmuty, &c. &c.

It will be remembered that in the first Tournament of 1857, Club competed against Club; and in 1858, single players entered against each other on equal footing; but this season an important alteration has been introduced. There are now two classes of players, paying the same entry money, one guinea; the first class consisting of the best golfers who neither receive nor give odds; and the second, consisting of those players who are handicapped and made equal to each other by a judicious arrangement of odd-strokes, adjudged by a select committee.

In the first class there were sixteen entries, and all played—viz., Captains Maitland Dougal, Hay, Fairlie; Messrs Mitchell, Glennie, Ord Campbell, R. Hay, W. C. Thomson, Williamson, Hamilton, Clark, H. Alexander, G. Condie, W. Playfair, Bethune, and D. M'Cuaig.

In the second class there were 31 entries, and 2 forfeits, Moncrieff Skene, Esq., and Major G. Whyte Melville. The remaining 29 were handicapped by the committee as follows:—1st division—Messrs Sibbald, J. Lindesay, C. M'Cuaig, M'Arthur, Anderson, and Cowan; receiving no strokes. 2d Division—Messrs G. Thompson, Romanes, Duncan, Whigham, Sutherland, J. Blackwood, and Scott; receiving a fourth, or 4 strokes. 3d Division—Captain Lyon, Lord Dupplin, Oswald, Macdonald, Everard, and Wolfe Murray; receiving a half, or 9 strokes. 4th Division—Messrs J. Whyte Melville, Burn, Kinloch, Inglis, Mann, Campbell of Ormsby, and General Moncrieff; receiving two-thirds, or 12 strokes; and the 5th Division—Messrs J. Grant, Turnbull, and Curwen; receiving one more, or 18 strokes.

The sweepstakes will be equally divided between the two classes, so that there is a prize in each. The only other important points of difference in the present Tournament regulation are, that there can be no tie, the parties halving the round requiring to play out till the match is decided by a hole, and that no player can run more than one bye. In the second class, members of the 1st and 2d division were drawn together as partners, and in the same manner, members of the 3d, 4th, and 5th divisions. The odds in the second class were taken in the usual manner; but when a third or less was given, the stroke was not permitted to fall on the first hole.

Thomas Paton, Esq., was elected umpire.

63 **St Andrews and District.** 1859

ROYAL AND ANCIENT GOLF CLUB.

THE AUTUMN MEETING.

Since the instituting of a tournament in connection with the Royal and Ancient Golf Club, the meetings of the Society come thick and fast, in the summer and autumn of the year. Beginning with the spring or May meeting, we have next—at least, for two years back—a tournament in the middle of July, the proceedings connected with which generally extend over the space of a week. These tournaments have certainly brought forth a great host of players from all quarters as competitors, and besides created an unusual excitement among golfers generally; but coming so close on the autumn meeting of the Society, the date of which has within the last few years been fixed nearly a month earlier, it just becomes a question whether a tournament yearly would not have a tendency to diminish the attendance at the autumn meeting in September, which is reckoned the principal meet of the Society. From the paucity of players previous to the meeting day, it was augured that this September would be a poor one. The tournament was blamed for this invariably. If the Committee think a tournament conducive to the interest of the Society, would it not be a better arrangement to fix the time for such to commence on the day after the medal competition at this meeting? The Royal and Ancient Golf Club, however, need no new phases in their meetings to draw a muster of golfers. The Society stands acknowledged as *the first* in the kingdom. Its medal competitions have always brought together a good field, and will continue to do so.

Tuesday was most favourable for golfing, and a great many partners were out. Wednesday, however, did not in the morning look very favourable. The wind had changed to south east, and several showers fell, which was rather against the play.

Amongst others on the Links on Tuesday we observed—Mr Wemyss, M.P.; Mr Moncrieffe Skene; Mr Cathcart, Pitcairly; Mr Wolfe Murray; Mr Campbell; General Moncrieffe; Captain Lyon; Mr Whyte Melville; Mr Everard; Colonel Campbell; Mr Guthrie; Mr Burns; Colonel Mackay; Mr Duncan; Mr Robert Hay; Captain Gough; Captain Morris; Captain M'Whannell; Captain Kinloch; Mr Campbell; Captain Hume; Captain Cox; Mr Robertson; Mr Lloyd; Mr John Blackwood; Mr James Blackwood; Mr M'Lachlan; Mr Sutherland; Captain Maitland Dougall; Mr Brown Douglas; Mr Abel Smith; Mr Mitchell; Mr Nicoll; Mr Oswald, Dunnikier; Sir Ralph Anstruther, Bart., and party.

Sir David Baird, Bart., of Newbyth, the Captain-Elect, arrived in St Andrews on Tuesday evening.

At the general meeting held as usual in the Club House before commencing play, the rule as to a ball landing into the burn, which made it imperative to tee a yard therefrom was altered, so as not to make it imperative to do so.

There were three new members admitted—Dr Gibson, Colonel Campbell, and Captain Preston.

It was also moved by Mr Wemyss, M.P., and seconded by Sir Hugh Lyon Playfair, Provost of St Andrews, that an expression of the loss sustained by the Club in the death of Allan Robertson, and the estimation in which he was held, should be recorded in the minutes, and a copy thereof be transmitted to his widow with the condolence of the club.

tribute to Allan

Pairs having been arranged about 11 o'clock, fourteen couples started in the following order in competition for the medals for disposal at this meet-

---

VALUATION OF LANDS AND HERITAGES (SCOTLAND) ACT, 17 AND 18 VICT., CAP. 91.

District of Kyle—County of Ayr.

No. 163 PARISH OF Monkton

To The Prestwick Golf Club

TAKE NOTICE, that the Property owned or occupied by you has been entered in the Valuation Roll at the sums after mentioned for the year 1855-56, for the purposes described in the Act. If you consider yourself aggrieved by such Valuation, you may appeal to the Commissioners of Supply for the County, giving me *intimation* thereof in *writing*, prior to the 4th day of September, 1855, that you are to maintain such appeal; which intimation must specify the amount of Valuation which you allege should be substituted for the sums stated in the Roll, as notified below;—or you may obtain redress without the necessity of such appeal, by satisfying me, *on or before the 8th day of September*, 1855, that you have well-founded ground of complaint.

JOSEPH ERSKINE, *Assessor*,
4, CASSILLIS STREET.

AYR, 24 AUGUST, 1855.

NOTE.—Parties having ground of complaint are requested to communicate with the Assessor, on receiving their Notices, with the view of an adjustment, thereby, in all likelihood, saving the trouble and expense of an appeal.

In all Communications repeat the No.

Description of Subject.	Proprietor	Tenants or Occupants.	Yearly Rent or Annual Value
House	Prestwick Golf Club	Thomas Morris	£6 0 0

1851

Valuation of Lands and Heritages.

To Charles Campbell Esq
Banker

Every year ↑ this would come through to Mr Campbell our Secretary

STUDENTS AT PLAY IN CHEAPES BUNKER
2ND. HOLE OLD COURSE

Photographs with the late Allan Robertson – sadly missed

Sandy Pirie, Keeper of the green. — Self. — Mr Robert Cathcart of Pitcairlie — Daw, My caddie — Allan — Mr Wallace — Mr Hay Wemyss

Allan in Mr Roger's Studio

James Wilson (clubmaker) — Bob Andrew ("The Rook") — Willie Dunn — Willie Park — Allan Robertson — "Daw" — Self — Bob Kirk

Posing for a match ← after the grand National Tournament of 1858 Self and Allan against Willie Park and Willie Dunn.

Two of
J. O. Fs sons

See
Page
81 + 82 → ↖ General
Sir Hope
Grant

The General's
son

Myself ↑
J. O. Fairlie

Captain at Prestwick
St Andrews
and Blackheath
Mr George Glennie
(above)

67

PRESTWICK.

XXIX.—PRESTWICK GOLF CLUB.

INSTITUTED 1851.

The EARL OF EGLINTON AND WINTON, *Patron.*
GILBERT MITCHELL INNES, *Captain.*
D. DUNLOP, Ayr, *Secretary.*
D. D. WHIGHAM, Ayr, *Treasurer.*

The Captain, Secretary, Treasurer *ex officiis;* Lieut.-Col. Fairlie of Coodham; E. A. Hunter; J. P. Wilson of Polquhairn; Major Phillips, R. A. Y. C., Ayr; Captain J. K. M'Adam; and C. F. Knower, Ayr—*Committee.*

ANDREW STRATH, *Custodier of the Links.*

XXX.—ST. NICHOLAS GOLF CLUB.

INSTITUTED 1851.

The Right Hon. the Earl of EGLINTON AND WINTON, *Patron.*

WINTER MEETING—1st January.—William Doleman, Glasgow, and George M'Arthur, Ayr, were equal for the Club Medal, having each completed the two rounds, or 24 holes, in 137. In a short match of five holes to decide the "tie," the first-named gentleman scored 24 against his youthful opponent's 30, thus winning the medal and first prize by six strokes.

William Doleman played in many tournaments as an amateur player

NORTH BERWICK.

XXV.—NORTH BERWICK GOLF CLUB.

Instituted upwards of 40 years.

SIR HEW DALRYMPLE, *President.* W. LITTLE GILMOUR *Captain.*
JOHN R. WHITECROSS, *Hon. Secretary and Treasurer.*

LIST OF MEMBERS.

Lieut.-Col. Aitchison	W. L. Gilmour	Jas. Moncrieff, M.P.
Sir R. Anstruther, Bt.	Hon. N. Hamilton	William Moncrieff
Sir D. Baird, Bart.	Sir Adam Hay	R. S. Muirhead
Sir James Baird	Samuel Hay	A. Campbell Renton
James Blackwood	Robert Hay	C. Robertson
John Bruce	Captain Hay	Moncrieff Skene
Duke of Buccleuch	Sir Thos. Hepburn	Gavin G. Suttie
Sir H. H. Campbell	C. C. Halket Inglis	Charles Tennant
Robert Cathcart	A. Mitchell Innes	George Thomson
Lord Elcho, M.P.	S. Mitchell Innes	George Warrander
Robert Cowan	N. Mitchell Innes	D. B. Wauchope
Earl of Stair	T. Mitchell Innes	James Balfour
Sir Hew Dalrymple	Lord Wm. Kennedy	Marquis of Beaumont
Alexander Duncan	Alex. Kinloch	Hon. H. Duncan
Lord Elphinstone	Sir J. Dick Lauder	J. W. H. Anderson
Colonel Fairlie	Sir Thos. Moncrieff	J. C. Wylie
John Fletcher	General Moncrieff	Hon. A. Cathcart

MEDAL HOLDER, 1866.

George Thomson, who completed the 14 holes in 86 strokes.

XXIV.—MUSSELBURGH GOLF CLUB.

INSTITUTED 1772.

JAMES MILLAR, *Captain.*
DR SANDERSON, *Treasurer.*

This old-established Club has recently been much reduced in strength; but it is expected that it will soon be recruited by an accession of new members. The present holder of the Cup is James Millar. It was not competed for in 1866, no decision having been come to regarding the terms upon which candidates for election will be admitted to the Club.

PERTH.

XXVII.—KING JAMES VI. GOLFING SOCIETY.

Instituted 1858.

Bailie R. H. ROBERTSON, *Captain.*
JOHN A. IMRIE, *Secretary and Treasurer.*

James Moir, Hunter Greig. Dr Buist, William Gray, George Kyd, Walter Stuart—*Committee.*

We may mention that this Society was the first to introduce these "home and home" matches; and they have now vanquished in succession the Warrander, Burgess, and Bruntsfield (Edinburgh), besides having twice defeated the Prestwick St Nicholas.

XXVIII.—ROYAL PERTH GOLFING SOCIETY.

INSTITUTED 1824.

PATRONESS—Her Majesty Queen Victoria.

The Right Hon the Earl of KINNOUL, *Captain.*
Rev. JOHN ANDERSON, *Chaplain.*
A. BURNS MACDONALD, *Hon Secretary and Treasurer.*

George Condie, R. C. L. Blair, William Marshall, and Fraser Thomson—*Council.*

GULLANE.

XVI.—EAST LOTHIAN GOLF CLUB.

INSTITUTED 1859.

SAMUEL SHIRIFF, *President.*
JAMES MILLS, *Vice-President.*
JOHN CALLANDER, *Secretary and Treasurer.*

T. Begbie, T. Aitchison, W. Palmer, and J. Todd—*Committee.*

There was also played for, and decided by the first round of the green, a drinking cup, the gift of a member, which was won by T. Aitchison in 69 strokes, his allowance of 7 strokes being of no use to him. Wonderful to tell, he only used his right arm, having met with an accident to his left hand in the early part of the season.

One round of Gullane hill (of 13 holes), measuring 2 miles decides the Medal and principal prizes.

LEITH.

XVII.—LEITH GOLF CLUB.

ROBT. M'INTOSH, *Captain.*
J. G. WALLACE, *Treasurer.* A. PORTEOUS, *Secretary.*
D. Geddes, D. M'Laren, Geo. Smith, Jas. Doig—*Councillors.*

XVIII.—THISTLE GOLF CLUB.

This Club was established in 1815, and was in active operation for 15 years up to 1830. After having been in abeyance for 36 years, it was resuscitated on 5th April, 1866. The members have a commodious Club-room, and the game has made great progress since Spring, the resident professional being Willie Dunn, whose services the Club was fortunate enough to secure.

THOMAS HAY (1824) *Captain.*

Joseph Cundell (1827), N. M. Mackie, Samuel Halket, Robert Chambers, jun., Jas. T. Hardie, and William Lindsay Wood—*Councillors.*

THOMAS SHIELLS, *Treasurer.* JOHN SCOTT, *Secretary.*
William Dunn, *Custodier of the Links.*

… a public-house by his mother … applications being made, the Court adjou…

St Andrews and District.

ROYAL AND ANCIENT GOLF CLUB.

The May meeting commenced here on Wednesday under most favourable auspices. The day was charming and highly favourable for the sport. The Links are somewhat dry for want of rain; and, in consequence, the putting-greens are tremendously keen.

It has been our custom generally to have a long list of arrivals, and note of matches played. On the two days previous to the meeting of the Golf Club there appeared to be no indication of a meeting at all on this occasion—no notice being given. The Links on Monday and Tuesday were no more frefrequented than usual. In fact, never perhaps was there less appearace of a good muster than at the May meeting. This may be accounted for, from the fact of the week previous being the Sacramental week in Edinburgh, when a number of Edinburgh golfers were here for a day or two. The Meeting week, coming immediately after, might have proved inconvenient for the attendance of such as were here then. There were numerous arrivals by train on Wednesday morning.

Amongst others on the Links on Tuesday and Wednesday we observed—Sir Thomas Moncrieff, Bart.; Lord Charles Kerr; Mr Fairlie; James T. Oswald, Esq.; Robert Milne, Esq.; Mr J. C. Lindsay; Mr P. Alexander, Colonel Low, Mr M'Whannel; Mr Ord Campbell, Mr Whigham, Mr Wolfe Murray, Captain Dougall, Mr Bethune (Blebo), Mr Gillan; Mr Jackson, Mr Wm. Thomson and Sheriff Gordon, Captain Playfair, Mr Samuel Thomson, Mr A. J. Sutherland, Major Dreghorn, Mr J. Bell (Dundee), &c. &c.

The competitors, twenty-eight, for the medals, were balloted for, and paired as under, starting thus, shortly after eleven o'clock:—Mr Guthrie and Dr Govan; Mr S. Thomson and Mr Rattray; Mr Patrick Alexander and Mr M'Whannell; Mr Bethune and Mr Robert Mitchell; Colonel Low and Mr Lamb; Sir Thomas Moncrieffe and Mr J. O. Fairlie; Sheriff Gordon and Captain Playfair; Mr Robert Milne and Mr J. C. Lindesay; Mr Wolfe Murray and Mr Whigham; Mr Jackson and Mr Wauchope; Captain Maitland Dougall and Mr Ord Campbell; Mr Whyte Melville and Mr Gillan; Mr William C. Thomson and Mr Andrew Nicoll; Lord Charles Kerr and Mr Oswald, Dunnikier.

The above having made the rounds of the course, the following returned least in strokes—namely,

Captain Maitland Dougall...... 98 strokes.
J. O. Fairlie, Esq. of Coodham 99 ,,
Patrick Alexander, Esq......... 99 ,,

Captain Dougall, being a Gold Medal holder of the Club, for the current year, is precluded from holding the Silver Cross, to whic he would have been entitled by the above score, but he is allowed to fall back on the Bombay Medal, the other honour for competition at this meeting. Messrs Fairlie and Alexander, having *tied* at 99, were sent out again to decide who should hold the Silver Cross. In their second round, they kept neck and neck all the way out, and wound up at the home hole *again a tie*, each having taken 105 strokes, on a second bout. They are to fight it out to-day (Thursday), commencing at half-past eleven o'clock forenoon. From the known excellence of each as a golfer, some fine play may be expected.

sonment. 1860

St Andrews and District.

ROYAL AND ANCIENT GOLF CLUB.

THE MAY MEETING.

In continuation of our report of the proceedings at this meeting, we will, before proceeding to detail several important matches played during the week, refer once more to the competition for the honours at stake. On Wednesday, the medal day, it will be remembered that the scores least in number were

Captain Maitland Dougall's of . 98
Major Fairlie's 99
Mr Patrick Alexander's . . 99

Captain Dougall being at present holder of the gold medal of the society, is precluded by rule from holding the silver cross, to which, as the highest honour for award at the May meeting, he was entitled by his score as mentioned above (98). He got, however, the Bombay medal, while Major Fairlie and Mr Patrick Alexander, as ties, had to fight their battle out for the silver cross. A second round on Wednesday afternoon resulted in another tie, at 105. Both having had enough for one day, it was arranged that a round for a decider should be begun on the day following, (Thursday). They started shortly after 11 A.M. Major Fairlie was declared the winner of the cross, after three bouts for it, by holing the course at 99 again, to his opponent's 112. And now that the medals are disposed of, we will proceed to detail several good matches which came off during the meeting week.

On the Monday previous to the medal day, a good foursome, consisting of Lord Charles Kerr and Tom Morris against Major Fairlie and Sir Thomas Moncrieff, was played. At the end of the day's play each party left off square. On Tuesday, a foursome, in which Mr Whigham, Edinburgh, and Andrew Strath, a professional of the Links here, tackled one of the couples mentioned above—Lord Charles Kerr, and Tom Morris—Mr Whigham and his partner had the best of it by two matches on the day—a result which was not expected, but Mr Whigham, it is said, played a tremendous game. On Wednesday, the medal day, there were several good matches entered into, and played, a note of which, however, we were unable to obtain, as the interest almost entirely centred on the competition for the medals, and the close run, betwixt Major Fairlie and Mr Alexander, for one of them, as detailed above. Passing on to Thursday, the first event on the card was the third round for the silver cross, the holder of which we have already named. A foursome was also played that day which deserves honourable mention, from the excellent play exhibited. It was arranged thus—Major Fairlie and Tom Morris against Sir Thomas Moncrieffe and Andrew Strath, who took the place of the lamented Allan as Sir Thomas's partner. Two matches played resulted in no advantage to either party.

We are reluctantly obliged to break off our report here for want of space.

… agst Julius, taken; 6 to 1 agst … taken … 7 to 1 agst Dragon, offered.

Winners of the Silver Cross

		Strokes
1836	James Condie, Esq., Perth	110
1837	John H. Wood, Esq., Leith	100
1838	C. Robertson, Esq.	108
1839	Do.	104
1840	Samuel Messieux, Esq.	109
1841	Robert Haig, Esq.	104
1842	Do.	104
1843	Captain David Campbell	103
1844	Robert Haig, Esq.	111
1845	Captain A. O. Dalgleish	99
1846	Robert Lindsay, Esq.	110
1847	Captain David Campbell	104
1848	Robert Hay, Esq.	101
1849	J. O. Fairlie, Esq., of Coodham	100
1850	George Condie, Esq., Perth	96
1851	George Glennie, Esq.	99
1852	Captain W. H. Maitland Dougall, Scotscraig	96
1853	Henry Jelf Sharpe, Esq.	96
1854	J. O. Fairlie, Esq., of Coodham	95
1855	Captain W. H. Maitland Dougall	98
1856	William Playfair, Esq.	102
1857	W. C. Thomson, Esq., Dundee	96
1858	Sir Thomas Moncrieffe of Moncrieffe, Bart.	95
1859	James C. Lindsay, Esq., Broughty Ferry	101
1860	James Ogilvie Fairlie, Esq., of Coodham	99

The Silver Cross

Among the variety of incidents that have accompanied the play for the medal was one which occurred in 1860, when an extraordinary tempest raged. The wind from the north was howling, and the rain lashing. Just as parties were about to start a cry was heard that a vessel was being wrecked in the offing. The play for the medal was postponed. The lifeboat was launched; but there was great difficulty in getting it manned. Maitland Dougall, who was about to play, when he heard of the difficulty, volunteered to go, and took the stroke oar. The men were rescued, and the lifeboat came ashore in the afternoon. The play for the medal was begun after the arrival of the lifeboat. The wind was still furious. It was to Maitland Dougall's credit that, though his arms were sore, and he was stiff and all wet, he gained the Club gold medal at 112 strokes. Gourlay, the Musselburgh ball-maker, who was present, remarked, "What nerve the Captain must have for the game!" that he (Gourlay) would not have gone out in that boat for a thousand pounds.

Maitland Dougall's heroic actions during the Club Medal

69 The St Andrews Mechanics Club from 1843 to 1860 and their trades - 8 cabinetmakers including - 11 Tailors
6 gardeners - 6 joiners
1 umbrella maker - 3 Innkeepers 4 Plumbers
- 2 Ballmakers

St. Andrews, 2nd May 1860.

Mr. Whyte-Melville moved the following resolution, which was seconded by Sir Thomas Moncrieffe, and agreed to unanimously :—That this Club consider some acknowledgment to be due to the eminent services of the late Allan Robertson in improving the game of Golf and extending its practice through-

Alex. Carstairs, cabinetmaker.
David Todd, jun., painter.
Peter Gorrie, engineer.
George Cunningham, tinsmith.
John Keddie, joiner.
Alexander Bruce, cabinetmaker.
John Robertson, cabinetmaker.
Thomas Peattie, plumber.
Robert Wilson, smith.
William Ayton, cabinetmaker.
Richard Lister, joiner.
David Thomson, upholsterer.
John Lynn, tailor.
Robert Patterson, slater.
John Ronald, cabinetmaker.
Adam M'Pherson, plasterer.
Allan Robertson, golf ball maker.
Walter Harris, joiner.
James Herd, mason.
Edward Herming, tailor.
William Halkerson, shoemaker.
James Berwick, mason.
James M'Pherson, residenter.
D. Auchterlonie, plumber.
James Sturrock, hairdresser.
George Bruce, cabinetmaker.
David Clark, plumber.
James Lorimer, plasterer.
Tom Morris, golf ball maker.
Archibald Howie, umbrellamaker.
David Gressix, golf ball maker.
David Clark, plasterer.
Andrew Manzie, shoemaker.
Alexander Clyne, tailor.
William Ayton, jr., joiner.
George Morris, weaver.
George Rutherford, tailor.
John Hastie, innkeeper.
Alexander Grieve, valet.
Charles Ritchie, innkeeper.
James Howie, glazier.

Adam Stewart, merchant.
Thomas Potts, caddie.
John Brown, gardener.
James Black, tailor.
Andrew King, do.
David Robertson, joiner.
John Morrison, do.
J. Bayne, cabinetmaker.
John Lynn, tailor.
Andrew Rolland, saddler.
Andrew Anderson, ostler.
Alexander Galloway, tailor.
Archibald Downie, painter.
John Bankier, groom.
David Lothian, baker.
James Wann, grocer.
Richard Farmer, cabinetmaker.
Elias Jones, tinsmith.
George Key, merchant.
Henry Kirk, gardener.
James Scott, café.
David Drummond, mason.
Alexander Greig, valet.
David Spence, baker.
Lawrence Thomson, innkeeper.
Thomas Howie, tailor.
George Rae, architect.
David Henderson, plumber.
William Patterson, slater.
Robert Patterson, tailor.
James Ireland, tailor.
John Christie, innkeeper.
Melville Fletcher, jun., stationer.
A. B. Harris, bank clerk.
Wm. Brown, baker.
David Grimmond, gardener.
Wm. Smith, baker.
A. Harrow, bank clerk.
Robert Forgan, clubmaker.
David Balsillie, coal agent.
George Scott, shoemaker.
John Wilson, ironmonger.
James Wilson, gardener.
James Walker, gardener.
Charles Manson, merchant.
William Hunter, ,, (?)
Robert Sanders, gardener.
David Balsillie, shoemaker.

PRESTWICK GOLF CLUB. (1860)

CHALLENGE BELT.

IT is proposed by the PRESTWICK GOLF CLUB to give a CHALLENGE BELT, to be played for by PROFESSIONAL GOLFERS; and the various Golf Clubs in Scotland and England are requested to name and send the best players on their Links, not exceeding three from any one Club, to compete for it. The Game to be 36 holes, or three rounds of Prestwick Links, the player who succeeds in holing his ball in the fewest number of strokes to be the winner.

The winner of the Belt for three successive years to keep it.

The Game to be played over the Links at Prestwi[illegible] *Twelve o'clock noon on Wednesday, the* [illegible]*th of current.*

Professional Players, not being Keepers of Li[illegible], [illegible] produce a certificate of respectability from the [illegible]surer the Golf Club to which they are attached.

All disputes to be settled by the Captain of the Prestwick Golf Club, or the person acting for him.

COLVILLE, Captain.
D. DUNLOP, Secy.
Prestwick Golf Club.

28, Wellington Square,
Ayr, 2d October, 1860.

Part of the Challenge Belt
Presented by the Earl of Eglinton 1860
a red morocco leather belt with a buckle
engraved with a golfing scene

Sir

It is proposed by the Prestwick Golf Club to give a Challenge Belt to be played for by professional Golfers –

You are requested to name and send the two best players on your Links to compete.

Announcement ↔
for the first
Open Championship

for it – ~~The winner~~

The game to be 36
Holes or three Rounds
of Prestwick Links –
the player who succeeds
in holing his ball in
the fewest number
of Strokes to be the
Winner –

The winner of the belt
for three successive
years to keep it –

The game to be played
over the Links at
Prestwick at 12 o'clock
noon on Wednesday
the 17 of October –

It is desirable that the
players shall be known &
respectable Caddies –
to the Secretary of the
Golf Club.

Blackheath

Ayr Advertiser
20th Oct 1860

GREAT GOLF MATCH.

A GREAT match at Golf was played on the Prestwick Links yesterday, for a Challenge Belt given by the Prestwick Golf Club, to be competed for by professional players. This match has excited great interest in the golfing world, and the best players in the kingdom, both from England and Scotland, entered the lists. A large number of spectators, including a sprinkling of ladies, assembled on the links yesterday to witness the contest. The game was arranged to be thirty-six holes, or three rounds of the Prestwick Links. The following crack players entered for the prize – William Park, of Musselburgh; Tom Morris, of Prestwick; Andrew (the Rook) from Perth; Steel, from Bruntsfield; Smith, from Bruntsfield; Brown, of Blackheath; Strath, of St. Andrews; and Charles Hunter, of the St. Nicholas Club, Prestwick. They started in four pairs, each pair having a marker appointed by the Prestwick Club. The following gentlemen acted in that capacity, viz., Mr Gillan, of Wallhouse; Capt. James; Capt. Pratt; and Major Fairlie. At the commencement of the game the interest was concentrated in Tom Morris and the Rook, who were paired together; but it very soon had came apparent that the struggle for supremacy would be betwixt Park and Tom Morris. Park made the best start, making 4 ahead of Tom in the first two holes. At the end of the first round Park had scored 55, and Tom 58. In the second round they scored equal, 59 each. The excitement at this stage became very intense. Park in the third round came home in 60, and Tom in 59 – the Musselburgh champion thus winning by 2, – the total number for the three rounds being: – Park, 174; Morris, 176. The Rook came next, and, though a crack player, was a good way behind Tom. The play, considering that a strong breeze blew over the links, was very fine; and afforded much gratification to the spectators. The belt is a very handsome and valuable one, being made of red morocco mounted with plates of silver, containing representations of players, clubs, &c. The terms of competition are that it must be gained by the same person for three successive years, before he is entitled to keep it.

The Course
as I laid it out
in 1851 – from
an Ordnance Survey
Map of 1858

73 **The members of the Prestwick Golf Club lately resolved to give a challenge belt, to be played for by professional golfers, and they invited the various golf clubs in England and Scotland to name and send the best players in their links, not exceeding three, from any one club, to compete for it. The game was viewed with great interest by professionals, both in England and Scotland, and during the last week a good number of them have been practising for the match on Prestwick Links. The game was to be 36 holes, or three rounds of the Links, the player who succeeded in holing his ball in the fewest number of strokes to be the winner, and the winner of the belt for three successive years to keep it. The match came off on Thursday, when there was a good turn-out of the lovers of this fine game to see the play of the crack professionals who had entered themselves for the prize. They were as follows:- Wm. Park of Musselburgh, Tom Morris of Prestwick, Andrew (the rook) of Perth, Steele of Bruntsfield, Smith of do., Brown of Blackheath, Strath of St Andrews, and Charles Hunter of the St Nicholas Club, Prestwick. The day was rather unfavourable for good play, the wind being high, and frequently blowing fitful gusts. The competitors started in four pairs, each pair accompanied by a marker appointed by the Prestwick Club. In the first round Park scores 55, and Morris 58, leaving three in favour of Park; in the next round they scored 59 each; in the third round Park made 60, Tom 59 – leaving the Musselburgh player to win by two holes.**

The 1st winner
Willie Park
beat me
by two shots

1. Thomas Morris Prestwick & Robert Andrew Perth
2. William Park Musselburgh and Alexander ~~Steel~~ Smith Brunlsfield
3. William Steel Bruntsfield & Charles Hunter Prestwick St Nicholas Club
4. George Daniel Brown Blackheath & Andrew Strath St Andrews

~~Thomas Morris completed~~

~~The~~ The Club appointed the following markers for the respective pairs &c

1st pair Mr Gillon of Wallhouse
2d pair Cap James
3 pair Cap Pratt
4 pair Major Fairlie

Thomas Morris completed the three rounds in 176 strokes

Robert Andrew in 191 strokes

Wm Park in 174 strokes

Alexander Smith in ~~196~~ 196 strokes

William Steel in ~~210~~ 232 strokes

Charles Hunter in 195 strokes

George Daniel Brown 192 Strokes

Andrew Strath 180

The Challenge Belt

Recognising the desirability of providing some annual test to guage the comparative merits of professional golfers, the Prestwick Club, with characteristic enthusiasm and liberality, lately subscribed for a Challenge Belt, open for competition to the three kingdoms. The trophy, which consists of red morocco, is an exquisite piece of workmanship, richly ornamented with varions devices in silver, and cost, we believe, 25 guineas But apart from its intrinsic value as the most enviable distinction available to the playing talent of the golfing world ranging above amateur excellence, its custody for the first year at least fired the ambition of the crack men of the best greens in the empire. Wednesday being the day fixed for the inaugural contest, there was a large number of aspirants whose praise was on all the links in the country; and, despite the unpropitious weather, a great concourse of the patrons of the ancient game was attracted to Prestwick to witness a contest which had excited an interest unprecedented in golfing circles. Eight celebrities preferred their claims to the honour, and were paired off as follows:—

1. Thomas Morris, Prestwick Golf Club, and Robert Andrew, Perth.
2. William Park, Musselburgh, and Alex. Smith, Bruntsfield, Edinburgh.
3. Wm. Steel, Bruntsfield, and Charles Hunter, St Nicholas Club, Prestwick.
4. George Daniel Brown, Blackheath, and Andrew Strath, St Andrews.

George Brown

Andrew Strath

Bob andrew

Self

Robert Hay, Esq., was chosen Umpire, and to each couple the following markers were appointed, viz.:—1. Capt. James; 2. Capt. Pratt; 3. Major Fairlie; 4. Mr Gillon of Wallhouse. The conditions of the match were three rounds of the links or 36 holes, and the prize to be retained by him who should gain it three years in succession. Making allowance for the high wind, there was beautiful play on the part of the whole competitors, although, ere the game had made much progress, it became evident to the veriest tyro that the tug of war would ultimately be fought between the Prestwick and Musselburgh champions. The former was the favourite, as much on account of his deservedly great repute as of the advantage he enjoyed in traversing his own ground. Accordingly hope beat high that the belt would remain at Prestwick. On going out the first round, however, this pleasing anticipation was dashed by the extraordinary good fortune of Park, who played a fine game, accomplishing the distance in three strokes fewer than his most formidable rival. Tom's admirers did not lose heart, buoying themselves up on his recovering himself in the second round, but he only succeeded in maintaining his own, both having scored the same number of strokes—59 each. At this crisis the excitement waxed most intense, many being sanguine that whatever might betide, a tie would be the worst contingency they had to fear. But in the third round, Tom made only one on his opponent, leaving the latter the victor by two strokes. No one who was a spectator of the struggle could refrain from feeling and expressing their high appreciation of Park's play; but on the other hand, the most veteran frequenters of the Links will also admit that in all their experience of Morris they never saw him come to grief so often, because it is well known that the battle of Bunker's Hill is an engagement which he has very seldom to fight. The competitors respectively finished the 36 holes in the following order:—

Park,	174	strokes.
Morris,	176	"
Strath,	180	"
Andrew,	191	"
Bro[illegible],	192	"
Hunter,	195	"
Steel,	232	"
Smith,	196	"

As might have been anticipated, a good deal of money changed hands on the event. It must be gratifying to the members of the St Nicholas Club to find one of their own number occupying such a creditable position among "the stars," as Mr Hunter achieved on Wednesday. The play on the whole was exceedingly good, and we have no hesitation in saying that the game of golf was never seen in such perfection as on the memorable 17th.

A fine "four-some" was played on Thursday between R. Hay, Esq., and W. Park, against Tom Morris and G. D. Brown. So equally were the players pitted, that

Willie Steel took 232 strokes – that's 16 over sixes

75

From George Glennie at Blackheath about the outcome of the Challenge Belt.

London 19th Octr. 1860

Letter to our Secretary Mr Campbell

My dear Sir,

I am very much obliged to you indeed for your great kindness in sending me such a full account of the very interesting, & must have been exciting, competition for the Belt. The Play was very good in such a day, and tho' I regret exceedingly that our Friend Tom was not successful yet he played the best Game — Park's first round of 55 gave him the victory and it appears to have arisen from the chance holing of the 4th hole in four — it was great chance, but still must have been well played — he had also been lucky in holing long Putts, but these are just the chances of the Game of Golf, & happen one day to one Man & another day to another.

Look at the steadiness of Tom's Game two 59s & one 58, nothing could be finer than that, & as I said before, tho' not the winner he proved himself to be the best Player — I do not know how they stood on the first round as to holes, but I see on the last two Rounds Tom was one hole ahead — There is no doubt that Park is a fine player but in all the Matches that I have seen him play, he is what I would call a lucky Player — he goes bold at every thing & is generally successful especially with his long Putts — & if his Ball missed the catch of the hole he would be out of holing — Tom must not get down in the Mouth about it, but "live to fight another day".

I have much pleasure in enclosing you another copy of the Rules of the Blackheath Golf Club —

We have a Medal day to-morrow but the weather is wretched — High wind & Rain — RETIRED. Again thanking you for your kind attention

Believe me

Yours very sincerely

Charles Campbell Esqr. } Geo. Glennie —

76

The Victor Vanquished

On Friday Park and Morris had a friendly match for £20, the course being the same as in the great game of Wednesday. The Prestwick hero took the head vigorously, allowing his opponent to get only one hole in the first round to his five and ultimately winning easily by seven holes and six to play. Tom has thus not only put some money in his pocket, but what is far dearer to him, retrieved his laurels and deepened the confidence reposed in him by his friends – the confidence not even shakened by his unexpected and accidental defeat on Wednesday. We are given to understand that he is ready to meet Park for any stake whenever his backer and himself are favoured with an explanation of the circumstances which led the Musselburgh champion to declare off by not lodging his money or volunteering the why and the wherefore of his inability to fulfil his last engagement.

↑ The week after the 1st challenge Belt 1860

GOLF – PARK AND MORRIS

Prestwick, November 22, 1860

Sir – Your impression of Monday contained a paragraph which stated, "that Mr William Park, who now takes the title of champion golf-player of Great Britain, and who represented the Warrender Club at the late great tournament at Prestwick, has exhibited to the members for the last three weeks the silver belt given by the Earl of Eglinton and others, and gained by him, and which is perhaps the finest thing of the kind ever competed for. Not however, from its intrinsic value, nor for its artistic merit, is the belt so much esteemed by the golfing community in our neighbourhood; but because it has been gained by a golfer representing an Edinburgh club – gained, too, from one of the best players in the world, at his own door, on his own ground." Far be it from me to derogate in the slightest degree from the reputation of the Musselburgh champion, enhanced as it has been by his recent victory over a distinguished golfer whom you justly characterised as, "one of the best players in the world." But perhaps you will kindly allow me to supplement the above statement by adding that the Friday after the contest for the belt (which the representative of Prestwick lost only by a single stroke), Park and Morris again met in a friendly match for £20, over the same course, when "the champion golf-player of Great Britain" was defeated by Morris, who in three rounds of the Links, or thirty-six holes, won by seven holes with six to play. Let my interest in the ancient game, and a pardonable jealousy for the honour of Prestwick, plead my apology for troubling you to give publicity to a fact which is not so widely known as it deserves to be. – I am &c.

STEMMY

1861 Sept

THE PRESTWICK GOLF MEET. 1861

THE CHALLENGE BELT.

On Thursday a brilliant field appeared as candidates for distinction. Heavy showers of rain having fallen early in the morning, apprehensions were entertained that the weather would be as unpropitious as it unfortunately proved upon a similar occasion last year; but the threatening clouds gradually rolled away, and long ere noon the day broke out exceedingly fine, without a breath of wind sufficiently strong enough to affect the play. It will be remembered that the belt was first competed for in October 1860, when it fell to the lot of W. Park, who carried it off from Tom Morris by a single stroke. The brothers Dunn of Blackheath, who have deservedly acquired a wide reputation, had undertaken a special journey from London, to show their old friends that their hands had not forgot their cunning during a protracted and profitable residence in the south. St Andrews, Perth, Musselburgh, and Bruntsfield were also well represented by first-class men. Availing themselves of the modification lately made in the conditions, several gentlemen players of high name, among whom we noticed Colonel Fairlie, Captain Stewart, Captain Hay, R. Clark, Esq., R. Hay, Esq., Robert Chambers, jun., Esq., and H. M. Buskin, Esq., entered appearance; but as few returns were given in to the Secretary, we have no reliable data from which to estimate the score—an incompleteness to be regretted, as it would have been interesting to contrast the figures with those given below:—

	1st Round.	2d Round.	3d. Round.
David Park, Musselburgh,	58	57	57
Robert Andrew, Perth,	58	61	56
William Dunn, Blackheath,	61	59	60
George D. Brown, St Andrews,	60	65	60
William Park, Bruntsfield,	54	54	59
Peter M'Ewen, do.,	56	60	62
Tom Morris, Prestwick,	54	56	53
Charles Hunter, do.,	67	64	59
James Dunn, Blackheath,	63	62	63
William Dow, Musselburgh,	59	58	54

The foregoing tabular statement represents the manner in which the ten professionals were paired, with the number of strokes respectively taken to complete each of the three rounds; and the following shows the grand aggregate score of the players, and the order in which they were ultimately placed:—

		Total.
1.	Tom Morris,	163 strokes.
2.	William Park,	167 ...
3.	William Dow,	171 ...
4.	David Park,	172 ...
5.	Robert Andrew,	175 ...
6.	Peter M'Ewen,	178 ...
7.	William Dunn,	180 ...
8.	George D. Brown,	185 ...
9.	James Dunn,	188 ...
10.	Charles Hunter,	190 ...

At a comparatively early stage of the proceedings the majority of the competitors were thrown out of the chances of success, and the crowds which followed Park and Morris showed unmistakeably that they must bear the brunt of the battle. Maintaining an equality on the first round, the result of the second was awaited very eagerly, and when it was found that the champion had placed another 54 to his credit against Tom's 56, the opinion became very prevalent that the former would be able to retain his laurels. In approaching the second hole of the final round, however, a daring attempt to "cross the Alps" in two brought Park's ball into one of the worst hazards on the green, and cost him three strokes—by no means the first occasion on which he has been severely punished for similar avarice and temerity. On arriving at the same point in his homeward journey Tom had made up all his lee-way, and in a few minutes he was a stroke a-head, a lead which was increased by two at the stone wall. This advantage was lost, however, at the fifth and sixth holes, at the latter of which he was again square with his opponent. Having played the eighth, ninth, and tenth holes indifferently, Park was passed by Tom at all of them, and was now three behind. The eleventh hole was taken by a fine iron shot, and a finer put in two, and the champion having scored three there, his Prestwick rival was now four strokes in advance, which allayed all further suspense respecting the issue. Driving a magnificent ball from the teeing ground towards home, it landed in a bed of fog at the edge of a pool of water accumulated in the hollow opposite the lunch-house by the late heavy rains. To come to grief at such a time was most provoking, and the spectators thought that Tom would pick out the ball and forfeit a stroke; but with self-reliance, rising to the emergency, he dexterously sent it bounding into the air, and ultimately halving the last hole, finished a splendid round for 53, and secured the national guerdon of golfing skill. Considerable disappointment was expressed that there should not have been a formal investiture of the belt by some of the officials of the club on the spot, although from the modesty with which Tom wears his honours, we presume it was more in consonance with his own feelings to have been relieved from participating in any such ceremony. It may be well to add that the championship was won last year in 174 strokes, or eleven more than the lowest figure on Thursday—Park being [illegible], and Mo[illegible] being 12 strokes better this season.

The Himalayas

PRESTWICK GOLF CLUB.—There was a large concourse of people on the Prestwick Links yesterday, to witness the annual competition for the Challenge Belt, given by the club. Five pairs of professionals, and an equal number of gentlemen players, started for three rounds of the course. The interest of the contest was centred in the professionals, who made a fine display of science and skill. We are glad to say that Tom Morris, the professional keeper of the Prestwick Links, carried off the belt in 163 strokes; W. Park, Musselburgh (who won it last year), 2d, in 167; W. Dow, Musselburgh, 3d, in 171; D. Park, Musselburgh, 4th, in 172; R. Andrew, Perth, 5th, in 175; P. M'Ewen, Bruntsfield, 6th, in 178; W. Dunn, Blackheath, 7th, in 180; G. D. Brown, St. Andrews, 8th, in 185; J. Dunn, Blackheath, 9th, in 188; and C. Hunter, Preswick, 10th, in 190. Several matches took place to-day; but in the afternoon the weather became wet and disagreeable, sending all but the keenest golfers off the Links.

my first win and by 4 shots from Willie

PRESTWICK GOLF CLUB.—The annual competition for the Challenge Belt given by the Club came off on Thursday, and attracted a large concourse of spectators. Five pairs of professionals; and an equal number of gentlemen players started at 12 o'clock for three rounds of the course. The following are the totals of the most successful competitors, who, as was anticipated from their professional standing and experience, made some fine play during the match:—Tom Morris, Prestwick, winner of the belt in 163 strokes; W. Park, Musselburgh, 2d in 167; W. Dow, Musselburgh, 3d in 171; D. Park, Musselburgh, 4th in 172; R. Andrew, Perth, 5th in 175; P. M'Ewen, Bruntsfield, 6th in 178; W. Dunn, Blackhead, 7th in 180; G. D. Brown, St Andrews, 8th in 185; J. Dunn, Blackhead, 9th in 188; and C. Hunter, Prestwick, 10th in 190. Park was the favourite, he having carried off the belt last year from his Prestwick rival by a single stroke, Tom Morris nobly retrieving his laurels, although two strokes behind his opponent in starting for the last round. We subjoin the rounds of the two champions in whose play nearly all the interest centred:—

	1st Round.	2d Round.	3d Round.
Tom Morris,	54	56	53
W. Park,	54	54	59

On Friday a foursome was arranged between Capt. Stewart and Robert Hay, Esq., against Colonel Fairlie and Tom Morris—the latter pair coming off successful in two matches. Some idea of the style of play may be inferred from the fact that one of the rounds was completed by the Colonel and his partner in 52 strokes—one less than Tom's best round on Thursday—a feat unequalled, we believe, by any couple, gentlemen or professionals, on Prestwick Links.—A match was arranged to come off on Saturday, between the brothers Park, against Tom Morris and W. Dow; but the Parks considered it prudent to take their departure for home on Friday night, and the match consequently did not come off.

"The Rook"

Self and Charlie Hunter
in the Earl of Eglinton's
foresters' jackets
for the Challenge

Studio portrait after winning the Challenge Belt in 1861

80

PRESENTATION OF THE FREEDOM OF THE CITY OF ST ANDREWS TO LIEUT.-GENERAL SIR JAMES HOPE GRANT, G.C.B., &c., &c.

In accordance with a resolution passed by the Town Council of St Andrews, that the freedom of the city should be presented to Sir Hope Grant, for the eminent services he has rendered his country, a meeting took place in the New Town Hall on Tuesday, the 23d inst. The Council occupied a position at the top of the hall, presided over by the Provost, at the side of which were seats reserved for Lady Hope Grant and party. There was a brilliant assemblage of spectators, but owing to the disagreeable state of the weather, the attendance was smaller than might otherwise have been. Among those present we observed:—Mr and Lady Lucy Grant of Kilgraston, and the Misses Grant; Lady Hope Grant; Lady Home; Mrs Graham Speirs; the Misses Shakspear; Miss Taylor; Mrs Low of Clatto, and the Misses Low; Mr and Mrs J. O. Fairlie; Mrs Bruce Gardyne; Mrs Skene of Pitlour; Mrs Milton, Mrs Ainslie, Mrs Briggs, Miss Burns, Miss Playfair, Miss Alexander, Miss Tribe, Misses Wemyss of Denbrae; Sir George Home, Bart.; General Moncrieff; Colonel Low, Cairney Lodge; Colonel Robert Campbell; C. Halkett Inglis, Esq. of Cramond; Principal Tulloch; Professor Mitchell; Rev. Dr Park; Rev. Dr Ainslie; Rev. David Playfair, Abercorn; Rev. John Anderson, Kinnoul; Dr Baird of Airston; John Jamieson, Esq. of Kingask; Dr Watson Wemyss of Denbrae; and Messrs G. H. Lamb, Walter Walker, George M'Gregor, and James Bain.

Provost MILTON said this meeting had been called for the special purpose of carrying into effect the resolution passed by the Council on the 14th of June last—namely, That the freedom of the city be presented to Lieutenant-General Sir Hope Grant, and an address along with it, in consideration of his eminent services. Sir Hope Grant was in the adjoining room, and he asked the Council if it was their pleasure to send for him.

Bailie BONTHRON then stepped out, and returned with Sir Hope Grant, who was received by the company standing.

The PROVOST addressed Sir Hope Grant, and said—When we knew you were going to take up your residence among us, the Town Council of St Andrews, as representing the community, unanimously agreed that the highest honour they have in their power to confer should be passed upon you, by presenting you with the freedom of the city, along with an address, expressive of their high appreciation of the services you have rendered to this country. They also add their admiration of you as a gallant soldier, and as an individual, for whom they entertain the greatest respect and esteem. (Applause.) In accordance with the resolution, I now call upon the city clerk to read the address, as agreed upon by the Town Council, and thereafter present to you the ticket of a burgess.

To Lieutenant-General Sir James Hope Grant, G.C.B., &c., &c.

St Andrews, 23d July 1861.

SIR,—In presenting you with your burgess ticket as a citizen of St Andrews, the Provost, Magistrates, and Town Council, are proud of the opportunity of expressing on behalf of themselves and their fellow citizens, the high sense entertained of your personal character, and your distinguished military achievements. A gallant and successful soldier from your youth, your earliest distinctions were gained in connection with that vast and remote empire which has been the scene of your latest triumphs.

In the second Chinese war, you served as Brigade Major, and then as Deputy-Adjutant-General, on the staff of Lord Saltoun, and were present at the taking of Chinkian-foo by storm. Afterwards you were engaged in both campaigns of the memorable Sikh war, and were present at the battle of Sobraon, Chillianwallah, and Goojerat, commanding on the two latter occasions your own regiment—the 9th Lancers.

During the unhappy Indian mutiny, your name was associated with the names of many other heroes, of whom our country has reason to be proud. You were present at the siege and capture both of Delhi and Lucknow. You co-operated with your distinguished countryman, Sir Colin Campbell (now Lord Clyde), at the battle of Cawnpore, and followed up the success there gained by a brilliant pursuit of the enemy across the Ganges, in which 150 of their guns were captured. In command of a separate force throughout the rest of the campaign you fought many actions, and did not sustain a single reverse.

But it was during the late Chinese war that you earned your highest distinction, and rendered the greatest services to your country. As Commander-in-Chief of the British forces on this occasion your name will be handed down to posterity in connection with one of the most triumphant yet bloodless campaigns of which history can boast. The attack and capture of the Taku Forts, notwithstanding the apprehension of the French General, and the subsequent march upon Pekin, in which you carried the British forces for the first time into the heart of an empire which had deemed itself invincible in its mysterious seclusion, and showed to the Chinese how a European army could at once be effective in conflict, and forbearing in victory, even while enacting condign punishment for barbarous cruelty. These are events which have carried your fame as a soldier throughout the length and breadth of the land.

It will, to a mind like yours, be not the least pleasing result of your success in China, that you have thereby not only vindicated the prowess of the British army, but extended the pathway of commerce—the great peace-maker of the world, and opened up to the very centre of an ancient idolatry, a road for the Christian missionary, and the life-giving truths of the Gospel.

It is the earnest prayer of your fellow citizens of St Andrews that you may be long spared to wear the laurels you have so gallantly won, and that in the distant country where you are about to assume a permanent command, you may enjoy continued health and happiness.

Signed in behalf of the Magistrates and Town Council of St Andrews, by

WALTER THOS. MILTON, Provost.

He then read the burgess ticket, which had been prepared by Mr William Anderson, writing-master, George Street, Edinburgh, which stated that the same was presented to Sir Hope Grant "in testimony of their high appreciation of his eminent public se[rvices] during the late mutiny in India, and thereafter as Commander-in-Chief of the British army during the recent war in China."

The reading of this and the address was frequently interrupted with bursts of applause.

Provost MILTON—It now remains with me to present you with this address, and to welcome you as a burgess of our ancient city, assuring you that wherever your lot may be cast, we will ever take a lively interest in all your proceedings; and every laurel gained by you will be hailed with joy by us, as one gained by a fellow citizen. He then handed the address and the burgess ticket to Sir James Hope Grant, amidst loud applause, the audience standing.

Sir HOPE GRANT, in acknowledging the presentation, said—I am very grateful to you, Provost, and to the other members of the Council, for the honour you have done me to-day in giving me the freedom of this city. I am not only grateful for this as a public testimony of your esteem and regard, but also because I look upon this compliment as coming from those whom I may call my friends—(cheers). Many a happy day I have passed in St Andrews in former times; and I can only say that during the last two campaigns in the East I have often felt, when I was far away from this country, that nothing would give me so much pleasure as to have another game of golf on the old links—(loud cheers)—but from the trouble and danger of war it seemed doubtful whether it would ever be realised. This pleasure has, however, arrived, gentlemen, and I already feel ten years younger—(cheers). You have been pleased to say that I have been of service to our Queen and country. Your approbation repays me for all the hardships that I have undergone; and I can only say that should war again break out between this country and a foreign nation, and should any command be intrusted to me, I will always be ready, and I hope fit, to do my duty—(loud applause). I must say gentlemen, I was exceedingly surprised and highly gratified the other day upon my arrival here to see two such fine companies of artillery and infantry volunteers assembled to meet me, and to do me honour—(cheers)—and with the Provost at their head. So long as we have such patriotism displayed in our country, the honour of our nation will always be supported—(cheers). I must now thank you, ladies and gentlemen, for the honour you have conferred on me by meeting me here to-day; and as you must be aware that it is a soldier's business to fight, and not to make speeches, you will excuse me for not detaining you longer—(loud applause).

Sir Hope Grant then went round and received the congratulations of the Town Council, after which Mr W. F. Ireland proposed three cheers for Lieutenant-General Sir James Hope Grant, which was most enthusiastically responded to, and the same was given for Lady Grant. This finished the business, and the audience retired.

THE BANQUET.

A banquet was given to Sir Hope Grant in the evening by the members of the Royal and Ancient Golf Club of St Andrews, in the Union Club House.

The noblemen and gentlemen present were:—J. Whyte Melville, Esq., Convener of the County; the Earl of Eglinton; the Earl of Rosslyn; Lord Loughborough; Sir Hugh Hume Campbell; Sir George Home; General Moncrieff; Colonel Mackay; Col. Low, Cairnie Lodge; Colonel Fairlie, Coodham; Colonel Anstruther, yr. of Balcaskie; Colonel Lyon; Colonel Maitland Dougal of Scotscraig; Mr Morris, Bengal C. S.; Major Briggs, Strathairly; Major Bethune; Major Boothby; J. Anstruther Thomson, Esq. of Charleton; Captain Oswald of Dunnikier; Captain J. D. B. Hay; Captain Kinloch, yr. of Gilmerton; Lieut. A. L. Playfair; James Balfour, Esq., W.S.; Mr Walkinshaw; Mr S. W. Lamb; Mr R. Kirkpatrick Howat; W. J. L. Gilmour, Esq. of Craigmillar; A. S. Sutherland, Esq., W.S.; Moncrieffe Skene, Esq., yr. of Pitlour; Mr Wm. Skene; E. J. Jackson, Esq., Largo House; John Grant, Esq., Kilgraston; Dr Watson Wemyss of Denbrae; Dr Baird, Airston; A. Bethune, Esq. of Blebo; Mr D. L. Burn; J. Purvis, Esq. of Kinaldy; A. K. Lindsay, Esq. of Balmungo; J. Haig, Esq., Cameron Bridge; D. Gillespie, Esq. of Mountquhanie; Halkett Inglis, Esq. of Cramond; Dr Wm. Playfair; George Gordon, Esq., Kinburn House; Mr Lumsden, of Lathallan; Wolfe Murray, Esq. of Cringlettie; D. Meldrum, Esq. of Kincaple; Dr Methven, R.N.; John Ogilvie, Esq. yr. of Inshewan; W. Pagan, Esq. of Clayton; G. H. Pagan, Esq., yr. of Clayton; Principal Tulloch; the Rev. A. Hill, St Andrews; Mr W. H. Haig; W. F. Ireland, Esq.; Mr Bairnsfather, Dunbarrow; George Thomson, Esq., Burn House; Provost Milton; Bailies Bethune, Lees, Richard, and Macpherson; Messrs R. Mitchell; James Blackwood; John Blackwood; Wm. Murray; George Hay; Ord Graham Campbell; S. C. Thomson; Patrick Arkley; D. M. Ogilvy Dalgleish; Wm. Blackwood; D. B. Wauchope; Samuel Hay; Stuart Grace; Wm. Horsbrugh, &c., &c.

The Chair was occupied by J. Whyte Melville, Esq. of Mount Melville, supported on the right by the guest of the evening, Lieutenant-General Sir James Hope Grant, G.C.B.; Earl of Rosslyn; Sir Thomas Erskine, Bart.; and J. Grant, Esq., of Kilgraston. On the left by the Earl of Eglinton; Lord Loughborough; and J. A. Thomson, Esq. of Charleton. General Moncrieff and Provost Milton acted as croupiers.

A blessing having been asked by the Rev. A. Hill, the numerous party partook of the excellent viands provided for them by Mr Davidson of the Star Hotel, who was purveyor for the occasion. The arrangements reflected the highest credit on Mr Davidson, and much of the comfort and pleasure was due to him for his excellent superintendence of the banquet.

The CHAIRMAN then proposed "The Queen." He said it was always usual on occasions like the present that the first toast should be that of the Sovereign of the realm, and that custom had existed for so long a period, it was almost considered a statutory enactment. But in the present day they had the great satisfaction of having a distinguished lady to sit upon the throne of these realms—distinguished alike for her public and private virtues. (Applause.) Therefore, that toast which might formerly have been drunk, merely as a matter of form, was now given from the bottom of their hearts. (Applause.) And when it was added that her most gracious Majesty was Patroness of the Royal and Ancient Golf Club of St Andrews, he required to say no more, but call upon them to drink the health of her Majesty the Queen, with all honours.

The CHAIRMAN then proposed "The Prince of Wales, and other members of the Royal Family," which was drunk with applause.

The CHAIRMAN said the next toast he had to propose was "The Army, Navy, and Volunteers." The army and navy had of late years so greatly distinguished themselves whenever they were called upon, that it was quite unnecessary to say anything regarding them. The volunteer force had, however, become an established fact, and he would drink a bumper to that toast, coupling with it the name of a distinguished officer and very zealous volunteer, Lieutenant-General the Earl of Rosslyn.

A great day for Sir James Hope Grant and the town.

This great affair Continued →

81

SIR HOPE GRANT.

Sir Hope Grant's reply

Sir. HOPE GRANT, who was re... with given cheering, rose to reply, and said—Mr. President, my Lords and Gentlemen—It is very easy to fight battles and even to conquer an enemy, but I can assure you it is much more severe work to make speeches and to partake of the splendid dinners which have lately been given to me, so I trust you will forgive me if I say little. I beg to return my most heartfelt thanks for the kindness you have shown me this evening, and for the great compliments you have paid me, which I feel I do not deserve, and did not expect. The army that I had the honour to command in China was of first-rate description. All the different branches were in most effective order, and the Chinese must have been surprised at a nation coming from the other side of the globe, landing in their country with such a splendid force of artillery, cavalry, and infantry, and I feel convinced they do not consider us in the light of barbarians, as they formerly did. (Cheers.) They are, however, a fine nation, and when we consider that the compass, gunpowder, and printing, were invented by them long before we knew anything of their use; and that we owe to the Chinese these discoveries, we ought not to think lightly of them as a nation. (Applause.) They, however, are not well versed in the arts of war; and, to prove my assertion, I will quote the following anecdotes, which took place in the first war:—At the taking of Amoy a despatch was found in the house of the Tartar General, written by him to the Emperor—"The unlearned Barbarians not knowing the use of fire arms took our guns in the rear, thereby rendering them of no avail." I, gentlemen, went on the same system in attacking them at the Takoo Forts, we took their guns in reverse, with comparatively little loss to our troops. Mr Melville has kindly complimented me on many points which I do not deserve, but, in regard to music, I flatter myself I am in some degree proficient in that acquirement, as it is always a source of great delight to me. With regard to the game of golf, I fear I am not the player I used to be, and I much fear I shall never regain the character of a good player; yet, with practice, I hope to improve sufficiently to prevent my antagonist defeating me easily. (Laughter and cheers.) Gentlemen, I beg to return my best thanks to you. (Sir Hope resumed his seat amid great applause.)

The Earl of ROSSLYN, who was received with applause, said, as senior military officer present, it was his duty to return thanks for the compliment paid to the profession to which he had the honour to belong. The prizes in the lottery of that profession were but few, and there were not many who would be able to obtain them. It was the boast of the British soldier, in accepting the services of the Crown, that he forfeited none of the rights and privileges of a British subject; and one of the highest honours that could be passed upon a soldier was the approval of his fellow-citizens. (Applause.) That approval was doubly grateful when expressed by the voice of the Houses of Parliament—grateful to him when, in this instance, it was re-echoed by his countrymen generally. They were assembled to offer their gallant friend upon his right their congratulations upon his return from his successful campaigns. (Cheers.) They may rest assured in whatever quarter of the globe this evening's proceedings might be recorded, and the object for which they had assembled, to do honour to the gallant General, would be a stimulus to his comrades—to every man in the army—in attaining the glory which he has gained. (Cheers.) He was afraid he would trench upon the duty of other officers present, who were superior to him in rank in the Volunteers, when he returned thanks for the honour they had paid to the Volunteer army of Great Britain. But having been under the gallant General Peel in a subordinate office in the War Office at the time when the Volunteer movement was originated, he had no hesitation in saying that their fondest expectations never anticipated that the movement would have acquired the enormous proportions it had now reached. Its object was to receive for the country the services of those who were not likely to give their services either in the militia or the regular army. The Government at that period did not anticipate that the patriotism of the country would have been excited to such a degree as to be prepared to abandon their time, spend their money, and trouble, to submit to the requirements of discipline and duty, to enable them to participate in the duties which would fall on the regular army in the event of any aggression. As the Chairman had assured them, that movement was now a great and an established fact. It was with no little pride, and with no little satisfaction, that the regular army saw that in the event of any aggression on the territories of Great Britain, they would be backed by such a gallant, and well disciplined army of volunteers. (Cheers.) He begged, in name of the two branches of the service, to return them his thanks. (Applause.)

Colonel MAITLAND DOUGAL replied on behalf of the navy, stating that although it was a long time since he left the navy, yet he was assured there were a great many of the right sort there. Jack had seldom an opportunity of showing his pluck, because the enemy fired from behind sand banks and batteries, but he was sure they would show their pluck if ever they had the opportunity, and he was certain that young Nelson's, Peel's, and Hope Grant's, would yet spring up. (Applause). These iron-plated vessels were rather too much for the wooden vessels, and the molten iron shells were sufficient to set any wooden vessel on fire, yet although they had only five of these new vessels to 15 of their friends on the other side, yet

One Frenchman lick two Portuguese,
One Englishman lick all three.

(Loud applause.)

Sir THOMAS ERSKINE proposed "The Earl of Eglinton and the House of Peers."

The Earl of EGLINTON, who was received with cheers on rising, said—On behalf of the House of Lords, with which you have done me the honour to couple my name, I beg to return you my most sincere thanks. It is always most grateful to any member of that House to find that he is believed to be acting upon conscientious motives, and by which, I believe, they are almost entirely actuated. (Cheers.) It is most essential and agreeable to any member of that House to find that they are approved of by those whom I will term the untitled aristocracy of Great Britain, of whom I cannot but think we are, even more than the other House, the representatives. (Loud cheers.) Though we don't sit to the same late hours that the other House does—(hear, hear)—though we don't speak so lengthy—my belief is, we do the business which comes before us perhaps almost as well as the other House of Parliament. (Applause.) If we are at different times accused by the papers, or by the appearance of the shortness of our sitting to the world at large, it is because they don't give us business to do. It is not because we are not ready to do that business which it is our duty to perform. Then there are many of our members—and, I need only mention the name of Lord Derby—who have descended from a long line of ancestors, and who have reflected credit not only upon that line of ancestors, but upon the country to which they belong. Still, I cannot but feel that the House of Lords would have to put that position as a monopoly and innovation, if they had not from time to time been replenished by additions from the outer world. (Cheers.) Among those additions to the roll—though it cannot be said that the House of Lords is strengthened when they are added to its numbers—we have had such men as the Duke of Wellington, Lord Gough, Lord Raglan, and Lord Clyde—noble honours to their profession—and from time to time, when necessary, we have had lawyers and statesmen brought in among us. (Cheers.) Our gallant guest has attained already, perhaps you may say, to the highest honours that can be awarded to a soldier—at all events to a soldier of his standing in the army. It is barely possible, in the high command which he is now about to fill, that on some future occasion which, I trust, he may live to see—if it ever occurs—but which, I trust, will not occur—some future war—it may be possible that our gallant guest may be added to that gallant list who have been enrolled among the peers. I will say this, that among the gallant men who have been enrolled, none will be received with greater acclamation, or with more open arms. (Loud cheers.) For myself I have only to say, that though I am not at present in a position for attending any public festivities—and this is the first I have attended this year—I felt I could not be the only golfer at St Andrews, staying here on such an occasion as this, that would not come to welcome our gallant guest. (Cheers.) I feel this the more, not only from my high appreciation of him as an officer, and as a man, but because he has long been a private friend. (Cheers.) I came to St Andrews to join in that pastime which I admire so much, but in which, I am sorry to say, I do not in the same way excel as our gallant guest. I came here expecting to enjoy that quiet and charming pastime, and I have also had the pleasure of adding my mite of approbation to our gallant guest, whom you have done yourselves the honour to invite to this entertainment this evening. (Loud cheers.)

The Earl's ← speech

The CHAIRMAN then rose to propose the toast of the evening, and said—However inadequate I may feel to do justice to the toast of the evening, which I am now about to propose to you, I beg to assure you, gentlemen, that it gives me the greatest gratification to have been appointed by you as your president, to congratulate Lieutenant-General Sr James Hope Grant upon his happy return to this country, as well as to assure him that we feel it a very great pleasure and a very great honour in having his company here this evening. (Cheers.) Gentlemen, having known that gallant soldier from his boyhood, I have watched his military career with very great interest, from the time he was a captain of Dragoons until the conclusion of his late glorious campaigns, and knowing the inherent talents of his family, I almost predicted that he having himself taken the profession of arms, he would—if circumstances occurred—if an opportunity took place, be sure to distinguish himself. Gentlemen, I think that prediction has not been a false one. (Loud cheers.) I am very unwilling, in the presence of Sir Hope Grant to speak as strong as I could do in his absence. In regard to the high estimation in which I hold his talents as a soldier, and his qualities as a man, I may be permitted to express to you very shortly the leading out... of his military career, which, commenced by his accompanying the lat... Saltoun—the gallant defender of the gates of ...mont—as Brigade-Major, when that General went out in command of a division to China ... end of the year 1841, or beginning of 1842. ... that occasion the two were very happily descri... by the talented author of "Golfiana," which many ... daresay, whom I have the honour to address m... have read, but which every person may not remember. I shall, therefore, repeat to you these lines, which he beautifully describes these two—Lo... Saltoun and Sir Hope Grant. He writes:—

The poor Chinese there cannot be a doubt,
Will shortly be demolished out and out;
But, oh! how blest beyond the common line
Of conquered nations, by the Power divine,
Saltoun to cut their yellow throats, and then
Hope Grant to play their requiem notes, Amen.

The talented bard did not anticipate that in twen... years after he wrote these lines of requiem notes th... would be so simply right. (Cheers.) After this ... Hope Grant rejoined his regiment—the 9th Lanc...—and was with it at the battle of Sobraon; a... thereafter commanded that regiment throughout t... greater part of the campaign in the Punjaub 1848-9, including the battles of Chillianwallah a... Goojerat. He then returned to this country, b... only for a short time, for he was out again previo... to the disastrous mutiny in India. Upon that occa...sion, as Brigadier-General, he commanded t... cavalry at the capture of Delhi, where he had ... horse shot under him, and otherwise greatly dist...guished himself. After that he commanded a di...sion under Lord Clyde at the relief of Lucknow, also subsequently in the Punjaub, until the ent... rebel army was defeated. His talents as a milit... commander were sufficiently appreciated at the W... Office, and he was appointed, as the fittest officer, ... take the command in China; and that appointm... was endorsed by the voice of the country. ("He... hear," and cheers.)

GREAT GOLF MATCH.

1862

TOM MORRIS v. WM. PARK.

£100 A-Side.

In accordance with the conditions regulating this the most important match that ever excited the general interest of the golfing world, the Champion and ex-Champion again met at Prestwick on Tuesday, when the second of the four games of 36 holes each was appointed to be played. Among a goodly concourse of spectators we observed the Marquis of Ailsa; Lord William Kennedy; Ord Campbell, Esq., Edinburgh, the general umpire; Col. Fairlie of Coodham, the champion of Scottish amateurs, who acted as local umpire; Major Shaw Kennedy of Kirkmichael; Major Fergusson, South Lodge; Major Phillips, A.Y.C.; D. D. Whigham, Esq.; Captain Kennedy of Bennane; Dr Sloan; Dr Knower, and other members of the Prestwick Club. The fact that the favourite had defeated his opponent at Musselburgh on Friday, in the first match of the series, influenced the betting to such an extent that there were no takers at even money against him on his own green, and scarcely any business was done, the little that was transacted being at odds on Tom. When the challenge was accepted, considerable regret was expressed that the lateness of the season should have marred the prospects of first-class play, and this regret was deepened on Tuesday, when, in many respects, the weather was anything but propitious for a satisfactory display of science on the part of either of the men. The links were in a perplexingly abnormal condition from frost, the usual velvet sponginess of the turf having been transformed into an unyielding surface, almost as hard as a macadamised road, along which the balls danced to a distance, even when driven from the wrist, that always excited the surprise of the onlookers, and often the chagrin of the players. On the putting greens the grass was so crisp as to render the short game more a matter of hap-hazard than anything else, equally defiant of judgment and ingenuity. But while these disadvantages increased the score, they also intensified the excitement, always attending the most delicate department of scientific golf, and by the very force of contrast, afforded all present a novel treat, the peculiarities of which will not soon be forgotten. Frequently when "halves" were looked upon as a dead certainty, holes were gained and lost, so inexplicably on both sides, that more than one novice in attendance audibly flattered himself that he could have done better if *he* had had such chances! As was expected, Tom made all the running, although the lead he took and kept through two thirds of the game was much stronger than could have been hoped for. On the first twelve holes he placed no fewer than three to his credit, a very respectable beginning; and on the second twelve he succeeded in adding the same number to the score. Six ahead at the commencement of the final round was a remarkable run of good fortune and a very unpleasant burden for his rival to carry with comfort. Here, however, Park appeared in his old colours. Of the first four holes going out for the last time he won three and reduced the lead by a half. At this stage the memory of his antecedents in similar adverse circumstances on the same links changed the possible into the probable; and the knowing ones forthwith began to speculate upon the likelihood of his being able to retrieve himself by once more coming in at the death. At the eighth hole, however, the suspense was over, Tom being five in advance with only four to play. The next two were halved, the eleventh fell to the lot of Morris and the twelfth to Park, who remained a winner of one on the third round, leaving him five behind on the day's performance. The general remarks we have to offer upon the progress of the game are necessarily few, because we have so often commented on the style of each of the celebrities engaged, and because there was really little calling for detailed notice. The driving comprised some of the greatest feats in the experience of both, and these were not confined to an occasionally brilliant shot or two, but extended over a succession of the longest balls ever struck by either on the Prestwick links. For the information of those who are of opinion that Park enjoys the advantage in this part of the game, we may add, what all present will corroborate, that Morris generally out-distanced him on Tuesday. The "putting," however, was proportionately deficient, as may be easily imagined from the causes to which we have already alluded. Afraid of running themselves out of certainty by the customary pith, they were both cautious to a fault, and generally weak, although, of course, there were some fine exceptions to this timid policy. One of these deserving special commendation was a dexterious "loft" by Park, who holed the ball with his iron over a dead "stimie" at the Barn. Indeed the majority of his iron shots at various distances could not have been surpassed. In approaching the putting-greens, making legitimate allowance for the nature of the ground, the quarter strokes were all but perfection on both sides. In the estimation of a number of the spectators the Champion should have been seven a-head at the lowest computation but for two indifferent "puts;" although like many of his friends he doubtless congratulated himself, in a retrospect of the day, in all being well that ends well. As regards the strokes, Tom completed the first round in 58, the second in 54, and the third in 57, making a grand total of 169, or only six more than the score at which he has twice carried off the Belt, an insignificant discrepancy when the frost tells upon the figures, and another proof of the steadiness for which he is so distinguished. Park's rounds stood at 62 for the first, and 57 for the third, there being no record of the second, from the circumstance of his having neglected to hole out on two occasions when he saw the attempt hopeless; and having momentarily forgotten that the strokes were being marked.

1862

GOLF MATCHES.—After the competition for the St. Andrews' medal, says the *Fife Herald*, Colonel Fairlie and Tom Morris played a capital foursome against Major Boothby and Bob Andrews. Colonel Fairlie and Tom were the winners. On Thursday, J. H. E. Wemyss, Esq., M.P., and Tom Morris played Mr W. Moncrieff and Andrew Strath. The first round the former beat by six holes, and the second round the latter beat by two. On the two rounds Mr Wemyss and Tom were victors by four holes. William Park and Andrew Strath played a two-some—one round. Strath beat Park 7 holes. Park challenged Strath for £5, but Strath declined to renew the contest. William Dow of Musselburgh, and Bob Andrews of Perth, played against each other one round. Dow beat Andrews by four holes. William Dow and William Park also played a single-handed match, which was halved. On Friday perhaps the best match of the week was played by Colonel Fairlie and Tom Morris, against Colonel Maitland Dougall and William Park, two rounds or thirty-six holes. It was an admirably contested match, though evidently Colonel Fairlie did not seem to be up to the mark of his usual good play. Col. Dougall and Park beat the former by five holes on the match. Mr Skene Moncrieff and Andrew Strath played two matches against Mr Whigham and Bob Andrews, and beat them both times. On Saturday, Tom Morris and Strath played Park and Dow, and beat them by two holes. Mr Cathcart of Pitcairly and Tom Morris played Mr John Blackwood and Strath, and beat them two matches.

83

A HUNDRED GOLFERS

AIR—"*A Hundred Pipers*"

Wi' a hundred golfers an' a', an' a'.—
The club, the cleek, an' the ba', the ba'.
O, Bruntsfield Links look braw, look braw.—
Wi' a hundred golfers an' a', an' a'.

The *Burgess* are auldest of a', of a'—
Wi' Robertson, Martin, an' Shaw, an' Shaw—
Fresh laurels they gain, which weel they maintain,
Though their vet'rans are wearin' awa', awa'.
The *Bruntsfield* comes next in the raw, the raw,
Wi' the *Burgess* they've oft a *fracas, fracas*:
To add to their honours most gallantly Chambers
Frae St. Andrew a prize brought awa', awa'.
Wi' a hundred golfers an' a', an' a'.—
The club, the cleek, an' the ba', the ba',
O, Bruntsfield Links look braw, look braw.—
Wi' a hundred golfers an' a', an' a'.

A HUNDRED GOLFERS

The *Warrender* lads are nae slaw, nae slaw—
Yule, Ballantine, Forbes, an' Law, an' Law—
Their golfing will stand wi' the best in the land,
An' their "Tournay" gaed aff wi' *eclat, eclat.*
The *St. Leonards* can rise at the daw', the daw':
They like weel to hear the cock craw, cock craw:
Let the mornin' wind blaw wi' rain, sleet, or snaw,
It stops nae Kinross's guffaw, guffaw.
Chorus—Wi' a hundred golfers, etc.

Though the *Merchiston* band ne'er blaw, ne'er blaw,
On the green they've nae fear ava', ava':
Wi' Sanson sae steady, an' Conn'ly, an' Peddie,
An' Calver, wha kept the Golf Ha', Golf Ha'.
The *Allied* come hinmost—hurrah! hurrah!
They're the chiels for drivin' the ba', the ba':
M'Ewan an' Robb, an' Stevens an' Hogg,
Are a foursome no easy to thraw, to thraw.
Chorus—Wi' a hundred golfers, etc.

Dec. 1862. T. R.

I find myself whistlin this tune a lot when workin on the course!

Ayrshire Express. Sept 13 1862

THE CHALLENGE BELT.

On Thursday the weather was all that could be desired for the important contest, the issue of which is decisive of the Championship of the golfing world. Open to all comers, the splendid Challenge Belt is the only national distinction for which the professionals of the United Kingdom can compete; and it is matter of regret that the disinterested enterprise and liberality of the Prestwick Club should not be more widely and warmly apppreciated by those for whose benefit this annual tournament was organised. Surely the representatives of the different links throughout the country are reprehensibly blind to their own interest, when they do not deem it their duty to enter an appearance on an occasion which affords them the most tempting opportunity of making a reputation among the patrons of the game. Possibly, however, the majority of them felt that the struggle would now, as formerly, lie between two of their number who are at the very head of their order; and that there was consequently little use in their undertaking a somewhat expensive journey to Prestwick only to flourish among the unsuccessful aspirants. This may account for the meagreness of the entries on Thursday, which comprised but three accredited professional players, the gentlemen who competed having kindly started to make a field. Shortly after noon four couples went off in the following order—1st, Mr Charles Hunter and Mr James Knight; 2d, Mr J. F. Johnston and Tom Morris; 3d, William Park and William Dow; 4th, Rev. R. Pollock and Mr William Mitchell. Although the betting was all in favour of the present holder of the Belt, the fine round made by his rival on the previous evening, showed he was in good fettle, and augured well for another closely contested run. But it will be seen from the subjoined return, that these anticipations were far from being realised—the favourite having taken the lead from the beginning and maintained it with remarkable steadiness throughout. On the cards being handed in to the Secretary, the five best scores stood thus:—

	1st Round.	2d Round.	3d Round.
Mr C. Hunter, ...	60	60	59
„ James Knight,...	62	61	63
Tom Morris..........	52	55	56
William Park,.......	59	59	58
William Dow, ...	60	58	63.

On the completion of the second round, it became evident that Park had failed to recover his lost ground; and, barring accidents, that the Belt was safe to remain in Prestwick at least for another year. We never remember to have seen him more unfortunate in his putting, many of his balls having lipped the hole and bounded back—a circumstance which told most materially on his score. This is all the more surprising, that the roughness of the green was considered advantageous to the bold style of play in this part of the game which is the great characteristic of the ex-champion. For a long time Dow made a plucky stand, being equal with Park when they set out for the final round. More brilliant driving could not be witnessed than that displayed by this, the most promising of all the young professionals. Many of his best balls were not sufficiently winded, and came to grief in some of the most formidable hazards with which the Links abound. As will be seen from the foregoing analysis, Tom Morris went to his work and prosecuted it with his accustomed caution and precision, worthily sustaining his old renown by varying surprisingly little in the entire three rounds, the majority of the holes having been all taken at the same figure. The champion has carried off the great trophy a second time, in precisely the same number of strokes as that by which he achieved his hard worn victory of last year—a singular proof of the steadiness for which he has been uniformly distinguished. Nor is it the least gratifying feature of his success, that his professional brethren cheerfully and unreservedly acknowledge that it is richly merited. Locally, it is specially noteworthy that Mr Charles Hunter was only two strokes behind

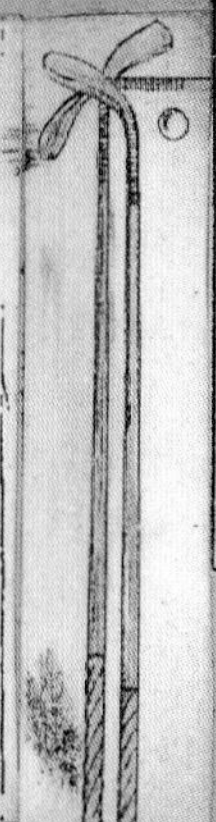

PRESTWICK GOLF CLUB.—The autumn meeting of this club took place on Wednesday last. Three new members were added to the roll; and the Earl of Eglinton was elected captain for the ensuing year, in room of Sir J. Hope Grant, who is abroad on foreign service. On Tuesday, the day previous to the general competition, as is usually the case, several matches came off. Col. Fairlie and Mr W. Park of Musselburgh pitted themselves against D. D. Cunnigham, Esq., and Tom Morris, in a "foursome," which resulted in favour of the latter pair. On Wednesday no fewer than ten couples started, amidst a drenching shower, for the Eglinton Gold Medal; and, after an exciting match, Col. Fairlie came in first, carrying off the medal by completing the two rounds in 134 strokes—Mr Gillon of Wallhouse being second in 147, and the Rev. Mr Pollock third. George Cunninghame, Esq. of Skeldon, won the first handicap sweepstakes, receiving 30 strokes of odds; and Major Phillips the second, receiving 28 strokes—the former making the creditable score of 149, and the latter following closely at 152.—On Thursday the Challenge Belt was competed for. Shortly after noon, four couples went off in the following order:—1st, Mr Charles Hunter and Mr James Knight; 2d, Mr J. F. Johnston and Tom Morris; 3d, William Park and William Dow; 4th, Rev. R. Pollock and Mr William Mitchell. After some brilliant driving, and an excellent game, the cards were handed in

The 1862 Challenge
I won by 13 shots

Shortly after the Earl was taken from us - a great loss to both Prestwick and St andrews. Report from Mr Balfour ↓

The late Lord Eglinton was a keen player at this, as at most other athletic sports. He was at St. Andrews in October 186~~1~~2 and on the day before the medal the weather was beautiful. He played three rounds with Mr. Grant of Kilgraston, Sir Francis Grant, and Mr. Little Gilmour. After Sir Hope and I had finished our match, he asked me to go out a few holes and walk in with his brothers and Lord Eglinton. We did so; his lordship was enjoying himself extremely. He expressed his delight with the scenery at the high hole—and indeed he frequently admired the whole landscape, as the descending sun lengthened our shadows on that October afternoon. He afterwards went out to Mount Melville to dinner. When coming away in the evening he complained to a friend, as they were passing through the library, that he had felt rather unwell in the drawing-room, but that he was now all right. When, however, he got to the hall, while the butler was helping him on with his great-coat, he fell down in a fit of apoplexy, was carried to a bedroom, never spoke again, and died two days after. As may be supposed, this cast a sad gloom over the gathering for the medal next day, this was one of my best matches ever against Willie over the 4 greens →

In 1862, Park once more challenged his old opponent to play another match over the four greens for £100—36 holes on each links, the winner of the greatest number of holes over all to be the victor—and the terms having been accepted with alacrity, arrangements were completed for commencing the contest on Friday, 21st November. Park having won the toss for choice of greens, naturally selected his own ground for the inauguration of the game.

At Musselburgh, Park gained the first round by one hole; Morris the second by two holes; Morris the third by two holes; and Park the fourth round by one, thus leaving Tom the victor by two out of the thirty-six played.

At Prestwick, on Tuesday the 25th, intense frost had transformed the velvet sponginess of the turf into an unyielding surface almost as hard as a Macadamised road, along which the balls danced to a distance, even when driven from the wrist, that excited the surprise of the onlookers and often the chagrin of the players. On the putting greens the grass was so crisp as to render the short game a matter of hap hazard, equally defiant of judgment and ingenuity. Morris made all the running; on the first twelve holes placing no fewer than three to his credit; and on the second twelve he succeeded in adding the same number to the score. Six a-head at the beginning of the final round was a remarkable run of good fortune, and a very unpleasant burden for his rival to carry with comfort. Here, however, Park appeared in his old colours. Of the first four holes going out for the last time he won three, and reduced the lead by a half. At this stage the memory of his antecedents in similar adverse circumstances on the same links changed the possible into the probable, and the knowing ones began to speculate upon the likelihood of his being able to retrieve himself by once more coming in at the death. But at the eighth the suspense was over, Tom being five in advance with only four to play. The next two were halved; the eleventh fell to the lot of Morris, and the twelfth to Park, who remained a winner of one hole on the third round, leaving him five behind on the day's performance.

At North Berwick, on Friday the 28th, the ground was covered with snow, but the umpire having decided that the play should proceed, the following was the result:—The first round Park was two holes up; the second Morris was three holes up; third round Morris five holes up; fourth round Morris three holes up—he being thus four holes in advance on the thirty-six.

At St Andrews, on Tuesday 2d Dec., Morris gained the first round by four holes, scoring 92 strokes against Park's 96. On the second round going out, the first hole was halved, and the second and third were won by Tom, thus finishing the match.

The following is the general abstract:—

	Holes.
Musselburgh, ...	2
Prestwick, ...	5
North Berwick, ...	4
St Andrews, ...	6
Majority for Morris, ...	17

According to the *Scotsman*, this "triumph is unparalleled in the annals of golfing, Tom having won on all the links, and by a heavier majority than ever fell to the lot of a golfer in such a match."

At the January dinner of the Prestwick St Nicholas Club, the Captain proposed the health of Tom Morris, congratulating him on his recent decisive victory over Park. In reply, Tom said "he would prefer playing Park to making a speech, for he was more at home on the links than in addressing a public company. With reference to the late contest for £100, he might use the freedom to repeat here what he had said in Edinburgh before it commenced, that, lose or win, it should be the last single he would undertake over four greens, as the training required inconvenienced him both personally and in his business. There was no disguising the fact that William Park was as good a golfer as ever lifted a club, and he was very glad that it was his great fortune to defeat such a formidable opponent on all the four greens."

OCTOBER, 1862.

Wm. Park encountered A. Strath, when Strath beat him by 6 and 4 to play. Wm. Dow defeated Bob Andrew by 4 holes. Wm. Park and Wm. Dow halved a round. Tom Morris and A. Strath played Wm. Park and Wm. Dow, and won by two holes.

Receipt for rent of Tom Morris House £5 —

22. Decr 1862

Ayr 22d Novr 1862

Received from Prestwick Golf Club by the hands of Charles Campbell their Treasurer Five pounds being half Year's rent to Martinmas 1862, and towards price of house in Prestwick occupied by Thomas Morris.

St. Andrews, 30*th Sept.* 1863.

His Royal Highness the PRINCE OF WALES having this day gained the SILVER CLUB (being represented by John Whyte-Melville, Esq., of Strathkinness), Mr. Whyte-Melville, in the name and at the special request of His Royal Highness, took the Chair as Captain of the Club.

£9-15/-

Thomas Morris

Quarter's Wages

12 Nov to 12 Feb 1863
1862.

Paid 12 Feby 1863

1863.

In April, Tom Morris gained a round by one hole against W. Dow, the scores being 55 and 59 respectively.

In September, A. Strath and David Park tested their merits over neutral Links. The former got so brisk a lead that he was 4 holes in advance of his opponent who, however, put on a spurt, collared, and passed; but Strath cleverly recovering his lost ground, came off the victor by 2 holes out of the 24, to the disappointment of those who laid 6 to 4 against him.

86

GOLF.—The St Andrews' May meeting was held on Wednesday when 19 couples competed. The Silver Cross, presented by Colonel Belshes in 1836, fell to Mr Gilbert M. Innes at 97 strokes. For the 2nd medal—presented by the Bombay Golfing Club in 1846—there were four ties, viz.:—Sir Thomas Moncrieffe, and Messrs A. Nicol, Hodge, and R. Clark—each notching 100. Another round was consequently played by these two couples, when the result was as under:—Mr Clark, 92; Sir Thomas Moncrieffe, 100; Mr Hodge, 100; Mr Nicol, (not known). Mr Clark accordingly won. There was a sweepstakes divided into two prizes, for which, as usual, odds were allowed, and which were gained by Sir Thomas Moncrieffe and Mr A. Nicol, both being equal. Perhaps, says the *Fifeshire Journal*, before the meeting, the only notable feat was done by Colonel Fairlie of Coodham, who tackled Sir Thomas Moncrieffe, and came in the last 9 holes at 40 strokes, there being a slight following wind. The only companion to this really remarkable score was that furnished by the late Allan Robertson, in his remarkable round with Mr Bethune of Blebo on 15th September, 1858, when he holed the Links at 79—going out at 40, and in at 39. It is immense play. Unfortunately, Colonel Fairlie had scarcely started on the medal round on Wednesday, when he gave himself a twist, which had the effect of putting him *hors de combat*. A very interesting single-handed match was played on Tuesday between Andrew Strath of St Andrews and David Park of Musselburgh—Strath beating his opponent by two holes in two rounds of the Links. William Dow, Musselburgh, desires us to say that he is ready to play William Park, whenever he likes and can get backers, over 4 greens. Dow thinks that Park has rather shuffled out of his last match with him, on the pretext that Prestwick was not to be one of the greens. He is willing, however, to make a new match. Tom Morris is presently at St Andrews; but we have not heard of any competitions in which the champion was engaged.

Ayr 12th February 1863.

Received from Charles Campbell Esq Treasurer of Prestwick Golf Club the Sum of Nine Pounds fifteen Shillings Sterling being wages due to me for the thirteen weeks from 12th November 1862 to 11th February 1863.

£9-15-Stg

Thomas Morris

1862

The ball was well attended, and, after supper, the Earl of Dalhousie proposed "The Hero of the Green, Col. Fairlie," in reference to which toast he remarked that Colonel Fairlie was the most distinguished golfer in Scotland, he being now decorated with three golf medals, which he had won in one year—first, Prestwick; second, North Berwick; and third, St Andrews. Colonel Fairlie replied.

GOLFING AT ST ANDREWS.—On Thursday week (says the *Fifeshire Journal*) a grand match, which had been made up on the day previous, was played, consisting of a foursome—Simpson Innes, Esq., and Tom Morris, against John Blackwood, Esq., and Andrew Strath, St. Andrews. The latter party gained the first round by two holes. On the second round they were again successful by a single 'put.' On Friday the grand match of Thursday was continued with Mr. Cathcart as colleague to Tom Morris, in place of Mr Simpson Innes. At the close these gentlemen were in advance of their opponents, John Blackwood, Esq., and Andrew Strath, by four with three holes to play. A fresh match gave the latter the advantage by one hole. Another match between Captain M'Whannell and Colonel Maitland Dougall, against Colonel J. O. Fairlie and Mr Gilbert Mitchell Innes, was twice played. The first round gave the victory to the first named couple by 4 holes with three to play. In the second round the victory lay with the latter pair by two holes. On Saturday Colonel Fairlie and Tom Morris beat Mr Gilbert Innes and Andrew Strath by one hole. Strath drove his tee stroke into the Burn coming in.

whereby her right arm was broken. She was [illegible] to the Royal Infirmary.

July 1863

ST ANDREWS.—*Golfing.*—Never in golfing history has such a number of gentlemen players appeared on the green and played, in any one day, as there were on Saturday. There were special parties from Edinburgh, Dundee, Perth, &c., irrespective of the numerous local, stationary, and erratic, and with Tom Morris, the champion, playing three rounds a-day in good matches, and generally successful, but none of them are champion brushes. Not fewer than about 300 gentlemen were playing. Included in this was the Madrid College competition, for which twelve couples started. The Silver Medal was gained by Mr Geo. Ballingall at 103. The Silver Cross, by Mr John M'Dougall, at 104. Sweepstakes—in playing for which odds were allowed—were gained by Mr H. Bruce.

Ayr Advertiser 30/4/1863

PRESTWICK GOLF CLUB.—On Wednesday evening week, a scurry stake, got up by a few gentlemen, was competed for by Tom Morris and W. Dow. A finer round has seldom been witnessed at Prestwick. At the close Morris was found to be victorious by one hole and four strokes, having made the round in 55 strokes, and Dow in 59 strokes.—On Thursday last a "foursome," between Colonel Fairlie and Tom Morris *v.* Mr G. M. Innes and W. Dow, came off at the links, and was a protracted one, consisting of 36 holes. The contest attracted a good many spectators. The Colonel and the Champion went off with the lead, being three a-head at the close of the first round, five a-head at the close of the second, and ultimately winning by three a-head and two to play.

87

1863

TOM MORRIS v. W. DOW.

Between five and six o'clock a scurry stake was got up by a number of the gentlemen, to be competed for by the two professionals, it being considerately arranged that the loser should get a fourth of the money. No sooner was the match mooted than the frequenters of the Links were on the *qui vive*, all being curious to know what stand the young aspirant could make against the champion. His play when coping with Park here at the autumn meeting, and his more recent challenge to the ex-champion, augured an interesting contest; and certainly the result did not belie these expectations. A finer round has seldom, if ever, been witnessed at Prestwick, the excitement of the onlookers being worked up to, and remaining at fever heat till nearly the close. Subjoined is the score:—

	MORRIS.	DOW.
1st hole,	6 strokes.	6 strokes.
2d "	5 "	5 "
3d "	4 "	4 "
4th "	7 "	7 "
5th "	6 "	5 "
6th "	4 "	6 "
7th "	4 "	4 "
8th "	2 "	4 "
9th "	5 "	5 "
10th "	4 "	4 "
11th "	2 "	4 "
12th "	6 "	5 "
	55	59

From the above return it will be seen that the start was almost unprecedented, the first four holes being halved. Dow succeeded in winning the fifth, an advantage that was soon lost by his having driven his ball from the tee into the bunker, known as "the pulpit;" and he never placed another hole to his credit until the one home, which was wrested from the champion, who came off victorious by one hole and four strokes. Tom's famed steadiness was again proved, 55 being his average round in such weather; but there can be no doubt that Dow has become a formidable player, for whom there are yet first-class laurels in store.

COLONEL FAIRLIE AND TOM MORRIS v. MR G. M. INNES AND DOW.

This foursome came off on Thursday, and was a protracted one, consisting of 36 holes. Fortunately, with the exception of one shower, there was no rain during the afternoon, although the wind was again high. The contest attracted a good few spectators, but on neither side was the play quite up to the standard of such excellent golfers. The Colonel and the champion went off with the lead, being three ahead at the close of the first round, and five ahead at the close of the second, and ultimately winning by three ahead and two to play. They should, however, have been more in advance, seeing that at one stage of the game they were not fewer than eight up. This disparity was cleverly reduced by Mr Innes and Dow, who pulled their opponents wonderfully, making a rush at the death too late to turn the tide of fortune.

PRESTWICK ST. NICHOLAS GOLF CLUB.

The annual meeting of this club was held on Saturday at noon, when the office-bearers were unanimously re-elected, the only change in the management being the substitution of Mr J. F. Johnston, Ayr, as a member of committee *vice* a gentleman who had in the interval removed to Glasgow. The accessions to the roll having been very numerous during the season, it was resolved to double the amount of the entry money, as well as the annual subscription; although it is thought that not even this pecuniary barrier will in the slightest degree affect the progressive prosperity of the club. About one o'clock the members repaired to the Links to compete for the medal presented by the late Earl of Eglinton, and for which nine couples started. Fortunately the weather proved most propitious, the ardent rays of a strong sun over-head being tempered by a refreshing breeze. By a singular coincidence the best of the teams made a very indifferent beginning; indeed, we doubt whether so many good players ever took so many strokes to the first hole out on a similar occasion. It is no disparagement to the majority of the competitors to say that the interest culminated in a contest between Messrs James Knight and Charles Hunter, who were the favourites at the start, both of them standing high among the most skilful amateurs in this part of the country. The latter went off with a creditable lead, and, so closely did rivals run each other that at the 23d or second last hole they were "all square." In going home Mr Hunter unluckily sent his tee shot into a whin, and his opponent holed out in a stroke less, taking 135 to the two rounds while Mr Hunter's score was 136. Everybody supposed that the medal had been won by Mr Knight, who had carried it off no fewer than twelve times, chiefly when it was competed for quarterly. But this expectation was disappointed in the first instance; Mr Wm. Reid, the successful candidate last July, having played such a very fine round that he had only a short "put," to bear away the honour of the day. Not holing out, however, his score reached 135 also; and there was no alternative left but to play a third round to determine who was to be the custodier of the medal. Mr Knight and Mr Reid accordingly again started amid considerable excitement on the part of the onlookers, the former getting the advantage at the commencement. When three holes from home there was only one stroke of difference, and in general estimation the match was now considered anybody's. But the next hole widened the distance, and ultimately Mr M'Knight added to his former laurels by completing the round at 66, his opponent scoring 70—thus winning by 4 strokes. The Club premiums presented by the captain, the secretary, and Messrs Knight Tom Morris, A. Crombie, Charles Hunter, J. Thomson, and W. Hunter were awarded as follows—1st prize a club, an iron and two balls to Mr A. Stuart, who scored 128, receiving 32 strokes of odds; 2d, two clubs and 1 ball to Mr J. Mackay who scored 132, receiving 24; 3d, an iron and 1 ball to Mr Ruthven Campbell Todd, who scored 133 receiving 30; 4th, a niblock and 1 ball to Mr Wm. Reid, who scored 135 with no odds; 5th, a club to Mr Charles Hunter who scored 136 with no odds; and 6th, 3 balls to Mr [illegible] Hutchison who scored 137, receiving 32 strokes of odds. It must be admitted that these figures are very high for the summer competition, but they are easily accounted for by the state of the green, which was anything but favourable to a scientific display of science, at the quarter game many well-designed shots in approaching the hole being somewhat wild in consequence of the hardness and keenness of the ground.

At five o'clock about 25 of the members of the club and their friends dined together in the Red Lion Inn under the presidency of the captain; Gordon Smith, Esq., Glasgow, officiating as croupier. The healths of the medal-holder, of Tom Morris, the champion; and of the officebearers of th club, and of the new members were cordially pledged among other appropriate toasts, and the evening was very pleasantly spent. After dinner, which reflected great credit on Mr and Mrs Hunter, a foursome was played in which the winners made the round at 65; and on Monday the medal holder's score in a private match was 58. An interesting single has been arranged for this day week between a distinguished member of one of the Edinburgh clubs, and a representative of the St Nicholas, the latter having accepted a challenge to have their respective powers tested. An exciting match may accordingly be expected.

ST ANDREWS. 1863

OCTOBER MEETING OF THE ST ANDREWS ROYAL AND ANCIENT GOLF CLUB.

The meeting of the St Andrews Royal and Ancient Golf Club was held in the Club-House yesterday forenoon at eleven o'clock for despatch of business. The Earl of Dalhousie was elected Captain of the Club for the ensuing year; and the following new members were admitted by ballot:—

A. B. Maccallum, Esq., Edinburgh; James Gibson Thomson, Esq., Edinburgh; William Wallace, Esq. of Auchenvale, Kilsyth, Dumbartonshire; Major G. A. St P. Fooks, St Andrews; Robert Lee, Esq., advocate, Edinburgh; A. C. Sellar, Esq., advocate, Edinburgh; John Jamieson, Esq., Kingask; David Pitcairn, Esq.; Alexander Balmain, Esq.; and John Smith, Esq., Chelton Lodge, Hungerford. After the meeting, the King William IV. Gold Medal and the Club's Gold Medal were competed for over the links.

The weather being fine, though a good stiff breeze was blowing, a large assemblage of ladies and gentlemen congregated on the green in front of the Club-House to witness the commencement of the competition, and amongst those present we observed the following ladies:—Mrs General Moncrieff; Misses Moncrieff; Mrs Captain Skipwith; Mrs Wemyss, Wemyss Castle; Mrs Dean and Miss Dean; Miss Tribe; Miss Thomson, Charleton; Mrs Dr Tulloch; Miss Tulloch; Mrs Colonel Maitland; Mrs Colonel Hunter; Mrs Dr Alexander; Mrs Methven; Misses Hodge; Misses Broughton; Misses Wemyss of Denbrae; Mrs and Misses Burn; Mrs Ferrier and Miss E. Ferrier; Mrs R. Mitchell; Mrs Bruce

BALL OF THE ROYAL AND ANCIENT GOLF CLUB OF ST ANDREWS.

—This annual assemblage came off in the Town Hall, St Andrews, on Thursday evening, and, as was anticipated, was a brilliant success in every sense of the word. The exterior of the hall was partially illuminated; the turretted gables fronting both Queen and South Streets being lighted up with numerous *padelles*, while in the centre of the spire was displayed a beautiful illuminated crown. The interior of the large hall was under the superintendence of Mr William Thomson, upholsterer, and was decorated in a style far surpassing former years. At the south end was a splendid transparency, showing in the centre the arms of the Prince of Wales, Captain of the Club, with the initials A. E. Below the arms were the silver clubs and balls belonging to the institutions, with a banner festoon. A similar festoon was displayed above, and the whole surmounted by a Prince of Wales Feather. On each side of the device was a Brunswick Star formed of swords and bayonets. At the opposite end hung the royal standard, in the centre of which was a splendid Danish star, formed of swords, bayonets, and rods. Colonel and Misses Moncreiffe—son and daughters of the General—contributed not a little to the success of the decorations. The company began to arrive about ten P.M., and dancing was begun before eleven. There never has been witnessed in connection with the Club such an assemblage of rank and fashion. The following ladies and gentlemen were present:—

The Hon. Mrs Cheape, Lalberken; Mr and Mrs Wedderburn, Birkhill; Mr and Miss Raith, Arniston; Miss Clark Rattray, Mr Clark Rattray, 92d Highlanders, Mr Stark Christie of Ballindean, Mrs and Miss Deane, Mr and Mr R. Deane, Mr and Mrs Birners, Mr and Miss Kinloch of Killrie, W. P. Adam, Esq., M.P., and Lady; F. H. Erskine Wemyss, Esq., M.P., and Lady; Lady Augustus Fitzclarence, Misses Fitzclarence, Captain and Mrs Goff, Mr Wallace of Auchinvole, Rev. A. Hill; Mrs and Miss Wright, Edinburgh; Mr William Reid, Mr and Mrs Graham Johnstone, Lieutenant-Colonel Moncreiff, Mr Henry Moncreiff, Mrs Stewart, General Richardson, Hon. E. Somerville, Hon. L. Somerville, Miss Wombwell, Mr R. B. Stewart, Dr Fork, Mr Ogilvy, Inchewen; Mrs Forbes, Misses H. and L. Granville, Mr Warburton, Mr and Mrs Bruce Jardyne of Middleton, Mr McGregor, Colonel Anderson, John Grant, Esq., of Kilgraston; and Misses Grant, L. R. Lumsdaine, Esq., of Leethallan; Mrs and Miss Ferrier, Mr John Ferrier, Mr Burnett, Mr Mrs and Miss Burn, Messrs Henry and D. B. Burn, Miss Leighton, Dr Adamson, Mr Stuart Grace, Sir John Richardson, Mr E. D. Smith, Mr Mrs and Miss Wildman, Mr G. Thomson or Burnhouse, Mr E. A. Hunter, Ayr; Mr and Miss Champion, Mr and Mrs Seton Stewart, Mrs Dunsmore, Captain Steih, John Whyte Melville, Esq. (acting captain of the Club); Right Honourable the Lord Advocate, General Sir John and Lady Low, Sir John and Lady Lindsey Bethune, Miss Low, Miss Selina Low, Miss Thackeray, Colonel W. Low, Lieutenant-Colonel Brown, General, Mrs, and Miss Moncreiff; Colonel Moncreiff, Fusileer Guards; Mr and Mrs Harrington Balfour, Sir George and Misses Grant Suttie, General and Mrs Christie, Major, Mrs, and Miss Boothby; Mrs Boothby, senr.; Provost Milton, Mr James and Mrs Farmer, Auckland, New Zealand; Mr F. Sprutt, late of R.H.A., and Mrs Sprutt, London; Miss Ayton, Tuchdownie; Mr R. F. T. and Miss Campbel, Craigie; Captain E. M. and Mrs Playfair, Captain and Mrs Lindsay, Miss Lindsay Carnegie, Miss Christie, Miss H. Cook; Miss Alexander, Mr Harry Edwards, London; Mr R. H. Playfair, John L. Arnall, Esq. of Foodie; Mr Inglis, Redhall; Mrs and Miss Chalmers, Oldbar; Mrs Govan, General and Miss Campbell, Mrs Fischer, Miss Ferguson, Mr James Stewart, Trinity College Cambridge; Dr Baird, Airston; Mr Whigham, Colonel Campbell, Mr and Mrs Wolfe Murray of Cringletie, Mr and Mrs Blackwood, Mrs Skene, Pitlour; Mr James Blackwood, Major Archibald Blackwood, Mr William Blackwood, Mr Charles Tennant, George Cheape, Esq.; Mr Wauchope, Mr Jackson, Miss Aytoun, Miss Lyon, Mr and Mrs Gardyne, Mr D. Gardyne, Captain Buckle, Mr Muir, Mr Ogilvy, Mr and Mrs Robert Mitchell, Miss Tribe, Miss Ochterlonie, Captain and Mrs Skipwith, Mr W. Horsburgh, Misses Lindsay, Balmingo;

1863
failed to win the Belt for a 3rd time

PRESTWICK GOLF CLUB.

The annual autumn meeting of this Club took place on Thursday last. Unfortunately, the weather was very unpropitious, fitful breezes blowing across the links during the greater part of the day, and rendering the play very uncertain. At noon the usual business meeting was held under the presidency of Major W. F. Hamilton, M.P., when, on the motion of Dr Sloan, Andrew Gillon, Esq., of Wallhouse, was unanimously elected to succeed the Earl of Eglinton as Captain of the Club for the ensuing year. A few gentlemen were then admitted members of the club. Afterwards, the members repaired to the links to compete for the Eglinton Gold Medal, for which fifteen gentlemen had paired off, and which was won by Robert Clark, Esq., Edinburgh, who completed the two rounds in 120 strokes—the fewest number, we believe, in which the October medal was ever won. The sweepstakes was gained by Mr Hugh Hamilton, Sundrum, who was handicapped at 45 strokes of odds. A number of private foursomes and single games were also contested during the day.

On Friday the competition for the Challenge Belt took place, when seven pairs started—the largest field that ever competed for the belt, and it is to be regretted that the day was so unfavourable for the contest. After the three rounds had been completed, the following was found to be the result—the four at the top winning respectively the Belt, £5, £3, £2:—

1.	Wm. Park, ...	168
2.	Tom Morris, ...	170
3.	David Park, ...	172
4.	Andrew Strath, ...	174
5.	G. D. Brown, ...	176
6.	Robert Andrew, ...	178
7.	Mr C. Hunter, ...	184
8.	Mr Knight, ...	190
9.	Mr Miller, ...	192
Tied.	Mr Johnstone, ...	197
	Mr Chalmers, ...	197
	James Paxton, ...	197
13.	Mr Mitchell, ...	206
14.	Mr Moffat, ...	233

It will thus be seen that Wm. Park has succeeded in carrying off the prize from his former successful rival, Tom Morris, who had won the Belt two years in succession, and who would have been entitled to retain it permanently in his possession had he been fortunate enough to come off victorious on this occasion. Several games of minor interest were played during the afternoon and on Saturday.

Sept 1863

Self and Mr Innes v Mr Blackwood and Andrew

A capital foursome was played betwixt Mr Norman Mitchell Innes and Tom Morris against Mr John Blackwood and Andrew Strath—all equal at the close of the round.

Major Boothby and Mr Hodge had a tough single, which was gained by the Major by two holes. Colonel Maitland Dougal played a good single with James Anderson, jun., a rising professional. The Colonel gained by a single put.

The bulk of the matches came off early in the day to make way for the grand champion match formerly arranged. For some reason William Park returned to Musselburgh on Friday evening, but the gentlemen accepted William Dow in his place, so that the match stood Tom Morris and Andrew Strath against David Park and William Dow. At the close of the first round, Morris and Strath were two holes ahead, having gone the round at ninety-one, their opponents being ninety-five. An immense crowd followed up the second heat, which was taken by Morris and Strath by seven holes, with six to play. These were played out, and resulted one hole in favour of Morris and Strath. The second round was gone by the winners in eighty-eight, the best score of the meeting; the others were again ninety-five. With Saturday's proceedings the May meeting is generally looked upon as having been closed.

The most exciting match of the season came on Thursday between four of the best professional golfers of the day,—viz., Tom Morris of Prestwick, and Andrew Strath, St Andrews, against the brothers William and David Park, Musselburgh. The match was got up by several gentlemen at the May meeting, and heavy bets were staked on both sides—the favourites being Morris and Strath, as much as six to four, and in some instances three to one, being offered and taken.

Shortly after eleven o'clock they struck off, and on going the first round Morris and Strath came in two holes ahead, both parties having gone the round in 88 and 89 strokes—Tom and Strath going out in 46 and coming in at 42; the Parks going out in 47 and in at 42. After a short refreshment, they again struck off. Morris and partner took the burn hole, making them three ahead; the next hole was halved; they also gained another hole upon the next two, which made them four holes ahead; but, at the hole across, their propitious stars began to wane—Tom chanced to miss a short putt, and the hole was lost. From this point the Parks shot rapidly ahead—taking the next eight holes running!—and on coming in were dormy at the fourth hole. Morris and Strath took the next hole, but the Parks took the one following—thus winning the match by four. At the corner of the dyke hole, they played in the two remaining holes—the brothers gaining these also—thus making them victors by six holes on the two rounds of 36 holes.

We understand that the same match is to be played on Saturday. It may be remarked that the day was beautiful, and the green in excellent condition, with no wind to interfere with the play. A large concourse of spectators followed the players both rounds. The scores of the second round were For the Parks, 45 out and 40 in—total, 85; Tom and Strath, 46 out and 49 in—total, 95.

Self and Andrew v Parks

The Red Lion where the Prestwick members dined

AYR.

Golfing at Prestwick.—The annual meeting of the Prestwick Golf Club took place on Thursday, when Andrew Gillon, Esq. of Wallhouse, was unanimously elected captain of the club for the ensuing year, in room of the Earl of Eglinton and Winton. The competition for the gold medal was gained by Robert Clark, Esq., Edinburgh, who completed the two rounds in 120 strokes. On Friday, seven pairs started for the champion's belt. It had been won for the past two years by Tom Morris, of Prestwick; and had he been successful at this competition, it was to become his own property. He was, of course, the favourite, but he was unlucky at starting, and never made up the lost ground. The consequence was, that he was defeated by two holes, by his old opponent, William Park, of Musselburgh. There was a large turn-out of professionals at this competition. The club was very unfortunate in so far as the weather was concerned, wind and rain being prevalent during the whole week.

21 Sept 1863

89 Perth Tournament for a week

April

THE GOLF TOURNAMENT. 1864

The past week will be a memorable one in the golfing annals of Perth. The grand tournament, for which arrangements had been making for some time previous, was opened on Tuesday. And, if the successful issue of any event can reflect credit on its promoters, certainly we must congratulate the gentlemen who projected and arranged this great competition on the result of their exertions. It has indeed been a great success. And by that success they cannot but feel in a great measure rewarded for the great trouble which they must have had. We believe to Mr Hay Robertson, captain of King James VI. Club, the community is largely, if not mostly indebted for the great feast of golfing. The weather was everything that could be desired; the green was in excellent order; and the play proved altogether first-rate. There was an unprecedentedly large number of crack professional players present, including Morris of Prestwick, the two Parks and Dow of Musselburgh, Brown and the two Straths of St Andrews, Morris of Carnoustie, Keddie of Leven, our own local champion Andrews, as well as McDonald and McPherson (the Herd Laddie) of Perth. Large crowds of intently interested and evidently highly gratified spectators accompanied the players. Among the gentlemen present we observed, Lord Dupplin, Sir Thomas Moncreiffe, W. Macdonald Macdonald, Esq. of St Martins; the Hon. John Rollo; James Condie, Esq.; Wm. Marshall, Esq. of Luncarty; George Condie, Esq., Frank Sandeman, Esq.; Archibald Turnbull, Esq. of Bellwood, &c.

The competition on Tuesday was for the professional players. The game was three rounds of twelve holes each. The prizes were, first, £10, second, £5, third, £3. Exactly at eleven fourteen couples started, including several of the gentlemen who were to play next day. The following are the scores:—

	1st.	2nd.	3rd.	Tot.
Morris, Prestwick,	57	57	54	168
W. Park, Musselburgh, ...	55	56	57	168
Andrews, Perth, ...	54	58	58	170
D. Park, Musselburgh,	57	62	51	170
Dow, Musselburgh,	57	59	57	173
Brown, St Andrews, ...	54	53	68	175
A. Strath, St Andrews,	58	57	62	177
Major Boothby,	57	60	62	179
Mr Marshall, Leven, ...	60	61	63	184
Mr Alexander, Perth,	64	57	63	184
Mr Charles Hunter, Prestwick,	57	62	65	184
Mr William Stewart of Perth, ...	58	65	63	186
W. Strath, St Andrews, ...	60	62	65	187
N. McPherson (the Herd Laddie),	64	63	63	190
Sergt.-Major Chalmers, Perth, ...	62	60	68	190
Mr Robert M'Gregor, Perth, ...	59	62	69	190
Mr N. Carse, ...	64	59	67	190

The remaining gentlemen came in with scores above 190, and stood, we believe, on the list very much in in the following order:—

Mr Robert Blair, Perth, } equal.
McDonald, Perth, }
Keddie, Leven,
Morris, Carnoustie,
Mr Hay Robertson, Perth.

The play was altogether very beautiful. The closeness of the figures shows its steadiness and precision. Of Morris and Park it is unnecessary to speak. Their play is well known, and their scores show how steady they were even upon strange ground. In regard to Brown and Andrews, however, a word of explanation is necessary. At the end of the second round it will be seen that Brown was winner by considerable odds, but at the outset of the third round something crossed his path which seemed to fret him, and so, loosing patience, lost his game. Brown is a beautiful player, and if he could command himself as he commands his club, he might be safely reckoned on for any match. Andrews, again, played, upon the whole, very like himself. His high scores in the second and third rounds were entirely attributable to misfortunes in a single hole in each. In the second round he lost as many as four or five at one hole. A similar catastrophe befel him in the third. He regained his laurels, however, in playing off his tie. But for these unfortunate occurrences he would have distanced all his competitors, as he ought to have done, and had the first prize by large odds. He seems to want nerve or confidence in himself for high pressure competition. In ordinary practice he takes the round almost as often at 50 strokes as any other number.

At the close of the competition, a very pretty match of one round was played between W. Park and Dow, which resulted in favour of the former by seven holes.

Tommy's first mention aged 13

Another match of great interest was Morris and Park against Andrews and A. Strath. The weight of this contest of cou[illegible] lay on the one part upon Andrews, who, althou[illegible] very well supported upon the whole by Strath, still suffered a little by the connection. The match was capitally played, however, and was well [illegible]ped. The last hole gave it in favour of Andrews [illegible] Strath.

But perhaps the most interesting match of the day was between Master Morris, son of the redoubtable "Tom," and Master W[illegible] Greig of, as it seems, Perth juvenile golfing celebrity. They are really wonderful players for their years, both of them. We had no idea that the young Perth could produce so proficient a golfer in Master Greig. He played with astonishing neatness and precision, but the honours of the day were in store for his competitor. Master Morris seems to have been both born and bred to golf. He has been cast in the very mould of a golfer, and plays with all the steadiness and certainty, in embryo, of his father. The juvenile competition was extremely interesting, and although the young Prestwicker gained the day, Perth has the very opposite of any reason to be ashamed of her youthful champion. ...

There were more folk ↖ watchin the boys' match than the tournament itself – "Master Morris seems to have been both born and bred to golf" – never a truer word spoken

The Wednesday I won again this time in yet another head to head with Willie

ROYAL AND ANCIENT GOLF CLUB OF ST ANDREWS.

May — 1864

SATURDAY'S PROCEEDINGS.

The weather to-day turned out remarkably well, but strong sunshine and a stiffer breeze from the northwest caused the play to be a little wider.

A grand champion single match began the day's proceedings, the competitors being Wm. Dow, of Musselburgh; and Bob Andrews, Perth. The two rounds of the Links were executed in two and a-half hours, not much over the usual time taken for one foursome. Both of the players were in excellent trim, but Dow managed to get a run of the first six holes and kept his vantage ground. The next two holes were halved, and Andrews gained the ninth. The players started, to return with three holes in favour of Dow. On starting the second round, Andrews took the first two holes, reducing his loss to three—and again the match turned in with five for Dow. At the third hole in, Dow was "dormy" at six, the next hole was halved, and thus "dormy" still—the next, or "Singer beer hole," was halved, and this decided the match, Dow being victor by five holes with four to play. The first round was taken at eighty-nine and ninety-four strokes—the second was not played out.

A capital foursome was played betwixt Mr Norman Mitchell Innes and Tom Morris against Mr John Blackwood and Andrew Strath—all equal at the close of the round.

Major Boothby and Mr Hodge had a tough single, which was gained by the Major by two holes. Colonel Maitland Dougal played a good single with James Anderson, jun., a rising professional. The Colonel gained by a single put.

The bulk of the matches came off early in the day to make way for the grand champion match formerly arranged. For some reason William Park returned to Musselburgh on Friday evening, but the gentlemen accepted William Dow in his place, so that the match stood Tom Morris and Andrew Strath against David Park and William Dow. At the close of the first round, Morris and Strath were two holes ahead, having gone the round at ninety-one, their opponents being ninety-five. An immense crowd followed up the second heat, which was taken by Morris and Strath by seven holes, with six to play. These were played out, and resulted one hole in favour of Morris and Strath. The second round was gone by the winners in eighty-eight, the best score of the meeting; the others were again ninety-five. With Saturday's proceedings the May meeting is generally looked upon as having been closed.

ROYAL AND ANCIENT GOLF CLUB.

AUTUMN MEETING. 1864

Yesterday was a great occasion on the Links of St Andrews. A stranger coming by the mid-day train to the "Ancient City" might have been sadly puzzled to understand why there should have been so many fair ladies and gallant gentlemen promenading on the grounds immediately in front of the Union Club House, and forming an assembly which, for beauty and fashion, would even have graced the Champs Elyséo themselves. It could not be a military display which occasioned the turn out; for though the red tunics might have suggested that, there was no regularly drawn-up body in soldier array in the field, and though they had *balls* and *clubs* in abundance—both emblems of war, the one of civilised and the other barbarian—the weapons of their strife were tokens rather of the blessings of peace than of warfare. What, then, could be the cause of all the pleasant excitement which animated every countenance, and was the all-absorbing topic of conversation? If the uninitiated, as he neared the centre of operations, had not learned that this was the great Autumn Gathering of golfers from far and near, to compete for the Royal and other honours in possession of the Club, his perplexity might have been set at rest as soon as he was able to decipher the beautiful figures adorning the new flag which waved from the top of the flagstaff. It was divided into quarters, the first containing the "Union;" the second, the "Royal Crown;" the third, the patron saint, "St Andrew on the Cross;" and the fourth, the "golfing arms"—the cross, clubs, and balls; the whole design being admirably adapted to indicate the nature of the proceedings. The weather—which is always an important consideration in a good day's game at golf—was really delightful. There was a refreshing breeze from the west, but so gentle as not to affect the driving of the ball, and though the sun smiled upon the smooth green surface of the Links, the rays were not by any means so strong as in any way to incommode the golfer's vision. There are few out-door pastimes—indeed we don't know that there are any, with the exception of angling—where those who engage in them are so fastidious about atmospheric conditions; yet the weather yesterday was everything that the keenest and most particular golfer could wish. The grass, too, from the fine weather of Monday and Tuesday, was in capital condition, being neither too keen nor too stiff—in fact, the field altogether was such as to give scope for the greatest skill and the most unbiased play. On no previous gathering do we remember seeing so many golfers forward. Last year twenty-six couples entered the competition, and that was considered a large number, but this year it was much larger, there being no less than thirty-two couples on the lists. As with the players, so with the onlookers. They are yearly increasing. Indeed these competitions form the occasion for one of the best exhibitions of the *beaux mondes* to be witnessed in this fashionable city, and in no former season have so many of the *élite* of our society turned out to see the start.

professional players on the ground were, Tom Morris, David Park, Musselburgh; and Andrew Strath, St Andrews.

At eleven o'clock, a meeting was held in the Union Club House, for the despatch of business and arranging for the match. J. Whyte Melville, Esq. of Bennochy and Strathkinness, presided in the absence of the Prince of Wales, the retiring Captain. Viscount Duplin, was unanimously elected Captain for the ensuing year;

THE LATE GOLF TOURNAMENT—PHOTOGRAPH OF THE PROFESSIONALS.—We have before us a photograph of the professional golfers who took part in the tournament here last week. It was done by Mr. Henderson, photographer, Marshall Place, and is a very fine specimen of his art. There are eleven figures in the group, all of them as natural as when they trode the North Inch the other day. It is one of the best specimens of photography we have seen in Perth.

St. Andrews, 4th May 1864.

Major Boothby moved, That Tom Morris of Prestwick, formerly of St. Andrews, be brought here as a professional Golfer, at a salary of Fifty pounds a year, on the understanding that he shall have the entire charge of the Golf Course under the Green Committee.

Colonel Campbell the Secretary at Prestwick looked after me well through those 13 years

91

The Challenge Belt
↓ my 3rd win

PRESTWICK GOLF CLUB.—The annual autumn meeting of this Club was held on Thursday last, when Lord David Kennedy was unanimously elected Captain. Twenty-two competitors started for the medal contest, when Major Phillips came in the winner with 133 strokes. The Major likewise carried off the sweepstakes. The match among the professionals for the Challenge Belt took place on Friday, and excited, as usual, no small degree of interest. Some fine golfing was displayed, and at the close, the game stood as follows :—

1st Prize, the Belt and £6	Tom Morris	167
2d Prize, £5	A. Strath	169
3d Prize, £3	R. Andrew	175
4th Prize	W. Park	117
5th Prize	W. Dow	181
6th Prize	W. Strath	182

The office of keeper of the links having become vacant on account of the resignation of Tom Morris —who is removing to St. Andrews, and who has done much to establish this favourite and scientific game in Ayrshire—it became necessary to appoint a successor, when Mr Charles Hunter, Prestwick, was the successful candidate, A. Strath being only six votes below him.

MAY, 1864.

Wm. Park defeated Wm. Dow by one hole on two rounds. Wm. Dow beat Bob Andrew by 5 holes. Tom Morris and A. Strath were successful against David Park and Wm. Dow in a match of two rounds by 7 holes.

In May, 1865, A. Strath and W. Dow tackled Tom Morris and Wm. Park, when the latter were vanquished by 3 holes a-head and one to play. [It is somewhat singular that the two professionals, between whom the Championship lay so long, have never been successful when associated together in a foursome against any of their brethren.]

Mr W. C. Thomson was thus declared winner of the Belshes' Cross, being the first honour; and Major Boothby having unintentionally infringed the rules of the game at a "hazard playing" at the "high hole," Mr Gilbert Mitchell Innes was declared winner of the Bombay Medal.

The sweepstakes, divided into two prizes, and for which, as usual, odds were allowed, were gained respectively by Professor Heddle, St Andrews, and Mr Richardson, Edinburgh.

The members of the club dined together in the club-house at half-past six o'clock—John Whyte Melville, Esq., occupying the chair.

Of "professional" players present at this gathering, besides the St Andrews ones, were Tom Morris, of Prestwick (the champion), William and David Park, and William Dow, of Musselburgh, and Bob Andrews, of Perth.

The matches during the week are expected to be numerous and of a very exciting character. On Tuesday, a good single-handed was played between William Park and William Dow, of Musselburgh. The first match, a round of the Links, was halved; and in a second, also of a round, Park beat his opponent by one hole. In two rounds of a "foursome," between Mr Hodge and Tom Morris against Mr Gilbert Mitchell Innes and Andrew Strath (of St Andrews), the first was halved, and the second gained by the first named couple by one hole. Mr G. M. Innes and Tom also played a round against Mr Hodge and Bob Andrews, and were victorious by five holes and three to play.

Of the matches to come to-day, one, a single-handed between Dow of Musselburgh and Andrews of Perth, has been arranged, and, from the money depending on it, promises to create much interest. An old favourite foursome, in fact *the* expected match of the week, is also arranged, with heavy bets, between Tom Morris of Prestwick and Andrew Strath of St Andrews against William and David Park of Musselburgh.

Between the close of the competition for the honours and the hour of dinner yesterday afternoon, several good foursomes were played, the most noticeable being a renewal of the match of the former day between Mr Hodge and Tom Morris against Mr Gilbert Mitchell Innes and Andrew Strath. The first named couple were victors by two holes and one to play.

The silver cross of the Club was therefore won by Mr Thomson, who performed the round in 95 strokes, a very creditable score. Last year at the same match, the champion score, made by Mr Clark, was 92 strokes, but this was in a second round to decide a tie, and the medal fell to Mr Gilbert Mitchell Innes at 97, Mr Clark and three other gentlemen being second in a tie of 100. The playing on this occasion was therefore fully equal to last year. The silver medal presented by the Bombay Golfing Club in 1846, would in due course have been won by Major Boothby, but his score was called in question, on the allegation that he had not complied with one of the rules. Major Boothby has since withdrawn his claim to the medal, and it falls to Mr G. M. Innes with 101 strokes. The point in dispute also affected the scores of other players, and among the rest, that of Mr Morrison, of Cupar, whom we have quoted at 112 strokes. One of the rules the Club provides in the following words 'that should a ball be driven into the river Eden at the high hole, or the sea at the first hole, the ball must be placed a club length in front of either sea or river, losing a stroke.' The balls of Major Boothby and of Mr Morrison, among others, went over the bank among the loose sand at the 'high hole.' The Major teed his ball at the front of the bank, thereby escaping the difficulties of extrication. Mr Morrison, on the contrary, played his ball out of the sand at fifteen strokes, so that had he taken the same advantage as Major Boothby he must have stood among the lowest in the notching. The sweepstakes (with odds), were won by Professor Bell, first; and Mr Richardson, second.

On Tuesday, the day previous to the meeting, some private matches were played. Mr Gilbert Mitchell Innes with Tom Morris, and Mr Hodge with Bob Andrews, went over the ground, when Mr Innes and Tom gained by five holes. A second match was then played—Mr Innes and Andrew Strath against Mr Hodge and Tom Morris. In the first encounter the players came in equal, and on a second round, Mr Hodge and Tom gained by a single *put*—or by one hole. Another match was played immediately after the conclusion of the medal contest on Wednesday—Mr Innes and Strath again opposing Mr Hodge and Morris. This match attracted considerable interest, and was followed by a large party of onlookers. In going out, Mr Hodge and Morris got four ahead of their opponents, but lost three about mid-game. In coming in, they made another hole, however, and the match was finished with Mr Hodge and Morris two holes ahead and one to play.

FAREWELL DINNER AT PRESTWICK IN HONOUR OF TOM MORRIS

Tom Morris, the well known custodier of Prestwick Links, being about to transfer his services in a similar capacity to the Royal and Ancient Golf Club of St Andrews, our local players, whom he has put under so many obligations, and other personal friends, resolved that the Champion should not be permitted to leave the district without some parting demonstration of respect. Arrangements were accordingly made for a public dinner in his honour, and the entertainment took place in the Burgh Council room on Saturday afternoon. Covers were laid for fifty. The chair was taken at 5 o'clock by Mr R.H. Smith, Captain of the St Nicholas Club – Baillie Gondie, Mr Prayne and Mr Gordon Smith, Glasgow, officiating as croupiers.

The chairman, in proposing the toast of the evening, after some preliminary remark, said it was now nearly fourteen years since golf was introduced to the West of Scotland by the late lamented Lord Eglinton and Colonel Fairlie of Coodham, who, recognising the rare facilities afforded for its prosecution, leased the lands adjoining the beach, and established the Prestwick Club. But not even the weight of the deservedly great influence, the force of the good example, or the advantageous connection of its promoters, could have crowned the scheme with success unless they had the forethought to secure the services of a professional pioneer. (Cheers.) That professional pioneer was Tom Morris, whom they had known and respected both as a man and a golfer at St Andrews. Already a player of distinction, and the favourite pupil of the late Allan Robertson, whose memory was revered as the father of modern golf, the selection then made was most judicious; and the links were a monument of invaluable aid which the guest had rendered in laying out the ground, which for compactness and variety of hazards was admitted to be unsurpassed throughout Scotland. (Cheers.) It was no exaggeration to say that the day of his departure would be a dark day for Prestwick; yet why should they repine if his fortunes were to be bettered and his labours lightened? Prestwick, it was true, was the birthplace of his children, the centre of the firmest friendships he had ever formed, and the garden of his golfing renown.

They should also remember that the ties of an earlier and stronger affection drew him Fife-wards to re-settle in his native county at St Andrews, known over the world as the headquarters of the grand old national pastime whose interests he had done so much to advance. Reluctantly and regretfully though they bade him farewell, nonetheless heartily would they wish him good speed; and they earnestly hoped that his luck would be brightened by every blessing which could make man happy. (Cheers.) And for Prestwick, their golfing *alma mater*, was there not a word of sympathy due in prospect of the heavy loss she was about to sustain, by being bereft of her founder and builder, her stay, her help, an her shield? Surely the least dutiful of her many loyal sons would say – peace be upon her Links, and prosperity either in or out her bunkers. (Laughter.) Health, long life and continued success to Tom Morris, with all the honours. (Loud cheers.) (The toast was pledged with every demonstration of enthusiasm)

Tom Morris on rising to reply, was greeted with repeated rounds of cheering, the waving of handkerchiefs, &c. He said the chairman, by the manner in which he had spoken of him, and the company, the way in which they had drunk the toast, had fairly put him in to the bottom of the "Cardinal"; and he was lying so deep that he was afraid his 'niblock' would not be able to get him out. (Cheers and laughter.) He would try and do his best, however, to thank them all for the honour they had done him. It was a proud thing for him to see so many gentlemen from the village and from a distance coming forward that night to wish him well before his removal to St Andrews. He was not sure that he had done anything to deserve such a mark of respect; and he took little credit to himself for doing all in his power to make the game take in this quarter. That was no more than his duty, placed there as he had been; but it has always been his study to consult the comfort of everybody who came out to the Links. (Cheers.) He had succeeded in pleasing his patrons, as he thought that meeting had proved, he had done all he had worked for during the thirteen years he had lived in Prestwick. When he first came to the village he was dull enough, for there was very little play, and he thought he had made a mistake in accepting the situation. But bye and bye one after another of his neighbours were tempted to try their hands, gentlemen came out from Ayr, and they with the visitors at Eglinton Castle and Coodham gave the game a good start, and kept him pretty busy. Within the past few years it had made great progress, and now it was both well liked and extensively practiced. He had the satisfaction, therefore, of leaving the district when golf had risen into a favourite amusement with all classes. (Cheers.) From both Clubs he had always received the greatest kindness, and particularly from his old master, Colonel Fairlie, who had done a great deal for the game and who, they would be glad to learn, had re-appeared on the Links on Friday, in good health and in first-rate play. (Cheers.) Nothing would give him greater pleasure than to hear that they were prospering in his absence; for although he would no longer be going in and out among the members, he would always take an interest in their welfare. He had spent many happy days in Prestwick, and he left it with regret, for he had much to be thankful for in his connection with the many friends he had made since he came to the west a total strange; and he would always be glad to return, as often as he could, to see those who had shown him so much kindness. (Cheers.) His feelings would not allow him to say more, because he was never a good speaker at any time; and if they would take the will for the deed, he would again offer them his best thanks for the honour they had paid him, an honour which he would never forget. (Loud cheers.)

One of the most memorable nights I ever had – and very satisfyin, after all that work knocking the course into shape – even being known as "Prestwick Tom" – I'll miss the setting sun and the walk along the beach with the dogs.

93 Many of the St Andrews members played in this match 1864

GOLF MATCH AT NORTHAM BURROWS.—The game of golf was introduced into the west of England in 1864 by some gentlemen in the north of Devon who saw the advantages of Northam Burrows as admirably adapted for "links" on which to play the noble game. A club, consisting of fifty gentlemen, was formed at that time, and the game has been prosecuted with vigour and spirit since then. Though the game of golf is a great favourite north of the Tweed, and has taken kindly in the north of Devon, yet it does not appear to have made any headway beyond the "links" at Northam. A game so scientific and invigorating, deserves a wider spread than it has at present attained in the west; and it is only to understand the game, where "links" can be formed, to secure its general practice. The West of England Golf Club in 1864 struck a gold challenge medal, to be won three successive years by the same golfer for him to retain it. The Moncrieff Cross and other prizes have also been offered. Mr. George Glennie, the medallist, and well-known player of the St. Andrew's "links," has held the gold medal for two successive years. The West of England Club has some long hitters who have shewn themselves skilful at the "quarter strokes," and several members played a tight game with the holder of the challenge medal last year. Thursday was the day for playing the annual match for the gold challenge medal and other prizes. The weather was delightfully fine, and the "links" were in the best possible condition. A large marquee was erected on the Burrows, and an excellent luncheon provided. Though the weather was fine, it was rather unfavourable for first-class play, there being a stiff easterly breeze. Some of the best players from Scotland and the St. Andrew's Club were on the ground. When we mention the names of Sir Hope Grant, Mr. George Glennie, Mr. Buskin, Mr. Bennet, and Mr. Adamson, the latter being the captain of the Blackheath Club and holder of the gold medal, it will be seen that the men in the North Devon Club had their work cut out, with apparently the remotest chance of retaining the challenge medal in the west. But, nevertheless, the holder of the medal was played a very tight game, and the chances of victory oscillated in the balance, but for an unfortunate "bunker" when success seemed easy by Mr. G. M. Molesworth, the foremost player in the West of England Club. The contest lay between Mr. George Glennie, Mr. Adamson, Mr. Molesworth, Sir Hope Grant, and Mr. Buskin. The two former scored 106, and the ties were played off, and Mr. Glennie was again declared the winner. It is a high compliment to Mr. George Glennie's skill as a golfer that he has held the gold challenge medal for three years in succession against all comers, and he now retains it as his own. It is no less creditable to Mr. Molesworth, as a member of the North Devon Club, he having lost by only one hole. The following is the score as played and returned:—

The first that paired off were Sir Hope Grant, G.C.B., and Mr. Adamson; the former scored 108, and the latter 106.

Rev. Lymbeare Harding, hon. sec. N.D. Club, met with an accident, and was unable to continue the game; Mr. Car Stevens, 116.

Mr. George Glennie, 106; Mr. Buskin, 109.
Mr. Molesworth, 107; Rev. J. O. Vincent, 122.
Rev. I. H. Gossett, 122; Rev. J. H. Kirwan, 141.
Mr. Freeman, 114; Mr. T. Purdie, 126.
Rev. E. Reynolds, 135; Mr. J. C. Oliver, no return.
Mr. Bennett, 118; Mr. Paul Wilmot, 117.
Capt. Didham and Mr. Bazeley, no returns.

The prize of a set of nine beautiful golf clubs, open to all comers, was won by Mr. Adamson, of Blackheath.

A handsome set of six clubs, open only to the North Devon Club, was won by Mr. Molesworth, with the Moncrieff Cross.

ST ANDREWS FROM
PUBLISHED BY

April 1865

We need scarcely add that the reappearance of the Champion was cordially hailed by the members of the Club and all his old friends; while the presence of a professional of A. Strath's standing invested the proceedings of the week with deep interest. On Wednesday the two played a single, which was won by Tom, who completed the round in 53, his opponent being only one stroke behind, and losing the match by one hole.

Yesterday Col. Fairlie and Mr Innes encountered Ord Campbell and Mr Clark a match of 24 holes, which terminated in favour of the former by three holes. Mr Clark and Mr Innes lost a similar match against Mr Whigham and Tom Morris by the same number of holes.

MATCH AT MUSSELBURGH FOR £20 A-SIDE.—A very exciting foursome golf match was played at Musselburgh on Friday 14th instant, between Andrew Strath, late of St Andrews, but who is now domiciled in Musselburgh, and William Dow, of Musselburgh, against the Brothers William and David Park, of Musselburgh—the match being 36 holes or 4 rounds of the Green. After the first round Strath and Dow were 1 hole a-head. In the second round the same parties were 2 holes a-head. The Parks then made some splendid play—winning 7 holes out of 9—which made them 5 holes a-head and 9 to play at the end of the third round. The next hole was halved; and winning the next 2 holes gave the Parks the match by 7 holes a-head and 6 to play. The Parks holed the third round in 34 strokes, which is considered great play.

Willie shows off the Belt at Bruntsfield Links

GOLF.—The interesting and much-contested struggle for the October medal and the Cannon medal, given at this time by the Warrender Golf Club, the original competition for which, it will be remembered, resulted on a former occasion in a *tie* between Mr Dudgeon and Mr Robert Kay, took place on Bruntsfield Links on Saturday afternoon. There was great anxiety manifested in the event, and it was therefore much regretted that proper intimation was not given of the time appointed for the match, which was not expected to come off on a day so unfavourable for the game. But it appears the Captain was warranted, in the present unsettled state of the weather, in taking advantage of the first fair day that presented itself. The play on both sides was considered very good, but the veteran of the two (Mr Dudgeon) who holed the two rounds in sixty-five strokes, was declared the winner. The more valuable of the prizes, therefore, becomes his property; the other is retained by Mr Kay for a year. We may here take opportunity to mention that Mr William Park, who now takes the title of champion golf-player of Great Britain, and who represented the Warrender Club at the late great tournament at Prestwick, has exhibited to the members for the last three weeks the silver belt given by the Earl of Eglinton and others, and gained by him, and which is perhaps the finest thing of the kind ever competed for. Not ... from its intrinsic value, nor for its artistic me... belt so much esteemed by the golfing commun... our neighbourhood, but because it has been gained a golfer representing an Edinburgh club—gained from one of the best players in the world at us door, on his own ground. The frequen... urrenc...

Back to Prestwick for the Challenge Belt
Tommy, aged 14 played.
He was still being schooled at Ayr Academy.
He retired when a shot ahead of me!
1865

Thursday dawned more propitiously than any morning which has yet been fixed for the match which determines who is to be the holder of the greatest trophy open to professional skill. Never since the Belt was competed for has the weather been so good, the only drawback being that some of the putting-greens were not so smooth as hitherto. It is well, however, to notice that the field comprised not only numerically, but also in golfing talent, the finest players who could legitimately aspire to the championship of Scotland, and therefore of the world. Not very long ago, although Strath stood second in the competition, being only two strokes behind the champion, there were many who predicted that he would never become the custodier of the Belt—not that his play was inferior to that of his most formidable rivals, but because it was supposed that he had not the nerve requisite to win a match of such importance. These misgivings have been falsified in the most practical way in which they could be by the result of Thursday's play. By a sort of poetical justice, the much-coveted distinction subscribed for by the Prestwick Golf Club remains in the village, and has been won by the professional who is now resident on the Links, which have been the scene of many spirited contests, for which our local golfers are indebted to the liberality and enterprise of the late Lord Eglinton, Col. Fairlie of Coodham, and their colleagues. Shortly after eleven o'clock the competitors started in the following order; and we subjoin the returns, in so far as they have been handed in to the Secretary:—

	1st Round	2d Round	3d Round
A. Strath, ...	55	... 54	... 53
Mr T. Hood...	66	... 66	... 66
Will. Park ...	56	... 52	... 56
J. Miller ...	63	... 58	... 66
W. Dow ...	56	... 61	... 54
J. Allan ...	64	... 65	... —
R. Kirk ...	64	... 54	... 54
W. Doleman	62	... 57	... 60
Tom Morris ...	57	... 61	... 58
R. Andrew...	61	... 59	... —
Tom Morris, jr.	60	... 57	... retired
W. Stirling	71	... 68	... do.

Andrew Strath 3 rounds	55-54-53	162
— Hood	~~3~~ 66×66×66	198
Wm Park	— 56+52+56	164
— Miller	63×60×66	189
— Dow	56-61-54	171
John Allen	64-66-59	189
		173
Bob Kirk	64-54-~~54~~ 55-	~~17~~ 2
Doleman	62-57-59	178
T. Morris	57+61+56	174

1865
Open
Andrew Strath
St Andrews

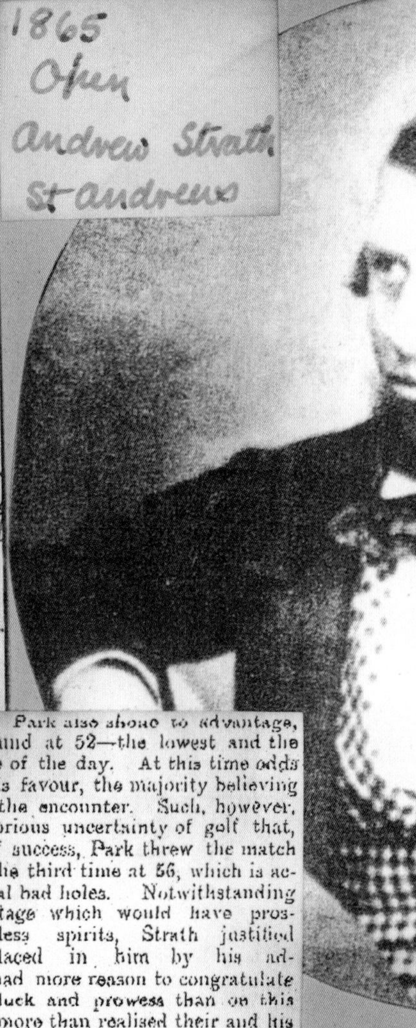

Andrew took over from me as keeper of the Prestwick course

Ayrshire Express report continued

As usual, the whole interest of this decisive trial of strength centered in the performances of Tom Morris and William Park, than whom, with all their faults, it must be admitted there are not two better golfers in the kingdom. But the late champion was not up to his own standard, having made the worst score which was ever registered against his name on a similar occasion. Starting well, he has seldom had the chance of appearing to greater advantage, and yet he took 57 to the first round. Such was the faith reposed, not unnaturally, in the old horse, that the spectators believed he would make up his lee-way in the second round—a hope warranted by the fact that he had holed the last four in 16—which was not surpassed, or even equalled, by any of his brethren. Getting into grief repeatedly during the second round, which was completed in the extraordinarily high figure of 61, his most ardent admirers foresaw that coming defeat which was inevitable. No little consternation prevailed among the backers of the favourite when it was known that he had been beaten by his own son on the first round and a-half of the links. With the honesty which seems to be a second nature with the ex-champion, he frankly admitted that he owed his unexpected defeat to bad play, and bad play alone. No sooner was Tom Morris put out of the chances of success than speculation ran high on the comparative merits of Strath and Park. Although not playing the game anticipated either by himself or his friends, the former went through the ordeal with a steadiness that was highly appreciated by the assembled spectators. Park also showed to advantage, holing the second round at 52—the lowest and the most creditable score of the day. At this time odds were freely laid in his favour, the majority believing that he would win the encounter. Such, however, seems to be the glorious uncertainty of golf that, with fair prospects of success, Park threw the match away by coming in the third time at 56, which is accounted for by several bad holes. Notwithstanding a physical disadvantage which would have prostrated less dauntless spirits, Strath justified the confidence placed in him by his admirers, who never had more reason to congratulate themselves on his pluck and prowess than on this occasion. He has more than realised their and his own expectations by carrying off the Belt, and in fewer strokes than it has ever been won before—Tom Morris having earned the proud title of champion twice in 163, while Strath has attained the same summit of professional ambition in 162. Bob Kirk, who is a stranger to the links, deserves a special meed of praise for having been placed fourth —a position which might have been improved had he not come to grief so frequently in the first round. To have had such limited opportunities for practice, Dow and Andrew made a very creditable appearance —the former being assigned the third place, and the latter narrowly escaping a corresponding honour by not giving in his last score. The amateurs who undertook the onerous duty of competing with the best professionals in the land are worthy of all commendation. Mr Millar's reputation is fragrant in all the golf clubs of the country, although, unfortunately, he did not approach his usual standard at this meeting; while Mr Doleman showed himself to be a very formidable competitor against players of his own stamp. Never was there a better muster of good players at the competition for the Belt; and so long as it remains open with substantial pecuniary inducements, it cannot fail to attract the presence and to fire the ambition of the best professional and amateur golfers in the three kingdoms. We append the gross scores of the prize winners in their order of merit:—

1st, A. Strath winner of the Belt and £8,		162
2d, W. Park, £6,	... ...	164
3d, W. Dow, £4,	... ...	171
4th, R. Kirk, £2,	... ...	172

Yesterday, the excitement was continued by a foursome, in which Tom Morris and Bob Kirk defeated the Champion and William Park, although 6 to 4 was liberally laid in favour of the latter couple. Later in the afternoon the same pair tackled Park and Dow, whom they beat by a number of holes. In a fine single for £5 a-side, Dow vanquished Bob Kirk. Mr Cunningham, London, and Mr G. D. Brown beat Mr Mann, Edinburgh, and Dow by four holes. Mr Miller and Mr G. D. Brown lost a match against Dow and Doleman, although the former were four ahead and five to play. Mr Whigham had also to succumb to Capt. Hay.

We understand that Park and Morris are to play a single this afternoon.

95

ROYAL AND ANCIENT GOLF CLUB.

THE AUTUMN MEETING.

There was great excitement on Thursday about a foursome between Tom Morris and Bob Kirk (one of the most promising young golfers anywhere), against the brothers Park. A hundred pounds were at issue among the backers, apart from the numerous smaller bets taken on. The Musselburgh men were the favourites at starting, and the confidence reposed in them was quite justified by their success the round out, as they gained two holes ahead of their opponents with seeming ease. It was clear, however, that Tom and Bob were in capital 'fettle,' and were not to be beaten without a struggle worthy the reputation of the players engaged, the play from the commencement and all through being the finest seen on St Andrews Links. Without going into details, we come to the result, which was that Tom and Bob came in two holes ahead, having finished the round in the brave play of 86 strokes. This victory may be considered as decisive regarding the superiority of Bob and Tom over all competitors, for, one way and another, they have successfully faced all the leading professionals in the country within the year. In May they faced Dow and Strath, with whom they halved a round, but from whom they took a second. In Prestwick they beat W. Park and Strath by five holes. On the same ground they beat W. Park and Dow by four holes, and now they have beaten the two brothers Park, one of the best couples going, by two holes. This seems decisive work, and meantime keeps all the honours in St Andrews.

The next great match was a single between Bob Kirk and William Dow, of Musselburgh, —two rounds of the Links. It was throughout a splendidly contested match, notwithstanding the 'putting' at first was indifferent. Bob, the first round, was as low as three holes behind, some saying that he was holding his man too cheap. The fact was, however, that he laboured under a defect of footing—a defect he remedied before going on the second round. Coming in, he made all square at the second last hole, and, but for a bad tee stroke which sent his ball into a cart rut, the round would have ended very differently from what it did. As it was, he lost the first round by one hole. After half an hour's repose parties again started with, if anything, confidence increased in Bob's prowess. This confidence he justified by placing four holes to his credit at the close of the match. In consideration that this was the third round the brave little fellow had made of the Links, there was no wonder that the crowd was inclined to cheer him as he handled over his club to his caddy, though, to be sure, he did not seem tired in the least. The play on his side all through was steady, cautious, and determined, on that of Dow, careful, deliberate, though occasionally ill-judged, probably arising from his comparative ignorance of the green. The driving by both was something to be seen, and the match, on the whole, will long be remembered for its equality and excitement. One of the results is, that Bob is now fairly looked on as a first-class man for his indomitable pluck, his coolness, and, therefore, his steadiness and safety as a professional to back. Tom and he are now the pair in the position to challenge all comers. The weather, we may state, for both the matches, was all that could be desired, and the few—compared to the numbers on the Links the day before—who were present, were thus enabled in comfort to follow the fortunes of the players.

THURSDAY, OCTOBER 5, 1865.

There were other matches played by amateurs, among these the following:—

Major Boothby and Mr Hodge had a close tie with Mr Clark and Mr Dunn. In the first round the former were gainers by two holes, the second round was halved, and in a short match they halved again.

Major Bethune and Mr Bethune of Blebo had a tie with Messrs Moncrieff and Bruce of one round.

Mr Thomas Peters and James Anderson took a match from Captain Ramsay and Andrew Strath.

The prize offered by Sir Hope Grant (divided) was competed for on Friday by ten professionals. The winner of the first prize was A. Strath, for the second there was a tie between James Anderson and Bob Kirk; on playing off, Bob won.

What followed of the meeting among the professionals showed how fickle fortune is in the distribution of her favours, and on the whole how fair our estimate of Tom Morris and Bob Kirk is from the proceedings of Thursday. On Saturday, Tom essayed Wm. Park one round of the Links, and after some of the finest play ever seen, beat his man by two holes. That the play was first-class is proved by the fact that Tom did the round in eighty-two strokes—or within three of the lowest number ever taken; Park in eighty-four. Park was the favourite—for Tom's age is getting to be against him among backers when pitted against such an agile player as Park; nevertheless, he is not to be beaten when he sets his mind on victory, and is in decently average condition. But there was even a more startling turn of affairs on Monday when plucky little Bob Kirk thrashed the Prestwick champion, A. Strath, by two holes. It was such a daring venture that hardly any one had the hardihood to back him, but the result was unmistakable, and it was left for him to finish the harvest of honours reaped by the local professionals. Tom and he have now defeated everybody, and that—if anything can add to the brilliancy of the autumn meeting—would do it. The probability is that this turn of affairs among the champions, ex and otherwise, will lead to new matches, and so give an impetus to the game throughout the country, as will gladden the hearts of all true golfers.

Meantime, we may here state that the professionals from a distance are not exactly pleased at the little temptation which has been offered them to come so far again. With the exception of the five pounds offered by Sir Hope Graut they had no means of getting their expenses paid unless through betting; and that at this meeting has been all against them. They point out that at Prestwick there is never less than £30 offered them in matches, and they go there always sure that, however the betting may go, they can always collar in prizes as much as will keep them free of loss. We are not aware whether any of the professionals have spoken on this point to any members of the Club this season, but we take the liberty of thus publicly mentioning the matter for their consideration. In fact, we may state that if better inducements are not held out on these occasions, William Park at least will hesitate before he come. For the sake of the game, and therefore for the Club, this is greatly to be deplored, especially since it can be easily remedied.

THE BALL.

This part of the programme is looked upon at all times as not the least important of the week's proceedings, and came off on Friday night with fully its usual *eclat*. The Town Hall with all its accessories and appliances was in requisition, and a very comfortable evening indeed was spent. The music was by the excellent assembly band of Mr Wallace, Edinburgh, who performed their parts admirably. The purveyors for the supper were the Messrs Hunter and Co. of Edinburgh, who even did their own former selves in the magnificent table of delicacies they produced, which were admired and relished by all.

Shortly after ten o'clock the carriages began to arrive, and the company when mustered were as follows:—

Sir John and Lady Low, Mr and Mrs Geo. Patton, Capt. and Mrs Low, Miss Low, and Miss Celina Low, Miss Makgill, Mr Irvine Low, Mr James Agnew, and Mr John Charles; Lord and Lady John Manners; Lord Kirkcaldy; the Right Hon. Lord Advocate, the Misses Moncreiff; Major-General, Mrs, and Miss Christie; Lieutenant-General Moncreiff, Mrs and Miss Moncreiff; Lieutenant-Colonel Moncreiff, Scots Fusilier Guards;

Lady M'Gregor, Miss M'Gregor; Mr John Whyte Melville; Mr Kermack; Mr and Miss Walkinshaw; Miss Lindsay; Mr W. J. Renny; Dr Morehead and Miss H. Morehead; Mr John Luke, Brownhills; Dr Watson Wemyss, Miss Wemyss, and Miss Catherine Wemyss; Mr Wm. Wood, Leith; Mr Adam B. Bannatyne; Mr T. Stark Christie, Ballindean; Mr John Grant, of Kilgraston, and the Misses Grant; Major Briggs, of Strathairly, and Mrs Briggs; Mr R. Ewen Curwen; Capt. R. Low; Major and Mrs Bethune; Miss Schlesinger; Mr Bruce Stark Christie; Mr Walter F. K. Lyon; Mrs Dean, Miss Dean, Mr Dean, and Mr R. Dean; Mrs and Miss Falconar; Mr Bryan W. Broughton; Dr Robert Chambers, Miss Chambers, and Mrs Priestly; Mr James Blackwood, Mr William Blackwood, Miss Blackwood, Mr and Mrs John Blackwood; Major Blackwood; Miss Hume Ewdarder; Mr Thomas Blackwood; Major-General Stewart; Mr and Mrs Purvis Russell; Miss Popham, of Gainsburgh; Mr and Mrs Robert Mitchell; Mr John Skelton; Mr and Mrs T. S. Baynes; Mr and Mrs A. D. Cockburn; Misses Maitland, Dundrennan; Mr Little Gilmour; Mr George Thomson; the Hon. Mrs Cheape, Lathockar; Mr Wedderburn, Birkhill; Mr H. Moncrieff; Mrs Maitland and the Misses Maitland; Mr and Mrs D. B. Wauchope; Mr and Mrs D. L. Burn and the Misses Burn; Misses Nicholson; Captain Coldwell; Mr D. Crawford; J. O. Fairlie, Esq. of Coodham, and Miss Fairlie; Captain Carey, Royal Engineers; Mr James Walker; Mr Clarke Walker; Captain Lindesay and Mrs Lindesay; Miss Chambers; Major and Mrs Boothby; Mr S. F. Muir; Mr Stair Agnew; Mr and Mrs Seaton Stewart; Lady Wallace; Mr, Mrs, and Miss Pitcairn, Cunnoquhie; Mr and Mrs Pitcairn, Pitcullo; Principal Tulloch, Mrs Tulloch, Miss Sara Tulloch, Miss Agnes Tulloch, Miss Lilly Tulloch, Mr William Weir Tulloch; Mr F. M. Hunter; Mrs Maidston Smith, Miss Smith, and Mrs Gillespie Smith, and Lieut. Wm. Clevland; Mr Hunter of Blackness; Major J. Thomson; Colonel Bethune; Mr A. S. Cook, Miss Cook, Miss Diana Cook, Haddington; Col. Wm. Low, and Col. Lyon.

About one o'clock the party retired to the Council Chambers for supper, but the accommodation was too limited, so that a few had to enjoy a *tete a tete* in the Hall until the proceedings of the evening were gone through. The gallant veteran, Captain of the Club, General Sir John Low, in full insignia, occupied the chair; supported on the right by Lord John Manners and Lieut.-General Moncrieff; and on the left by Mr John Whyte Melville and Colonel Low.

The Captain in giving 'The Queen' as first toast remarked that all the ladies who had now happily favoured them with their presence had reason to be proud of their sex in her Majesty's person; in every sense of the word, and as patroness of the Club, she was entitled to a hearty bumper. The toast was pledged with right loyal goodwill.

In the giving of the next toast to 'The Prince and Princess of Wales and the rest of te Royal Family,' the connection of the Prince as a former captain of the Club was referred to and the excellent manner which his delegate Mr Whyte Melville had performed the duties. The toast was hailed with the greatest enthusiasm.

Mr WHYTE MELVILLE called for a full bumper. It afforded him much pleasure to refer to the happy selection of a Captain they had now made. It was but a just tribute to the merits of the gentleman, whether as military or a civilian; and he hoped all would join in wishing him 'long life, health, and happiness.' The toast was most cordially received.

In the reply, the gallant GENERAL said that he tried his best to keep out of this post, but here he was. He would do what he could to fulfil the duties devolving upon him.

The CAPTAIN than gave, in a facetious speech, 'the health of the Right Hon. Lord John Manners,' which was replied to in equally becoming terms.

The CHAIRMAN then called for a *bona fide* bumper, and, in a very knacky speech, gave 'the Ladies,' which was gallantly responded to. The company then retired to the ball-room, where dancing was kept up until about four o'clock.

A grand affair
Carriages arrive - 10m
Supper 1. A.M.
- Dancing till 4. A.M.

ST. ANDREWS.

9TH OCTOBER, 1840.—The late Allan Robertson beat the late Tom Alexander, Musselburgh, one round of the Links by 4 holes.

JULY, 1843.—Allan Robertson and Willie Dunn played a match of twenty rounds, two rounds each day, for ten consecutive days. On the tenth day the veteran Allan was declared victor by two rounds ahead, and one to play.

20TH OCTOBER, 1843.—Allan Robertson defeated Willie Dunn in a match of 36 holes by 8 holes.

IN OCTOBER, 1850, Allan Robertson and Tom Morris played a foursome against the brothers Dunn for £50 a-side. The former were victorious at the burn hole.

23D OCTOBER, 1852.—A match for £100 a-side came off between Mr Robert Hay, Edinburgh, and Willie Dunn, against Allan Robertson and Tom Morris, two rounds of the Links, when the latter won by 6 holes.

ON 9TH MAY, 1853, the only single played between Allan Robertson and Tom Morris took place, when the latter had the match by three holes. The reason is that these two generally played great matches on one side, and except in this case, never had occasion to be pitted against each other.

IN OCTOBER, 1857, Allan Robertson and A. Strath gained a match from Tom Morris and David Park by 7 a-head and 5 to play.

IN MAY, 1858, a very excellent match was played between the brothers Wm. and D. Park against the brothers Tom and George Morris—two rounds of the links. The latter never were a hole ahead till the last hole, when they gained the match therefore by one hole, after uphill work the whole game.

Professional matches

Willie, Self and Allan

PRESTWICK.

In October, 1860 (the day after the first competition for the Belt), Tom Morris challenged the Champion to a match of three rounds, or 36 holes, for £20. The Prestwick man took the lead vigorously, allowing Park to get only one hole in the first round, and winning easily by 7 a-head and 6 to play.

1861.

At the May meeting W. Park defeated Tom Morris by 4 holes out of 12, their respective scores being 53 and 57 strokes.

W. Dow and G. D. Brown were successful against David Park and R. Andrew by two holes on the round.

In June a most extraordinary single came off between W. Park and Tom Morris, which the former gained by one hole out of 48, although the latter was 7 ahead with 18 to play. Before the third round closed 3 of the crushing majority were cleverly rubbed off by Park who, however, started for the final circuit of the Links 4 holes behind. At the seventh hole coming home, the positions of the rivals were reversed, Park being now one in advance with 5 to play. And now came the tug of war. He halved the eighth in 4 strokes, and gained the ninth in 5. The tenth was also halved; and he upon whom fortune seemed to have turned her back so long was now "dormy"—2 ahead and 2 to play. Tom took the eleventh by a fine cleek shot and a put in 2. Hopes were now entertained that the match would result in a triumph for neither, but Park making sure of a longish put halved the last hole in 5, otherwise the battle would have been drawn. In strokes, too, the winner had the advantage, as follows:—

	Park.	Morris.
1st Round, ...	54	56
2d ,, ...	56	50
3d ,, ...	54	55
4th ,, ...	53	59
	217	220

1862.

At the September meeting W. Park beat W. Dow by 4 holes out of 12; completing the round in 52 strokes.

The following day the same parties played a match of 24 holes, Dow getting 3 to 2 in money. Though Park was 2 ahead at the fifth hole of the second round, Dow reduced the lead gradually, and ultimately gained by 2.

A purse, subscribed by the members of the Prestwick Club, for competition between the second and fourth placed aspirants to the Challenge Belt, was competed for on Saturday, and was won by W. Park, who defeated Dow by 6 ahead and 5 to play on the three rounds. A short match of 5 holes home terminated in favour of the latter. Another round, making the fourth that afternoon, was also gained by the "young-'un." Not content with the result of the week's contest, the same pair had a series of matches again on the Monday, Park having the superiority, but pecuniarily Dow was very nearly equal with his opponent.

MONTROSE.

A goodly number of the professional golfers in Scotland had a trial of skill over the Montrose Links, on Wednesday 24th October, 1866, when the Royal Albert Club offered £10 to the player who completed 25 holes in the fewest strokes—£5 and £3 being awarded to the second and third successful competitors. The Tournament was open to all-comers. The weather was very wet, but towards noon—the time of starting—it fortunately cleared up. In consequence of the rain the ground was rather slippery, but the competitors were unanimous in pronouncing the course one of the best in Scotland. If it has any fault it is that too few hazards exist. The following were the players with their scores:—

1.	W. Doleman, Glasgow, ...	112
2.	Wm. Park, Musselburgh, ...	115
3.	Robt. Kirk, St Andrews, ...	117
Tied {	Andrew Strath, Prestwick, ...	120
	James Anderson, St Andrews, ...	120
6.	Tom Morris, Do., ...	121
7.	Jno. Allan, Do., ...	122
Tied {	Robt. Dow, Montrose, ...	127
	Mr T. Hood, Musselburgh, ...	127
10.	Robt. Andrew, Perth, ...	128
11.	Wm. Dow, Musselburgh, ...	129
12.	Stewart Petrie, Montrose, ...	132

First honours were thus taken by Mr Doleman, an amateur, who, as he expressed himself, "drives a baker's van in Glasgow every day"; the second and third places being occupied by Wm. Park and R. Kirk respectively. Several heavy bets were lost in consequence of the turn the play took. Strath and Anderson went out six additional holes to decide their tie, when the match was once more halved, the former holing a fine put about 12 yards, and ultimately dividing with his opponent the sweepstakes of £3.

George Whyte Melville. Prominent member of the R & A and writer.

PERTH.

April, 1864.—Andrew Strath and R. Andrew having accepted a challenge from Tom Morris and Wm. Park to play 24 holes, the latter laying £6 to £5, a most exciting game was witnessed. The Champion and ex-Champion were the favourites, and the contest was so keen that neither couple had the advantage at any stage by more than two holes. The younger pair, however, pulled through admirably, and wrested the laurels from their celebrated rivals by one.

A. Strath gained a match of 36 from David Park by 5 and 4 to play—£6 to £4 having been laid upon the latter.

A match of 36 holes was played between W. Dow and R. Andrew, the latter of whom was the favourite, and although 4 ahead at the completion of the second round, the Musselburgh man reduced the lead, and ultimately won by 2.

April, 1866.—Tom Morris and Bob. Kirk were defeated by A. Strath and R. Andrew in a match of 36 holes, for £5 a-side, by 6 a-head and 4 to play.

MUSSELBURGH.

In February, 1865, Wm. Park challenged A. Strath, laying him £10 to £6, a match of 36 holes, which was gained by the latter, who was 3 a-head and one to play.

In April, 1865, Wm. and David Park defeated A. Strath and W. Dow in a match of 36 holes, by 7 and 6 to play.

The same month, David Park beat A. Strath by 5 and 4 to play out of 36 holes.

MONTROSE.

October, 1866.—A. Strath and Wm. Dow beat Tom Morris and Bob. Kirk by one out of 19 holes.

1865.

In April Tom Morris gained a match against A. Strath by one hole, the scores being 53 and 54 strokes.

In September R. Andrew and W. Doleman beat Bob Kirk and Jno. Allan by one hole out of 24—the first-named couple holing the first round in 53 strokes, the best score ever made in a foursome over Prestwick Links by strangers to the green. In fact, it has only been surpassed by Colonel Fairlie and Tom Morris, who, in double matches, twice completed the 12 holes in 52.

Tom Morris and Bob Kirk gained a match against W. Park and A. Strath, although 6 to 4 were freely laid on the latter.

W. Park, having been backed for £5 against Tom Morris, pulled off the stakes by 4 holes out of 24, his gross score being 105—a 54 and a 51; that of his opponent 108, or two fifty-fours.

1866.

On the 4th May an open competition for professionals took place. The play was excellent, as the following scores testify :—

1. Tom Morris, St Andrews, ... 83 strokes.
2. A. Strath, Prestwick, and... / Bob. Kirk, St Andrews, ... 87 ,,

In playing off the tie A. Strath beat Bob. Kirk, holing the round at 83 strokes.

On the 5th May a very closely contested foursome took place, when Tom Morris and Bob. Kirk, St Andrews, beat A. Strath, Prestwick, and R. Andrew, Perth, by one hole on two rounds, or 36 holes.

In October the second open competition for professionals came off, when the following was the order of merit :—

1. Bob. Kirk, ... 86 strokes.
2. Tom Morris, ... 89 ,,

On the 26th October a match was played between Bob. Kirk and James Anderson, St Andrews, against W. Dow, Musselburgh, and A. Strath, Prestwick, for two rounds of the Links. At the end of the first round the former were 4 holes a-head, but during the second round their opponents managed to reduce this number gradually, until they were "all even" and one to play. After considerable excitement in the last hole, the St Andrews men were beaten by this one hole on the match.

Novel Match.

A match, of a somewhat novel nature, was played in May, 1866. Robert Clark, Edinburgh, and Gilbert M. Innes, Edinburgh, opposed Tom Morris. Each played a ball, and the two former were allowed at the end of each hole to choose the ball they preferred to count against Tom's. On a first consideration this would appear quite favourable to Morris ; but no one has the least conception of the many difficulties and chances against him, unless he were himself taking part in the match. The game was well contested for two rounds.

↑ Two against one! during the R & A Spring Meeting

Extra Scores made during 1866.

1. Professional Scores.—The lowest professional score for the year was made on the 6th of July, by Tom Morris, when playing against Colonel Maitland Dougall of Scotscraig. It may be remarked here that the score *out* is the lowest on record ; and that the total round ties with the late Allan Robertson as the champion professional score of the Links. It is as follows :—*Out*—4 5 3 3 6 4 4 3 4—36 ; *In*—4 4 5 5 6 5 5 5 4—43 ; total, 79.

My best round on the old course. Out in thirty-six with a three at the fourth! ↑

TO

COLONEL J. O. FAIRLIE

OF COODHAM,

DESERVEDLY DESIGNATED

BY

THE EARL OF DALHOUSIE

THE

"Champion Amateur of Scotland,"

AS HAVING HELD

THE

Prestwick, St. Andrews, and North Berwick Medals

DURING THE SAME SEASON,

These Pages

ARE DUTIFULLY DEDICATED.

J. O. Fairlie with his sons – two of them future captains of the R & A

98

INCIDENT IN GOLFING—QUERY.

A member of the Manchester Club, whom nature has blessed with luxuriant hirsute appendages, in playing a match 14th December, 1866, struck his ball when lying against a tuft of grass. The ball rose straight up, and, without touching his dress or face, lodged firm and fast in his beard. Query—Was he bound to play it out, or could he drop it, or should he lose the hole?

THE CHALLENGE BELT.

A look back at the 1st seven championships

Recognising the desirability of providing some annual test to test the comparative merits of professional golfers, the Prestwick Club, with praiseworthy enthusiasm and liberality, subscribed for a Challenge Belt, which should be open for competition to the world, and held permanently by the player who should carry it off three years in succession. The trophy, which consists of red morocco, is an exquisite piece of workmanship, richly ornamented with massive silver plates bearing appropriate devices, and cost about thirty guineas. Thirty-six holes, or three rounds of the Prestwick Links, is the prescribed course for the Championship. We subjoin the scores annually since the Belt was instituted:—

1860.

WEDNESDAY, October 17th.

		Strokes.
1.	W. Park, Musselburgh, ...	174
2.	T. Morris, Prestwick, ...	176
3.	A. Strath, St Andrews, ...	180
4.	R. Andrew, Perth, ...	191
5.	G. D. Brown, Blackheath, ...	192
6.	C. Hunter, Prestwick, ...	195
7.	Alexander Smith, Bruntsfield, ...	196
8.	W. Steel, Do., ...	232

1861.

THURSDAY, September 26th.

		Strokes.
1.	T. Morris, Prestwick, ...	163
2.	W. Park, Musselburgh, ...	167
3.	W. Dow, Do., ...	171
4.	D. Park, Do., ...	172
5.	R. Andrew, Perth, ...	175
6.	Peter M'Ewan, Bruntsfield,	178
		Strokes.
7.	W. Dunn, Blackheath, ...	180
8.	G. D. Brown, Do., ...	185
9.	James Dunn, Do., ...	188
10.	Charles Hunter, Prestwick, ...	190

1862.

THURSDAY, September 11th.

		Strokes.
1.	T. Morris, Prestwick, ...	163
2.	W. Park, Musselburgh, ...	176
3.	C. Hunter, Prestwick, ...	178
4.	W. Dow, Musselburgh, ...	181
5.	Mr Knight, jun., Prestwick, ...	186

1863.

FRIDAY, September 18th.

		Strokes.
1.	W. Park, the Belt, ...	168
2.	T. Morris, £5, ...	170
3.	D. Park, £3, ...	172
4.	A. Strath, £2, ...	174
5.	G. D. Brown, St Andrews, ...	176
6.	R. Andrew, Perth, ...	178
7.	C. Hunter, Prestwick, ...	184
8.	Mr Knight, jun., Do., ...	190
9.	Mr Miller, Musselburgh, ...	192
Tied	Mr J. F. Johnston, Ayr, ...	197
Tied	Mr Chalmers, Perth, ...	197
Tied	James Paxton, Musselburgh, ...	197
13.	Mr Mitchell, Prestwick, ...	206
14.	Mr Moffat, Musselburgh, ...	233

1864.

FRIDAY, September 16th.

		Strokes.
1.	T. Morris, the Belt and £6, ...	167
2.	A. Strath, £5, ...	169
3.	R. Andrew, £3, ...	175
4.	W. Park, ...	177
5.	W. Dow, ...	181
6.	W. Strath, ...	182

1865.

THURSDAY, September 14th.

		Strokes.
1.	A. Strath, the Belt and £8, ...	162
2.	W. Park, £6, ...	164
3.	W. Dow, £4, ...	171
4.	R. Kirk, St Andrews, £2, ...	172

The only championship I was out of sorts in

1866.

THURSDAY, September 13th.

		Strokes.
1.	W. Park, the Belt and £6, ...	169
2.	D. Park, £3, ...	171
3.	R. Andrew, £2, ...	176
4.	T. Morris, ...	178
5.	R. Kirk, ...	180
6.	A. Strath, ...	182
6.	Mr W. Doleman, Glasgow, ...	182
7.	John Allan, St Andrews, ...	183
8.	Tom Morris, jun., ...	187
9.	W. Dunn, Leith, ...	189
10.	Mr T. Hood, Musselburgh, ...	191
11.	James Hutchison, Do., ...	194

PRESTWICK GOLF CLUB.—The autumn meeting of this club came off at Prestwick on Wednesday. The business meeting was held at noon, and among the gentlemen present were:—Col. Fairlie, Major W. F. Hamilton, MrGillon of Wallhouse, Mr Evan A. Hunter of Belmont, Mr D. D. Whigham, Mr Ord Campbell, Dr Knower, Mr Harvie of Castlesemple, Capt. Stewart, Major Phillips, &c.,—Mr Gillon, preses, and Mr D. Dunlop, secretary. The general committee of the club submitted a number of new rules and regulations, which were unanimously approved of and adopted. One of the rules provided that the captain shall in future be appointed in April, and accordingly Mr Gilbert Mitchell Innes was reappointed Captain until April. The Treasurer reported that there was a balance in bank at the credit of the club of £87. Business over, the members proceeded to the links, and engaged in competition for the Eglinton Gold Medal, which was ultimately won by Dr Clark Wilson, Ayr, in 121 strokes. The chief sweepstakes (£2 15s) also went with the medal, the other (£1 5s) falling to the lot of Captain Stewart, who, however, was not up to his usual mark, figuring as he did for 128. Mr Peter White, jr., Newark Castle, stood third at 129, receiving 12 strokes of odds. In the afternoon the medal-holder and Captain Stewart were victorious in two matches over Mr Ord Campbell and Mr Whigham. W. Park had a single with Mr Hood, whom he defeated. R. Kirk won two matches from Mr W. Doleman. On Thursday the Champion Belt was competed for, and won, after some fine play, by Wm. Park, of Musselburgh, in 169 strokes—7 more than last year, when it was won by Mr Strath in 162. Mr D. Park was second in 171; Mr R. Andrews 3d, 176; Mr Tom Morris 4th, 178; Mr R. Kirk 5th, 180; and Mr A. Strath 6th, 182. The wind was rather high, which accounts, no doubt, for the scores not being quite so good as last year.

George McLachlan

Tom Morris is consolidating himself in St Andrews. He purchased on Tuesday the property of Mr G.D. Brown – who retires to London – golf-club and ball maker, for the purpose of carrying on that trade in all its branches and perfection. Tom is to be congratulated on his worldly prosperity, but most of all in his possessing in all who frequent the Links, friends, ever ready to help and encourage him. 1866

The clubmaking shop to the side of the new 18th green

99

—THE ROYAL AND ANCIENT GOLF CLUB OF ST. ANDREWS. some members 1866

INSTITUTED 1754.

The Club was in 1837 presented with a Gold Medal by His Majesty King William IV. to be competed for annually, and in 1838 with a Gold Medal by the late Queen Adelaide, to be worn by the Captain.

THE QUEEN, *Patroness.*

H.R.H. The PRINCE OF WALES, *Patron.*

Sir ROBERT ANSTRUTHER of Balcaskie, Bart., M.P., *Captain.*

THOMAS HODGE, *Holder of the Royal, or King William the Fourth's Medal.*

DAVID LAMB, *Holder of the Club Gold Medal.*

WILLIAM C. THOMSON, *Holder of the Silver Cross.*

THOMAS D. M'WHANNELL, *Holder of the Bombay Medal.*

The Very Rev. Principal TULLOCH, *Hon. Chaplain.*

STUART GRACE, *Honorary Secretary.*

Council.—All the old Captains of the Club, and the Medal-holders for the time.

TOM MORRIS, *Custodier of the Links.*

Those marked * have been Captains.—Those marked † have been holders of the Club Medal.—Those marked ‡ have been holders of the Royal Medal, the gift of his late Majesty.—Those marked § have been holders of the Silver Cross of St. Andrew, the gift of Colonel Belshes.—Those marked ‖ have been holders of the Bombay Medal.

1805 * Leut.-General Sir John Low of Clatto
1810 * C. M. Christie of Durie
R. B. Dalgleish of Rires
1811 Capt. Alexander Nairne, H.E.I.C.S
Lieut.-Col. Alexander Hay
1815 James M. Melville, W.S
1816 Capt. David Briggs, R.N
Rear-Ad. Ramsay, C.B
And. Stein, jun., Kirkliston
Admiral Geo. Scott, R.N.
* J. W. Melville of Strathkinness
Major J. Wemyss of Wemysshall
Alex. Aitken of Thornton
1817 Major A. Douglas
1818 Col. J. Dalgairns of Balgavies
Dr Alexander M'Kenzie
J. O. Dalgleish of Woodburne
† Wm. Wood, Leith
1819 Hugh Bruce, Advocate
Mark Sprot of Garnkirk
†† Sir Charles Shaw
1820 Hon. A. Leslie Melville
Frederick Hope
Patrick Hunter
Major-General Sir John Cheape
* John Grant of Kilgraston
1821 Wm. Maxwell, Lieut., R.N
B. W. Morrison of Fawfield
John Carnegie of Southesk
1822 *‖ G. Dempster of Skibo
Thomas Paton, W.S., of Glenalmond
John Murray
1823 R. A. Nisbet Hamilton
Rev. Julian C. Young
John Hay of Morton, R.N.
James Rait of Anniston
Mungo Murray of Lintrose
Rev. Dr Wm. Menzies, Maybole
J. Haig, Cameron Bridge
C. Guthrie of Taybank
John Hay of Letham
Sir Francis Grant, Kilgraston
D. A. Lindesay of Wormiston
1824 Edward B. Glass, H.E.I.C.C.S.
W. Pitt Dundas, Advocate
Capt. W. G. Scott, E.I.C.S.
William M. Logan
Geo. Logan, Madras Infantry
1825 James H. Anstruther
1826 ‡ Lieut.-General Sir Hope Grant
* Henry Stewart of St. Fort
Bazette D. Colvin, London
Major-General S. Balfour
1827 B. J. Colvin, H.E.I.C.C.S.
H. Gillespie, Colonel, Royal Marines
Alex. Cheape of Lathockar
Colonel C. Cheape, H.E.I.C.S.
W. Holcroft, Seven Oaks
Arch. Butter of Fascally
1829 Capt. D. Littlejohn, late 48th Regt., Madras Infantry
* F. L. S. Wedderburn of Wedderburn
* John Balfour of Balbirnie
Richard Henry Vade Walpole
M. Clerk of Westholme
1830 Capt. R. K. Trotter, 17th Lancers
Rev. Dr. J. Cook, Haddington
Henry Inglis, W.S.
H. H. Glass, H.E.I.C.C.S,
†† R. Oliphant of Rossie

Hastings D. Sands
* Lieut.-General G. Moncrieff, late of the Guards
Samuel Horsley
1831 Patrick S. Kier, yr. of Kinmont
* David Gillespie of Mountquhanie
†‡§ John H. Wood, Leith
Andrew Richardson
Col. W. Low, E.I.C.S.
Charles Willing
1832 T. W. Webster, London
D. Laird of Strathmartine
J. Macgregor of Glengyle
The Hon. and Rev. John Bailie
Lieut.-Colonel R. Fergusson of Raith
Major-General John Christie, Bengal Cavalry
T. E. M'Ritchie of Denork
W. Burn, architect, London
Sir D. Dundas of Dunira, Bart.
1833 C. R. Scott, Edinburgh
Chas. E. Allen, Edinburgh
J. R. Robertson, London
W. Woodcock of Mountville
Charles Scott
* G. Makgill of Kemback
Lieut.-Gen. W. Beatson, Bengal Cavalry
† William E. C. Wood
Capt. Paton, R.N.
1834 Patrick F. Robertson, M.P., Halton, Hastings
Captain Alexander Chrystie, H.E.I.C.N.S.
† James Skelton, W.S.
Colonel John Kinloch of Kilrie
Alex. Corstorphine of Pittowie
†§‡‖ James Condie, Perth
Wm. Peddie of Blackruthven
Sir Howard Elphinston
Rev. Thomas Marjoribanks
1835 James Dalyell
Captain Alex. Robertson
Sam. R. Fergusson, W.S
H Cook, H.E.I.C.C.S
Jas. F. Scott of Commiston
Lieut. Stuart E. Rolland
Jas. Blackwood, Edinburgh
Geo. Gray, Writer, Perth
Earl of Camperdown
Captain Hamilton, R.N
L.-Col. Geo. Lyon, Dalruscan
Honourable John Murray
Captain Isaacke, H.E.I.C.S
John Guthrie of Guthrie
1836 Alexander Tod, W.S
David Muir, Advocate
William Jollie
William Greig, Edinburgh
John Cook, W.S
His Grace the Duke of Buccleuch
Alex. Mackenzie, W.S
James Foreman, barrister
Richard Jobson, Dundee
W. L. Gilmour of Liberton and Craigmillar
Jas. Anstruther of Tillicoultry
* J. A. Thomson of Charlton
Captain Thomas Chrystie
Hon. John Rollo
George Thomson of Burnhouse
R. S. Fleming of Moness
Geo. Stewart of Murthly
§* R. Lindsay of Straiton
Captain J. Maitland, R.N
1837 Alex. Allen, Advocate
Thomas Sprot, W.S
A. Shank Cook, Advocate
Rev. Geo. Cook, Bathgate
Capt. Macniel, Montrose
Dr Lyon Playfair, C.B
Dr John Adamson, St Andrews
William Kennedy
Henry Maitland, late of the 60th Rifles
G. P. Houghton, Kilmarnock
John Sprot, Edinburgh
Colonel W. Ogilvie

Hon. Captain Arbuthnot
1838 *§‖‖§‡§‡ J. O. Fairlie of Coodham
Capt. W. H. Hunter, Perth
J. C. Fernie
James Caw, Glasgow
J. Wood, Banker, Colinsburgh
Sir Wm. Stirling Maxwell of Keir, M.P
William S. S. Crawford of Milton
Capt. Cox, R.N., hon. member
1839 W. Dundas
Sir John Wauchop of Edmonston, Bart
Jas. Walkinshaw, London
James Montgomery of Whim
Viscount Strathallan
* G. Whyte Melville, yr. of Mount Melville
G. Simson of Pitcorthie
John Peter, Kirkland
1842 R. Maidstone Smith, M.D
‖ Alex. Bethune of Blebo
R. Chambers, L.L.D., Edinbur.
John Alexander, Banff
Patrick Wilson, Edinburgh
Major Jelf Sharp, Perth
1843 Lieut.-Col. N. Christie
George Maclachlan, W.S
John Purvis of Kinaldie
Samuel Kay, Edinburgh
Alexander Mitchell Innes
Sir Coutts Lindsay, of Balcarres, Bart.
William Murray, St Andrews
W. Thompson, Calcutta
James Daun, H.E.I.C.S.
W. T. Milton, St. Andrews
W. S. Mitchell Innes, Edinr.
Lord Archibald Seymour
Alex. W. Wemyss of Denbrae

J. S. Menzies of Chesthill
Sir W. Baillie, Polkemet
A. Turnbull of Bellwood
‡‡‡ J. Calvert, Montrose
J. M'Connell, Penrith
Sir J. Richardson of Pitfour, Bart
E. M'Millan, W.S
J. Pitcairn of Pitcullo
1840 John Jameson, Dublin
Right Hon. E. Horsman, M.P
Thomas Whitson, of Parkhill
Sir W. H. Fielden, Bart
* J. Wolfe Murray of Cringletie
Hon. Mr Duncan
W. F. Ireland, St Andrews
Alex. K. Lindesay of Balmungo
1841 John Ogilvie of Inshewan
Lieu.-Col. Brewster, 76th Regt.
Stuart Grace, St Andrews
James Hadow, London
H. E. Pattullo, H.E.I.C.S
'§* Sir Thos. Moncreiffe, Bart
Earl of Caithness
Henry Peter, Kirkland
‡‡‡†††§§§‖‖‖‖‖ Capt. W. H. M. Dougall of Scotscraig
F. B. Douglas, advocate
Captain Miller, Edinburgh
1845 James Webster of Balmuir
Angus M'Laine
§§ J. Lindsay, Broughty Ferry
Duncan M'Lachlan, Dundee
David Small, writer, Dundee
Gregor M'Gregor, St Andrews
F. M. Heriot of Ramornie
John Dudingston, Earlsferry
Alex. Grace, London
Capt. E. M. Playfair, E.I.C.S.
James Wilson, M.D. Brighton
W. G. Bonar of Greigston
Isaac Horsford Cockburn, Edinburgh
Robert Fergusson, Kilkerran
†§‡ George Condie, Perth
Sir William Dunbar, Bart.
Alex. Morgan, Kirkcaldy
John Berry of Tayfield
††† James Balfour, W.S., Edinburgh

1846 Wm. Ponsonby Barker, Kilcorby Abbey, Tipperary
Captain Johnstone, Bengal Infantry
* E. James Jackson, Edinburgh
Thomas M. Stirling, Manchester
A. H. Dreghorn, Perth
Hon. Lieut.-Col. Chas. Lindsay
Duncan James Kay, High Leigh, Herts
John Ogilvie, Edinburgh
Henry Jameson, Clonmel
Captain Francis Hawkins
Captain Skene, Edinburgh
John Bayley, London
Reginald Craufurd of Craufurdland
1847 James Kidd, Airdrie
Melville Jameson, Perth
Captain J. Orr, Edinburgh
Jas. R. Hope Scott of Abbotsford, Q.C.
‡ O'Brien Peter, Kirkland
J. Blackwood, Edinburgh
Capt. H. W. Welman, 17th Foot
Sir H. H. Campbell, Bart.
Geo. More Gordon of Charleton
Pat. M'Dougall, Musselburgh
‡†§ Sir Robert Hay, Edinburgh
David Hunter of Blackness
William Keillor, Perth
Jas. A. Hunt, Pittencrieff
Wm. Horsburgh, Cupar
John Ord of Howtell
1848 James Balfour, Leven
Wm. Mason, merchant, Dundee
Robert Hodder, Leith
Richard Cowan, Leith
Wm. T. Monypenny of Pitmilly
James Kennedy, Ayr
J. T. Oswald of Dunnikier
Roger S. Aytoun of Inchdairnie, M.P.
1849 Major George Playfair, H.E.I.C.S
Robert Methven, St Andrews
Robert Berry, Tayfield
John Bell, Newcastle
Lord Charles Lennox Ker
Wm. R. Frazer, New Zealand
George H. Pagan, Cupar
Captain J. Milward Reeve of Edenpark
Major Robt. Bethune of Nydie
Robert Peddie, Advocate
John L. Campbell of Achalader
Hugh Alexander, Glammiss
Ord G. Campbell, Edinburgh
Chas. E. Cundell, Leith
Rodham Home, Edinburgh
John D. B. Hay, yr. of Morton
†Thomas Peter, Kirkland
C. F. Shand, Advocate
* The Earl of Kinnoull
1850 F. Campbell of Aros
John A. Wood, Advocate
J. Lumsdaine Small of Foodie
Robert Cowan, W.S
G. F. Montgomery, Edinburgh
Sir James Burnett, Bart
D. Graham Johnstone, London
Geo. Mackay, M.D., H.E.I.C.S
Major C. M. Govan, Royal Artillery
Norman Mitchell Innes, Parsonsgreen
§‡§ G. M. Innes, Parsonsgreen
Sir James G. Baird, Bart
Norman Uniacke
1851 Major P. J. Chiene
Wm. Marjoribanks, Leith
§‡ G. Glennie, C.E., Blackheath
D. Greenhill Gardyne, of Glenforsa, H.E.I.C.S
Robert Hebden, Orkney
Alex. Duncan, Montrose

List of members continued

A. S. Leslie Melville, Lincoln
Chas. Hugh Lyon, St. Andrews
And. R. Clark, Advocate
S. R. Lumsdaine of Lathallan
Lord Colville of Culross
John Bruce, W.S
Charles Arnot, Balcormo
Joseph Hume, St Andrews
* Sir Robert Anstruther, Bart. of Balcaskie, M.P
Geo. Moncrief Govan, M.D
1852 John Thoms of Pitscottie
George Taylor of Kirkton Hill
W. Chambers of Glenmoriston
Aw. Gillon of Wallhouse
Frederick Pitman, W.S
W. Douglas Irvine, of Denino
§ Henry Jelf Sharpe, jun.
W. Alex. Campbell of Ormsary
John F. Reoch, Edinburgh
Francis Lindsay, Leith
Andrew Taylor, banker, Cupar
Geo. F. Buist, Edinburgh
‡† Patrick Alexander, Edinr.
Lieut.-Colonel T. B. Butt, 79th Highlanders
Thos. M. Innes, Parsonsgreen
Capt. Wm. Briggs, H.E.I.C.S
His Grace the Duke of Beaufort
1853 Hon. G. E. Lascelles
‖† Major Robert T. Boothby, St Andrews
C. G. Scott of Malleny
Viscount Kirkaldie
‡ Capt. J. C. Stewart, 72d Highlanders
Earl of Leven and Melville
A. Kinloch, yr. of Gilmerton
1854 C. C. Tennant of Glen
* Earl of Dalhousie
Frederick Playfair, H.E.I.C.S
Lt.-Col. J. Hunter, H.E.I.C.S
§ Capt. W. Playfair, H.E.I.C.S
A. Gordon Sutherland, Edinr.
William Thomson of Balgowan

Henry Abel Smith, London
‡‡†‖ Thos. M'Whannel, Perth
Rev. J. A. Honey, Inchture
Sir Thomas Milles Riddell, Bart
* Earl of Rosslyn
John Thomson, Melbourne
1855 George S. Simson, yr Pitcorthie
John Campbell, H.E.I.C.S.
William Haig, St Andrews
* Robert Cathcart of Pitcairly
James Bell, Dundee
‖§‡§§ W. C. Thomson, Broughty Ferry
Dr Geo. R. Playfair, H.E.I.C.S.
Robert A. Dalyell, Lingo
A. Hay Milne, of Woodhill
Chas. Balfour of Newton-Don
* Sir D. Baird of Newbyth, Bart.
Henry Everard
Thos. A. Hogg of Newliston
Capt. James Briggs, 96th Regt.
Hon. Francis Drummond
Wm. Graham Sandford, late Perthshire Rifles
Thomas B. Blair, Dundee
1856 Major J. E. Thomson, Bengal Army
Geo. Henry Lamb, St Andrews
Professor W. Y. Sellar, Edinbur.
† Robert Mitchell, St Andrews
Robt. Chambers, jr., Edinburgh
A. W. Russell of Kenley Green
Wm. Crossthwaite, jr., Dundee
Henry M'Kechnie, Canada
Rev. Dr John Tulloch, Principal of St Mary's College
Andrew Nicoll of Bonnyton
James M. Paton, Dundee
David Wauchope, Edinburgh
James B. Gardyne, Middleton
Wm. Pagan of Clayton
James Walkinshaw, St Andrews
Sir Chas. M. Ochterlony, Bart. of Ochterlony
Wm. B. Skene of Pitlour

T. M. Bruce Gardyne of Middleton
Ralph Dalyell, Lingo
Lieut.-Colonel G. H. Moncrieff, Scots Fusilier Guards
William Ogilvie Dalgleish, yr. of Woodburne
George Dunlop, Gogar House, Edinburgh
General Phillip Anstruther, C.B. of Thirdpart
Lieut. H. L. Dempster, Madras Artillery
George Gordon, St Andrews
Major William Ross King (unattached) of Tertowie
Robt. T. Pattison, Ayton House
Captain W. D. Ogilvie Hay, 72d Highlanders

Professor Oswald Bell, M.D., St Andrews
Fountaine Walker of Foyers
William Reid, M.D., St Andrews
David L. Burn, St Andrews
Wm. Blackwood, Edinburgh
David O. Dalgleish, Woodburne
Joseph H. Lee of Redbrooke
Robert Tennent, Edinburgh
Lieut. A. L. Playfair, H.E.I.C.S
Thomas Ivory, advocate, Edinr
Patrick Arklay, Boston
John Hunter, jun., advocate, Edinburgh
W. L. Fielden, yr. of Feniscowles
James Baird Hay of Belton
1859 John Skelton, advocate, Edinburgh
Professor J. C. Shairp, St Andrews

Admiral D. Bethune of Balfour
1857 Captain Robert Webster, H.E.I.C.S.
Lieut.-Col. Robert L. Playfair, H.E.I.C.S.
Alex. Dunn Pattison, Edinburgh
The Right Honourable J. Inglis, Lord President
Colonel Douglas Jones
William Inglis of Sypsies
*Sir Thomas Erskine of Cambo, Bart.
James Wyllie Guild, Glasgow
Charles Walker, London
D. Dundas Whigham, Ayr
W. Moncrieff, Edinburgh
P. Brown, civil engineer, Perth
James Erskine, H.E.I.C.C.S
1858 Thomas Bruce of Arnot
George Lamb, R.A.
George Lees, LL.D., St Andrews
Robert Stewart, yr. of St Fort
Rev. Wm. M'Culloch, Carnbee
Viscount Stormont
Henry Montgomery, Rankeillour
Lord William Kennedy
Alex. W. L. Lindsay, H.E.I.C.S

Wm. P. Adam, of Blair-Adam, M.P
Wm. M'Donald, H.E.I.C.S, Pegu Light Infantry
Dr Wm. M'Donald, Professor of Natural History, St Andrews
Major John Patrick Briggs, late H.M. Bengal Army
George Hawkins Dempster of Dunnichen
Major D. Briggs of Strathairlie
J. H. S. Christie of Teasses
Sir Alex. Muir Mackenzie, Bart. of Delvine, 78th Highlanders
Robt. Ewing Curwen, London
Alex. Robertson, London
Henry Inglis, late 78th Highlanders
J. H. Morris, Bengal C.S
George Bayley, Edinburgh
Dr P. C. Gibson, Edinburgh
Col. Robert Campbell, London
R. Wardlaw Ramsay of Whitehill
Frederick Elliot, 36 Jermyn St., London

W. Baird Airston of Broomrigg
1860 John Ogilvy, yr. of Inshewan
J. P. F. Tytler
James Richard, St Andrews
W. F. Lindesay, yr. of Balmungo
Dr David Smith, Bengal Army
P. Bairnsfather of Dunbarrow
D. Meldrum, of Kincaple
Harry Smith, Advocate, Edinr.
Evan B Gardyne, Bombay Army
Dr William S. Playfair, London
Lieut. Lorn Macdonald, H.M. Indian Army
Jas. Stirling, C.E., Edinburgh
P. C. Baldwin, China
W. Malcolm Low, yr. of Clatto
John A. Lindsay, Balmungo
Capt. W. Keir, China
Lieut.-Col. Maitland, Bengal Army
James Mure, of Caldwell
Hamilton Anstruther, Balcaskie
Bruce Stark Christie, Teasses
Arbuthnot Guthrie, London
Capt A. Stewart, late of 11th Hussars
1861 Capt. Crabtree, F.M. Rifles
Capt. Forrest, late 79th Highlanders
Sir P. A. Halkett, Bart. of Pitfirrane
W. A. Brown, advocate, Edinburgh
J. S. Wilson, yr. of Auchineden
‡§‖ Thomas Hodge, St Andrews
David W. Balfour Ogilvy, late 24th Regiment
Captain G. Sinclair, Edinburgh
Captain Douglas Herbert, R.N.,

Robert Richardson, Restalrig, Edinburgh
Lt.-Col. E. Maude, 109th Foot
George Mercer, Edinburgh
Captain Falconer, St Andrews
Major General Stuart, C.B., late 14th Dragoons
A. Smith, yr. of Carbeth Guthrie
A. D. Cockburn, Coates House
W. H. Haig, Cameron House
George Clerk Cheape of Strathtyrum
D. Archibald, M.D., St Andrews
William Morrison, Procurator-Fiscal, Cupar
J. Lindesay Keir, Brunton House
Edward Broughton, Calcutta
Lieut. Wauchope, H.M. Indian Army
Henry R. Kynaston, Blackheath
Captain Thomas William Goff, late 7th Dragoon Guards
George C. Cheape, jun., 11th Hussars
Major Archibald Blackwood, Indian Staff Corps
1862 Wm. Traill of Woodwick
A. Henderson Chalmers, W.S.
D. Bryan Webster, Edinburgh
†‖‡‖ Robert Clark, Edinburgh
Henry Moncrieff, Great Stuart Street, Edinburgh
Andrew G. Merson, Oriental Bank, Melbourne
David G. Bruce Gardyne, Trin. College, Oxford
Col. Brown, H.M. Indian Army
The Lord Elphinstone, R.N., Carberry House, Musselburgh
Dr J. Walker, Cupar

100

I'm called "Old Tom" with Tommy coming to the door

"TREASON!"

GOLFERS have, it seems, agreed to forgive Allan Robertson for his nefarious and Satanic caper in inventing a crime; but I must say I never expected that Old Tom would have made himself a partner to this outrage on the sanctity of the Royal game. It may be a photograph—it may be a daguerreotype. Who knows—who cares? But what will the pious golfer of Boodrapoor, say, or the reformed putter of the Sing-Sing recreation ground think when they recognise in this masquerade the face they have brought up their lambs to reverence? What would Old Sutherland have thought of this untoward development of ribald levity, or Allan, or even Old Philp? As to Old Gourlay, I have not the least doubt, from a careful perusal of his recorded pranks, that his remarks would have done full justice to this melancholy ploy.

Let us draw the curtain silently and with as few tears as may be over this wayward freak of Old Tom's! His partner—and, no doubt, his evil genius—in this fleeting iniquity was a Mr. Hastie, of the old Cross Keys Hotel, St. Andrews; and as he seems to have been much liked in his day and generation, it is perhaps best that we forgive him also.

10

Tommy
aged 16 years
was attracting a
lot of attention.

Tournament in Leith 1867
Willie
Bob Kirk
Tommy
Jamie Anderson
Brother George
Jamie Dunn
Sandy Greig
Allan Strath
Self posing with the ball
Willie Dunn

103

Copyright Photograph, published by J. K. Home Crawford, Photographer, Portobello, Edinburgh. Woodbury Gravure.

W. Dunn. Geo. Morris. Tom Morris, Jun. David Park. Jas. Anderson. Bob Kirk. W. Dow. A. Strath. Tom Morris. Jas. Dunn. Alexr. Greig.

GRAND GOLF TOURNAMENT BY PROFESSIONAL PLAYERS

On Leith Links, 17th May, 1867.

Andrew Strath Davy Park Bob Kirk Jamie Anderson Jamie Dunn Willie Dow Willie Dunn Greig Self Tommy George

Article about this photograph on page 190

players extant; made the running by finishing the first round in 55, and had he not come summarily to grief in the second, he would have been honourably placed. Bob Kirk , too, one of the best professionals in Scotland, made a creditable beginning, but, falling off, was nowhere, notwithstanding numerous bets that he would be one, two, three. Bob Andrew, a first class player, looked like the winner for a while, but the fates were against him, and he had to content himself with a position very much disproportionate to his merits. Dunn and Dow, from whom much was expected, both played a good though unfortunate game. Park came out in his old style, and astonished those who thought that his chance was *nil.* The veteran Tom Morris, against whom any odds were pitted, vindicated his former repute by carrying off the Belt, his next formidable antagonist, Park, being only two strokes behind him.

The following are the details of the three rounds –

1. Tom Morris, the Belt, £7	58	54	58 -	170
2. W. Park, £5,	58	56	58 -	172
3. A. Strath, £3,	61	57	56 -	174
4. T. Morris, jr., £1	58	59	58 -	175

The Challenge 1867
my 4th win

Thursday dawned most auspiciously, although as the hour approached, the sky was overcast, threatening rain, which, however, kept off till *the* event of the meeting, and indeed of the golfing year, was decided. A smart breeze blew from the south-west – the most favourable wind for the Prestwick Links. There was a great muster of professionals and more than an average attendance of spectatora. No competition excites more interest among the lovers of the grand old national pastime than that for the Challenge Bel, open as it is to the world. For the first time since it was instituted, the *cognoscenti*

were in perplexity, not knowing whom to back. There were no favourites, four to one being freely laid upon the field, although the two most distinguished professionals in the country had entered the lists. The hesitation generally manifested to put money on those who had alternately made good their claims to the championship, was accounted for by the fact that the "rising talent" had lately proved themselves dangerous rivals to the most experienced golfers in the kingdom. It would seem, however, that there is as much glorious uncertainty on the green as there is proverbially in the courts of law. An amateur – Mr Doleman – than whom there are few, if any, better

Prestwick Golf Club 1867

The Champion Belt

The play on the whole was very good. So much, however, cannot be said for the next day's match for the champion belt. The weather was most suitable but somehow everyone seemed to be below their game. The consequence was that the scores were considerably above the average of good play. On this occasion, Tom Morris had the fortune to regain his lost laurels, the belt and £7 falling to him with a score of 170. Park came in second with 172; Andrew Strath, third, 174; and Tom Morris jun., fourth, 175. The other competitors were R. Kirk, 177; M. Doleman, 178; R. Andrew, 179; W. Dow and T Hunter, 184 and W. Dunn, 189. Considerable disappointment was expressed that there should not have been a formal investiture of the belt by some of the officials of the club on the spot, although the modesty with which old Tom Morris wears his honours, we presume it was more in consonance with his own feelings to have been relieved from participating in any such ceremony.

After the belt Tom Morris Jun., challenged Park to a round the latter winning by two out of twelve holes.

IX.—CARNOUSTIE AND TAYMOUTH GOLF CLUB.

Instituted more than 30 years ago.

JAMES SMITH, *Captain.*

JAMES LAIRD, *Treasurer.* ALEX. SPARKS, *Secretary.*

James Hogg, David Hogg, Alex. Kyd, Robert Gray, William Rae, David Mitchell, William Japp, Alex. Butchart, George Milne, Andrew Gray—*Council.*

13th October.—The closing match for the season took place, being an annual game between the Bachelors and Married Men in the Club, and resulted in favour of the Bachelors by 11 holes.

Brother George now the Professional

Tommy won the first tournament on the new course (10 to 18 holes) conversion

The Royal North Devon and West of England Golf club

Of the Links themselves, it is enough to say that Tom Morris, St. Andrews, on visiting Northam shortly after the institution of the Club, to lay out the course, pronounced them the finest he had ever seen.

Mr Glennie Colonel Fairlie and General Hope Grant are members

Re-laid out the course in 1867

Tommy wins The Belt

- Son and Father winner and runner-up

I was as proud that day as if I'd won it myself

1st oct 1868

The belt was played for on Thursday. Twelve competitors (six couple) came forward. It was won by Tom Morris, jun., St Andrews, at 154. The following came next in order. Tom Morris, sen., St Andrews, 155 and C. Hunter, Prestwick, 172; R. Andrews, Perth, 159, and R. Fergusson, Musselburgh, 165; W. Park, Musselburgh, 162 and W. Dow, Musselburgh, 180; R. Kirk, Blackheath, 171 and W. Dunn, Leith, 183; W. Doleman, Glasgow, 181, and T. Dunn, Leith, 167. It will be seen that Young Tom Morris carries off the belt, and first prize of £6, with a score of 154; Tom Morris sen., the second prize of £4, with a score of 155; and R. Andrews, Perth, the third prize of £2, with a score of 159. Consolation stakes £5, nine competitors - 1st, R. Fergusson, Musselburgh, score 51; 2d and 3d tie between J. Allan, North Devon, and R. Kirk, Blackheath, 52. On Friday a match was played by Tom Morris jun., and J. Allan, against W. Park and R. Kirk, in which the former gained by 4 up and 2 to play. The winner of the belt was the youngest competitor on the Links. - *Ayrshire Express*

Ayr advertiser 23rd Sept 1869

PRESTWICK GOLF CLUB.– The competition for the champion belt of the Prestwick Golf Club came off on the Prestwick Links on Thursday, and was witnessed by a large number of spectators. The weather was very favourable for the game, and great interest was manifested in it. The course for the belt is three rounds of the Links or 36 holes. The match is open to the members of any established Golf Club as well as to professionals. The trophy, the possession of which is coveted by all golfers, is made of red morocco, richly ornamented, and is a fine piece of workmanship. Seven couples started for the belt on Thursday viz., Mr G. Mitchell Innes and Doleman; D. Strath and Jamie Anderson; Charley Hunter and Tom Dunn; Dr McQuaig and Tom Morris, jun.; Bob Kirk and Tom Morris, sen.; Mr C. McArthur and W. Doleman; Mr George McArthur and James S. Imrie. There was some capital play. After the first round, however, it was almost certain that Tom Morris, jun. would repeat his last year's performance by carrying off the belt – he having made the first round in 50 strokes. Curiously enough the station hole was made by him in one stroke.! The second round he made in 55 strokes, and the third in 52. With this total of 157 strokes he proved himself the champion for the present year. Should he win it next year, and thus be the victor three years in succession, he will retain the belt. Bob Kirk was second in 168 strokes, and D. Strath, third in 169. On Wednesday evening, after the contest for the Eglinton Gold Medal, a foursome match was played btwixt Tom Morris, jun., and Jamie Anderson, against Bob Kirk and Strath – the former couple winning by seven holes in two rounds.

PRESTWICK GOLF CLUB.

THE CHAMPION BELT. ~~1869~~ 1868

Mr T. Morris Junr

1st Round. Strokes.		Holes.		2d Round. Strokes
5	/////	1	/////	5
5	/////	2	//////	6
4	////	3	////	4
5	/////	4	//////	6
5	/////	5	/////	5
5	/////	6	////	4
3	///	7	///	3
4	////	8	////	4
4	////	9	/////	5
4	////	10	////	4
3	///	11	///	3
4	////	12	/////	5/4
				54
		1st Round.		51
		Total.		105

Tommy's winning card for 1869 was in fact, the 1868 card – his 1st win

106

1st

Tommy

2nd

Bob Kirk

John allan

June 1870 ↓

GOLFING AT DEVON.

The following is from an esteemed correspondent:– —When golf champions wend their way from Scotch Links to the far off south and west quarters of the noble game in North Devon, it may probably interest the inhabitants of Fife, and the golfers of that elk, to hear how it fared with the golf champion from St Andrews, Thomas Morris, jun., with Bob Kirk, the Blackheath professional; and with John Allan, formerly of Prestwick, Aberdeen; and St Andrews, the professional curator of the N. Devon Links. These three met on Friday on the Westward Ho! Links, North Devon, when the following single matches were arranged and played:—

Morris v. Kirk. →
Morris v. Allan.
Allan v. Kirk.

The matches were one round of the links of 18 holes. The competition was by holes and not strokes—to each single, two prizes were allotted, the results of a subscription—a first prize of £3, a second prize of £1. While to the best round of the six, a further prize of £1 was allotted. The games were finely contested, and gave one more proof of the glorious uncertainty of golf—each man winning one match. Morris beating Kirk—Allan beating Morris—Kirk beating Allan—while Morris made the best round. The wind was fresh but not boisterous, in the north-west—some little rain fell during the first match—but there was very litttle during the second, and none during the third. The day was grey, and in all other respects a good one for the professional competition. I proceed to record these matches as I took them down to the best of my ability, anxious to do honour to the brave, and rejoicing over no man's griefs—with this exception that a professional's trials and failures always afford some comfort to the sufferings and afflictions of the amateur, buried in bunkers or rushes, and awfully punished:—

Kirk v. Morris. →

Hole 1—Halved in five.

Hole 2—A cleek shot from the tee landed Morris in a good place to play over the yawning high hole bunker. He played a good shot with his cleek on the flag, about 90 yards off, and on reaching the hole found his ball in it! Kirk made a fair hole in four. Morris one hole up.

Hole 3—Morris holed out well in four. Kirk's first was wild to the left and fell in a rushy place. He made a good shot under difficulties, but went short to the right of the hole—a good long putt brought him within reach of a half—which he nearly secured with a second putt that caught the edge of the hole, but failed to fall into the trap. Morris two holes up.

Hole 4—Kirk proved the truth of the old golf adage that a bad tee shot generally brings grief in its train. He tapped his ball from the tee, and put it behind some rushes—thence a spoon shot carried him into a second rushy bottom near the hole. A first iron shot failed to lift the globe out of its grief. Three more iron shots landed it on the green, and two putts wound up the sad history in eight. Morris holed in four. Morris three holes up.

THURSDAY, JUNE 16, 1870

107

YOUNG TOM WINS THE CHAMPIONSHIP BELT OUTRIGHT →

Hole 5—In appr aching this green, Kirk got into the bunker his second shot—thence he made a fine iron stroke on to the green, and holed out with two putts. Morris reaching the green with his second holed in two more. Morris four holes up.

Hole 6—Kirk holed in three. Morris got a bad fall from his tee shot, but making an excellent iron stroke, holed out also in three with a brisk putt.

Hole 7—Kirk had the best position after the tee shots; both parties made fine iron strokes on to the green, and holed in two putts.

Hole 8—In this, Morris played a short iron stroke from a sandy hill side, while Kirk played his second shot with the iron beyond the green, and holed in two putts—Morris making a second iron stroke and two putts before he h ed out—Morris three holes up.

Hole 9—Morr hitting a wild tee shot got into a bad bunker, with another similar sandy grove between him and the hole—his niblick admirably played laid him on the green. Kirk was still nearer the hole with an excellent iron shot, but failing to hole in one putt, a close shave, the hole was halved in four.

Hole 10—Two long drives from the tee landed both players over the alps, and amid some closely adjoining sandy peeks. Morris holed out the best in four strokes in all to Kirk's five—Morris four holes up.

Hole 11—Two long tee shots left both players on a little green basis among surrounding bunkers and rushes—a very narrow escape from serious trouble. Morris, half topping his next stroke put it under a bunker's face—but drove out sideways into a place of safety with his niblick—he then played two iron strokes, and ended by holing a fine hill side putt of about five paces. Kirk, taking one stroke less, won the hole. Morris three holes up.

Hole 12—Both parties holed in four. Morris interfering what nearly proved a stymie. Kirk put on his mettle, holed out, scraping his opponent's ball in passing.

Hole 13—Kirk drove into the bunker near hole his first shot, but, lying well, played out on green, and holed in two more. Morris was not so fortunate, failing in an iron shot across the bunker, he fell in the sand too near the face to be comfortable—a failure with the niblick left the ball so bad against the wall of bunker, that Morris was obliged to come out sideways with niblick — the ball reaching the green, and eventually, after rolling some way, falling again into the bunker. Its position worse than when it first fell into this sand. A fine niblick shot, at last, laid it safety, and two putts played it in the hole. Morris holes up.

Hole 14—Kirk topped his tee shot, but the second shot laid the combatants side by side in a grassy hollow. Kirk taking his fourth heavy on a sandy hill side, made little progress, and fell in sand—but with his iron reached the green, running beyond the hole. Having to cross a hillock he then used the cleek, and ended with three puts of a somewhat feeble character. Morris's third shot fell luckily on a small grassy edge of a bad bunker, and thus avoided punishment, thence with an iron shot on to green, when he holed out in two putts, doing this hole in two less. Morris three holes up.

Hole 15.—Morris hooked his tee shot to the left among rushes—whence however he made a clever spoon shot, falling again somewhat luckily just above some small bunkers—following up another spoon shot with one from his iron. he laid his ball dead with the putter from abo yards off, and halved in six with Kirk, who w very short in his first putt, and expended three strokes on the green, being hindered by a stymie. Morris dormy three.

Hole 16—Morris topped his second shot, and barely avoided the bunker, lying on the sward above it—thence he played a fine iron shot on to the green, and holed in one putt. Kirk, balked by some bystanders moving near him, played his third shot short with the iron, and taking two putts to hole out, lost the hole. Morris wins the m tch by four holes.

Hole 17—Morris holed out in four strokes. Kirk taking one more, getting into sandy road from off the tee, the first iron shot failing to transplant the ball. The niblick laid the ball on the green. An iron and a cleek stroke made up the num of five.

Hole 18—Morris won this la hole in eight—Kirk taking nine. Kirk tipped his ba the third shot, thereby losing his chance of the hole.

Thus the champion golfer heavily beat the Blackheath professional. The contest, though not a close one, embraced many points of interest, and gave untold satisfaction to the assembled golfers.

After twenty minutes' refreshment, Morris and Allan put in an appearance on the teeing ground, and the second professional match of the day commenced.

Thus ended three very interesting matches.

The scores were as follows: –

	1st Round.	2nd Round.	Total.
T. Morris	35	49	84
B. Kirk	42	51	93
T. Morris	38	48	86
J. Allan	44	44	88
B. Kirk	39	48	87
J. Allan	40	50	90

Tom Morris carried off the Exeter prize for the best round—84.

I trust that our professional guests will have so pleasant a recollection of our course, and of their own interesting competitions, that we may see them again on future occasions. It may, I think, be worthy of consideration whether great and grave professional matches, like the late one of the champion's father and W. Park, might not with good reason and some advantage be played here, as on a neutral links. We will offer to all combatants a fair field and no favour.

As strangers may like to know something of our links, I venture to add that Thomas Morris, senior, of St Andrews, will shortly be supplied with excellent lithographic plans of our links, published from an original ur y.

ST ANDREWS.

The "Westward Ho!" Meeting.—The *Exeter Telegram* of Saturday says:—"The golf medal week of the Royal North Devon and West of England Gold Club will be held in Whitsun week. Already the men of North Devon are working up for the struggle. The Royal Blackheath Club have put off their medal day, in order that they may be well represented on the North Devon links, and not only are the flower of amatuer players expected, but Bob Kirk, the professional, has signified his intention of being present, and the exciting encounter of last year, in which John Allan, the professional of the Royal North Devon Club, was victorious, will be renewed. An attempt is being made to induce young Tom Morris, the champion, to give battle to John Allan, and if the distance from St Andrews does not form an impediment, we may hope to see him.

…In 1868, Tom Morris, jun., won the belt with the lowest score then on record - 154, and repeated his success last year with the score of 157. Considerably more than the usual interest in the belt was manifested this year, as it was known that Young Tom was in excellent form, while other players were in equally good play, and all determined to do their best in order to prevent the young champion from permanently retaining the belt, which he would do if he won it on the present occasion. The weather on Thursday was beautiful, and in every way favourable for playing the ancient and national game. There was scarcely any wind, and the heat was tempered by light, fleecy clouds, which hid the sun's face. The large number of spectators who assembled on the green testified to the general interest which was felt in the contest, and from the Cardinal's Nob and other coigns of vantage, knots of ladies and gentlemen watched the play. Others, again, accompanied the combatants, and took hints from the play of the professionals, as they advanced from hole to hole. The favourite, and the player who had the largest following, was young Tommie, whose careful and steady play was the theme of general admiration. In fact, he never played better in his life, and the manner in which he drove was as wonderful as his short game. Nine couples started at ten o'clock for the three rounds, which were not finished till shortly before three o'clock. At the conclusion of the second round it would observe that the →

victor would turn up in either of the three juniors – Tom Morris, Bob Kirk, and David Strath – all of whom were playing very steadily. In the first round young Tom took 47 strokes to the twelve holes, the lowest score on record, and in the two following rounds he only scored 51 each – his total for the three rounds being 149, the smallest with which the belt has yet been won. It is also worthy of note that during the three successive years on which the young champion has gained the belt it was with the lowest scores hitherto made since the institution of the contest – his totals being 154, 157, and 149, in 1868, 1869, and 1870 respectively. Tom Morris, sen.'s, lowest score in his champion years was 163, while Willie Park's lowest total was 168, and that in 1863. Andrew Strath won the belt with the score of 162 – the same as was made on Thursday by Tom Morris, sen. D. Strath and Bob Kirk tied for second honours with the score of 161, and they played a round of twelve holes in order to decide the claimant for the second prize of £4 – the third being £2, while £6 was given along with the belt. The tie resulted in the victory of Bob Kirk, who took 56 strokes to the round, compared with 60 made by Strath. The play of these young players was first-class, and Strath accounts for his longish score of 58 in the third round by getting into the Cardinal's Nob bunker. He took 54 strokes in the first round, and only 49 to the second. Bob Kirk did the first two rounds in 52 each, while his third was only achieved in 57 – he also having come to grief in a bunker.

As Young Tom carries off the belt to St Andrews and retains it, a new champion trophy will require to be furnished if a wholesome spirit of emulation is to be kept up among the professional golfers of the country. We understand that it is the intention of the Prestwick Golf Club to order another belt, but we have not learned what the design will be, or the probable cost. If a suggestion might be allowed, we would say that the trophy should be made perhaps less valuable than the one so honourably won by the young St Andrews champion, and that the money prize which always accompanies the championship should be increased. Why should not at least £20 be given to the annual champion? That sum would be more commensurate with the importance of the contest and the honour of winning the belt than the present paltry £6, while we daresay there would be even more numerous competitors than at present.....

......Our correspondent says – "Young Tom has won the belt for the third time," were the words in everybody's mouths when the news arrived of his success, and they seemed to convey the *acme* of satisfaction. A flag was displayed from Mr Morris's workshop, and when it became known that the champion would arrive on Saturday night with the 10 o'clock train, a number of his friends awaited his arrival, and he had scarcely set foot on the railway terminus ere he was hoisted shoulder high and borne in triumph to Mr Leslie's Golf Inn, where his health was drank with every honour.

1870

GOLF MATCH AT MONTROSE.—On Monday forenoon a match was commenced on the Montrose Links between Tom Morris and Robert Dow for 36 holes. At the outset, Tom took the lead, and gained the first six holes in succession. Dow gained the seventh hole, but Tom again took the lead, and won the next four holes. Dow was successful in gaining two holes and halving other two successively; but Tom, by some beautiful putting, gained other two holes; Dow also gained another. Tom was therefore the gainer by eight holes. There were two holes halved, twelve won by Tom, and four won by Dow. Tom was very fortunate in putting, and some extraordinary fine putts were made. In the second round, Dow won first a hole with four, while Tom required six. At the eleventh hole Tom stood at eight up, being the same as at the conclusion of the first round. There being only seven to play, Dow decided to settle the match and thus terminated one of the most interesting matches ever played on Montrose Links.

ROYAL AND ANCIENT GOLF CLUB.

The October meeting of this Club came off on Wednesday with very great success. There was a very large attendance of spectators, and the number of competitors for the honours was upon a scale beyond that of former years. The wind was against what may be called the average play, and was in going out about equal to a third on the round. In other respects no day could have been better, either for those engrged in the game, or for those looking on. The green, thanks to Tom Morris, was in splendid condition. The usual meeting of the members took place in the Club House at 11 o'clock, under the auspices of the retiring Captain, Sir Robert Anstruther, Bart., M.P., at which a number of new members were admitted. Sir John Bethune of Kilconquhar was duly elected Captain for the year. Shortly before noon the newly elected Captain played off the first ball, which secured him the Silver Club and the Royal Adelaide Medal, after which the competition commenced. The result was a tie between Mr Hodge and Dr M'Cunig, of Edinburgh, at 96, Mr Robert Chambers, of Edinburgh, scoring 97. It was precisely 4.30 when the last couple, Messrs Thomson and Lamb, came in, and it was felt desirable that the tie should be played off at that time. Some difficulty, however, seems to have arisen, which was referred to the committee, who decided, very much against the general opinion, to postpone competing for the tie till next day.

1867

The tie for the medal was played off on Thursday, by Mr Hodge and Dr M'Cunig. The wind was as boisterous and unfavourable for golf playing as on Wednesday. A keen interest was manifested in the result of this round, and many ladies and gentlemen followed the two competitors the whole round of the golf course. The result was Mr Hodge made the round in 99 strokes, and Dr M'Cunig in 105. Mr Hodge was accordingly declared the winner of the medal.

The only other match of importance was a keenly contested foursome, by Tom Morris and his son Tom against Andrew Strath and Bob Kirk. The play on both sides was exceedingly good, when taking into account the state of the weather. And so closely contested was the first round, that either party considered themselves lucky if they got a single hole ahead; and when they did so, it was generally to be brought down the next one to "all square." They were all square coming in the first round at the burn hole; and on playing out the last hole Tom Moris, sen., made a long put in playing the odds, which fell a good distance short of the hole. Strath failed to hole his ball by his next put, and young Tom, by an excellent put, holed his ball, which made them equal on the round. On coming back the second round, the father and son gained the match by three holes and two to play. Young Tom played a splendid game, and was admired by the large concourse of spectators as a youth of great promise. A good deal of betting was on this match.

109

The competition for the belt was originated by the late Earl of Eglinton and Colonel Fairlie of Coodham in 1861. The game is three rounds of 12 holes each. The belt, which becomes the property of young Tom, is made of red morrocco, and is an exquisite piece of workmanship, richly ornamented with massive silver plates. Among other appropriate devices it bears the Burgh of Prestwick Coat of Arms. The trophy, we believe, is worth about thirty guineas, and has been won as under:—

	Strokes.
1860—W. Park, Musselburgh,	174
1861—Tom Morris, sen., Prestwick,	163
1862— Do. do. do.	163
1863—W. Park, ...	168
1864—Tom Morris, ...	160
1865—A. Strath, St Andrews, ...	162
1866—W. Park, ...	169
1867—Tom Morris, St Andrews, ...	170
1068—Tom Morris, Jun., ...	154
1869— Do. do., ...	157
1870— Do. do., ...	149

From the above it will be seen that young Tom has secured the belt this year with five strokes less than ever it was won with before. It is worthy of notice that the champion this year made the round in 47 strokes—a feat which has never been equalled. In previous years the lowest number was 49, which was performed by young Tom and the late Andrew Strath. Tom Morris, junr., besides securing the belt, won the first prize of £6. For the second prize of £4 Bob Kirk and D. Strath tied, and played a round of the links, to decide, with the following result:—

	Strokes.
R. Kirk, ...	56
D. Strath, ...	60

Kirk was therefore declared winner of the second prize, and Strath received the third prize of £2.

Yesterday the links again presented an animated appearance; and a number of interesting matches were played. For the Consolation Stakes, one round, the following professionals started:—C. Hunter, C. Brown, Tom Morris, Jamie Anderson, and Willie Park. After splendid play, Allan and Anderson tied at 50 for the first prize—and divided first and second—Morris being third, and Park fourth. An interesting foursome was played between J. Bennet, Esq., London, and Tom Morris, jun., against Mr Denniston and Charlie Hunter. Over two rounds the latter couple won by 4 holes. Another foursome was played, which resulted in a tie. E. A. Hunter, Esq., and young Tom played three matches against Mr Wilson of Polquhairn and Charlie Hunter, when the former pair gained one match on the day's play. Mr Craig and J. Allan played three rounds against J. S. Muir, the winner of the medal, and ended all square. A foursome, in which Rev. Mr Syme and Willie Park opposed Tom Morris, senr., and Mr. D. D. Whigham, resulted in a victory for the former couple.

The initiatory stage of what promises to be a very interesting contest for a sum of money, was commenced on Prestwick links yesterday [illegible] Tom Morris and Bob Kirk—3 rounds for 36 holes. After some magnificent play Kirk gained 4 holes on the day's play. The match is to be finished on St Andrews links during the ensuing week.

THE CHAMPION BELT.

Of all the days in the year the Belt Day is the most exciting on the picturesque Links of Prestwick. The belt was instituted as a prize in 1860—the object of the Prestwick Golf Club, by whom the thirty guineas which the belt cost was subscribed, being to afford an annual test as to the comparative merits of professional golfers. The competition is open to the world, and on almost every occasion since the prize was offered, amateurs as well as professionals have taken part in the great annual championship contest. The belt is of red morocco, ornamented with massive silver plates—that on the centre having two golfers and two caddies represented in the act of playing golf, in relievo. The back plate has the common seal of the burgh of Prestwick exquisitely engraved upon it, and surrounded with scroll-work. There are also two massive clasps, with golf clubs and balls in relievo. The belt, on the whole, is a beautiful trophy, and is well worthy of the keen emulation displayed by the different players during the past ten years. The conditions of the contest for the belt were, that it should be won three times in succession by the same player, and that the course should be three rounds of Prestwick Links, or thirty-six holes. It was won in 1860 by Willie Park, Musselburgh, and on the two following years by Tom Morris, sen.—then custodier of the Prestwick Links. Willie Park won it in 1863 and again in 1866, and Tom Morris, sen., secured the championship in 1864 and 1867—the trophy going in 1865 to Andrew Strath. In 1868, Tom Morris, jun., won the belt with the lowest score then on record—154, and repeated his success last year with the score of 157. Considerably more than the usual interest in the belt was manifested this year, as it was known that Young Tom was in excellent form, while other players were in equally good play, and all determined to do their best in order to prevent the young champion from permanently retaining the belt, which he would do if he won it on the present occasion. The weather yesterday was beautiful, and in every way favourable for playing the ancient national game. There was scarcely any wind, and the heat was tempered by light, fleecy clouds, which hid the sun's face. The large number of spectators who assembled on the green testified to the general interest which was felt in the contest, and from the Cardinal's Nob and other coigns of vantage, knots of ladies and gentlemen watched the play. Others, again, accompanied the combatants, and took hints from the play of the professionals, as they advanced from hole to hole. The favourite, and the player who had the largest following, was young Tommie, whose careful and steady play was the theme of general admiration. In fact, he never played better in his life, and the manner in which he drove was as wonderful as his short game. Nine couples started at ten o'clock for the three rounds, which were not finished till shortly before three o'clock. At the conclusion of the second round it was observed that the victor would turn up in either of the three juniors—Tom Morris, Bob Kirk, and David Strath—all of whom were playing very steadily. In the first round young Tom only took 47 strokes to the twelve holes, the lowest score on record, and in the two following rounds he only scored 51 each—his total for the three rounds being 149, the smallest with which the belt has yet been won. It is also worthy of note that during the three successive years on which the young champion has gained the belt it was with the lowest scores hitherto made since the institution of the contest—his totals being 154, 157, and 149 in 1868, 1869, and 1870 respectively. Tom Morris, sen.'s, lowest score in his champion years was 163, while Willie Park's lowest total was 168, and that in 1863. Andrew Strath won the belt with the score of 162—the same as was made yesterday by Tom Morris, senior. D. Strath and Bob Kirk tied for second honours, with the score of 161, and they played a round of twelve holes in order to decide the claimant for the second prize of £4—the third being £2, while £6 was given along with the belt. The tie resulted in the victory of Bob Kirk, who took 56 strokes to the round, compared with 60 made by Strath. The play of both these young golfers was first-class, and Strath accounts for his longish score of 58 in the third round by getting into the Cardinal's Nob bunker.

Players.	1st Rd.	2d Rd.	3d Rd.	Tl.
1st, Tom Morris, jun., St Andrews	47	51	51	149
2d, Bob Kirk, Blackheath	52	52	57	161
3d, David Strath, St Andrews	54	49	58	161
Tom Morris, sen., Do.	56	52	54	162
William Doleman, Musselburgh	57	54	58	169
William Park, Do.	60	55	58	173
Jamie Anderson, St Andrews	59	57	58	174
J. Allan, North Devon	61	58	57	176
A. Doleman, Musselburgh	61	59	58	178
C. Hunter, Prestwick	58	56	64	178
T. Brown, Musselburgh	66	55	59	180
J. Miller, Do.	66	63	54	183
T. Hunter, Do.	62	63	60	185
F. Doleman, Do.	65	64	60	189
W. Boyd, Prestwick	65	59	67	191
J. Hunter, Do.	62	65	64	191
W. Dow, Musselburgh	68	64	66	198

As Young Tom carries off the belt to St Andrews, and retains it, a new champion trophy will require to be furnished if a wholesome spirit of emulation is to be kept up among the professional golfers of the country. We understand that it is the intention of the Prestwick Golf Club to order another belt, but we have not learned what the design will be, or the probable cost. If a suggestion might be allowed, we would say that the trophy should be made perhaps less valuable than the one so honourably won by the young St Andrews champion, and that the money prize which always accompanies the championship should be increased. Why should not at least £20 be given to the annual champion? That sum would be more commensurate with the importance of the contest and the honour of winning the belt than the present paltry £6, while we daresay there would be even more numerous competitors than at present.

Among the gentlemen on the Links yesterday were the Earl of Stair, Captain E. A. Hunter, Mr Gibson-Craig, Mr Pettigrew Wilson, of Polquhairn; Mr D. Dundas Whigham; Mr W. J. Mure, Edinburgh; Mr Hay Newton; Captain Lindsay, Captain Campbell, of Craigie; Mr D. B. Wauchope, Rev. J. Sime, Dundonald, Rev. Mr Rennie, Glasgow; Dr Wilson, Ayr; Rev. Mr Gray, Glasgow; Bailie Salmon, Glasgow; Bailie Wilson, Glasgow; Bailie Goudie, Ayr; Mr Charles Dalrymple, M.P.; Mr A. Crombie and Mr W. R. Crombie, Glasgow; Mr Mitchell, of Sauchrie; Mr Hart, secretary to the Prestwick Golf Club, &c. The belt was formally presented to Young Tom by the Earl of Stair.

1870

THE GOLD MEDAL.

The annual business meeting of the Club was held on Wednesday, but the business brought forward was of little importance. After the business meeting, the members of the club proceeded to play for the Eglinton Gold Medal, the competition for which is confined to the members. The weather was fine, with a fair breeze of wind, and there was a good turn-out of spectators, including a number of county ladies and gentleman. About one o'clock eleven couples started on the journey of a round and a half, the gentlemen playing in pairs as follows:—Mr Gibson Craig and Mr Ogilvy Fairlie; Rev. Mr Sime and Mr Whigham; Mr Lamb and Mr A. Crombie; Dr Knower and Mr Shand; Mr W. Wilson and Mr G. Smith; Mr W. Houldsworth and Mr W. H. Houldsworth; Rev. Mr Rennie and Mr H. Hart; Mr Muir and Mr Wauchope; Mr Wallace and Mr W. Crombie; Mr Pettigrew Wilson and Dr Gibson; Dr Wilson and Captain Lindsay. At the conclusion of the game, Mr W. J. Muir, Edinburgh, was found to be the winner of the medal with a score of 96 strokes. Mr W. R. Crombie was second, with 100 strokes; and Rev. J. Rennie, third, with 105 strokes. The medal was won last year by Mr M. Innes, with 119 strokes of two rounds of the links.—There was also a sweepstake incorporated with the medal, which was tied for by the Rev. J. Rennie and Mr W. J. Muir. After deducting 9 strokes, the prizes were divided.

MATCHES.

Several matches were played during the week. On Monday J. Anderson and Bob Kirk had a contest with Tom Morris, jun., and J. Hunter, when the former couple won by four holes in two rounds. A short match of two holes was won by the same couple. In a match between the same pairs, two rounds, Anderson and Kirk giving their opponents a fourth, Morris and Hunter won by a hole. On the same day, Mr Whigham and D. Strath played J. Allan and Dr Wilson three matches, when the latter couple won by one match. On Tuesday, Tom Morris, sen., and Bob Kirk played a single of 24 holes, when "Old Tom" won by 4 holes. John Allan and D. Strath had a single of 24 holes, which was gained by the latter by 6 holes. The Earl of Stair and Mr Whigham had two matches with Mr E. A. Hunter and C. Hunter, which finished "all square." On Wednesday, Tom Morris, jun., and J. Allan had a single, when the latter won by 3 holes, the scores being 54 and 57. Park and Hunter played one round, when the former won by 3 up and 2 to play. Young Tom Morris and Bob Park played a single of 12 holes, which resulted "all square." Tom Morris, sen., and Mr Whigham played a couple of matches against the Rev. Mr Sime and Bob Park. The first match was halved, and the second was won by Morris and Mr Whigham.

Ayr Observer
Sept 1870

CONSOLATION PRIZES.

On Friday, the weather being again auspicious, five couples started for the consolation Prizes given by the Club for the non-successful professionals. The following were the five competing couples: John Allan, North Devon, and F. Doleman, Musselburgh; T. Brown, Musselburgh, and T. Hunter, Musselburgh; Tom Morris, sen., St. Andrews, and James Anderson, St. Andrews; W. Doleman, Musselburgh, and W. Park, Musselburgh; W. Dow, Musselburgh, and W. Boyd, Prestwick. The game was one round of twelve holes. At the close, John Allan and James Anderson stood equal, having each holed the round in 50 strokes. They halved the first and second prizes. The third prize was gained by Old Tom Morris, who made the round in 52 strokes; and the fourth by William Clark, who holed in 55 strokes. T. Brown stood next, at 57 strokes.

Several matches were also engaged in on Friday. Mr E. A. Hunter and Young Tom Morris played two matches against Mr J. Pettigrew Wilson and Charley Hunter, which finished square—Mr Hunter and Young Tom having gained the first match, and Mr Wilson and Charley Hunter the second. Mr J. L. Bennet and Young Tom Morris played two matches against Mr Denniston and Charley Hunter. Mr Denniston and Charley won the first match, and halved the second. Mr D. Dundas Wigham and D. Strath played a match of one round against Dr Wilson and James Anderson, which was won by Mr Whigham and Strath by five holes. The same parties afterwards played a short match of three holes, which Dr Wilson and James Anderson won. Mr Ritchie and the Rev. John Sime played a round of twelve holes, in which Mr Ritchie was victorious by one hole. Mr Whigham and Old Tom Morris played a match of one round against the Rev. Mr Sime and W. Park, which was won by Mr Sime and Park in three holes.

PRESTWICK GOLF CLUB.

THE CHAMPION BELT, 1870

Mr. T. Morris Junr.

1st Round. Strokes.		Holes.		2nd Round Strokes.
3	123	1	12345	5
5	12345	2	12345	5
3	123	3	12	2
5	12345	4	12345	5
6	123456	5	123456	6
3	123	6	12345	5
3	123	7	123	3
3	123	8	1234	4
4	1234	9	12345	5
3	123	10	123	3
4	1234	11	1234	4
5	12345	12	1234	4
47				51
		1st Round, ...		47
		Total, ...		

Tommy's winning card to keep the Belt

Record Score never to be beaten on that 12 hole course

Morris

3rd Round.

Holes.		Strokes.
1	12345	5
2	12345	5
3	123	3
4	1234567	7
5	1234	4
6	12345	5
7	123	3
8	123	3
9	12345	5
10	1234	4
11	123	3
12	1234	4
		51
	1st Round, ...	47
	2nd Round, ...	51
	Total, ...	149

GOLF MATCH AT LUFFNESS.

An interesting match came off yesterday over Luffness Links, between young Tom Morris of St Andrews, and Fergusson of Musselburgh. The match, which has been looked forward to with great interest in the golfing world, was for £20 a side, and was witnessed by a large number of spectators, among whom we noticed Captain Hope of Luffness, Captain Kinloch, yr. of Gilmerton, and other gentleman who take an interest in the national game. Both players had their backers, but at starting Tom was the favorite, the odds in his favour being given at 6 to 4. The match of yesterday was not the first encounter they have had together, Tom having on two, if not on three, previous occasions had the better of his antagonist. Fergusson, however, with a pluck which did him credit, entered into the match with a determination to do his best to wipe off old scores, and though he failed, his style of play yesterday showed that Tom had to do with a very formidable opponent. Both men handled their clubs with consummate ease and dexterity. The "swiping" on both sides was magnificent. In the half and quarter strokes with the "cleek," there was also little perceptible difference—though in this nice part of the game it was rather in favour of Tom, his St Andrew's experience telling to his advantage. The weak point of Fergusson was in his "putting," particularly in the first round, where he used his cleek rather too freely, and was punished in consequence. It was precisely here where the science and calculation of young Tom told most decidedly in his favour. His putting was deadly, and before the match was half over, the result had almost become a foregone conclusion. In the first round (17 holes) of the links, Tom led the way by taking the first three holes in succession. The fourth was halved, but the next three were again taken in succession by the youngster—making him six a-head. After the eighth hole, which was halved, his opponent, by careful and fortunate play, wiped off four from his score, leaving Tom only two a-head with five holes to play on the round. The next three were won by Tom, his beautiful putting once more giving him the superiority. He was now five a-head, and two to play. The sixteenth hole was halved, and the last on the round w[on] by Tom, who came in six holes a-head. After a brief breathing time, the second round was commenced. Tom again leading the way by taking the first two holes. The third was gained by Ferguson, and the fourth halved. The next t[wo] were wrested from Tom, who lost a stroke over the hill bunker, and gave the chance to his antagonist. At this point Tom was five a-head with eleven to play. His backers were now confident of their man, and their expectations were not belied. Tom, by careful playing of his short game, and the admirable use of his "putter" at the far hole added two out of the next three to his score, halving the third. The match was now won, with eight a-head and seven to play in favour of the St Andrews champion. In coming home, Tom added other two holes to his score, beating his opponent on the two rounds by 10 holes. Though the play was excellent on both sides, the round has been frequently done in a less number of strokes. Tom's score on both rounds was 77, Ferguson's respectively being 83 and 81, making a difference of ten strokes in all. A high wind from the north, which swept across the course, to some extent affected the play, and helped to swell the scores on both sides; but apart from this, the play was superb, and fi[ner] golfing, we believe, has never been seen over any links in Scotland. Young Tom is the holder of the champion belt, and as he is but a youth not more than eighteen, it may be assumed that at the present moment he is the best player in Scotland, which of course means that he is the best player in the world.

We believe that a "foursome" match has been [arr]anged between the Morrises, father and son, [and] Park and Ferguson, to take place on [Musselbur]gh links to-morrow (Saturday) f[or]

1869

110

111

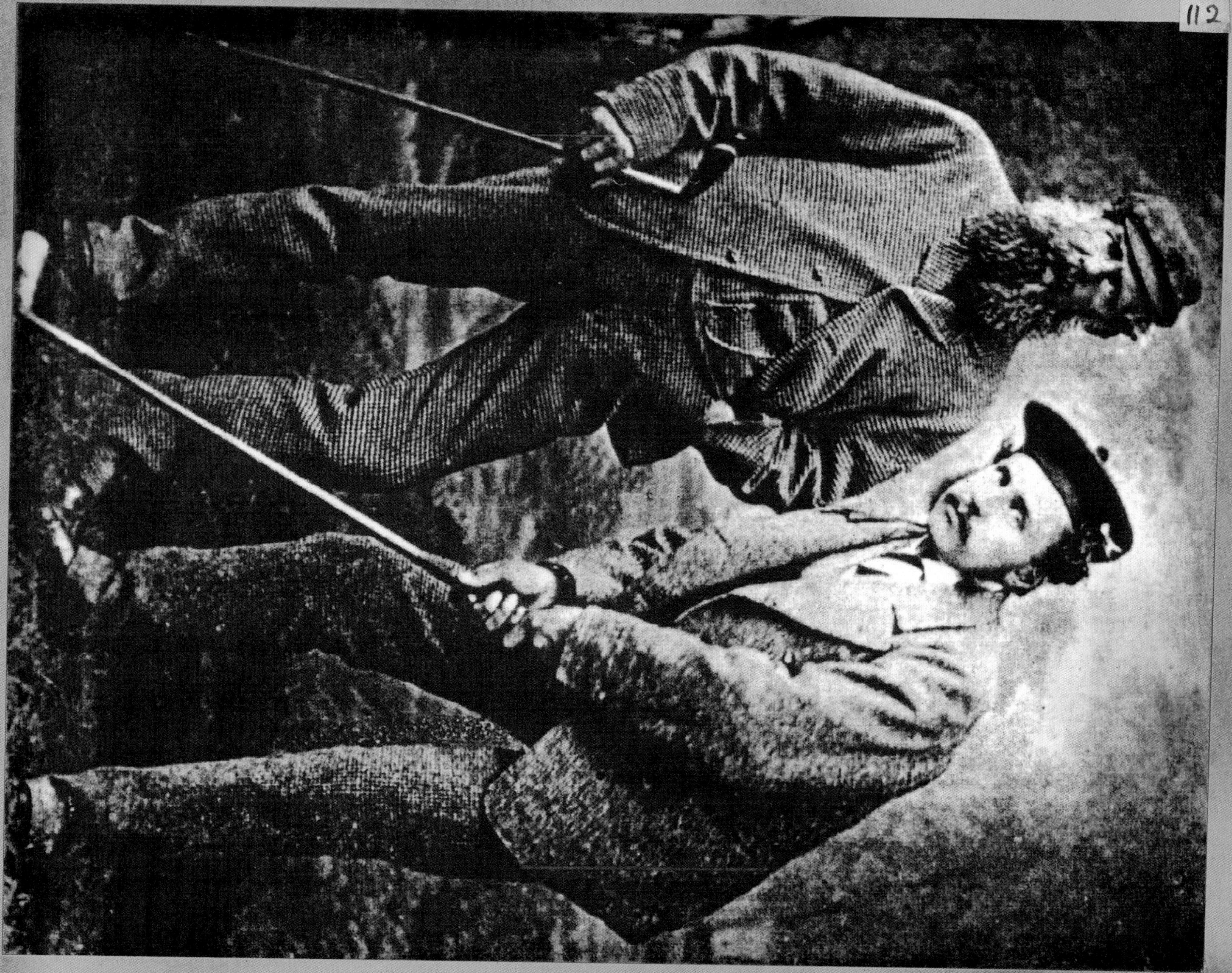

113

Four in a row!
Sept 1872

The Field

The competition for the challenge trophy came off last Friday, for the first time, over the Prestwick links. A competition has not been held since 1870, when the Belt, presented by the late Earl of Eglinton, fell into the hands of the younger Morris who that year scored his third successive victory. The competition for the championship in former years was fruitful of considerable interest, and tended to keep the 'royal game' before the public. It was, therefore, deemed advisable that these annual professional contests should not cease, and several lovers of the ancient game resolved to revive the championship competition. An appeal was consequently made, and sufficient funds raised among the members of the Prestwick Golf Club, the Royal & Ancient Golf Club of St Andrews, and the Musselburgh Club, to procure a cup for annual competition; the competition to be open to all comers, and to be played for annually over one of the following links, viz, Prestwick, St Andrews and Musselburgh alternately. Unlike the Belt, this trophy can never become the absolute property of any winner, but along with the custody of it for one year, he gets a medal to be specially retained, and also a money prize. It will thus be observed that the championship competition is now thoroughly established, which will tend to increase the popularity of this elegant and healthy pastime.

Tom Morris jun *St Andrews*	**57**	**56**	**53**	**166**
Davie Strath *St Andrews*	56	52	61	169
Mr W Doleman *Musselburgh*	63	60	54	177
Tom Morris sen *St Andrews*	62	60	57	179
David Park *Musselburgh*	61	57	61	
Charlie Hunter *Prestwick*	60	60	69	189
Hugh Brown *Prestwick*	65	73	61	199
Mr William Hunter *Prestwick*	65	63	74	202

The new trophy - a fine claret jug
and Tommy medal

Wallace, getting a stroke a hole, beat Master J. O. F. Morris by four holes. Mr Wallace and Master J. O. F. Morris beat Mr Lundie by four holes. Mr Lundie and Mr G. Wilson lost a round to Mr Wallace and Master J. O. F. Morris by two

J. O. F's 1st mention in a newspaper
Tommy's younger brother.

Scotland v England
1872

LIVERPOOL GOLF CLUB.—The Spring meeting of the Royal Liverpool Golf Club was continued on Thursday at Hoylake, near Liverpool, there being a good attendance of players. The chief event of the day was a grand tournament open to professionals, for which 26 players entered. Prizes to the value of L.55 were offered. Play commenced at 11.30, and after several interruptions from the showers of rain, terminated about five with the following results:—Tournament, open to professional players—1st prize, L.15 and silver medal, taken by Tom Morris, jun., in 167 strokes. The other players came in as follows:—Davie Strath, 168, L.10; Robert Anders, 171, L 8; John Allan, 172, L.7; James Anderson, 172, L.6; Thomas Dunn, 174, L.5; Thomas Morris, sen., tied with Davie Park for the last prize of L.4 at 176 strokes. Of the gentlemen who competed in the match, Dr Argyle Robertson, of Edinburgh, completed the rounds in 184 strokes, and Mr John Dun, of Warrington, in 194. The game between the young champion and Strath was an extremely close one, the latter just losing making a tie with him. Anders, Allan, and Anderson played a steady game throughout, though hardly so brilliant as on previous occasions. Dun was very unfortunate. A foursome by Colonel Kennard and Mr J. C. Fowlie against Captain Molesworth and Mr J. C. Baldwin resulted in the victory of the former couple. Upon the conclusion of the day's proceedings the members of the club dined together. On Friday, Tom Morris, jun., and Bob Ferguson, representing the Scottish Clubs, and Bob Kirk and John Allan, representing the English Clubs, played a match of 36 holes, when the former won by 8 holes and 7 to play. Colonel Kinneard and Tom Morris, jun., *v.* Mr Dun and Davie Park, played a match of 18 holes, when the former won by 8 and 7 to play—the Colonel playing a splendid game. The Consolation Stakes were won as follows:—Tom Morris, sen., and Bob Kirk tied at 83 for 1st and 2d prizes; Willie Dun, 3d. Mr Fowlie and Tom Dun won a match of 13 holes from Mr John Ball and John Morris by 3. Mr James Tweedie and R. Andrews played two matches against Mr E. K. Barnes and James Anderson. Mr Tweedie and R. Andrews won the first match by 3 holes, and the second match by 4 holes on the two rounds. Mr James Tweedie and R. Andrews played Mr George Bell and James Anderson two matches. The latter won the first match by 6 holes, and Mr Tweedie and R. Andrews won the second by 2 holes.

GOLF.—On Thursday:—Captain Allan and Mr Whyte-Melville against Mr Walkinshaw and Mr J. L. Small. Two rounds played. The former couple won the first round by two holes, but lost the second by three. Lord Carnegie and Mr M'Whannell were beat in two rounds by Mr Elliot and Mr Chambers, by two in the first and three in the second round. Captain Carnegie and Mr Gardyne beat Mr Fred Fair playing his own ball by three holes in a match of nine holes. The match in was halved. Captain Carnegie and Mr Gardyne beat Mr Fair and Mr M'Kenzie by one hole. Mr Fernie lost a round with Major Bethune by four holes—the Major also won the bye. In the afternoon, Mr Sinclair and Young Tom Kidd beat Major Bethune by one hole. Mr Sinclair and Young Tom Kidd vanquished Captain Herbert and the Rev. J. G. Macpherson, Ph. D. (Ruthven), by four, and three to play. Mr Fernie beat Captain Herbert by two holes

The First 'Open' at St. Andrews
1873

The annual competition for the Champion Golf Trophy (a Silver Challenge Cup and Gold Medal to remain the property of the winner) and money prizes to the value of £25, came off at St. Andrews on Saturday. The weather, after several days' constant rain, cleared beautifully up, and proved very favourable for the competition. The Links were much saturated with water and proved heavy to play over in consequence. The match consisted in two rounds of the Links or 36 holes, and was decided by strokes, not holes. The spectators on the green were very numerous, and seemed deeply interested in the result. Thirteen couples competed.

At the close of the second round the result was found to be as follows:—

Tom Kidd, 179—Champion and 1st prize.
Jamie Anderson, 180—2nd prize.
Tom Morris, jun. } 183—3rd and
Bob Kirk } 4th prizes
David Strath, 187—5th prize.

The next best were: Tom Morris, sen., 189; Mr H. A. Lamb, 192; Robert Martin and William Fernie, 194; Mr Robert Armit, J. O. F. Morris, and James Fenton, 195; Mr Mure Fergusson, 199; and T. Mansie, 200.

Tom Kidd, who has by the result of this competition won for himself the high honour of champion, has already proved himself to be an excellent player, and distinguished himself in many singles and foursomes, and the honour thus gained will consequently be grudged him the less, although he has won it with so high a score.

Tommy was 3rd which was a surprise I was 6th and J.O.F. 11th

The course and clubhouse from the West Sands 1873

Tom Kidd The Winner of the 1st championship here.

My second oldest son

J.O.F starting to make a name for himself

115

Jack Morris my nephew at Hoylake

From behind the R & A at Martyrs Monument

We were that busy playing exhibition matches and challenges throughout the country that I forgot to get a cutting of the 1874 open - the 1st at Musselburgh - Willie's brother Mungo 1st - Tommy was 2nd - I didn't play.

Young Tom's Marriage Entertainment
25th November, 1874

On Wednesday evening, Mr Thomas Morris entertained at supper his workmen and a few friends in the Golf Hotel (Mr Honeyman's) on the occasion of the marriage of his son, Tom Morris, Jun., which tool place that day. After a substantial repast and the usual toasts being drunk, Mr Mitchell proposed the health of Tom Morris, Jun., who they must no longer call Tommy, remarking on his distinguished career as a golfer, and the many victories and trophies he had won. These marked him out as the champion pars excellence. He had carried off the "belt" in three successive years against all comers notwithstanding that he was then out of his "teens". His performance had not in the least abated as shown by having twice this autumn defeated Willie Park, certainly the most formidable opponent who could be brought against him. No doubt much of his success was due to that amiability of temper, together with fixed determination, which made him so much a favourite both on and off the green, and which would be carried into the new relationship he had that day formed. The health of "The Bride" "Mr. And Mrs., Morris Sen., and the usual shop toast, "Long may the Hammer Strike and the Lathe Turn", brought the proceedings of a very agreeable evening to a close.

St. Andrews, 30th Sept. 1874.

Which day the Royal Medal, the gift of His late Majesty King William the Fourth, was played for over the Links of St. Andrews, and gained by Samuel Mure Fergusson, Esq., by holing the course at 91 strokes.

Same day the Gold Medal of the Club was played for over the Links of St. Andrews, and gained by Leslie Melville Balfour, Esq., by holing the course at 97 strokes. W. P. Adam, *C.*

REGARDING

PAY AND DISCIPLINE OF CADDIES,

ADOPTED BY

THE ROYAL AND ANCIENT GOLF CLUB OF ST. ANDREWS,

At a Special General Meeting of the Club, held on 3rd February, 1875.

I.—All Caddies shall be Enrolled,—none being admitted under 13 years of age.

II.—Members of the Club shall employ only Enrolled Caddies.

III.—A List of Enrolled Caddies shall be placed in the Club Hall, and also in the Clubmakers' Shops.

IV.—Caddies shall be divided into Two Classes, according to skill or age, and their services shall be rated as follows:—

First Class Caddies,—Eighteenpence for First Round, and One Shilling for each following Round, or part of Round.

Second Class Caddies,—One Shilling for First Round, and Sixpence for each following Round, or part of Round.

V.—No Caddy, unless previously engaged, can refuse to carry for a Member, under penalty of suspension for a stated time.

VI.—Names of suspended or disqualified Caddies shall be posted.

VII.—Complaints regarding Caddies shall be made through the Keeper of the Green to the Green Committee, who shall award an adequate penalty.

VIII.—The penalty shall be awarded by not less than two of the Green Committee.

IX.—The Keeper of the Green shall have charge of the Caddies, and Members shall apply to him when in want of a Caddy.

X.—Members are particularly urged to report all cases of misconduct on the part of the Caddies, whether during their time of service or otherwise,—such as incivility, bad language, abusing the Green, or any other form of misdemeanour,—which may merit censure or penalty.

XI.—Tom Morris shall be Keeper of the Green, and Superintendent of the Caddies.

Mr Balfours reminiscences of the Links before the great changes - see pages 19 an 20 for illustrations

The course is marvellously adapted to the game. It used to be flanked by high whins for the greater part of its extent, and these formed an interesting hazard. The turf is smooth and fine; the subsoil is sandy; the surface sometimes undulating and sometimes flat. There are beautiful level putting-greens, while the course is studded with sand-pits, or bunkers, as golfers call them. These, with the ever-recurring hazards of whin, heather, and bent all combine to give endless variety, and to adapt the Links at St. Andrews for the game of golf in a way quite unsurpassed anywhere else. If there be added to its golfing charms the charms of all its surroundings—the grand history of St. Andrews and its sacred memories—its delightful air—the song of its numberless larks, which nestle among the whins—the scream of the sea-birds flying overhead—the blue sea dotted with a few fishing-boats—the noise of its waves—the bay of the Eden as seen from the high hole when the tide is full—the venerable towers and the broken outline of the ancient city; and in the distance the Forfarshire coast, with the range of the Sidlaws, and, further off, the Grampian Hills, it may be truly said that, probably, no portion of ground of the same size on the whole surface of the globe has afforded so much innocent enjoyment to so many people of all ages from two to eighty-nine, and during so many generations.

The changes that have taken place on the course during these forty-five years have been very considerable. First of all, the course is much wider. Formerly there was only one hole on each putting-green, and players played to the same hole both going out and coming in. The party first on the green had the right to finish the hole before the match from the opposite direction came up. This naturally kept the course narrow, but when players began to multiply it was found to be inconvenient, and now it would be impossible. To obviate this it was resolved to have two holes on each putting-green, one of them being played to on going out and the other on coming in; or rather there were two distinct putting-greens parallel to one another, and a hole in each. This was virtually making two courses all along the Links—one for playing out and the other for coming in; thus the breadth of the course for golfing was gradually increased, till now it is about two-thirds broader than it used to be. This was probably unavoidable, owing to the increased number of players, but it has taken away much of the interest of the game. The only other plan that was suggested was to extend the course round the other side of the Links, and thus make it a circular one; but this was very properly rejected. To that there are many objections. It would have made the course shorter; it would have abolished all the present holes on the homeward line, some of which are so charming in themselves, and full of associations; it would also have deprived parties of the pleasure of meeting their friends, and hearing how their matches were getting on. It is to be hoped that such a proposal will never be renewed.

Description of each hole

Let us now consider the changes that have taken place on each of the holes individually, and we shall do so by following the medal round, taking the course out by the right.

1. The first hole used always to be on the green beside the road. Its hazards were the road across the Links, the burn, the bunker on one side of the putting-green, as well as the turnpike road on the other—making thus a limited green with a narrow approach to it flanked by severe hazards.

The holes

The first hole on the medal round now is quite different. It is placed just beyond the burn, on a flat, smooth, broad green to the right of the course. The only hazards in the hole are the road across the Links and the burn. There are none whatever close to the hole.

2nd hole

2. The tee for the second hole used to be, of course, near the road. There was then no separate teeing-grounds, but the rule was to tee within eight club-lengths of the hole. The ground between the wall and the bunkers towards the corner of the dyke, which is now often preferred as the shortest approach to the hole, was covered with thick whins, and was then quite unplayable. Consequently players were obliged to cross the course, and approach the hole by the right of the bunkers. The whins on the right made the course narrow in that direction, and the low ground to the right of the putting-green could not be played on on account of whins and rough grass, so that the hole was much more difficult both in playing and approaching than now. The putting-green, too, which was formerly on a slope, has been made quite level.

At present the tee of this hole is on the right of the Links, while the whins having been driven back, and the low ground to the right near the hole made quite playable, the hole can be played without any bunkers intervening, or any hazards of any kind. Of course if the player goes off the line he has to encounter some hazards. The putting-green, as has been said, is now on a flat and not a slope.

3rd

3. There used to be a thick bank of whins all along the left of the course by the side of the present railway, and the whins and rough grass on the right made it necessary to play straight in the centre, where was the Principal's Nose, with its little satellite of "Tam's Coo" (now filled up). The smaller bunker too, short of these, presented together with them dangerous traps. There was very little room indeed to pass them on either side. The hole was always in the *centre of the green*, so that the bunker which crosses the Links beside it had to be played over, else a considerable distance was lost by going to the right or left of it.

The tee is now on the right side of the green, and the ball from it is easily played to the right of the Principal's Nose, while the hole being to the right of the putting-green, it is readily approached without crossing the bunker.

4th

4. Formerly the whins encroached so much on either side that it was necessary that the tee stroke should be played on or over the table in front of the tee, and then a very narrow course was left up to the hole, which was on a narrower putting-green than now, and it was usually placed nearer the bunkers.

The whins having been now driven back, the ball can be played to the right of the table. The course is clear for the second stroke, and the hole is placed to the right, far from the bunkers.

5th

5. This hole is more altered than any other on the Links, and sadly destroyed. The tee stroke used always to be played to the right of the big bunker with the uncouth name, unless when now and then some huge driver "swiped over h— at one immortal go." The second stroke was always to the left on to the Elysian Fields, where the grass was then short and smooth like a putting-green. The third had to navigate the intricate "Beardies," and the fourth was across a wide, staring, horrid bunker, beyond which was a beautiful putting-green. Altogether, this used to be the finest golfing hole, certainly on the Links, and probably in the world. There were beautiful lies when the play was correct, very difficult hazards, and a perfect putting-green.

Now the play is quite different. The Elysian Fields are avoided, and the hole is played on a lower level, where high whins formerly grew, which made play there impossible. There is hardly any hazard; there are no bunkers of any consideration, and the approach to the green is a blind stroke without any bunker between. The hole is altogether much tamer, and less interesting, as well as easier. The young laird of the Links would do the game of golf an unspeakable benefit if he would plough up the low course, or honeycomb it with bunkers, so as to compel players to return to the old line on the Elysian Fields.

6th

6. The sixth hole is also much altered. It used to be one of the most dangerous on the Links, but two or three large and important bunkers have been filled up to make a double course. This reduces the number of hazards materially, and the whins have so much disappeared that it is safe to go round the bunkers, playing well to the right, instead of being compelled to play over them. The putting-green, too, is greatly changed. Formerly it had no turf, but was merely earth, heather, and shells, from which it got its name of the heather hole, or the "hole o' shell," but it has now been turfed, and, like the other greens, is carefully kept.

7th

7. The course here was a narrow one, so that the first stroke was necessarily played over—very often, unfortunately, into—the bunker that crosses the green; but there was not much room to go on either side of it. The putting-green at the high hole, which was always placed near the Eden, was then surrounded with thick, bent grass, leaving a very limited space near the hole. Besides, the ground was sandy and soft. The deterioration of this putting-green has been averted by the growth of rank sea-grass on the banks of the Eden,

8th

8. The short hole is not much changed, except that the putting-green is wider than it used to be.

9th

9, or last hole going out, used to be principally heather, but a large portion of that heather was some years ago taken up and relaid with turf. The putting-green is now also much broader than formerly.

The homeward nine

Having now reached the end hole, let us retrace our way and compare the holes going home as they now are with what they used to be. This may be thought to be unnecessary, as exactly the same ground has to be travelled over as has been already described. This is quite a mistake. Although the ground is the same, the various holes are as different as if they were on different Links.

10th

1. The principal difference on the first hole home is that the course was formerly narrower, and the heather has been replaced by turf. If a ball was at all drawn to the left, it used to be either lost in the whins or so imbedded among them that it had to be played out at the sacrifice of at least one stroke, if not more; but now it often lies very tolerably even there, and can be played forward. Near the hole, too, the ground short of it and to the left was so covered with thick grass that if a ball got there it had an exceedingly bad lie. Now the ball has a fair lie where the grass used to be so heavy.

11th

2. The short hole home is not much changed, except that the bents have disappeared, as already stated, while the putting-green is much harder and broader.

12th

3. In driving this hole there is now plenty of room to pass the bunker that crosses the green on either side of it. The rough ground at both ends of the putting-green has disappeared, and the putting-green itself has been turfed, and is no longer shelly.

13th

4. The next hole used to be one of the most difficult on the Links, and more medals have been lost at it than at any other. It has a good many hazards yet, but two of the largest bunkers have been filled up to make a course to the left, as well as one to the right. In former times Allan Robertson used to play the first stroke often with the short spoon short of all the bunkers, and the second with the short spoon over the bunkers, and the third from behind the hill with the short spoon also, on to the green. Now there is plenty of room to avoid the bunkers, both on the right and left: players can have a long stroke off the tee, while long drivers may be on the green in two, and some of the worst bunkers not played over at all.

14th

5. The long hole home, like the long hole out, has been entirely changed. The big yawning bunker in front of the tee, that was ready to catch a topped ball and to hold it, is almost entirely avoided, while the "Beardies," where so many balls used to be kid-napped, and from which escape was not always made with the loss of only one stroke, are never looked at.

Now the play is on the low ground to the left of the Elysian Fields, thus crossing the bunker diagonally. This line used to be absolutely impossible. There are now no hazards there, or only trifling ones. The hole itself is always placed on the right or left of the putting-green instead of the centre, just between two bunkers, the approach to which used to be at the sacrifice of some distance to circumvent the bunkers.

15th

6. The whins on the left, where the first stroke was played, protruded far on to the Links, and the ball was either caught in them or had to be played right in the centre. There was no possible play to the left of the table, and the second stroke had to go straight over that table; if that stroke were at all short, the ground, which sloped down towards dangerous bunkers, drew the ball into them. Now the hole can be played to the left or right without much risk.

16th

7. Formerly, there was little room to pass the "Principal's Nose" on either side from the tee, and it, and "Tammy's Coo" beside it, were ugly hazards. The line of whins alongside the present railway was an additional difficulty if the right-hand course was adopted; and if the left, the ground which is now clear was then impracticable from whins. The putting-green itself, as has been mentioned before, has been levelled, so that the hole, instead of being on a slope as formerly, is now on a flat table, and the low ground to the left of it is no longer covered with whins.

17th

8. Playing off from the hole at the dyke, the ground in front is now cleared of the dense clump of whins that used to be immediately in front of the tee. There has been no other alteration on this hole of great consequence, except that the grass, which is sometimes long and heavy after much rain, is mowed with a scythe, and a large bank of rushes has been removed.

18th

9. The principal difference on the last hole is on the putting-green. That has been quite changed by the formation of an artificial table-land, which forms a beautiful green. Formerly the hole was on broken ground in a hollow, with the ground sloping down on both sides. Shortly before my time, there was another serious hazard made by the sea, which came up to the stair of the present Club-House. That hazard was a very serious one, as the sand at that place was as deep as at the high hole. The last hole being often placed near the edge of the green was close to the sand. But the Links have now been made much wider by the rubbish from the town having reclaimed a large portion from the sea, and there are no hazards on that side.

Having now gone over the golf-course both going out and coming in, it only remains further to say on this head that the Links are far more carefully kept than they used to be. Tom Morris superintends this with great assiduity, and he has two men under him who are constantly employed in keeping the bunkers at the proper size, in filling up rabbit-scrapes or other holes, and in returfing places which have given way. The putting-greens also, instead of being left in their natural state as formerly, are now carefully rolled with a heavy roller, — mowed with a machine,—and watered in dry weather from a well that has been sunk near each of them. The putting is made smoother and better, and much truer.

A separate teeing-ground has also been provided at each hole, which preserves the putting-greens from being broken by the tee strokes. A wooden box filled with sand for the tee, and placed at the teeing-ground, is a novelty and an additional refinement.

Fine golfing outfit for me playing at the North Devon club

No wonder they chose a claret jug for the new trophy!

WINE (NOT WHISKY) THE ANCIENT DRINK OF THE SCOTS.

(From the Morning Star.)

It is generally supposed that whisky has always been the national drink of Scotland; but this is a very erroneous idea, for, even until 1690, when a relaxation was granted to make fourteen hogsheads for the use of the public, it was enacted and provided by the Town Council of Edinburgh, that "na person, man nor woman within this burgh, mak nor sell any aqua vitæ within the samyn, except the malsters, brethren of the craft of surregerey, and barbouris." This shows that it was regarded as a medicine and the sale confined to medical men, as chloroform, &c., now is. Ale and wine were then the universal beverage. The following statement shows at what extraordinary low prices wines of France sold in olden times in Scotland. These may be entirely relied upon, but it should be remembered that the population of Scotland was, in the first period, about three quarters of a million.

At that time, and for long afterwards, what is now called claret in England, and in everywhere else vin de Bordeaux, grown in the Medoc, was produced in other parts of the South of France, for the Medoc was then a sandy desert, and there is every reason to believe that the wines then imported were generally the strong, full-bodied kinds, which France can still furnish in large quantities, at low prices.

In 1520, the Town Council of Edinburgh, which then, and indeed for centuries, professed to regulate the retail prices of everything, framed an act of council, enacting that the prices of French wines, both red and white, be sold at sixpence, Scottish money, or one halfpenny sterling, the Scotch pint, under the penalty of having the head of the cask beat out.—(Maitland's History of Scotland, page 12.) A Scotch pint is about a third of our imperial gallon, or rather more than two ordinary wine bottles of the present day; so that a quantity equal to a bottle of wine could then be got for a farthing of our money. Of course it was not bottled, but was sold from the cask as beer now is; and when a large quantity was imported casks were often hawked through the town on sledges, the carts of that day, and sold in the streets in gallons or pints, in the same way that buttermilk is now frequently sold in Scotland.

There is an Act of the Parliament of Scotland (Maitland, p. 13) fixing the price of Bordeaux wine at 8d the pint, and Rochelle at 6d. As the Scotch money is one-twelfth of the English, this Parliamentary retail price was two-thirds of a penny of our present money for a quantity equal to two bottles; and the white, or Rochelle, at a halfpenny of our money for two bottles. As an instance of the comparative price of other things, as fixed by the same Act, I quote some of them, giving the equivalent sums in our present sterling money:—

The best pig	1½d.
The best tame goose	½d.
The best capon	1d.
The best hen	⅔d.
The best chicken	⅓d.

In the following year, 1552, there is an act of the Town Council fixing the price of the carcase of the best sheep at 10d sterling, the second at 8d, and the third at 6d. Of course all the sheep were very small in those days, and therefore to compare the prices of sheep and wine is perhaps hardly fair. In the case of poultry the comparison will probably be more correct. The price of red wine was at the rate of three bottles for a penny; and of white, four bottles. A man selling a goose, therefore, could then buy, with the price he got for it, four and a half bottles of claret, or six bottles of white. The price of a capon would purchase three bottles of claret, or four bottles of white; and the price of a hen, two bottles of claret. In 1609, the Town Council obtained power to levy four pounds Scotch (6s 8d sterling) on every tun (four hogsheads) of wine sold within Edinburgh.

In these documents there is no reference to wines from any other country than France; and until these were driven out of use by the enormous increase of duty at the latte[r] part of the 17th century, and by the Methuen Treaty in [the] beginning of the 18th, and then by the suppression of sm[ug]gling in Scotland and Ireland, little else was drunk th[an the] wines of France, and also the brandy from that cou[ntry]

The Bruce Embankment.- as you can see below the sea could encroach on to the course before George Bruce (Provost) in 1870 decided to create a breakwater using old boats as its foundation

SEPTEMBER 6, 1875

INTERESTING GOLF MATCHES AT NORTH BERWICK.

But for a melancholy occurrence, of which intelligence was received in the course of the afternoon, and which damped not a little the spirits of all then on the green, the foursomes with which the professional play at North Berwick was on Saturday brought to a close for the season, might be said to have passed off with an *eclat* pleasantly contrasting with the disputes of the previous day. The more important fixture was that noticed in Saturday's *Scotsman*—a match between the Morrises, father and son, and Willie and Mungo Park, for £25 a-side—and it having become known that the Parks had wisely resolved to go on with the play, notwithstanding what they had said on Friday, there was a very large number of spectators in waiting at the starting point at eleven o'clock in the forenoon ready to accompany the players round the course. The day fortunately was pleasant for outing, and the opportunity for watching the game consequently seemed to be much enjoyed by every one in the crowd, whose numbers were, despite the use of a long rope behind which they were kept, at times rather difficult to manage. The prevailing enthusiasm may be guessed from the fact that in the throng the young lady visitors to North Berwick were numerously represented, all of them resolutely sticking to their posts abreast of the rope during the four rounds which the foursome comprised. Among others present were noticed the Lord Justice-Clerk and Lady Moncreiff, Lord and Lady Ruthven and party, Mr Hope of Luffness and party, Sheriff Crichton, Sheriff J. H. A. Macdonald, Mr Laidlay of Seacliff, Mr Spens and the Hon. Mrs Spens, Dr Littlejohn, Dr Orphoot, Provost Brodie, North Berwick.

The players being forward in good time, the game was punctually begun, with the circumstances of the green on the whole favourable, although the turf was rather keen in the neighbourhood of some holes, and a strong breeze blew from the west. In going out to Point Garry neither couple did very brilliant work, as a stroke was added to each by Mungo's second drive not being very clean, and by Young Tom being short in the approach with his iron. On the way to the second disc both drives carried into sand, from which Willie and Young Tom played very nicely out. Again, the fourth shot was well played with a spoon by the elder Park, but was ill-fated enough to be caught in a bunker, out of which, however, Mungo played a capital "odds." Old Tom in his "like" to this was heavy and short, and a half was recorded in 7. Another half was next secured, this time in 4, neither the second shot of Willie nor that of Young Tom having been up to much. The first blood was, however, drawn by the Parks at the fourth hole, where the balls were about equi-distant from the pin after the third shots, and where Willie holed out in 4, against the 5 scored by the St Andrews men, through Young Tom having hard lines—the ball just running round the hole in his "like." At the fifth hole neither party had the advantage, the play being without a mistake, and on the next putting green some very middling work brought about another half. Here the "tee" shots were lying fairly on the putting green, to the extreme end of which Mungo had driven, while Old Tom's ball was short on the near side. To play the "odds" fell to Willie, and being fully 9 yards to the far side of the pin, he left Young Tom an excellent opportunity for making good the hole. In his put, however, the youngster was not up to form, and the hole was halved in 4. By being a little short in a longish put for his fifth, Willie Park, who had been left too much to do by Mungo, allowed Young Tom to pull down the lead on the next green by holing in 5; and again, in the tussle for the eighth hole, the St Andrews men had the better of it, showing a really unexceptionable game. In three, Old Tom lay nicely on the putting green, with a fine long draw left for the youngster, which being taken to perfection, finished the hole in 4, against the 6 run up by the Parks through a less clever performance. The match now stood one up for St Andrews, but Willie having sent away a beautiful "tee" for the home hole, followed by an equally long drive by Mungo, the Parks' ball lay well within sight of this hole in two, while the Morrises, having taken the wrong road, were only there in three. The "holing out" was managed without a flaw by the Musselburgh men, and the players finished all even on the round, the hole going to the Parks in 4 against their opponents' 5. The scores were:—

Morrises................................	674534545—43
Parks................................	674434664—44

After some capital play in the first hole, which was halved, the Parks were unfortunate on the way to the second in having a run of ill-luck. Willie, in the first instance, lay badly for his third, and played into sand; Mungo out of this bunker drew a capital shot, but, as ill-luck would have it, the ball again found a resting-place in a hazard near the hole, from which Willie did not lift it in his fifth, and the hole was therefore thrown up, as the Morrises were "home" in 4. By a clever long put Old Tom increased the lead to two at the third hole, while the Parks gave the succeeding hole to their opponents, first through Willie bein[g] ... in his approach, and then through Mungo fai[ling to] "hole out" in a feasible enough draw of about a[...] length. Making a bad beginning from th[e ...] where the old man struck off, the [Parks found them]selves all through too much to do ... drive of the elder Park's gave Mungo a chance of ho[l]ing out in 2—an opportunity which was well taken a[d]vantage of by "the champion," whose put quite deserved to have been "in." As it was the figures were—Parks, 3; Morrises, 4. By missing a put which should easily have been taken, Mungo failed to secure a half of the next hole, and through his brother's shortcomings Willie had the pleasure of seeing the eighth also go to the Morrises, making their lead "three up." Once more Mungo was wanting in driving to the "home" hole, and dropping into sand, gave Willie some heavy work; while the Morrises, being well forward in their swiping, were "dead" in 4, and added another to the long bill now standing against their opponents by finishing in 5.

Morrises................................	563454565—43
Parks................................	584543677—49

120

After an interval of an hour, play over the last two rounds was commenced at two o'clock. At this time the lead of the Morrises was, as has been seen, 4 up, and by some it might have been thought that the match was virtually over. By those more acquainted with the chances of the game, however, the matter was not received with such certainty, and the second start was therefore made with little, if any, abatement in the interest manifested by the onlookers. The prospects of the Musselburgh players were far from being improved at the beginning of the third round, the first hole going to the Morrises in 6, against an 8 credited to the other side, through bad play and ill-luck. On the way for the second hole fortune changed sides. Here Old Tom swerved to the left in his "tee" shot, and brought his son into using the niblick. Again the ball lay badly for Old Tom's third, which was so short that the youngster had then to play "two more." The Parks, on the other hand, were "home" in 4, and as their opponents in approaching the hole came to grief in a bunker, they at once stopped playing. Game—Morrises four up. After the next had been halved in 4, Young Tom gave the fourth hole to his opponents. For the second "like," the youngster had an easy iron lift over a hazard to the green, but taking his putter, and trying to run the ball across the bunker, he failed, was caught in the sand, and placed his father and himself at a disadvantage from which they did not recover. By some indifferent play the fifth hole was halved in four, as was also the sixth. This last hole, however, should have gone easily to the Parks. With his swipe, Old Tom carried the ball into a bunker, while Mungo lay in the "like" within nine yards of the pin. In the odds, Tommy did not get clear of the sand, thus leaving his father to play "two more." This the veteran did beautifully, dropping his ball "dead," but the Parks had now two in which to make the hole theirs. Willie, accordingly

121

In going "home" all were in better form, the driving of Mungo and Old Tom, and the putting of Tommy and Willie being equally good. This hole was halved in 4, leaving the Morrises' lead of four up with which they had started undiminished. The following were the scores :—

Morrises	684544564—46
Parks	864444574—46

Following a remarkably plucky game, the Parks pulled down their opponents a peg at the outset of the last round by strong play all the way to the side of the hole. Again, in making for the second pin, the Morrises found luck against them, as Old Tom had to play the first "odds" from a bunker, while a promising swipe of his son's was afterwards caught and spoiled on the top of a knoll. The Parks, however, made themselves deserving of the hole by their work on the putting green, where Willie stole a beautiful long draw to within half-a-dozen yards of the pin, and Mungo followed by holeing out in 6 against the 7 of their opponents. Game—Morrises two up. In the third hole, the St Andrews men were in danger of further losing their lead, but this Tommy avoided by pulling himself together on the putting green, and a half was declared. Through weak play, the Parks lost the next hole, but the fifth was gained to them by an admirable long put of Mungo's, which somewhat redeemed the champion's character. The state of the game, which stood two up for the St Andrews men, was further altered by the Parks taking the sixth hole in 3, and reducing the lead to one up—the Musselburgh men having in this case driven to the disc from the "tee," whereas Young Tom played into a nasty hazard to the left of the green. The excitement among the onlookers was now intense, and it was doubly increased at the next hole, where Willie, having on the putting green the "like" to play to a capital "odds" put down within a few feet of the disc by Young Tom, drew a beautiful ball, and holed from fully a dozen yards' distance, making the match "all even." The next hole, however, went to the St Andrews men, who took a capital road for the pin, were within eight or nine yards of the hole in 3, and finished in 4. Willie's "tee" shot, on the other hand, was off the line to the left, and the ball lay in sand, from which Mungo could only lift it, thus placing the scoring at a disadvantage, which there was not an opportunity of redeeming. The Morrises were in this way "dormy," but the game for the last hole was watched with the greatest closeness by every one on the green, the spectators crowding in at times and giving expression to their sympathies in a not very becoming way. After the "tee" shots things did not look too well for the Musselburgh players, as their ball lay rather badly, but, notwithstanding, they got well forward in the "odds."

Morrises	774445545— 45
Parks	864533465— 42

Last year, it may be remembered, a foursome between the same men was gained by the Parks with 3 up and 2 to play. Saturday's game was, it should be stated, a whole scarcely so good as that of last season.

Later in the afternoon a single was played by Willie Park and Davie Strath. During first round Strath was by no means in form and Park at one time easily ran up a lead of 4. In the second and concluding round, however, Strath pulled himself together, reducing the "odds" till at the eighth hole the game stood "all even, and one to play." By driving into the sea beach, Davie lost the last hole and the match at the same time. Curiously enough a single played between this couple last year finished in precisely the same way as did Saturday's. The scores were :--

Park—1st round	574444665—45
2d round	575544555—46
Strath—1st round	684545555—47
2d round	665434556—44

In connection with these matches it is to be regretted that a very affecting incident has to be noticed. Just as the balls were holed out on the last putting green of the concluding round, and the match declared won by the Morrises, a telegram was put into the hands of Young Tom announcing that his wife was dangerously ill, and requesting that he should get back to St Andrews with all possible haste. No train being available till seven o'clock in the evening, the Morrises were about to start for Edinburgh by road, in order to catch the last train for Fife, when Mr Lewis, one of the summer residents in the town, hearing of the news that had been received, suggested that they should sail across in his yacht, which was lying in the harbour. Accordingly Tom and his father, without a moment's delay, got on board of this craft, and they had just cleared the harbour and were hoisting sail, when a messenger reached the pier bearing another telegram stating that Mrs Morris had given birth to a son, but that both mother and child were dead. The purport of the message being made known to a number of Tom's friends who had been seeing him off, they agreed, although the yacht was within easy hailing distance, to allow it to sail without acquainting those on board with the distressing news, fearing that the shock to the unhappy husband would be too great. Meanwhile rumours of what had taken place found their way to the green, where the match between Park and Strath was in progress, and spreading among the groups on the Links, cast a gloom over the remainder of the play, much sympathy being everywhere expressed for Morris, who has been married scarcely a year.

11th September 1875

St Andrews Citizen

GOLF NEWS

FINE PROFESSIONAL GOLF MATCH AT NORTH BERWICK

On Saturday an interesting professional foursome was played over the North Berwick Links between Tom Morris, senior and junior, against Willie Park and his brother Mungo, the present holder of the champion trophy. The match was for a stake of £25 a side, and was contested throughout with varying success. At the close of the first two rounds the Morrises were four up, but during the remainder of the game their opponents succeeded in bringing them down. At the second last hole from home the Parks were only one behind, but the last being halved, the sire and son secured victory by one hole. The play was of a high class, and some excellent driving and putting were exhibited.

A sad incident occurred at the close of the match. Just as the last hole had been played, a telegram was handed to Young Tom stating that his wife was dangerously ill. He and his father at once left, and, there being no train, they got a gentleman to take them across the Firth in his yacht, and as they were sailing another telegram came with the melancholy intelligence that she had died after giving birth to a child.

2.—TOM MORRIS.
The G.O.M. of Golf.

I start up this scrapbook
again after my retirement
as Keeper of the green - Custodian
of the Links of St andrews
in 1902

26.—TOM MORRIS, JNR.

As you will understand as you look through the next few pages - my heart just wasn't in it after the trauma and sad passing of Tommy - taken in his prime - 27 years later I stick down some bits and pieces to fill up this scrapbook.

St Andrews Citizen
4th December 1875

Golf Match

A golf match which is attracting considerable attention was commenced on the Links here on Tuesday forenoon, between Mr Arthur Molesworth, Westward Ho, and Young Tom Morris. The match consists of twelve rounds; and is to be continued over six days, the former being allowed a third. The stakes are £50, one half going to the side winning most holes, the other half to the side winning most rounds. On playing the opening round, the first hole fell to Young Tom, and the second to his opponent, and they continued to give and take. The first round terminated in favour of Young Tom by one hole. The play was fair despite the unfavourable nature of the weather. A large number of spectators accompanied the combatants round the green. On Wednesday Tom added to his advantage – being twelve holes ahead over the whole and victor in four rounds.

St Andrews Citizen
11th December 1875

The golf match, on which £50 in stakes depended between Mr Arthur Molesworth, Westward Ho, and Mr Tom Morris jun., which has been so much trumpeted in the daily newspapers, has ended as everybody expected it would end – in favour of Tom. The last round was played on Tuesday, when Tom won the stakes easily, both as the winner in rounds (being six above his opponent) and also in holes, having won eleven and ten to play. It is somewhat extraordinary that such a match should have been played with a thick covering of snow on the ground. The referee wished to delay the match; but Mr Molesworth decided to go on. The circumstances of the game rendered the scores, as a matter of course, somewhat high; but looking to the weather – the game being often played amid blinding snow – the play was good.

The Death of Tom Morris Jun.

The sudden death on Saturday morning at his father's house, Pilmour Links, of Young Tom Morris, a golfer whose reputation was world-wide, will be very deeply regretted by all who knew him. Retiring a little after eleven o'clock on Friday evening apparently in his usual health, he was found in bed next morning a lifeless corpse. A little blood had oozed from his mouth, and the doctor who was called said that death had resulted from internal haemorrhage. A post mortem examination having been made, it was discovered that a blood vessel in the right lung had burst. Though to all appearances, as we have remarked, he was previous to his demise in good health, we understand that he had never quite recovered the prostration caused by the death of his wife in September last. With his parents, on whom the blow falls heaviest, much sympathy is felt. On St Andrews Links, as well as on many another green in the kingdom, a great blank will be experienced. Born in the spring of 1851 at Prestwick, he was only in his 25th year. Early – indeed when quite a boy – he attained a prominent position among golfers. When but 16 years of age he carried off the champion belt. The same feat he performed on the two succeeding years, and so the belt became his own property. Since then he has always been regarded as the foremost golfer. Tom or Tommy, as he was sometimes familiarly called, was a thorough gentleman, and his many amiable qualities gained him a large circle of friends.

Some account will in time be made of his matches, many of them of singular excellence, but one has been brought to our notice by a St Andrews golfer, himself one of the best, which, it may well be believed, deserves record. Our correspondent says that he saw young Tommy once play his own ball against Davy Strath and Jamie Anderson, who were both in good form, but he beat them. "I do not hesitate to assert," he adds, "that no one but Tommy could or ever will, be able to do the same."

The remains of poor Tommy were yesterday followed to the grave by a large cortege of persons from all quarters, and the city, usually dull at this season, wore its gloomiest as the mournful procession deployed through the streets. The warmest sympathy is felt for the deceased's family, who are held in high esteem by all who frequent the Links.

THE LATE TOM MORRIS JUN.

A painful feeling of surprise was experienced in the city and elsewhere on Saturday, when the report spread that one so well known and respected, both on his own account and that of his father, had died suddenly that morning. The deceased had returned home on Thursday after two days' absence in his usual health. The following evening – Christmas eve - he supped at a private party with a few friends and was in cheerful spirits. On returning home at eleven he sat and spoke for some time with his mother, who is an invalid. After retiring to bed in an adjoining room his father, according to custom, went and bade him goodnight. The following morning his parents heard his usual movements, and about an hour later upon his being called for breakfast, and no answer being obtained the sad fact then became apparent that he had passed away, and so quietly that he did not appear to have been awakened out of sleep. The cause of so sudden and peaceful an end appears from a minute medical examination to have been the sudden bursting of an artery under his right lung.

"Tommy", by which name he was so universally known was born at St Andrews, and not at Prestwick as has been incorrectly stated. He is therefore a native of the place with which he has been so long associated, and will be long remembered. He was 21 years of age. Shortly after his birth he removed with his father to Prestwick, and returned with him in 1864, when shortly afterwards he began to display those wonderful golfing powers of which mention will presently be made.

A little more than a year ago he was married, a union of the strongest in mutual affection which promised to be both long and happy. It will be in the recollection of our readers that at the close of a victorious golf match in September between his father and himself against the Brothers Park at North Berwick, he received intelligence of the sudden illness of his wife, and ere he had time to leave for St Andrews in a yacht, kindly put at his disposal by a gentleman, a second telegram announced her death, and also that of his child, which had just been born.

To all who knew Tommy and his fine sensitive nature it will not be difficult to understand, that he received a blow from which the result that has just taken place shows that he never recovered. His next public appearance was after the October Meeting, when he played with his father against Strath and Martin, and after bringing it so near a successful close as to be four holes up, and five to play, he unexpectedly and so completely broke down as to lose the five holes and consequently the match. After this he was seriously unwell and no effort availed to rouse him from the recollection of her with whom all his interest in life had passed away.

On the challenge of the late match with Mr Molesworth being given, Tommy's friends readily entered into it with the view that it might happily rouse him and do him good, although it was manifest he was far out of condition for such a match, and those who witnessed it could not fail to observe a strange wont of that spirit and determination which characterised all his previous performances on the green, and, indeed, he more than once observed to the writer of these lines that but for the interest of his friends and backers he would not have continued it.

my dear wife Nancy died the following year – God rest her soul

People said that Tommy died of a broken heart – but if that was true I wouldna be here either

125.

Inauguration of Monument to Tommy Morris

An event which was looked forward to with a degree of mingled feeling was the unveiling of a memorial stone to Tommy Morris in the Cathedral Cemetery, a ceremony which was arranged to take place at half – past five on Tuesday evening, after the annual business meeting of the club. Several hundreds of spectators assembled around the stone – Tommy's father and brother modestly taking their stand near the grave. Shortly after the hour named, the Lord Justice – General stepped on a small platform in front of the stone, and previous to its being unveiled,

The Lord Justice – General Inglis said: -

Ladies and gentlemen, the monument which we are met to inaugurate is dedicated to the memory of the late Tommy Morris, younger. It is a simple, modest, and characteristic erection, and I think it adequately expresses the sentiments of the members of not less than sixty golfing clubs, by whose subscriptions the requisite funds have been obtained. It is inscribed with the familiar name of "Tommy", a name by which he was best known to all his numerous friends and admirers. There is something in these familiar names of great significance; and in this case, I think the name expresses the kindly regard which he secured from all who knew him by his amiable disposition, by his simple and unaffected manners, and by his manly independence. It would be idle to an audience such as I see around me, to speak in detail of his golfing achievements, for they are known to you all; but I think I shall not be accused of extravagance when I say that he was the greatest golfer of his day. In 1860, if I am not incorrectly informed, the Prestwick Club instituted a champion belt, which was competed for annually for a good many years, and always changed hands every year; but at length Tommy succeeded in gaining the belt for three years successively, and according to the rules of the competition he was entitled to hold it in absolute property; and I have no doubt it remains in the hands of his family as a most precious possession. It is also recorded of him that he went round the Links of St Andrews in the unparalleled score of 77 – 37 going out and 40 coming back. Every true golfer mourns his loss most sincerely, for he was not only a prime golfer, but a very fine young man cut off in the prime of his life. But the time of grief has now gone by; and all that remains of Tommy is a pleasant memory. I think also that you will allow me to say that we have some consolation still, for although we have lost him, we have still a Tom Morris left – old Tom, and I think that I may venture to say that there is a great deal of life in that old dog yet. Long may he live and retain thereputation he has made, I have nothing further to say, except to ask you to vote thanks to two gentlemen who have been mainly instrumental in having the monument erected – I mean Major Bethune, the honorary treasurer, and Mr Denham, the honorary secretary. I now desire the monument to be unveiled.

The stone was then unveiled by Miss Phelps on behalf of Mrs Hunter, Tommy's only sister. It revealed a figure of the well – known golfer in the attitude of putting. Clad in a closely buttoned coat, and having on his favourite Glengarry bonnet, his eye seems fixed upon the hole, the knees are slightly bent, and every energy is concentrated on taking a steady accurate aim. The club, ball and turf are capitally managed, and the whole reflects no little credit on the designer and sculptor, Mr John Rhind of Edinburgh.

Underneath the figure is the following inscription, composed by Principal Tulloch: - In memory of Tommy, son of Thomas Morris, who died 25th December 1875, aged 24 years, deeply regretted by numerous friends and all golfers. He thrice in succession won the Champion Belt, and held it without rivalry, and yet without envy, his many amiable qualities being no less acknowledged than his golfing achievements. This monument has been erected by contributors from sixty golfing societies.

Two Interesting Relics of Young Tom Morris.

OPEN CHAMPIONSHIP BELT—WON OUTRIGHT IN 1870 BY YOUNG TOM MORRIS.

A PATHETIC interest attaches to the accompanying illustrations, two of which we are enabled to give by the kind permission and courtesy of Old Tom Morris.

The first is from a photograph of the Champion Belt, presented in 1860 by the Prestwick Golf Club as the First Open Championship Trophy. It was held by the winner for the year and became the property of any player who should win it three times in succession. This feat was accomplished by Young Tom Morris in the years 1868, 1869, and 1870, and in the latter year the Belt accordingly became his property.

In 1872 the present Championship Cup was given by the Royal and Ancient, the Honourable Company, and the Prestwick Clubs for annual competition, and Young Tom again won the title, this making his fourth successive win. This is a record which has never been equalled in the history of the competition.

YOUNG TOM MORRIS,
Wearing the Champion Belt.

It need hardly be said that the Belt is one of Old Tom's most cherished possessions, for in addition to his famous son's name, his own appears no fewer than four times on it.

The second picture has a still deeper personal interest. It shows Young Tom's locker as he left it at the time of his death with the famous player's clubs as they were last placed in it by his hand. We may state that until the other day the locker had not been opened since Young Tom passed away twenty-four years ago.

On the shelf above can be seen the club-making tools which Young Tom used.

In looking at these relics of the great player the following lines, which appeared in *Chambers's Journal* on the occasion of his early death, recur to one with a singular fitness:—

ELEGY ON TOM MORRIS, Jun.

Beneath the sod poor Tommy's laid,
  Now bunkered fast for good and all;
A better golfer never played
  A further or a surer ball.

Among the monarchs of the green
  For long he held imperial sway;
And none, the start and end between,
  Could match with Tommy in his day.

A triple laurel round his brow,
  The light of triumph in his eye;
He stands before us even now
  As in the hour of victory.

Thrice belted knight of peerless skill
  Again we see him head the fray;
And memory loves to reckon still,
  The feats of Tommy in his day.

The names inscribed on this historic Belt are as follows:

1860—W. Park, senr.	1865—A. Strath.
1861—Tom Morris, senr.	1866—W. Park, senr.
1862—Tom Morris, senr.	1867—Tom Morris, senr.
1863—W. Park, senr.	1868—Tom Morris, junr.
1864—Tom Morris, senr.	1869—Tom Morris, junr.
1870—Tom Morris, junr.	

YOUNG TOM'S LOCKER.

127

St. Andrews, 27th Sept. 1876.

His Royal Highness PRINCE LEOPOLD having this day gained the SILVER CLUB, he was duly installed as Captain of the Club and took the Chair accordingly.

WHEN PRINCE LEOPOLD WAS CAPTAIN.

Prince Leopold, who played himself in as Captain of the R. and A. on 27th September, 1876, was the guest at Mount Melville of Mr John Whyte-Melville. The above photo shows the Prince standing at the top of the steps at the door of the house, with Lady Catherine Whyte-Melville on his right and Miss Wolfe-Murray on his left. Mr Whyte-Melville sat on the steps below the Prince with the Countess of Rosslyn and Miss Jackson on either side, while the Hon. A. York and Dr Royle stood on the bottom step. This photo was taken by Mr Fraser, photographer, St Andrews, and has been loaned to us for reproduction by Mr Baptie, St Andrews.

129

SELF PRINCE LEOPOLD V JOHN WHYTE MELVILLE. SIR RALPH ANSTRUTHER
SIX HOLES — WE WON!

PRINCE LEOPOLD'S CAPTAINCY OF THE ROYAL AND ANCIENT GOLF CLUB.

His Royal Highness Prince Leopold was Captain of the Royal and Ancient Golf Club, St Andrews, in 1876-7, and faithfully discharged the duties for the year. The Prince's visit to Fife in September 1876, when he became the guest of Mr and Mrs Skene of Pitlour, near Strathmiglo, was the occasion of great rejoicing. In driving to St Andrews His Royal Highness passed through Cupar, which was profusely decorated, as was also the "Ancient City" in honour of Royalty. The members of the Golf Club, as might be expected, mustered strongly for their usual competitions on the 27th September. On that day Prince Leopold was installed as Captain, one of whose duties is to play off the first ball. The incident is thus described by the *Fife Herald*:—"The "ball was 'teed' for His Royal Highness by Tom Morris, and the "Prince opened by striking off the first ball, and so became holder of "the Royal Adelaide Medal and Silver Club. His Royal Highness "struck the ball very fairly, sending it over the heads of the spectators. "The Prince, as is well known to golfers, is by no means a novice in "the Royal game. A round has been specially laid out for his use in "Windsor Park, to which, induced alike by his liking for the 'gentle "craft' and medical advice, he occasionally resorts for an hour's "recreation." Our artist has faithfully depicted this scene. The figures of Tom Morris, Mr Whyte-Melville, and Sir Robert Anstruther will be distinctly recognised. In September 1877, when the Prince's Captaincy for the year expired, he again visited St Andrews, and graced the competitions by his Royal presence.

A GOLFER'S IDEA OF HEAVENLY BLISS. An esteemed octogenarian golfer, who does his two rounds a-day on Leith Links like any other man, and enjoys his rubber afterwards, hopes "Heaven will be golf all day and whist all night!"

BLACKHEATH, 1876
Oil painting by F. P. Halikins

By courtesy of the Royal Blackheath Golf Club

XXXII.—ST ANDREWS GOLF CLUB.

INSTITUTED 1843.

There are four quarterly meetings for general business and election of members. The Medal is played for in October, and the Cross Clubs in May; but both cannot be held at one time by one man; and on both days a dinner is held.

JAMES AUCHTERLONIE, *Captain.*
DAVID SPENCE, *Croupier.*
GEORGE MOTION, *Secretary,* WILLIAM AYTON, *Treasurer.*
The Captain, Croupier, Secretary, Treasurer, and John Lynn, Robert Harvie, and J. G. M'Pherson, M.A.—*Council.*

Honorary Members.
Tom Morris
Robert Kirk

David Strath
-Tommys friend
Refused a play off with Bob Martin in 1876 Open
-Also died a young man

Clubmaker and caddie with me
Bob Martin won in 1876 and again in 1885 in the Open

131

SINGULAR GOLFING INCIDENT.

The following narrative should have been included in our chapter on Golfiana, but is worthy of being reproduced yet:—In 1880, four gentlemen were playing from the eighth to the ninth or last hole outwards on St Andrews Links. One of them played a fair tee stroke along the left side of the course, the ball falling near rough grass where a few crows were. To the amazement of the golfers one of the crows lifted the ball. The players at once shouted at the audacity of the creature, and it dropped the ball; but no sooner had it done so than it returned to its prey, and again lifted the ball, carrying it the full length of the hole, though about thirty yards to the left, where it finally dropped it. This was claimed and allowed to be a "rub on the green." A letter from one of the players narrating the incident appeared in the *Scotsman* and the local papers recording the fact, and we have as our authority for the incident as here recorded the gentleman who played the "tee" stroke.

"*PUT* IT OUT, MINE ENEMY."

St. Andrews, 26th Sept. 1877.

Which day the Silver Club given by the Royal and Ancient Golf Club of St. Andrews, and the Royal Adelaide Medal, were played for over the Links of St. Andrews, and gained by the Right Hon. John Inglis of Glencorse.

ONE OF ALLAN ROBERTSON'S.—Allan was partnered in a foursome with an amateur who, if the truth must be told, was very unreliable. Notwithstanding, Allan and his companion had managed to square the match at the second last hole in on St Andrews Links. Between the "tee" ground and the last hole the burn intervened. It was Allan's partner to drive off, and ten chances to one he would go into the water. Allan whispered to him to miss the ball. The advice was followed. Allan now drove a splendid ball, sending it well home, and he and his companion won the match.

SINGULAR INCIDENTS.—A party were playing a foursome over Monifieth Links on a Saturday afternoon some 15 years ago. In the course of the play one of the golfers found his ball "cupped." He took the long spoon to it, and heeled the ball, which went off with considerable "side," and struck a village cow some distance in front in the region of the tail. The cow started off whisking her tail, and after running some twenty yards she was seen to drop the ball. This story is at least as credible as that of the sheep which got a golf ball under its tail in similar circumstances and went and dropped it in the hole!

133

1st. TEE WITH THE NEW GOLF BAGS IN 1889

1882

Prestwick
Converted to 18 holes
in 1882
Charlie Hunter supervising

1st HOLE Prestwick

THE "CARDINAL" BUNKER - PRESTWICK

Prestwick Clubhouse

The "Bridge" Hole – 4th

Prestwick
Himalayas Out
5th Hole

Bunker + Green - 17th

THE LATE J. WHYTE-MELVILLE, ESQ.

St. Andrews, 25th Sept. 1883.

At this the first meeting of the Royal and Ancient Golf Club since the death of John Whyte-Melville, Esq., Chairman of the Committee of Management, it was agreed unanimously to record in the Minutes an expression of regret at Mr. Melville's death, and of the deep sense entertained by all the Members of the Club of the services rendered by Mr. Melville during his long connection with it of upwards of sixty years, and particularly of the uniform urbanity and courtesy with which he had discharged the duties of Chairman of Committee of Management for a period of over thirty years.

Self

TECHNICAL TERMS
EMPLOYED IN THE GAME OF GOLF.

BAFF.—To strike the ground with the "sole" of the club-head in playing.

BUNKER.—A sand-pit.

CADDIE.—A person who carries the Golfer's clubs, and, if necessary, gives him advice in regard to the game.

CUP.—A small hole in the course, probably made by the stroke of some previous player.

DEAD.—A ball is said to be "dead"—1st, when it falls without rolling; 2nd, when it lies so near the hole that the "put" is a *dead* certainty.

DORMY.—One party is said to be "dormy" on the other when the former is as many holes a-head as there remain holes to play. (This word is fancifully derived from *dormio*, to sleep, owing to the security enjoyed by the *dormy* party.)

DRAW.—To drive widely to the left hand. (Synonymous with Hook and Screw.)

FACE.—1st, The sandy slope of a bunker; 2nd, the part of the club-head which strikes the ball.

FLAT.—A club is said to be "flat" when its head is at a very obtuse angle to the shaft.

FORE!—A warning cry to any person in the way of the stroke. (Contracted for "Before.")

FOURSOME.—A match in which two play on each side.

GOBBLE.—A rapid straight "put" into the hole.

GRASSED.—Said of a club whose face is "spooned" or sloped backward.

GREEN.—1st, The whole Links; 2nd, The Putting-ground around the different holes.

GRIP.—1st, The part of the handle covered with leather by which the club is grasped; 2nd, the grasp itself.

HALF-ONE.—A handicap of a stroke deducted every *second* hole.

HALVED.—A hole is said to be "halved" when each party takes the same number of strokes. A "halved match" is a "drawn game;" *i.e.*, the players have proved to be equal.

HANGING.—A "hanging" ball is one which lies on a downward slope.

HAZARD.—A general term for bunker, whin, or other bad ground.

HEAD.—This word is a striking specimen of incongruity and mixed metaphor. A head is the *lowest* part of a club, and possesses, among other mysterious characteristics, a *sole*, a *heel*, a *toe*, a *nose*, a *neck*, and a *face!* These features are briefly described in this Glossary, and the curious inquirer may easily have them pointed out to him by any one who knows the secrets of Golf-craft.

HEEL.—1st, The part of the head nearest the shaft; 2nd, To hit off this part.

HOLE.—1st, The four-inch hole lined with iron; 2nd, The whole space between any two of these.

HONOUR.—The right to play off first from the tee, which belongs to the winner of the last hole. After the tee-stroke, the party whose ball is furthest from the hole must play first.

HOOK.—See Draw.

JERK.—In "jerking" the club should strike with a quick angular cut behind the ball, and *stop* on reaching the ground.

LIE.—1st, The inclination of a club when held on the ground in the natural position for striking; 2nd, The situation of a ball—good or bad.

LIKE.—See under Odd.

LIKE-AS-WE-LIE.—When both parties have played the same number of strokes.

LINKS.—The open downs or heath on which Golf is played.

LOFT.—To elevate the ball.

MATCH.—1st, The parties playing against each other; 2nd, The game itself.

MISS THE GLOBE.—To fail to strike the ball, either by swinging right over the top of it, or by hitting the ground behind.

NECK.—The crook of the head where it joins the shaft.

NOSE.—The point or front portion of the club-head.

ODD.—1st, "An odd," "two odds," &c., per hole means the handicap given to a weak opponent by deducting one, two, &c., strokes from his total every hole. 2nd, To have played "the odd" is to have played one stroke more than your adversary. Some other terms used in counting the game will be most easily explained here all together:—If your opponent has played one stroke more than you—*i.e.*, "the odd," your next stroke will be "the like;" if two strokes more—*i.e.*, "the two more," your next stroke will be "the one off two;" if "three more"—"the one off three;" and so on.

ONE-OFF-TWO, ONE-OFF-THREE, &C.—See under Odd.

PRESS.—To strive to recover lost ground by special exertion—a very dangerous thing to attempt.

PUT.—To play the delicate game close to the hole. (Pronounce *u* as in *but*.)

RIND.—A strip of cloth under the leather to thicken the grip.

RUB ON THE GREEN.—A favourable or unfavourable knock to the ball, for which no penalty is imposed, and which must be submitted to.

SCARE.—The narrow part of the club-head by which it is glued to the handle.

SCREW.—See Draw.

SET.—A pack of clubs.

SOLE.—The flat bottom of the club-head.

SPRING.—The degree of suppleness in the shaft.

SQUARE.—When the game stands evenly balanced, neither party being any holes ahead.

STEAL.—To hole an unlikely "put" from a distance.

STIMY.—When your opponent's ball lies in the line of your "put." See Chap. III., page 30.

SWIPE.—A full driving stroke.

SWING.—The circular sweep of the club in driving.

TEE.—The pat of sand on which the ball is placed for the first stroke each hole.

THIRD.—A handicap of a stroke deducted every *third* hole.

TOE.—Another name for the Nose.

Glossary of Technical Terms.

TOP.—To hit the ball above its centre.

TWO-MORE, THREE-MORE, &C.—See under Odd.

UPRIGHT.—A club is said to be "upright" when its head is not at very obtuse angle to the shaft.

WHINS.—Furze or gorse.

WHIPPING.—The pitched twine uniting the head and handle.

St Andrews Citizen
29th April 1882

We ought not to omit noticing the additions to, and alterations on, the well – known premises of Mr Thomas ("Old Tom") Morris at the Links. The mason work is now completed – Mr Wm. Ness, builder, being contractor – and is after designs by a rising young townsman, Mr Archibald Downie. The alterations are a marked improvement on 'the Road'. The comparatively recent introduction of 'concrete' in connection with building operations, outside and inside, forms a very noticeable feature. Operations with this material have been very successfully carried on by Mr Alex. McPherson, son, and successor to the business, of our late much respected Dean of Guild James McPherson.

CHAMPION SCORES.

1872—Tom Morris, jun., St Andrews, - 166—at Prestwick.
1873—Tom Kidd, do., - 179—at St Andrews.
1874—Mungo Park, Musselburgh, - 159—at Musselburgh.
1875—Willie Park, Musselburgh, - 166—at Prestwick.
1876—Bob Martin, St Andrews, - 176—at St Andrews.
1877—Jamie Anderson, St Andrews, 160—at Musselburgh.
1878—Jamie Anderson, do., - 157—at Prestwick.
1879—Jamie Anderson, do., - 170—at St Andrews.
1880—Bob Fergusson, Musselburgh, 162—at Musselburgh.

From this list it will be seen that Jamie Anderson has won the Cup thrice in succession; and it may be mentioned that he was not present at the last Competition. Although the conditions of the Cup's tenure differ from those of the Belt, in that it is not permitted to become any one's absolute property, nevertheless Anderson's achievement entitles him to be placed in the foremost rank of living golfers.

JAMIE ANDERSON

In the great matches in which he has engaged he has generally proved too much for his opponent; and Bob Kirk, St Andrews, and Jamie Allan, Westward Ho! have both fallen before him.

At various Scotch and English greens there are one or more distinguished professional players well worthy of notice, but the facts we have given, and the names we have mentioned, make up, on the whole, the history of Champion Golfers down to the present time.

The 5th on the Old - just a rough sandy area from the tee before I shaped in "the Seven Sisters" - a group of bunkers.

See page 116 to 118 for details of how all the holes were played

THE CLUB HOUSE,
ST ANDREWS,
N.B. 16th Octr. 1884

Dear Sir,

I must apologize for not having answered yours of 4th curt: but I delayed in the hope of being able to learn something from Tom Morris regarding the block of ebonized wood on which the Challenge Trophy used to stand. - The cup was placed in the Royal Bank

Letter from Mr Grace Secretary of the R & A to Mr Hart in Prestwick

St. Andrews, 24th Sept. 1884.
Which day the Silver Club given by the Royal and Ancient Golf Club of St. Andrews, and the Royal Adelaide Medal, were played for over the Links of St. Andrews, and gained by George Glennie, Esq.

← Mr Glennie still playing well 33 years on

139

St. Andrews, 3rd March 1886.

The Committee of the Royal and Ancient Golf Club of St. Andrews cannot allow their first business meeting after the lamented death of the Very Reverend Principal Tulloch to pass without placing on record their deep regret at the loss of their associate and colleague in the management of the Club, of which for about 30 years he has been an honoured Member—in which he took so much pleasure, and where he was wont to unbend from the cares and anxieties of his busy life, and where his dignified presence and genial manner endeared him to all who had the pleasure either of his friendship or acquaintance.

← Principal Tulloch a fine man

RETIREMENT OF MR. STUART GRACE.

St. Andrews, 4th May 1886.

The following Minute, which had been prepared by the late Principal Tulloch and Major Bethune, as requested at the last General Meeting of the Club, was read and approved of, viz.—"The Royal and Ancient Golf Club cannot part with Mr. Stuart Grace, who has so long and with so much acceptance filled the office of Honorary Secretary to the Club, without recording their most cordial thanks to him for his long-continued and faithful services.

here, but without any stand. and I cannot say where it can be.. I don't even know who deposited the Cup but it is certain that no stand accompanied it.-

I do not know who won the cup on the last two occasions here, but I shall endeavour to find out from Tom Morris and will write to you again when I have seen him.-

Yours truly
p. Stuart Grace Hon: Sec
Chas. Stuart Grace

Harry Hart Esqr.
Prestwick Golf Club
Ayr

– the stand for the Claret Jug never did turn up!

– it was Bob Ferguson from Musselburgh

THE GREATEST UNPLAYED GOLF-MATCH.

The photograph mentioned here is on page 65

A GOLFING curiosity has recently been sent us by that most enthusiastic player, W. G. Roy, S.S.C. It is a photograph of the four greatest professionals who were ever alive at the same time, with their four characteristic caddies. A calotype of these celebrities was taken about 1858 by Thomas Rodger of St Andrews; and soon afterwards this photograph was taken from that calotype. It represents the players in a match which never came off, but which would have been the most famous in the annals of the game. Often was it spoken about by veteran players as the grandest foursome of the day; but, somehow, this photographed calotype is all the outcome of the talk. But with what keenness would every golfer worthy of the name have perused the report from some unearthed manuscript of the details of the match between Allan and Tom against Dunn and Park! This is all we have of the projected match; yet we can think of what might have been.

The eight characters here represented, as standing at the first hole of St Andrews Links, are Allan Robertson, Tom Morris, Willie Dunn, and Willie Park as principals; and Da' Anderson, Bob Kirk, Jamie Wilson, and Bob Andrews as their respective caddies. They are all evidently standing for their portrait, so fixed are most of their features. Allan is in a cranked position, as if he had just played off his tee-shot, and was holding up his driver over his left shoulder, his favourite red jacket open (whereas he generally had it buttoned), the deep dimple of intense humour in his chin. Tom is holding his putter, the leather in the right hand, the whipping in the left, as a standing protest against the modern use of the cleek in putting. Dunn, in his checked suit, is addressing himself to his ball, as if about to take one of his unrivalled swipes, with his hands in the model position, though his legs are just too straight to be natural. Park is quietly standing behind with his driver in his right hand, the tip of the handle on the ground and the head on his right arm, in a meditative attitude, as if calculating the possibilities of the match. Da' has his peculiar smile on his face, his mouth being well drawn up to the left side, as if he were certain of the issue. Bob's features are fixed in gloomy sternness, his right thumb carefully put down to the bottom of his right vest-pocket — a statue of determination. Jamie's features are particularly contemplative; he is carrying for a foreigner, yet he is an ardent admirer, and the conflict is evident between patriotism and real worth. The Rook stands leaning on the cleek, the head of which he holds in his right hand. All are shaven except the whiskers, a pretty large stock encircles each neck, and all are fixed upon a mighty struggle.

Allan stands in front, *facile princeps* of golfers. Never was he beaten. He came of a golfing race, his grandfather and father being ball-makers and golfers. He played with toy clubs when a child, and when a youth he rushed out while the dew was on the grass on the undisturbed Links and practised with his coat off, not unlike the modern enthusiasts Professor Tait and Colonel Ogilvy. No one who ever saw the champion can ever forget him. Frank and open to all, yet firm in his judgment, he was as polite as a Brummel and as politic as a Metternich. Small of stature, thick-set, short-necked, he stored a tremendous amount of energy and pluck, but the humour never ceased to play round his happy features. His style was invariably elegant and faultless. He was exceptionally temperate; though kindly, he was firm. Pawky was he, yet he lacked the diplomacy of his father. Of old Davie it was written after his death:—

> "Sound be his slumbers! yet if he should wake
> In worlds where golf is played, himself he'd shake,
> And look about, and tell each young beginner,
> 'I'll gie half-ane--nae mair, as I'm a sinner.'"

But Allan's game was pure, unadulterated science. He could not hold the candle to Dunn at driving; but his quarter-strokes were deadly, and his putting was perfect. Let him come within the reach of Sir David Baird, or the Doctor, or the Thraw-cruck (favourite clubs), to say nothing of the Frying-pan (iron) or cleek, and he had it all his own way; he could *play* with the ball. In 1843, he showed his superiority over Dunn in the greatest test match on record — a match of twenty rounds — when he beat his Musselburgh opponent by two rounds to one. His name will never be forgotten; and many are still living who heard, or heard about, old Sutherland's most pathetic remark, when the bells of the old city were tolling as the champion's remains were being taken to their last resting-place: "They may toll the bells and shut up their shops in St Andrews, for their greatest is gone."

140

Of the four players in the photograph, Tom was then the weakest. His style had never the sweet ease of Allan's; but he had the good sense to look up to Allan as his superior, and play into the champion's hands. Now this is one of the secrets of successful foursome play. For the common good one must give in and be directed. The writer well remembers the particular tact which Major (now Colonel) Boothby exhibited in thus yielding for the time being. We played many matches with uniform success against Clark and Innes, and other powerful couples; but that was *the* secret of our success. I may also mention in passing that in a big foursome it is a mistake, at St Andrews, to make the secondary player (even when he allows this) play off at the first hole: calculate the number of likely quarter-strokes (the most deadly part of the game), and you will find that more come to the weapon of the player who strikes off at the first hole. We also acted upon that, which was a long-calculated scheme of the Major's. Tom's character and work are familiar to our readers. Now in his seventieth year, a worthy elder of the Church of Scotland, and a very highly respected man, he bears his long list of honours with genial humility. The veteran still gives evidence of his first-class world-known play, as well as of his lifetime's weakness (confoundedly true of the writer also) for missing short putts. Tom three times won the challenge belt, open to the world; and in 1866 he equalled Allan's score of 79 at St Andrews. Many a tussle had he with Willie Park, whom he publicly called "as good a player as ever lifted a club"; but his most brilliant victory was in 1862, when he defeated Park on all the four greens of Musselburgh, Prestwick, North Berwick, and St Andrews, —a triumph unparalleled in the record of golf.

Allan and Tom were the strongest pair that ever played over any green. Once they were tried in true style. The brothers Dunn in 1849 challenged them in a match of £400 over the links of Musselburgh, St Andrews, and North Berwick. On the first green the Dinnies won at a canter, but on their home green Allan and Tom retrieved their loss. On the neutral (test) green the Dinnies were four holes ahead and eight to play. But the innate

Continued —

141 continued

strength of character, marvellous training, and pure skill of the St Andrews men came to their rescue just when wanted. By an unequalled game of brilliancy they won the first and the second, halved the third, won the fourth, halved the fifth, and won the sixth, making them all even and two to play. These two also fell to Allan and Tom, and they won the match. This was the most magnificent and extraordinary run of brilliant play ever known in the annals of the game. In a second test, during the same year, the two beat the Dunns at St Andrews, holing the round in 88, a marvellous foursome score in those days.

Of the brilliancy of Willie Dunn's style no language can give any adequate description. He stood more straight up than Tom (with his half-hunker) or even Allan (with his long flat clubs). His driving was simply unrivalled, without any forcedness to detract from its sweetness. Tennant of the Glen so admired Dunn's style that he was determined to get his flat clubs (long for his short stature) made more upright. Old M'Ewan looked at the little man and the long club, and told him that this was impossible. "What?" asked Tennant; "can't I have my clubs altered and made more upright like Dunn's?" "It wu'd be oncommonly onconvenient," answered the pawky club-maker. "Why?" "Because if ye played wi' them mair upright, withoot cuttin' the handles, ye wu'd need to play aye on a stool."

Of Park we have already written. He had in him the innate power of being the finest and most powerful of all players. But he was more of the "potato-soup" style of feeder, whereas Tom was more of the "ham-and-egg" type. His weakness was never in style, in pluck, or in golfing resources as to all the niceties—for in all these he was perfect—but in pure physical shortcoming at the crucial point in a great match. Had this match come off, of which we have an indication in our photograph, I have no doubt—patriot though I am—that Dunn and Park would not have been beaten, as were the two Dunns. As far as I can ascertain, they never played on a side; but I am confident that in their day they would have faced the world if they had managed to agree upon the directorship of the game. Of these eight players and caddies the golfing "world's victor's victor" has bunkered three—Tom, Park, Da', Bob, and the Rook alone remain.

myself and Daw from the photograph on page 65

AN HERCULEAN GOLFER.—A golfer, well-known on various Links, made a magnificent swipe on one occasion, except that the ball was sadly off the line, and a donkey in front, which gave no heed to the warning cry of "fore," was struck with such violence in the head that it died. To avoid the imputation of fratricide, the *cuddy* was dubbed a pony. This same golfer, when practising his swing in the lobby of the Union Club at St Andrews, brought down the handsome lamp about his "lugs."

CLUBS EMPLOYED IN THE GAME.

WHY are so many clubs necessary? This is usually the first question asked by a novice witnessing the game. To satisfy this pardonable curiosity, by giving a description of the various clubs and their special advantages, is the object of the present Chapter. Before proceeding to this, however, let us say that it is not owing to mere whim or caprice that the Golfer carries so many heavy weapons along with him when in pursuit of his favourite pastime. With a view to increase the interest and risk of the game, the surface of the Links on which it is played is generally broken by hollows and hillocks, and large sandy holes or "bunkers," to cope with which special clubs are required; and this fact, combined with the necessity for long or short strokes, according to the distance of the ball from the hole, satisfactorily accounts for the number and variety of the clubs employed. To the description of these and their special uses we now return.

The total number of different clubs is sixteen. Of these, however, some have become almost obsolete, while others are new-fashioned, fanciful, and useless; so that an ordinary set does not contain more than eight or nine. The following table shows at a glance the classes (genera), species, and varieties into which clubs are divided, the obsolete or useless being enclosed in brackets:—

I. WOODEN CLUBS........	*Drivers.*	Play-Club.
		Grassed Driver.
	Spoons.	Long Spoon.
		Middle Spoon.
		Short Spoon.
		[Baffing Spoon].
		Wooden Niblick.
	Putters.	Green Putter.
		[Driving Putter].
II. IRON CLUBS.	*Cleeks.* ...	Driving Cleek.
		[Putting Cleek].
	Irons. ...	Light Iron.
		Sand Iron.
	Niblicks.	Niblick proper.
		[Mashy].
		[President].

I.—WOODEN CLUBS.

Wooden Clubs are commonly employed to propel the ball when it lies in free and open ground, where there is a good chance of getting it well away, and little fear of breakage. We give this as a general rule, though, as we shall have occasion to show, some of the stronger wooden weapons may frequently be used with advantage in rather difficult situations.

Drivers.—Of all the clubs in the "set" the Drivers are the longest, most delicately constructed, and yet most powerful from a "swiping" point of view. They derive their name from being the clubs used to *drive* or propel the ball when the longest possible stroke is required. The handle or shaft of a full-sized Driver measures 3 ft. 7 in., and is carefully tapered from the "grip" to its junction with the head, in order to give it the proper "spring" or degree of suppleness. The head weighs 7 oz. or 8 oz., and is distinguished from those of the "Spoon" family by its "face" being straight and almost perpendicular. In the choice of this club these points should be attended to, and will generally be found in a weapon which is easily handled, and over which the player feels complete mastery. There are, however, two varieties of Drivers, and these must be distinguished from one another.

1. The "Play-Club" is chiefly used for "swiping off the tee," but may likewise not unfrequently be employed in playing through the green when the ball has a "good lie," and a full stroke is required. By the peculiarity of its construction, this club does not *sky* the ball too much, so as to waste its velocity "in the desert air," but only so as to accomplish the greatest possible distance, and is accordingly the club best adapted for that "long driving" which is the envy of all who cannot exhibit it, and the glory of all who can.

2. The "Grassed Driver" is likewise used to effect distance, and is a club very often in the Golfer's hands in playing the longest holes of the course. It differs from the Play-Club in having a slightly stiffer handle and heavier head, and in its face being sloped back a little from the perpendicular. When the ball is situated among soft grass, or on a downward slope, or when a hazard looming in front demands a well-elevated stroke, the Grassed Driver's services are properly called in, as it raises the ball to a considerable height, and also sends it well away, which the Play-Club in such cases would fail to do.

Spoons.—Spoons are a rather numerous family. They are employed in a similar way to the Grassed Driver, but do not send the ball so far. Their very suggestive title is taken from the great slope in their face, which distinctive characteristic is meant to enable them to raise the "gutta" to almost any height required, even out of very difficult ground. They have accordingly been described as most useful fellows, doing much of the "sapper and miner" work of the game. Each member of the family has its special duties to perform.

1. The "Long Spoon" comes into play when the "bad lie" is too much for the Grassed Driver to overcome; *e.g.*, when the ball is found among long grass, in a hollow, or on a declivity; and likewise, of course, when the distance to the hole is just such as this club will best accomplish. The Long Spoon handle is an inch shorter and considerably stiffer than that of the Grassed Driver, while the head is also heavier and more sloped in the face.

2. The "Middle Spoon" is a very strong club, and is especially useful in "forcing" a ball out of a grassy rut, and in playing a three-quarters stroke. It is shorter, stiffer, and heavier than its elder brother.

3. The "Short Spoon," as its name implies, is not so long as either of the preceding. It is still more sloped in the face, and is employed in similar predicaments when the distance required is not so great. Many players also call in its services when about a half-stroke from the hole, where others, as we shall see, use the Driving Cleek.

4. The "Baffing Spoon" is so called from the sound produced by it as it smites the ground in making the stroke; but it is now seldom met with except in the set of an oldster. Its use is, or rather *was*, to elevate a clear-lying ball over a hazard at a very short distance from the hole, and with this view it is very much spooned out in the face. Since Allan Robertson's * day, however, this function has generally been usurped by the Light Iron—a club which has yet to be described.

5. The "Wooden Niblick" is closely allied to the Spoon family. About thirty years ago this weapon had become almost extinct, but it has recently renewed its youth by the addition of a "brass-sole," and is at present very popular. It is of about the same length and "lie" as the Long Spoon, but its head is exceedingly small and more scooped out. Its special duty is to excavate the ball out of a rut or "cup," into which the "diminished head" easily makes its way. The brass-sole is of great advantage for playing on hard and stony ground, on which the club might otherwise be broken. This weapon may, however, be easily dispensed with, as a Spoon or an Iron club often answers the same purpose equally well.

Putters.—The two varieties of Putters are used for very different purposes. They are the most "upright" fellows in the set—that is to say, their shaft, when the sole of the head is laid flat on the ground, stands nearly vertical, so that the Golfer in handling them has to place himself very close to his ball.

1. The "Green Putter," as its name indicates, is employed on the putting-green when the ball is so near the hole that the player is able to calculate with considerable certainty the strength required to reach it. This club will accordingly be found preferable to all others at any distance within thirty yards, if the turf is tolerably smooth and level, and no obstacles or hazards are in the way. It is likewise the *only club* to be used in ordinary circumstances in "putting out" within a few feet of the hole, though some attempt this stroke with the Putting Cleek. The head of the putter is very heavy, the face quite perpendicular, and the handle short and perfectly stiff and slightly curved in the back. This construction gives the player complete command over his implement, so that he requires to exert very little force in manipulating it, and may accordingly devote his whole attention to that nice calculation which is the secret of all really scientific putting.

2. The "Driving-Putter" differs from its companion of the green only in the length of the shaft, which in the one measures 3 ft. 6 in., in the other 3 ft. One function of the Driving-Putter is to "cheat the wind" by sending a low "skimming" ball—a most desirable virtue in boisterous weather; another is to force a ball out of long grass; another to play a half-or quarter-stroke, and so on. These duties are, however, performed equally well by other clubs in the set, and so the Driving-Putter is fast falling into disuse.

II.—IRON CLUBS.

Iron Clubs are distinguished from their wooden neighbours, as regards construction, only by their heads being of that metal; the shafts of both being, of course, made of wood. Speaking generally, they are used to extricate the ball from those situations (bunkers, whins, ruts, &c.), in which a wooden club would be unavailable, and, moreover, would probably break. Skill as well as force may, however, be displayed in the manipulation of the iron weapons, and, accordingly, perhaps the most telling and deadly part of the game—that of "approaching the hole"—has likewise been assigned to them.

Cleeks.—There are two varieties of clubs known by this rather expressive name.

1. The "Driving Cleek," or Cleek *proper*, is ubiquitously useful. In very bad lies throughout the green, in cups and ruts, in open whins and sand, wherever the player desires to extricate his ball and effect distance at the same time, this is the safest and surest weapon to employ. It is further of great service in playing half strokes to the hole, and in "putting" out of bad lies or cups on the green. The handle is much shorter than that of the Driver, is very little tapered, and ought to have no perceptible spring. The construction of the head, however, is not so easily described; in fact it requires to be seen to be understood. It usually weighs about 10 oz., and is sloped in the face like a spoon to enable it to elevate the ball.

2. The "Putting Cleek" is a club which few good players use, and is only mentioned here to be condemned. Its head is almost perpendicular in the face, but in all other respects it resembles the Driving Cleek. It is employed on the putting-green, but is a very treacherous weapon, since if either heel or point catch the turf a moment before the rest of the head—and this is a very common occurrence—the ball is sent "off the line" to the right or left of the hole. The club is, in fact, a usurper, and deserves to be dethroned. The Green Putter fulfils the duties of its office far better.

Irons.—In olden times this species of club was very uncomely and unwieldy, and afforded scope for the display of mere brute force rather than of skill. In fact, it is almost laughable to place an antiquated iron—a relic of fifty years ago—alongside of a modern weapon of the same name. One could scarcely believe, unless he were told it on good authority, that they were meant to serve the same purpose. The ancient implement seems more fitted to destroy the turf than to drive a ball. Irons, however, as they are now made, are anything but unscientific tools; indeed, skill and calculation are at no time more needed than in handling them. The two varieties of Irons are employed for different purposes, but are distinguished from each other only by the weight of the head.

1. The "Light Iron" appears to an inexperienced eye almost identical with the Cleek, but is in reality considerably different from it. Their handles, indeed, are much the same, but as regards the head, they differ in two important respects, that of the Iron being both broader at the point and more sloped back in the face. Owing to these peculiarities the Light Iron skies the ball higher, and so does not send it so far as the Cleek; and this fact gives us a clue to its distinctive functions. It is employed in "approaching the hole" when the Cleek would drive the ball too far, or when special elevation over hazards is required. In this way it is a most useful weapon at half-and quarter-strokes, and frequently also a very deadly one, as the brilliant driver may find to his cost when his opponent—an adept at playing "off the wrist"—snatches from his grasp

2. The "Sand Iron," as may be at once inferred from its name, is mainly employed to extricate a ball from sandy ruts and bunkers. It ought, however, to be likewise used in whins, and all those other difficult situations for which no club is specified, where great force must be exerted, and the risk of breakage is considerable. With a view to these duties, the handle ought to be very strong, and the head heavy and well sloped back in the face.

Niblicks.—Of this species there are three varieties, which, however, do not essentially differ from each other.

1. The "Niblick" *proper* performs functions similar to those of the Sand Iron. It is specially employed to "jerk" the ball out of the steep face of a bunker, or to extricate it from rough stones or stiff whins, or the deep track of a cart-wheel. To accomplish these special duties a peculiar construction is required, by means of which the weapon may find its way into the most difficult situations. The handle is accordingly made very tough and strong, while the head is very small and specially distinguished by a rounded-off sole and a concave face.

2. The "Mashy" is used for the same purposes as the Niblick proper, and only differs from it in its sole and face being straight instead of rounded. It thus looks exactly like a Sand Iron with its head cut short. The Mashy, however, is one of those fanciful clubs that have been invented in recent years, and is entirely unnecessary in the Golfer's set.

3. The "President" is a still more fanciful weapon. It is distinguished in appearance from the ordinary Niblick by an oval-shaped hole right through its face—an addition, alas! neither ornamental nor useful. The hole is, we believe, intended to allow the sand to pass through in playing in a bunker, but what particular advantage is hereby to be gained we cannot imagine, and have never heard stated. The President is, in fact, better at hacking the "gutta" than at anything else.

We have now passed in review a complete set of Golfing utensils. There may, indeed, exist in the packs of some oldsters one or two monstrosities

A BALLADE OF THE GAME OF GOLFE.

There are laddies will drive ye a ba'
To the burn frae the farthermost tee,
But ye mauna think driving is a',
Ye may heel her, and send her ajee,
Ye may land in the sand or the sea ;
And ye're dune, sir, ye're no worth a preen,
Tak' the word that an aul' man 'll gie,
Tak' aye tent to be up on the green !

The auld folks are crouse, and they craw
That their putting is pawky and slee ;
In a bunker they're nae guid ava',
But to girn and gar the sand flee.
And the lassie can putt—ony she—
Be she Maggie, or Bessie, or Jean ;
But a cleek shot's the Billy for me,
Tak' aye tent to be up on the green !

I ha'e played in the frost and the thaw,
I ha'e played since the year thirty-three,
I ha'e played in the rain and the snaw,
And I trust I may play till I dee ;
And I tell ye the truth and nae lee,
For I speak o' the truth I ha'e seen—
Tam Morris, I ken, will agree—
Tak' aye tent to be up on the green !

ENVOY.

Prince, faith, you're improving a wee,
And, Lord, man, they tell me you're keen ;
Tak' the best o' advice that can be,
Tak' aye tent to be up on the green !

Andrew Lang.

AN EXCEPTION TO THE RULE.—The "caddies" of the Links can generally be depended on as most trustworthy in all matters connected with the game ; but the following story (the accuracy of which can be vouched for) must, from the cool impertinence and audacity it displays, be regarded as a decided exception to the rule. Two of Edinburgh's most brilliant legal luminaries, who, however, by no means shone on the Links, used now and then to visit St Andrews to enjoy a few days' play. On one of these occasions, requiring "caddies" as usual to carry their clubs and watch the game for them, they were instantly taken in hand by two worthy members of that profession, who evidently knew well the measure of their masters, at least in respect of their golfing capacities. What that measure was may be gathered from the following dialogue. "They's twa gey lads we've gotten the day," says worthy No. 1. "Aye ar' they," replies worthy No. 2. "We'll niver be able tae coont them, I doot," says No. 1. "Coont them !" exclaims No. 2, "we may as weel attempt tae coont the stars in the firmament." "A-weel than," says No. 1, "we'll jist ha'e tae auv'rage the thing. Your man 'll get the first hole an' mine 'll get the second, an' so on." "Aye, aye, jist that !" acquiesces No. 2. And so they set to work, and successfully hoodwinked their unsuspecting victims !

GOLF BY MOONLIGHT.

145

at Montrose

A GOLFING SONG.

JAMES BALLANTYNE, in "Golf," by Messrs R. & R. Clark.

AIR—"*Let Haughty Gaul.*"

Come leave your dingy desks and shops,
Ye sons of ancient Reekie,
And by green fields and sunny slopes,
For healthy pastimes seek ye.
Don't bounce about your "*dogs of war,*"
Nor at our *shinties* scoff, boys,
But learn our motto, "*Sure and Far,*"
Then come and play at golf, boys.

Chorus—Three rounds of Bruntsfield Links will chase
All murky vapours off, boys;
And nothing can your sinews brace
Like the glorious game of golf, boys.

a Golfing Song by Mr Ballantyne of Edinburgh

Above our head the clear blue sky,
We bound the gowan'd sward o'er,
And as our balls fly far and high,
Our bosoms glow with ardour.
While dear Edina, Scotland's Queen,
Her misty cap lifts off, boys,
And smiles serenely on the Green,
Graced by the game of golf boys.

Chorus—Three rounds, etc.

We putt, we drive, we laugh, we chat,
Our strokes and jokes aye clinking,
We banish all extraneous fat,
And all extraneous thinking.
We'll cure you of a summer cold,
Or of a winter cough, boys,
We'll make you young, even when you're old,
So come and play at golf, boys.

Chorus—Three rounds, etc.

When in the dumps with mulligrubs,
Or doyte with barley bree boys,
Go get you off the green three rubs,
'Twill set you on the "*Tee*" boys.

HOME HOLE, ST. ANDREWS, ABOUT 1850.

→ See page 33 for the photograph

THESE Calotypes bring back pleasant memories to me. I just remember the particular associations here delineated for the calotype taken by Dr. Adamson, about 1850. Dr. Adamson, the father of Mrs. Dr. William Tulloch, was an enthusiast in photography. I remember him working with the afterwards famous Thomas Rodger in the development of the then mystic art. When a youngster I was subjected to their particular calotype work. I have a faint recollection of having to sit for about two minutes for the positive glass impression. My mother said to me before the historical ordeal: "Mind, noo, an' keep yer een open, for they're faur back i' yer heid." I attended to this well-intended maternal injunction, and stared till everything was black and meaningless. Of course I dared not wink. That calotype I saw the other day in the house where I was born, and I could not have recognised myself but for the authentic evidence in favour of the production. Dr. Adamson was a most distinguished medical practitioner during my childhood and, acted for some time as lecturer in chemistry in the University. It is, therefore, with great pleasure that I go over these pictures from his famous calotypes. I may mention that the doctor's wife was a sister of the well-known Patrick Proctor Alexander, whose portrait appeared in a recent issue. I shall, if permitted, devote an article to him as a golfer.

This first drawing represents the Home-Hole at St. Andrews, about 1850. The railway from St. Andrews to Leuchars had just been completed. My ancient friend, Ancra Jack, collected in coppers sufficient to purchase a mimic railway, in primitive wooden blocks, with "sclarges" of paint for carriages, connected by wire couplings, set on rails slanted about three degrees to make sure of the exciting descent of the whole rickmatick when once let loose. I remember that celebrated *denouement* on the part of my "natural" friend, after the opening of the branch line. Here are represented the old Stationmaster's House, and the celebrated Stationmaster's Garden, in honour of which a special rub had to be made when a delinquent transgressed in his erratic driving. In the distance is "Lucklaw Hill," over which the late Rev. Dr. Park witnessed brilliant sunsets, unsurpassed in his favoured Wordsworth country. Nearer us we see clothes bleaching in the whins. No longer are the whins there; a new course takes their place. The burgesses of St. Andrews had a special right to have that place reserved for bleaching clothes. There was a famous law plea when that right was disputed. The County Session (Second Division) did not recognise the right, though Lord Young gave an exhaustive opinion in favour of the servitude. When I was young I saw the clothes lying on both sides of the Swilkin Burn, and "Gubb's House"—a wooden erection—was shifted about on the east side of the Burn to give him ample room for detecting thieves during the moonlight nights.

Near us is the first hole. I think the man playing on the right hand is Allan Robertson, the one next him is old Mr. Wallace, of Kildrummie, who ran Mr. Robert Chambers so hard in the first tournament. Old Wallace took an enormous time to play; back and forward would he wander at every putt, and thereby he wearied out all his opponents up to the final. But Mr. Chambers was too many for him. "Give me a novel and a campstool," Mr. Chambers said to a friend, when the deplorable delaying skill of his opponent was mentioned to him, "and I'll tire him out." Mr. Chambers won by being not put out of temper as others were. I remember the finish; and I will have something more to say about it at another time.

The last picture represents the lie of the Home Hole from the opposite direction. Our back is to the old railway station. The calotype shows us the Green about 1850, for the present club house at the first hole is not introduced. Had it been in existence, Dr. Adamson would certainly have introduced it, as it would give a set off to the picture, besides being a necessary appendage. I just remember when Mr. John Whyte-Melville, afterwards a Captain of the Royal and Ancient, laid the foundation-stone of the fine Club House, with full masonic honours in presence of a vast number of the craft.

The historical house in this calotype is Allan Robertson's. There feather balls were made for three-quarters of a century. There the gutta balls were successfully initiated, though against Allan's grain. There the famous Peter Davie and Allan Robertson lived in succession as ball makers and professional golfers. The house is no more—a hotel takes its place. Right opposite is the old Union Parlour, the Club House of the Royal and Ancient for many years. Golfing signals went between the two houses on many a morning. Caddies would be moving up and down on the left side of Allan's house. Campbell, of Saddell, would issue from the Union Parlour in hot haste and ask "Lang Willie," an authority on the weather, who looked so wise with his long tile hat on, "Is it to be fair; how's Allan's glass?" "Well, sir," would cautious Willie answer, "the gless's mair doon the day than she wass up yestreen." "What does that mean, Willie?" "That it'll be aither vera wat or more rain."

A little below Allan's house on the picture is the shop of Hugh Philp's.

PREPARING FOR A ROUND.

North Berwick Oct 1887
Willie Park Jnr.
Willie Fernie
Bob Ferguson
Willie Campbell
Archie Simpson
Ben Sayers
Self
Tom Dunn
Willie Dunn
Davie Grant
Cosgrove and Crawford

147

ST ANDREWS LINKS THIRTY YEARS SINCE.

1850's

THE Links, over which thousands have won their laurels, and which ever retain their dear associations, are not what they were thirty years ago. The reminiscences of that time come up to our mind with an ever-gladdening glow. But the historical link has been snapped. As to old wranglers of Cambridge the historical connection of that brilliant struggle in pure reasoning has been severed with a heartrending shock by the new system, which seems only to delight in change, so to old golfers at St Andrews the connecting bond of historical rivalry has been ruthlessly severed by fashionable committees and increasing numbers. The niceties of the game are minimised, and force is taking the place of skill.

The time was when a mistake at any place was severely punished; now, the course can be "skuttered" without much loss. Then the course was narrow, the bunkers were yawning traps for topped balls, the whins were deadly snares for screwed or heeled gutties; now, one can slip along the side without risking anything. I remember old George Glennie looking sadly at the filling-up of "Tam's Coo" bunker, as a knight of old would regard the dead body of an honoured and valiant rival; and he was the best golfer of his day. Where now is the nervous danger of crossing "Hell" on to the Elysian fields? Where the sure punishment of the "Beardies" for a missed stroke? Both are left as historical terrors; no one now requires to risk them.

The putting-greens, too, are quite changed. Then, there was a variety of surface which brought out the greater skill; now, all are nicely turfed over and artificially dressed like billiard-tables. Then, at the "Heather-hole" one had to dodge about and watch the lie of the green, carefully noting any hollow to catch or "soo-back" to avoid in the gentle stroke; thereby, as old Robbie Paterson used to say, "wilin' the wether into the hoose." Now, no caddy's advice is needed, no look is required from the ball end and then from the hole end to "study" the ground; a dead, straight putt suffices. The "Sandy-hole" puzzled the uninitiated with its heavy putting surface; now it is a stroke easier. The "Corner o' the Dyke" was most precarious; now it is easily approached. The "Home-hole" had its treacherous undulations to tax the ability of the player; now all is a dead plateau. Such changes have broken the score-chain—six strokes on the round are at least saved. Allan Robertson's 79 is not now understood or properly estimated. George Glennie's famous 88 medal score will stand against a modern 82.

Then, the clubs were made more for skill than force. With what affection did Allan look on his stock! Old Hugh Philp had polished at an apple-tree head for a whole afternoon, when modern makers would have considered it quite finished; and this Allan seized, reduced its weight to suit the thin handle, until it looked like a toy. But when, with wide sweep—always holding the leather by the very extremity—the little man came "whisk!" upon his small 26 ball, it left like a rocket; or, when half-topped against the wind, it rose so gradually that at last it rested in the air before falling. Allan once struck with his club a boy who happened to be standing behind him; afterwards he instinctively cast his eyes behind before the stroke, however important the match was.

Before Allan's day the baffing-spoon was the weapon of approach to the hole, if a bunker intervened (and no one handled it more neatly and adroitly than did Sir Robert Hay); but Allan introduced the deadly "iron," which he wrought with miraculous accuracy. Instead of the putter for long green-approaches, Allan began to use the "cleek," unless he had some precarious putt to hole. No man could more scientifically miss a putt. Allan had the happy knack of making an opponent pleased with himself; he would carry the player on (a small bet of a couple of balls being involved) by occasionally missing an advantage, though unobserved by his friend, until he "snoddit him at the burn"—that is, was two holes up and one to play. "Is there ony chance o' yer freend the Kornel gawin' oot i' the efternuin, Major?" "No, I hardly think it, Allan." "Aweel, we'll juist snod them at the burn." It was amusing to see Allan chuckle when an opponent was bunkered. "It appeals," he used to say, "to the higher feelings of humanity to see your rival in a bunker." Such a calamity could be "devoutly wished." Old Tom Morris had not yet left Prestwick to take the Links under his control; and Allan was monarch of all he surveyed. His "swing" was for a long time hereditary among the best golfers; now a different style prevails. During the medal week, Erskine Wemyss and Allan had always a keen tussle with J. O. Fairlie and Tom, from Prestwick. There was no beating about the bush—every stroke told. In the Club the whole game would be played over again; though the golfer's rare shots are never so exceptional as the angler's trouts.

Then Maitland Dougall's peculiar style was easily noticeable, playing for pure love of the game with James Balfour. The former frequently gained the Club medal; the latter once, by sheer steady play. No one could mistake James Blackwood, as he fell forward on his ball in striking; or John Blackwood, with his twisted swing. Cathcart, strangely, began golf by placing the left hand under, and played in this way afterwards with surprising steadiness. Old Sutherland, with his continual question to his caddy, "Is that right, Anera, eh?" might be seen playing with old Walkinshaw, a left-handed veteran. Both names have been perpetuated in the bunkers of the fourth and sixth holes. Pat Alexander was then not easily beaten, his cleek approaches being played to perfection. Old Wallace would have carried the championship at the final tussle of the first tournament by his wearisome style, had not Robert Chambers's temper been particularly easy-going. "Give me a novel and a camp-stool, and I'll let the old chap do as he likes," was his remark when pitted against the slow-coach.

Robert Clark's determined wrist play with "30" balls, and Gilbert Innes's steady brilliance, were equally successful. George Condie was a player of intense power, though his father was better on the green. Whyte-Melville's continual "waggle," when aiming at the ball, would have told who he was a mile away; and George seemed to have inherited a part of the special style. Wolfe Murray could then play a fair game. Captain Stewart, however, with a famous black-headed grass-club, could jerk out a ball from a cup in more brilliant style than could be seen.

"IT tak's a heid to write a poem," we lately read in the visitors' book of a hotel in Inverness. This wise remark at once called up to mind the inimitable criticism of the St Andrews caddy, when he was disgusted at the miserable play of a learned Professor: "Ye jist skutter at gowf; it's easy eneuch teachin' laddies Greek an' thae things; but it needs a *heid* tae play gowf." Yes, sensible Skipper, that is true! For there is a grand study in the game; and more than mere handicraft is sometimes brought in at the "turning-point" of a golf-match. Far more calculation and nerve and seizing of the occasion are required than nine out of ten players would at first conceive.

SKIPPER FENTON - ONE OF MY CADDIES

149

My son J.O.F at the top of his swing

Lining up a putt

We reproduce an excellent likeness of the youngest son and worthy representative of the great golfing family. He, too, is a very fine player, and although fate has hitherto been unpropitious to him in the matter of championship honours, still the latter have on more than one occasion been almost within his grasp. As with his famous brother, putting is one of his strongest points.

Among his more noteworthy feats were his two successive rounds at St. Andrews in 78 and 77, with every single half below 40. This is superb play.

IN 1887 JOF equalled Tommy's lowest score set on the St Andrews Links in 1869 77 strokes which no other had bettered.

Tommy out	Tommy in	JOF out	JOF in
4	3	4	4
4	3	4	3
5	4	4	3
6	6	4	5
4	5	5	5
4	4	5	5
3	5	5	5
3	5	3	5
4	5	4	4
37	40	38	39

So both sons - joint Record holders of the Old course.

A Proud father!

HAZARDS IN GOLF.

THE deep interest in the game of golf consists in the capital balance of chance and skill in its play. More of the chance element would reduce the pleasure to the petty excitement of gambling; and more of the skill element would give it too much of chess-like exactness. The critical point cannot be definitely fixed; yet all golfers know what this balance means. And the most important producer of the chance element is the variety of hazards. No doubt skill is also most signally tested by this necessary accompaniment of the game; yet the ever-present contingencies occasioned by the hazards contribute to the concentrating enthusiasm. A dead-level green, with no bunkers and destitute of whins, would be the field for some sort of games, but it could never be the arena for the true golfing contest.

A model golfing-green is not easily met with. Nature must benignly come to man's help in forming it. It should be of an undulating character—not like Montrose or Perth in many parts—and it should abound in suitably arranged hazards of every description. These are necessary to bring out the powers of the first-class golfer. Duffers may potter about where there is always plain sailing, and where mistakes are never punished; but the true golfer despises such a course. Even a long driver is not satisfied with his swipes over an even stretch of green; he delights in seeing the hillocks and projecting bunkers over which his ball must carry, to be in safety. The undulations are the first and simplest means of securing hazards. If the ball is half-topped it will run the risk of being stopped most effectually by the brae-side, unless against a strong wind, when this scientific hit produces one of the most beautiful, Allan-like strokes to be seen, the ball slipping along until it reaches the hillock, to rise majestically over the hazard. In the latter case the wind is the hazard; but

"The well-struck ball the stormy wind beguil'd,
And like a swallow skimmed along the field."

The undulations produce grassy graves, from which the player has to drive with skill.

Of the hazards which come first to one's mind, bunkers are the most essential for the interest and fascination of the game. These sand-pits have not been cut out promiscuously or without meaning; they are far too important to be thus carelessly produced. They range from two to six feet in depth—from slight impediments to gulfs of despair. They are not meant to punish a fault too mercilessly, but they are educators also in giving a good player the opportunity of retrieving his character by driving his ball well out again. Of course in the old greens we cannot tell when they were formed or what geniuses constructed them. Who formed the Alps at Prestwick, Pandy at Musselburgh, the Redan of North Berwick, or Hell at St Andrews? But in the new greens considerable skill is needed to lay them out properly. On some, where the holes are comparatively short, there is a scratch bunker between them. A tall red flag is placed at the spot behind which a good driver ought to carry his tee-shot; and a tall blue flag at the spot for which the ball of a secondary player, who wishes to avoid the bunker, should be played. As in a strongly opposing wind, some of the bunkers are too far for even the best swipers to carry, two teeing-grounds are laid out at every hole; the backward one for calm days or with a following wind, and the forward one for an opposing wind. Of course "carrying" the scratch bunker secures a great advantage.

Bunkers are capital tests of play. Sometimes a ball is drawn into a bunker by the continued inclining bearing of the ground, though the shot be good; but generally it is a trap for a bad shot, and more skill is displayed in getting well out of it than in avoiding it. In any case, however, the temper must be bridled. When one makes a mistake, he needn't blame his club, or the troublesome boys; such epithets as "scoundrels," and "to the devil," betoken anything but coolness or success in the player. Of course old and weak players must avoid the bunkers altogether. It was pitiful to see Dr Traill playing seven more in the "Principal's Nose"; Sir John Low, with his faithful pony, would pawkily dodge round the corner. Players who smash away in bunkers without carefully studying the proper means of getting out their balls, will soon have to repeat Ballantine's lines:—

> "We banish all extraneous fat
> And all extraneous thinking."

The golfers bridge over the Swilken burn

If the bunker is shallow, with perhaps a little grass in the bottom, the player may show his skill by driving his ball with his middle spoon through a slicket of the bunker's edge. If it is deep, he calculates his situation. First of is playing against a slight wind, a drop from off the middle spoon or the iron is beautiful and deadly. If one is playing out of this bunker, to lay dead is a most successful and paralysing stroke.

Strange is it that most players have a particular bunker in the course which they cannot easily avoid! Walkinshaw, Sutherland, and Deacon Sim have their names handed down at St Andrews. And Carnegie thus very satirically compares the game to the human race:—

> "The tee, the start of youth—the game, our life—
> The ball, when fairly *bunkered*, man and wife."

Whins form the next important hazard; but, alas! how mercilessly are they being cut down! In St Andrews the whins have ceased to mark with their golden bloom the heathery boundary of the course. Yet what skill was needed—especially with a side wind—to avoid the Scylla of the whins without being caught by the Charybdis of the bunker! It was once no joke to extricate the ball from a "dour" whin; but this has been ruthlessly removed for a different style of play. In the middle of the course whins are a nuisance, not a hazard. The heather at the sixth and ninth holes is scarcely worth calling a difficulty. Where are the rushes at the second hole?

Besides these, players have to contend with streams, roads, and railways; and in some greens with trees, hedges, and walls. The last can be dispensed with. Unplayable snares like rabbit-holes should not be called hazards, because no one can remember where these are.

elastic sand:—

> "The pond'rous club upon the ball descends,
> Involved in dust, th' exulting orb ascends."

A bunker near the hole brings out some fine skill. If one all he must get the ball out; but forward, or sideways, or even backward. He observes his distance from the hole, and the *lie* of the green. The good player never thinks about a bunker facing him; he simply drives over it if his ball is lying clean. But if it is lying bad, and the bunker is at a distance, with a considerable risk of not being able to carry over the hazard, he may find that he can reach the putting-green by playing the short stroke first, and then approaching the green with his second, instead of blazing away—very likely into the bunker. Judgment is here brought in. When Allan had a bad player for his partner, he would either make his duffer putt the ball forward near the bunker or miss the ball altogether. Hugh Philp, too, would say to an unsteady partner, "*Ye* stick tae the driving putter, and leave the bunkers tae *me*, syne we'll snod them." Once when victorious by this ruse, Hugh was thus attacked by his irascible opponent: "D'ye ca' that gowf, soopin' the ba' alang wi' a besom?" To which Hugh coolly replied, "Gowf or no gowf, it's been owre guid gowf for you; for ye've lost yer temper an' yer bet forbye."

One has to observe the nature of the sand in different greens: in some, like St Andrews, it is elastic; in others, like Musselburgh, it is dead. The niblick iron is most effective in both cases. Skill is needed to aim at the ball without marking the sand; this alters the style. Generally the pick-axe style is not so effective, as in the diagonal slant the iron is brought heel down close to the ball, yet not touching it, so as to make it spring from the

I'm sitting on a bench surrounded by some braw golfers!
Jack Burns, on my right hand side, had won the Open at St Andrews the year before (1888).
David Brown, on my left, won it in 1886. Hugh Kirkaldy (3 along from me on the left) would also win an Open at St Andrews in 1891 with his brother Andrew runner-up (5th left middle row) Ben Sayers from North Berwick is at my feet to the left and Davie Ayton, a fine St Andrews player, to the right

153

St. Andrews, 4th May 1892.

Which day the Silver Cross of St. Andrew was played for over the Links of St. Andrews, and gained by Francis A. Fairlie, Esq., by holing the course at 86 strokes. * one of J. O. Fairlies sons

RALPH ANSTRUTHER, *C.*

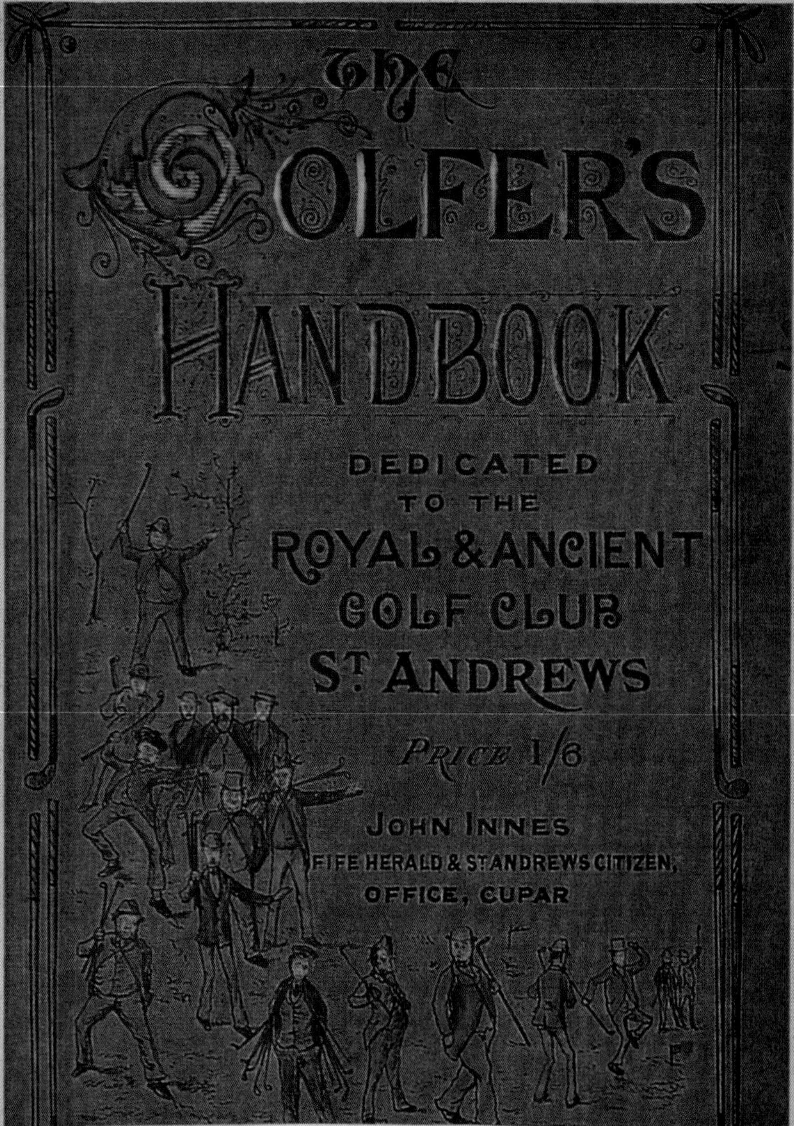

St. Andrews, 28th September 1892.

Which day the Silver Club given by the Royal and Ancient Golf Club of St. Andrews, and the Royal Adelaide Medal, were played for over the Links of St. Andrews, and gained by Andrew Graham Murray, Esq., M.P. RALPH ANSTRUTHER, *C.*

1st Golf journal

GOLF.

A Weekly Record of "ye Royal and Auncient" Game.

"Far and Sure."

No. 1. Vol. 1.] FRIDAY, SEPTEMBER 19TH, 1890. *Price Twopence.*

10s. 6d. per Annum, Post Free.

Fixtures.

ROYAL AND ANCIENT GOLF CLUB OF ST. ANDREWS.—FIXTURES, 1890.

AUTUMN MEETING.

The Business Meeting will take place on Tuesday, 23rd September, at 5 p.m.

The Silver Club, the Royal or King William IV. Medal, the Royal Adelaide Medal, and the Gold Medal of the Club will be competed for on Wednesday, 24th September. Entries close on Tuesday, 23rd September, at 5 p.m.

The Annual Ball will take place on the evening of Thursday, 25th September.

SEPTEMBER.

Sept. 20.—Littlehampton; Mr. Tod-Heatley's Prize.
Sept. 21.—Alnmouth; Handicap Cup.
Sept. 27.—Luffness; President's Medal and Mr. Tait's Star.
Buxton and High Peak; Competition for Medal; also Handicap Sweepstake.
Littlehampton; Mr. A. J. Constable's Medal.

OCTOBER.

Oct. 4, 5, 6.—Alnmouth; Autumn Meeting.
Oct. 4, 7, 8, 10.—Royal North Devon; Autumn Meeting.
Oct. 4.—Clapham; "Cronin" Medal.
St. Nicholas, Prestwick; Bailie Watson's Medal.
Oct. 7, 8, 9.—North Berwick; Amateur Golf Tournament.
Carnoustie and Taymouth; Sweepstake Competition.
Oct. 8.—Royal Liverpool; Autumn Meeting.
Oct. 11.—Tantallon Autumn Meeting; Club Medal, Victoria Jubilee Cup.
St. George's (Sandwich); Autumn Meeting.
Oct. 13.—Royal Isle of Wight; Autumn Meeting.
Oct. 18.—Ashdown Forest and Tunbridge Wells.
Clapham; Autumn Meeting.
Oct. 25.—Luffness; Wemyss Challenge Handicap Medal.
Buxton and High Peak; Monthly Competition, under Handicap, with Sweepstake.
Oct. 26.—Alnmouth; Final Competition for Handicap Cup.

NOVEMBER.

Nov. 1.—Great Yarmouth; Autumn Meeting.
Carnoustie and Taymouth; Sweepstake Competition.
Clapham; "Cronin" Medal.
Nov. 4.—Great Yarmouth and Cambridge University; at Yarmouth.
Nov. 29.—Royal Liverpool; St. Andrews Meeting.
Buxton and High Peak; Monthly Competition, under Handicap, and Sweepstake.
Royal Isle of Wight; St. Andrews Meeting.

DECEMBER.

Dec. 6.—Clapham; "Cronin" Medal.
Dec. 23.—Royal Isle of Wight Christmas Meeting.
Dec. 26.—Bembridge Gold Medal, Eaton Memorial Putter and Fisher Prize.
Clapham; Challenge Handicap Cup.
Dec. 27.—Buxton and High Peak: Monthly Competition, under Handicap, with Sweepstake.

JANUARY.

Jan. 18.—Royal Epping Forest Golf Club, Quarterly Meeting and Monthly Competition.

To Golfers!

SURELY no apology is necessary for bringing before the public a weekly journal devoted to the doings and sayings of golfers, both past and present.

The extension of what has been justly termed the National Game of Scotland has made such rapid strides in the last few years, that there is hardly a place of any notoriety in the British Islands, and in India and many of the Colonies, that does not boast of its Golfing Green, either in its immediate vicinity, or, within easy reach; and yet, although it is a game in which more interest is taken than in any other pastime, with the exception perhaps of Cricket and Football, there is at present no journal in existence which makes the "Royal and Ancient" and now popular Game its principal subject of attention.

Our object is to supply this great want. As we cannot possibly clash with any other interest, and as we have been promised the support of many of the "learned and witty" of our golfing brethren, we boldly and unhesitatingly launch our "bonny bark" on that "happy sea" which is now crowded by sailors, whose distinguishing feature has been, and we trust may long continue to be, that of "GOOD FELLOWSHIP."

Mr. A. J. Balfour putting out

A Modern Gutta Ball

PROFESSIONALS AND CADDIES.

Of club-makers, no man has ever approached Hugh Philp, and even now to possess a club of his is a treasure like an old Cremona violin to a musician, or a Toledo blade to a swordsman. He was a quiet and thoroughly respectable man, had a fine eye for a club, with exquisite taste, while he was simple and natural in his manner. His assistant, James Wilson, who worked with him for many years, and after his death opened an establishment of his own, was also much liked.

Let me recall some of the professionals and the old caddies. First among these was Allan Robertson, the prince of golfers. He and his father and grandfather had been ball-makers, when feather balls were the only balls, for more than a hundred years. He was a short, little, active man, with a pleasant face, small features, and a merry twinkle in his eye. He was universally popular, not a bit forward, but withal easy and full of self-respect. He generally wore a red, round jacket, and played constantly with gentlemen, both in matches of great importance, and in those that were only more or less important. His style was neat and effective. He held his clubs near the end of the handle, even his putter high up. His clubs were light, and his stroke an easy, swift switch. With him the game was one as much of head as of hand. He always kept cool, and generally pulled through a match even when he got behind. He was a natural gentleman, honourable and true.

155 Self and the Captain Broughton Story

Next to him was Tom Morris, now called "Old Tom." He began by helping Allan to make balls, and was very nearly his match at the game. His style I need not describe, as all golfers of the present generation know it. He still flourishes on the Links, and is still a fine player. He and Allan were together the champions of their day. Tom has always been respected, not only as a player, but for his excellent private character. There is an anecdote told of him, which I have great pleasure in repeating, because it is so honourable to him. On one occasion he was playing with the late Captain Broughton, and when at the high hole Tom's ball was lying in the bents that used then to surround it, the Captain said, "O Tom, you had better give up the hole; you are playing three more, and you are in the bents." "No," said Tom; "I'll perhaps hole this." "I'll give you £50 if you do." "Done with you, Captain," said Tom, and he holed it! Next morning the Captain brought £50, and handed it to him. "What is that?" said Tom. "What you won yesterday." "Take it away," exclaimed Tom, "I would not touch it. We were both in fun." This was exceedingly creditable to Tom, and showed real good feeling. If he had taken it, no one could have found fault with him, and £50 offered to a tradesman was a temptation. I had often heard the story from Campbell of Saddel, who was present, and other gentlemen, but I once asked Tom himself about it. He said it was all true, and he laughingly added, "You should have seen the Captain's face when I went in!" Tom, as is well known, is now the Conservator of the Links, and has a large establishment for making both clubs and balls.

His son, "Young Tommy," was perhaps the best player that ever appeared on the green. He was a tall, handsome athlete, and unmatched at all parts of the game. His victorious career began in 1867,

Among the older professionals were the twin brothers Dunn of Musselburgh. They were beautiful golfers, and fought many pitched battles with Allan and Tom. They ran them hard, but could not beat them.

Referring to the caddies, there were Sandy Pirie, who carried for Sir Hope Grant, and Sandy Herd, who carried first for Saddell and afterwards for Mr. Whyte-Melville; Charlie Thomson, once a crack player, as most of the others were; and many other most respectable men. But perhaps the greatest character among them was "Lang Willie." He was very tall, about six feet two, with bent knees and a slouching gait, a tall hat, swallow-tailed blue coat, and light trousers. His look was rather stupid, but he was in reality wide awake. He used to insist that he drank nothing but sweet milk, greatly to Allan's amusement, who knew better.

A daft solution for a tricky shot

156

CADDIES.

A STRANGER, passing the corner of Allan Robertson's house in St Andrews, about the year 1856, at eleven o'clock in the forenoon of any of the six days of the week, would wonder at the positions of a dozen or two of men and boys there located. Some would be leaning against the north wall of the house, gazing over the Links to Lucklie Hill, anxious that the wind should be "aff that airth," as a sign of good weather. Others would be walking up and down the slight descent for a score of yards, with hands in pockets, calmly meditating upon their "chance" that day. Younger lads—especially "Punch"—would be constantly swinging a club and driving away a cork, as they imitated the styles of the best players. Who were they? Those were the caddies of olden times. They had not entirely shaken off their habit of sentry-standing or sentry-walking in sight of the Old Union Parlour over the street, in order that the golfers who came out for their game might select a suitable attendant to carry their clubs. If it was a doubtful morning, Allan would send Charlie Thomson—an authority in weather-lore—to the Parlour to ascertain what "the gless said." On his return Charlie would demurely say, "I'm o' opeenion that she's fawther doon the day than she was up yestreen." "What does that mean, Charlie?" Schiehallion—one of the keenest of old golfers—would remark. "Weel, sir, I'm jist dootin' that it 'll be aither verra wat or mair rain." But even a remark of that kind would not daunt the ardour of the player bent on his match.

By this time Sandy Herd had been down at Hugh Philp's—then the only maker of clubs in the place—rubbing up Whyte-Melville's "irons." A bit of old emery-paper—the older the better, as it did not scratch—was in the faithful caddy's hand, as he first rubbed along the blade, front and back, and then across at the point and heel of the face, so as to leave the centre with a different shade from the rest, that the eye might be more easily caught when aiming at the ball in the wrist-stroke or the long putt. He took a pride in having all the clubs nicely oiled with a hare's foot (slightly dipped in linseed-oil, which hardly covered the bottom of an old tin can on the spare back bench of the shop). A polish would thus be put on them "like that on the back of an otter"—according to James Wilson's constant simile—and a "skin" got on the handles which made them "weather" any rain. Three days a-week did the master take his two rounds; and, before he died, the servant received a beautiful silver watch as a token of his faithfulness.

Sandy Pirie was also in Hugh's, getting ready Captain Maitland Dougall's instruments of war. Sandy had an idea that nobody could beat the Captain. No one ever saw Sandy try a shot himself; yet he knew every foot of the green, and every point of the Captain's "play." He had the grand merit of *silence* during a match. He knew his master's mind by a sort of trained clairvoyance, and put into the Captain's hand the right club without being asked. Close behind he would faithfully follow, earnestly bent upon the match, carrying the clubs in his left hand, instead of the time-honoured method of carrying them within the left arm. On a passing player asking about the game, Sandy would remark, "We're twa ahint; but we'll mak' it up; we're no' in oor play the day." The "*we*" showed the fidelity and interest of the old caddy.

Watty Alexander would slip quietly down to the first hole, cleaning the old balls upon the side of his coat, waiting with the clubs on Ord Campbell. Old Bob Kirk, who had just had his "forenoon" at John Morris's, was ready for the coming of Campbell of Saddell. Lang Willie, the most credulous of all, wore a long chimney-hat, and was a character in his way. He had a weakness for "sweet milk," which had the uncommon property of making his head lighter. As a tutor of the game he was useless, for he took his eye off the ball, and threw it round when swinging. Yet he had an unusual power of encouragement. It mattered not whether his master "sklaffed," or "topped," or "heeled" his ball, a word of comfort was always given by Willie: "Ye'll sune get intilt, sir; it micht hae been waur." Once he unconsciously made this remark when his master "missed the globe." Mathy Gorum was the most loquacious of all. During the winter—when there was little doing on the Links—he would take to selling razors or songs, or "reading heids," which gave him the "gift o' the gab." Years before, no one could equal him for steadiness of eye and nerve. He could drive a ball from the top of a bottle. It was a common amusement, however, for the young caddies to get him to undertake the celebrated feat of his better

days and see him smash the bottle. Long Jamie and Geordie Brown were very steady, cautious men, who gave instruction in the game to beginners.

Who at that time could fail to see "The Skipper," with his big mouth and little nose; Bob Mo—, with his continual stutter; Auld Da', so named to distinguish him from his son of the same name, who was also a caddy; Farnie, who used to fluently discourse to his fellows on varied topics, as he had been six years at College; Andrew Strath, the "Anera" of Old Sutherland, whose whole soul was in the game; or Kidd, who cautiously went about the even tenor of his way? In their day the servant identified himself with his master, and had a personal pride in securing victory for his side. Then there was no lagging behind to gossip. The caddy kept his eye on the ball when struck till it stopped, and—especially when it was off the course—he never removed his glance till he came up to it. Now, the master has in most cases to look after it himself. So well did a good caddy, after studying it, know the "game" of a golfer, that his "advice" was usually asked in a critical position, or when an important putt had to be made. Accordingly, it was among the "Rules of Golf" that a player could ask his caddy's advice, but not that of any outsider. The caddy was part and parcel of the player, as were his clubs. But a strike for higher wages altered the state of matters. Broken-down artisans interfered with the rights of the hereditary caddy, and times changed. Communism leavened the noble mind: *actum est de honore.*

An attempt was made by General Moncreiff and others to entice the caddies to read; a nice wooden erection was put up round the base of the flag-staff in front of the New Club, and ladies gave them coffee and instruction alternately. But "the article would not be improved." The reading-room was put to an ignoble purpose, and the instruction was useless when the coffee was stopped. Instead of the due respect of other days, Lonie would roar after Captain Ogilvy, "Efter the ba' yersel'; ye're on the hie road to Bedlam;" or Bill Strath would remark, when asked by one passing, if he saw a certain Professor on the green, "Ou ay, he's at the Ginger-beer Hole, tappin' his ba's and d—ning awfu'." No longer are they treated as of old, when Pat Alexander would give a dozen of them an annual treat in John Morris's. Once their master's bunkered ball was a personal calamity; now they commonly care not, or chuckle at the annoyance. The Pedant seems justified in saying of his modern caddy :—

"An' O it's past ma poo'er to tell
Hoo muckle I dislike yersel'!"

Registered caddies

Temporary green down the Home Hole

a now familiar pose on the 1st tee.

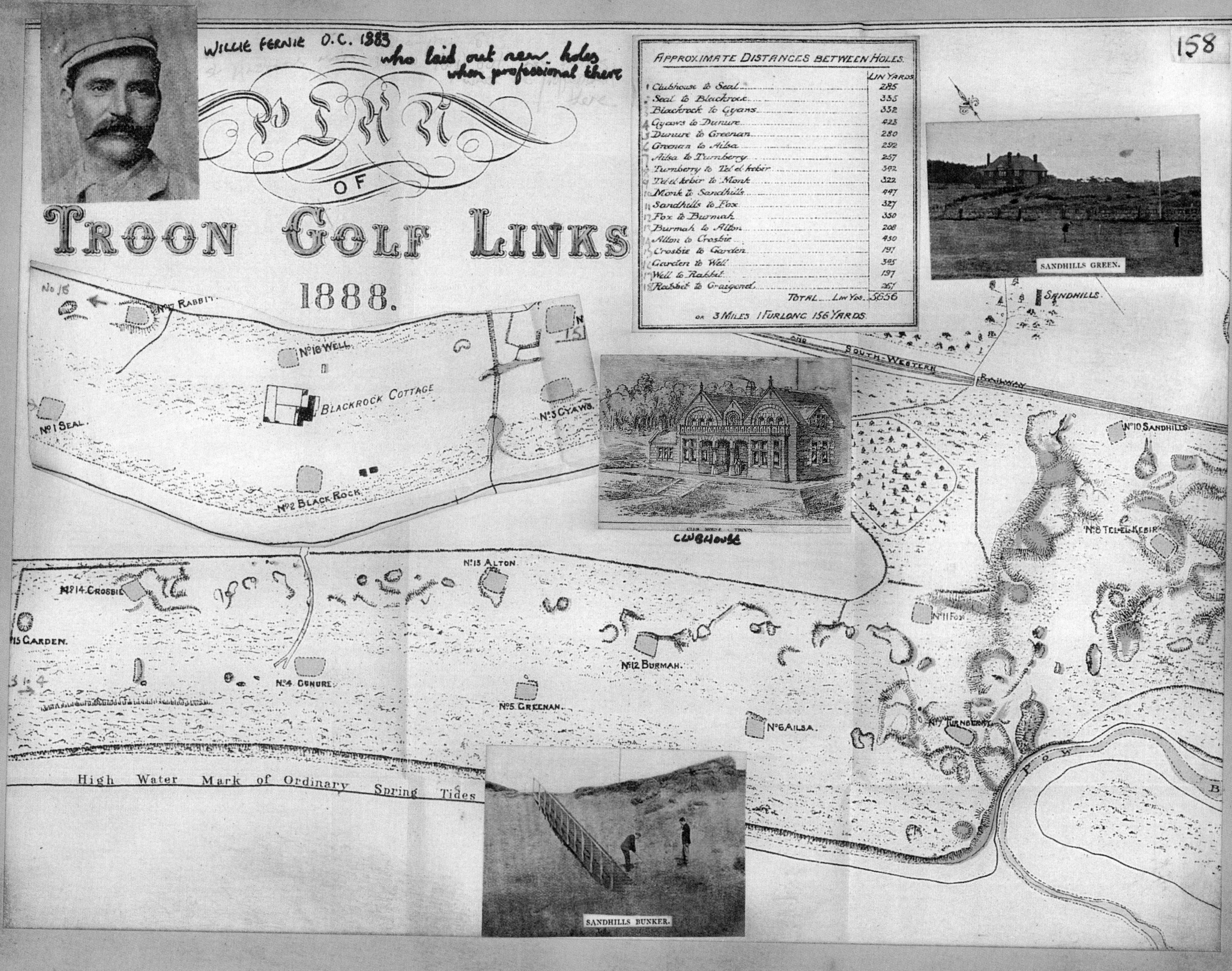

WILLIE FERNIE O.C. 1883 who laid out new holes when professional there

PLAN OF TROON GOLF LINKS 1888.

APPROXIMATE DISTANCES BETWEEN HOLES.	LIN YARDS
1 Clubhouse to Seal	285
2 Seal to Blackrock	335
3 Blackrock to Gyans	332
4 Gyaws to Dunure	423
5 Dunure to Greenan	280
6 Greenan to Ailsa	292
7 Ailsa to Turnberry	257
8 Turnberry to Tel el kebir	392
9 Tel el kebir to Monk	322
10 Monk to Sandhills	447
11 Sandhills to Fox	327
12 Fox to Burmah	350
13 Burmah to Alton	208
14 Alton to Crosbie	430
15 Crosbie to Garden	197
16 Garden to Well	395
17 Well to Rabbit	197
18 Rabbit to Craigend	261
TOTAL ... LIN YDS.	5656

OR 3 MILES 1 FURLONG 156 YARDS.

SANDHILLS GREEN.

CLUBHOUSE

SANDHILLS BUNKER.

ST. ANDREWS, 6TH OCTOBER, 1891.

No.	Players	1st Round	2d Round	Total
1	A. F. Macfie, Royal and Ancient and Wm. Young, Monifieth			
2	Tom Morris, St. Andrews and J. Kay, Seaton-Carew	92	94	
3	Henry A. Lamb, Royal Wimbledon and J. Hunter, St. Andrews G.C.			
4	A. Tingey, St. Andrews and J. Cuthbert, St. Andrews G.C.			
5	R. Martin, St. Andrews and W. Greig, St. Andrews G.C.	89	94	183
6	J. Simpson, Earlsferry and L. Auchterlonie, St. Andrews G.C.	87	93	180
7	J. E. Laidley, Honourable Company and G. G. Smith, Gullane			
8	D. McEwan, Musselburgh and David Anderson, Panmure			
9	R. Munro, Aberdeen and Peter Anderson, St. Andrews University			
10	J. M. Williamson, Musselburgh and J. Burns, St. Andrews			
11	George Pearson, Earlsferry and L. Ross, Edinburgh			
12	W. Anderson, St. Andrews and David Ayton, St. Andrews	94	87	181
13	R. H. Johnston, Honourable Company and H. S. C. Everard, Royal and Ancient			
14	D. Anderson, Jun., St. Andrews and J. Kinsman, St. Andrews	90	91	181
15	Hugh Kirkcaldy, St. Andrews (1st) and T. Carmichael, St. Andrews University	83	83	166
16	D. Mason, Kinghorn and — Anderson, North Berwick			
17	W. D. More, Chester and Ben Campbell, Musselburgh			
18	James Kirk, Thistle, St. Andrews and T. Gilroy, Dublin			
19	Robert Scott, Carnoustie and H. H. Hilton, Royal Liverpool			
20	Alex. Stuart, Honourable Company and D. Sheppard, Carnoustie			
21	R. B. Sharp, Royal and Ancient and Andrew Kirkcaldy, St. Andrews (2nd)	84	84	168
22	W. Campbell, Bridge of Weir and J. Ball, junr., Royal Liverpool	94	83	177
23	David L. Lamb, Royal and Ancient and A. Tait, Edinburgh University			
24	Archie Simpson, Carnoustie and W. Park, junr., Musselburgh	88	85	173
25	David Anderson Sen., St. Andrews and B. Sayers, North Berwick			
26	S. Mure Fergusson, Royal and Ancient and R. Simpson, Carnoustie	86	84	170
27	J. Kirkcaldy, St. Andrews and Robert Tait, Musselburgh			
28	F. Paxton, Eastbourne and Horace G. Hutchinson, Royal and Ancient			
29	D. Cuthbert, St. Andrews and James Anderson, junr., St. Andrews			
30	A. Lawson, Musselburgh and George Fernie, Troon			
31	Charles Hutchings, Royal Liverpool and D. Herd, St. Andrews			
32	H. S. Colt, Royal and Ancient and F. G. Tait, Royal and Ancient	94	88	182
33	E. R. H. Blackwell, Royal and Ancient and A. Herd, St. Andrews			
34	A. Sommerville, Dunbar and T. Chisholm, Scarborough			
35	C. Randall, St. Nicholas, Prestwick and Cyril Plummer, Sandwich			
36	W. Fernie, Troon (2nd) and David Leitch, St. Andrews G. C.	84	84	168
37	W. Auchterlonie, St. Andrews, G. C. and David Brown, St. Andrews	85	90	175

Play will commence in the First Round at 9 a.m., and in the Second Round at 12.15 p.m.
Parties not present when their names are called will be placed at the bottom of the list.
Approved Markers must be provided.
As the days are short it is particularly requested that all Competitors will play with as little delay
By Order of the Green Comm

WILLIE PARK, Jun.,

↑ JACK BURNS 1888 WINNER HERE

WILLIE PARK JNR - WON OPEN IN 1887 + 89
(LAID OUT SOME FINE COURSES)

← HUGH KIRKALDY, St. Andrews.

HERE we have another member of yet another golfing family. His successes are too numerous for us to chronicle; but we should note that it is he who first broke Young Tom's St. Andrews record of 77 with a wonderful 74. Nay, more, within nine months he actually reduced this to 73.

161

Forgan's factory next door to my shop

Sudden death of a son of Tom Morris

Those who frequent our world – famed Links have learned with much regret of the sudden demise of Jack Morris, youngest of the surviving sons of "Old Tom". Deceased was actively engaged making golf balls up to a late hour on the previous evening, and on retiring to rest was in his usual health. It is understood death was caused by a spasm at the heart. Jack had a natural deformity in his lower limbs, which debarred him playing at the game in which his father is such an adept; but, nevertheless, he took an active interest in everything appertaining to the game, and was looked upon as an undoubted authority. Much sympathy is expressed for his veteran father and the other members of his family.

St Andrews Citizen 25th Feb 1893
Jack R.I.P.

St. Andrews, 3rd May 1893.

Which day the Silver Cross of St. Andrew was played for over the Links of St. Andrews, and gained by Allan Fullarton Macfie, Esq., by holing the course at 82 strokes.

1st Amateur Champion in 1885 A. GRAHAM MURRAY, C.

163

TOM MORRIS,

Wholesale & Retail Golf Club Manufacturer,

ST. ANDREWS.

Printed Price List from 1894

REPAIRS EXECUTED BY EXPERIENCED WORKMEN.

GOLF COVERS AND ALL REQUISITES FOR THE GAME OF GOLF. . . . .

Morris' Machine-Made Balls.

PRICE-LIST.

ALL GOODS HAND MADE.

	EACH.
Drivers, ...	5/
Long Spoons, ...	5/
Mid Spoons, ...	5/
Short Spoons, ...	5/
Putters, ...	5/
Brassys, ...	6/
Irons, ...	5/6
Cleeks, ...	5/6
Iron Niblicks, ...	5/6
Mashies, ...	5/6
Iron Putters, ...	5/6
Morris' Patent Cleek, ...	7/6
Bulgers, ...	5/
Broad-headed Bulgers, ...	5/6
Morris' Patent Niblick, ...	7/6
Bulger Heads, ...	3/
Broad-headed Bulger Heads, ...	3/6
Driver, Putter, Long, Mid, and Short Spoon Heads, ...	3/
Brassy Heads, ...	3/6
Cleek, Iron, and Niblick Heads, ...	3/6
Morris' Patent Cleek Heads, ...	5/6
Morris' Patent Niblick Heads, ...	5/6
Shafts, ...	2/
Special Do., 6d. extra.	

BALLS RE-MADE, 4s. PER DOZEN.

	EACH.
Balls, ...	6d. and 8d.
Morris' Agrippa, ...	1/
Morris' Machine-Made Balls, ...	1/3
Morris' Special Balls, ...	1/9
Hickory Headed Drivers, ...	6/
,, ,, Bulgers, ...	6/6
,, ,, Brassys, ...	7/6
Dogwood Headed Drivers,... ...	5/
,, ,, Bulgers,... ...	5/
,, ,, Brassys,... ...	6/
Persimmon Headed Drivers, ...	5/
,, ,, Bulgers, ...	5/
,, ,, Brassys, ...	6/
Special Iron Putter,...	6/6
,, Mashie, ...	6/6
,, Cleeks, ...	6/6
Gun Metal Putters, ...	6/
Ladies' Drivers, ...	5/
,, Bulgers, ...	5/
,, Brassys, ...	6/
,, Putters, ...	5/
All Ladies' Iron Clubs, ...	5/6
Boys' Clubs, from	3/6
,, Cleeks and Irons, from ...	3/6
,, Toy Clubs, ...	1/6

BALLS RE-MADE, 4s. PER DOZEN.

ALL GOODS HAND MADE.

SPECIALTIES.

	EACH.
The New Socket Clubs, ...	6/
The New Socket Brassys, ...	7/
The "Tom Morris" Long Faced Bulgers, ...	5/
The "Tom Morris" Long Faced Brassys,...	6/
The "Tom Morris" Long Faced Socket Bulgers, ...	6/
The "Tom Morris" Long Faced Socket Brassys, ...	7/

Mr Tait

THE TERRACE

1 Charles Leslie Melville.
2 Major W. B. Craigie.
3 W. C. Thomson.
4 D. Argyll Robertson, M.D.
5 W. A. Henderson.
6 A. E. Henderson.
7 H. B. Simson.
8 Captain J. R. Scott.
9 *J. Cumming Macdona, M.P.*
10 E. J. Jackson.
11 D. M. Macnab.
12 Major Randle Jackson.
13 H. S. Wedderburn.
14 J. Anstruther Thomson.
15 W. B. Skene.
16 Hon. G. Waldegrave Leslie.
17 L. B. Keyser.
18 W. D. Bovill.
19 John Goff.
20 E. S. Balfour Melville.
21 Major-General Grahame.
22 R. Dalyell, C.B.
23 Major-General G. H. Moncrieff.
24 Col. E. H. Kennard.
25 J. Lindsay Bennet.
26 John Dun.
27 *Rt. Hon. Sir H. E. Maxwell, Bart., M.P.*
28 J. Tulloch Tarver.
29 F. Tarver.
30 Lt.-Col. W. Marshall.
31 C. E. S. Chambers.
32 *R. N. Fairlie* *
33 H. Seton-Karr, M.P.
34 C. L. Anstruther.
35 H. A. Bethune.
36 John Penn, M.P.
37 Rev. W. W. Tulloch, D.D.
38 A. N. Stewart.
39 E. C. P. Boyd.
40 Lt.-Col. A. Boyd.
41 Hugh M. Alexander.
42 James Mellor.
43 Col. J. McGregor Kerr.
44 Lieut.-Gen. F. M. Playfair, R.A.
45 F. C. Crawford.
46 F. D'A. O. Wolfe Murray.
47 David I. Lamb.
48 D. B. Wauchope.
49 T. T. Oliphant.
50 Viscount Dalrymple.
51 James G. Baird Hay.
52 Sir Alexander Kinloch, Bart.
53 R. Whyte.
54 Capt. W. Cunningham.
55 Ernest Lehmann.
56 J. L. Ridpath.
57 Professor G. G. Ramsay.
58 Hon. A. H. Grosvenor.
59 Capt. J. A. Middleton.
60 Bruce E. Goff.
61 Surgeon-Major Duncan.
62 E. L. I. Blyth.
63 A. Marshall.
64 E. M. Protheroe.
65 H. H. Longman.
66 A. Gray.
67 J. W. B. Pease.
68 C. S. Grace.
69 Rev. A. K. H. Boyd, DD., LL.D.
70 Henry Cook.
71 — *Robb*
72 A. R. Paterson.
73 R. H. Johnston.
74 W. G. Bloxsom.
75 A. G. G. Asher.
76 A. Cowan.
77 C. E. Gilroy.
78 Earl of Kinnoull.
79 F. Burgoyne Wallace.
80 Capt. John Stott.
81 W. R. Kermack.
82 G. Tertius Glover.
83 Stuart Oliphant.
84 *W. Park*
85 *W. Auchterlonie.*
86 *H. Kirkaldy*
87 *D. Rolland.*

Professional Players

ON THE STEPS

88 Stuart Grace.
89 Thomson Glover.
90 Major Chalmers.
91 E. A. Burchardt.
92 H. G. Fellowes Gordon.
93 *A. Denman.*
94 J. L. Low.
95 W. F. E. Blackwell.
96 Wm. Tulloch.
97 *J. Taylor*
98 Harry Cheyne.
99 F. M. Heriot.

ON THE GREEN

100 G. C. Wylie.
101 P. C. Dalmahoy.
102 Maj.-Gen. P. Dalmahoy.
103 J. W. Moir, M.D.
104 Robert Moir, M.D.
105 *Rev. W. Proudfoot.*
106 *Rev. J. Kerr.*
107 W. L. Purves, M.D.
108 *N. Foster.*
109 Sir Uthred Dunbar, Bart.
110 Col. W. Cleland.
111 Lt. W. Maitland Dougall, R.N.
112 W. Logan.
113 *Capt. H. J. Fairlie.* *
114 J. O. Wallace.
115 Rt. Hon. Lord Moncreiff.
116 *Capt. H. Kinloch.*
117 Sir A. B. Hepburn, Bart.
118 F. Kinloch.
119 J. Wharton Tod.
120 E. B. H. Blackwell.
121 John Oswald.
122 Major C. H. Morris.
123 John C. Watson.
124 Rev. E. D. Prothero.
125 G. M. Cox.
126 Rev. R. A. Hull.
127 *A. N. Ross.*
128 C. F. Deans Dundas.
129 J. H. Aitken.
130 Col. R. T. Boothby.
131 R. T. Boothby.
132 Col. A. D. Fordyce.
133 John Murray.
134 James Cunningham.
135 M. P. Fraser.
136 W. H. Fowler.
137 J. H. Blackwell.
138 E. H. Buckland.
139 Peter Wood.
140 W. Gilbert Mitchell-Innes.
141 E. R. H. Blackwell.
142 H. S. Colt.
143 Andrew Lang.
144 H. S. C. Everard.
145 W. M. De Zoete.
146 W. E. Fairlie. *
147 Frank A. Fairlie. *
148 T. Mackay.
149 S. Mure Fergusson.
150 *'The Skipper.'*
151 *Corstorphine.* – caddies
152 W. J. Mure, C.B.
153 Sir David Baird, Bart.
154 Gilbert Mitchell-Innes.
155 C. Hutchings.
156 *W. Dunsford.*
157 C. Anderson.
158 R. B. Sharp.
159 Robert Cathcart.
160 Alexander Bethune. *
161 J. Ogilvy Fairlie.
162 Sir J. L. E. Spearman, Bart.
163 D. W. Lambe.
164 F. W. Fison, M.P.
165 Leslie Balfour Melville.
166 James Balfour Melville.
167 Major D. A. Kinloch.
168 Rt. Hon. A. J. Balfour, M.P.
169 Sir Ralph Anstruther, Bart.
170 Major Robert Bethune.
171 Rt. Hon. Lord Kingsburgh.
172 B. Hall Blyth.
173 Rt. Hon. A. Graham Murray, Q.C., M.P.
174 *Tom Morris.*
175 Hon. Stormont Finch-Hatton.
176 *Aytoun.*
177 *Andrew Greig (Scorer).*
178 *P. C. Anderson.*
179 Hon. Ivo Bligh.
180 C. Eric Hambro.
181 Capt. W. H. Burn.
182 William Gordon.
183 *A. J. Robertson.*
184 *J. P. Croal.*
185 *A. Kirkaldy.*
186 W. T. Linskill.
187 A. F. Macfie.
188 Horace G. Hutchinson.
189 J. E. Laidlay.
190 F. G. Tait.
191 Alexdr. Steuart.

J.O.F.'s sons *

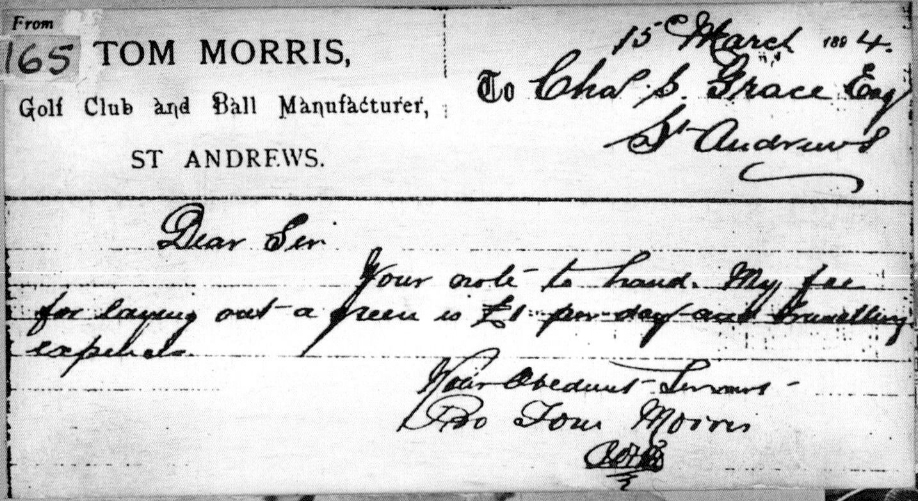

From

165 TOM MORRIS,

Golf Club and Ball Manufacturer,

ST ANDREWS.

15th March 1894.

To Chas S. Grace Esq

St Andrews

Dear Sir

Your note to hand. My fee for laying out a green is £1 per day and travelling expenses.

Your Obedient Servant

pro Tom Morris

Lady Margaret Scott

TEXT ABOUT TRAVEL

Harry Vardon's Clubs

Driving the last

Golf bags and umberellas ar now familiar sights on the links

15th

Playing to the 17th green

Two views of the 17th

16th

17th

4th

12th

167

In reply to your of June 15, anent stymies, I beg to state that I have always been in favour of stymies being abolished. I think a modification could easily be made. A motion was proposed by Captain Burn at a meeting of the Royal and Ancient Golf Club that a rule as follows should be made: - 'A player may, on the putting-green, remove his opponent's ball, but such act of removal should be equivalent to the opponent having played his stroke and holed.' This would do for one, but, of course, the Royal and Ancient would have many suggestions brought before them if the subject was put to them by other Clubs.

Letter to "Golf" 3-6-1894 by myself about the stymie rule.

"The Himalayas" Ladies Putting green

Building in progress on the Grand Hotel →

LADIES' PUTTING GREEN—CLUB-HOUSE—GRAND HOTEL.
THE LINKS, ST ANDREWS.

168
Entertainment on the Bruce Embankment
- travelling players (Actors and Jugglers)
Bathing Huts

Taking the air on the West Sands
Rusacks Marine Hotel
R+A
Grand Hotel
masons golf Hotel
my shop

The starters box

A fine Amateur Champion Horace Hutchison

who wrote well of the game – including his book. The British Golf Links

Tom Morris, now in his 75th year, who for more than half a century has occupied so prominent and so honourable a position in the golfing world." A Committee was formed to procure Tom a comfortable annuity, and as the result of the appeal to golfers £1250 was raised. Tom continued to play a good game until he had reached an advanced age. As late as 1885, on his 64th birthday, he registered an 81 for a round of the Old Course, and in August 1892 he had two rounds of 83 in one week.

Enjoying a glass of milk
at the ginger beer stand.

14th

15th

16th

P. C. Anderson
won the amateur
in 1893 representing
St Andrews university
"Daw"

Well done St andrean
Willie Auchterlonie
who won
the Open aged 19 years
at Prestwick

Minutes of the R & A by Mr Everard

171

Tom Morris Testimonial Fund!

The Open Championship: Revision of Conditions.—Testimonial to Tom Morris.—Completion of New Course.—Tournament.

In November, 1892, the Prestwick Golf Club had entered into correspondence with the Royal and Ancient and with the Honourable Company, and made certain suggestions with a view to the Open Championship being placed upon a new and wider basis. As a result of their communication, a representative of the club was deputed to attend a conference of the three clubs, and was instructed to report the result of the deliberations.

In September, 1893, the report was laid before a general meeting. It bore that the competition should take place annually in succession on the greens of the three clubs as hitherto, and in order to meet a generally expressed wish that the competition should be extended to England, it was resolved to include the greens of the Royal Liverpool Golf Club at Hoylake, and the St. George's Golf Club at Sandwich in turn with those of the three Scottish clubs. The succession was fixed as follows: 1894 at Sandwich, 1895 at St. Andrews, 1896 at Muirfield, 1897 at Hoylake. The competition was to be one of 72 holes, or four rounds of 18 holes each, two rounds to be played each day for two days. Each competitor to pay 10s. entry money, to be used as part of the prize fund, to which each of the associated clubs should contribute £15 annually. The prizes to amount to £100 annually, divisible as follows:—

First, £40 to the winner, of which £10 to be expended on a gold medal, and £30 to be given in money to a professional, or in plate to an amateur golfer; second, £20; third, £10; fourth, £7; fifth, £5; sixth, £4; seventh, eighth and ninth, £3; tenth and eleventh, £2; twelfth, £1.

No prize except the first to be open to an amateur.

The general arrangements in each year, including the date of the competition, to be left to the club on whose green the competition would be held, that club to defray incidental expenses.

In September, 1897, the allocation of prize money was somewhat altered in details. The amounts to be received by the first and second men, respectively, remained as before, but the [illegible] of prizes available was restricted to six, instead of twelve; to the third man was allotted £15; to the fourth £10; and to the fifth and sixth £7 10s. each. The number of competitors having by this time increased to an inconvenient extent, a weeding-out process had become necessary. Accordingly it was resolved that any competitor who should be twenty strokes behind the leading score at the end of the second round on the first day should be compulsorily retired. A *proviso* was added, that if there should not be 32 professionals within this limit, then the first 32 professionals might compete, and if among them there were a tie or ties for the last place on the list, then all who had so tied might compete.

In July, 1895, a committee was appointed to report as to the best means for carrying out a proposal to present Tom Morris with a testimonial. Accordingly, an extraordinary general meeting was called, at which the following resolution was unanimously adopted: "That the sum of £100 be voted from the funds of the club towards the Tom Morris Testimonial Fund"; and the committee were instructed to issue a fresh appeal for subscriptions, and to notify the adoption of the resolution. In April, 1896, after hearing a letter from Mr. George Todd Chiene, C.A., the committee agreed to recommend that £500 should be applied in the purchase of an annuity of £80, and that the balance of the money subscribed, about £700, should be invested in the names of the Trustees of the Club, and the interest thereon paid to Tom during his life; that thereafter the sum remaining should be applied for the benefit of his daughter, Mrs. Hunter, and her children, in such manner as the trustees might decide.

At the general meeting in May, 1896, the report was adopted, subject, however, to the deletion of the provision in favour of Mrs. Hunter and her children. By this time the subscriptions had amounted to £1,240, with the prospect of a slight increase before the close of the lists, which it was proposed should be on May 15th. The result therefore would be that Tom would have an income of over £100 a year, in addition to what he received as greenkeeper, and from other sources.

On September 24th, 1895, the convener of the sub-committee appointed to lay out the new course reported that the capital sum expended up to April 10th, when the course was open for play, amounted to £1,763 1s. He stated further that the sub-committee were of opinion that they could now be discharged, and that the course should be placed under the charge of the Green Committee. At an extraordinary general meeting held on October 25th, it was resolved that there should be an annual competition played on the new course, open to members of the club; accordingly, in May, 1896, the Green Committee reported that they were of opinion that no new medal should be instituted, but they would recommend that the Calcutta Cup Competition should be transferred to that course, the competition to take place at the usual time. This recommendation [illegible] carried out, though not without some opposition; two motions in favour of a return to the old course have [illegible] been brought forward, but not carried. It may be added that in June, 1895, immediately after the Open Championship, held that year at St. Andrews and won by J. H. Taylor, a tournament had been held on the recently opened course. It resulted in favour of Sandy Herd, who scored 86+86=172; W. Fernie second, 86+87=173; Andrew Kirkaldy, Tom Vardon, and Mr. F. G. Tait next, with 175.

We now come to the history of the preliminary correspondence and proceedings which led up to the eventual election of the body known as the Rules of Golf Committee, but as the matter cannot conveniently be dealt with within the limits of the present article, we reserve it for the next.

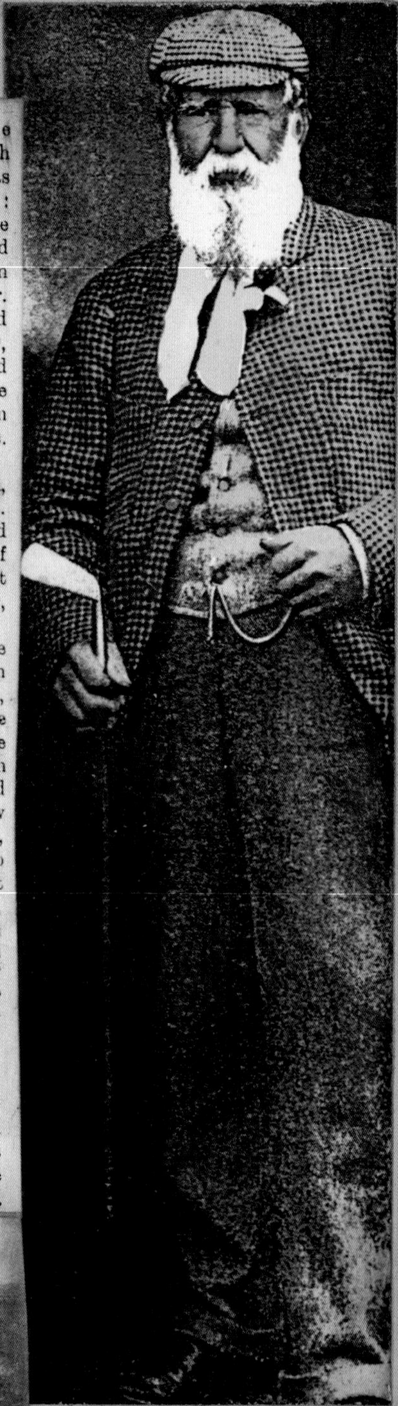

TOM MORRIS.

IT must have struck more than one golfer that many of Wordsworth's lines in eulogy of the Wanderer are wonderfully applicable to the respected veteran of whom we all affectionately speak as Old Tom.

"Rich in love.
And sweet humanity, he was himself,
To the degree that he desired, beloved:
Greetings and smiles he met with all day long
From faces that he knew."

And again:—

"And surely never did there live on earth
A man of kindlier nature. The rough sports
And teasing ways of children vexed not him;
Nor could he bid them from his presence, tired
With questions and importunate demand."

(Of course, it is obvious that the poet intended to refer here to golfers. No doubt, the benighted English printer of that day was unfamiliar with the word; but in spite of the substitution, the meaning is clear.)

This feeling of affection characterises all references in golfing literature to Old Tom. We find the veteran Mr. Thomas Peter writing in the same strain as the more modern Mr. A. J. Balfour, Mr. Lang, Mr. Hutchinson, Mr. Everard. All who have known him love and reverence him. It is only because the words of the first are probably less familiar than those of the talented contributors to the *Badminton* that we reproduce them in preference. Writing from his home in the far West, Mr. Peter says:—

"Tom Morris I need hardly describe. Who has ever handled a club and does not know him—his genial countenance, penetrating eye, which never failed to detect a cunning road to the hole, imperturbable temper, unflinching courage, and indomitable self-control under circumstances the most exasperating? He must now be a septuagenarian, but is still, I am delighted to see, able to wield his clubs. Long may he continue to do so—an honour to himself and the game which he has so much adorned!"

And the echo of this runs through Mr. Balfour's: "Perhaps the most distinguished professional of the century—a man known by name to all golfers, even to those who have never visited St. Andrews—Old Tom Morris"; Mr. Lang's: "The historian cannot but chronicle the merits, so kindly and genial, of famous Tom Morris, the Nestor of Golf, 'and wale o' auld men'"; Mr. Hutchinson's quotation: "Born in the purple of equable temper and courtesy"; and lastly, in the words of Mr. Everard, the one, perhaps, best qualified to speak of all, in his most readable sketch: "Courteous he is to all alike, as much at ease in the presence of Royalty when piloting a Prince of the Blood round the links as when playing a match with his own particular crony." And surely we should note, in passing, the testimony of A. K. H. B. to his venerable elder: "He is a great and good man"; and Mr. Everard:

"Most sincere, though unobtrusive, are his religious convictions, and no amount of persuasion was ever known to be successful in tempting him to play golf on a Fast Day"; or in Wordsworth's phrasing once more:—

"The Scottish Church both on himself and those
With whom from childhood he grew up, had held
The strong hand of her purity."

As Mr. Everard, his best biographer, says: "Old Tom is a character, an institution, a subject on which a most interesting monograph might be written. Wherever golf is played his name is a pass-word; interviewers have interviewed him, journalists made copy out of him; photographers photographed him (including in this latter connection at least one very skilful lady amateur, who confesses to an absorbing admiration for him); artists have sketched him, with sometimes astonishing happy results"; and it may be added that when the eminent amateur, Mr. Charles Anderson of Fettykil, succeeded in perfecting his improved hole-cutter, now in universal use, he, like a good and leal golfer, very properly presented the first made to Tom Morris.

It would weary the reader were a mere outsider, however warmly intentioned, to endeavour to go over again the oft-told tale of Old Tom's doughty deeds on many a famous links; but, as there is still a widely current belief among golfers that the mighty Allan Robertson was never beaten in a match played in singles in his life, I should like to draw attention to the two cases cited by Mr. Everard on page 334 of the *Badminton* where he was beaten by Old Tom himself.

KIND WORDS

OLD TOM.

OUR little barque has spread her wings—
Is heading for the sea;
Be ours to breathe a last God-speed,
A triple health to thee!

Where'er—out o'er—our wandering kin
May clink o'er barley-bree,
Their first maun aye be due to Rob,
Their next, Old Tom, to thee.

A kindly Scot—the sweet old words—
But and his courtesie—
Where'er the songs of Scotland win,
Be ours to drink to thee!

Where'er the Game of Scotland runs—
It and its minstrelsie—
When hearts yearn hame to breezy links,
There's a kindly wish for thee.

When fond, old folk—as old folk will,
Throughout all Christentie—
Prattle o' eld, they aye upbring
A thocht, Old Tom, o' thee.

And lissom wee things—(lily or rose—
But aye wi' the sunny e'e)—
Will whisper aft to tender joes
What they ha'e heard o' thee.

Our ae, ae wish is a lang, lang wish
(But it comes frae a braid countree)
An' aye the burden o' its sang
Is a blessing, Tom, for thee.

W. DALRYMPLE.

173

GOLF – AN INTERESTING FOURSOME

St Andrews Citizen Sept 1896

On Monday evening a more than usually interesting foursome was played here, the players being Mrs Asquith and the Right Hon. A. J. Balfour, and the Right Hon. H. H. Asquith and "Old Tom." It is curious to note the admixture of politics merged in this golf match – Mrs Asquith, of course, holding her husband's views, yet fighting alongside the Leader of the House of Commons at the royal and ancient game; while their opponent, Mr Asquith, whose Radical opinions are so pronounced, played with Tom Morris, whose leanings are decidedly Conservative. Mr Balfour only paid a flying visit to the city, and was, we were informed, *en route* for Balmoral. The match attracted a large crowd of followers, and great interest was evinced in it. Mr Asquith and his partner had rather the best of it the first half of the round, and turned three holes to the good. Homewards they still kept the lead, and won the match by 4 and 3 to play. Mrs Asquith was not quite up to her usual form; while Tom, on the other side, was playing an extra good game.

1st Hole "Well" at Nairn
I laid down the green there

The last green Old course

Mr. Balfour Melville putting.

Mr Ball - the first Englishman to win the Open with Mr J. E. Laidlay

Mr Balfour Melville driving off on the second - He won the Amateur Championship here in 1895

The Grand Hotel

Captain Baird Hay 1896 - 1897

Mr Grace The Hon. Secretary

7th – High Hole and 11th

The Captain – Mr Oswald putting on the 15th 1895–96

Mr John Oswald

Hell Bunker 14th Hole –

Hell Bunker 1856

J. H. Taylor – winner of the 1895 Open here – He broke my son's long standing course record

Taylor won again at St Andrews in 1900

1st Hole – New Course – opened in 1895

The New Course – 1896. The first time the Calcutta Cup is played for on it

Alyth – Perthshire – I helped them lay out the course in 1894

The Moray Links – which with my assistance was laid out by 1892 at Lossiemouth

The Clubhouse at Nairn

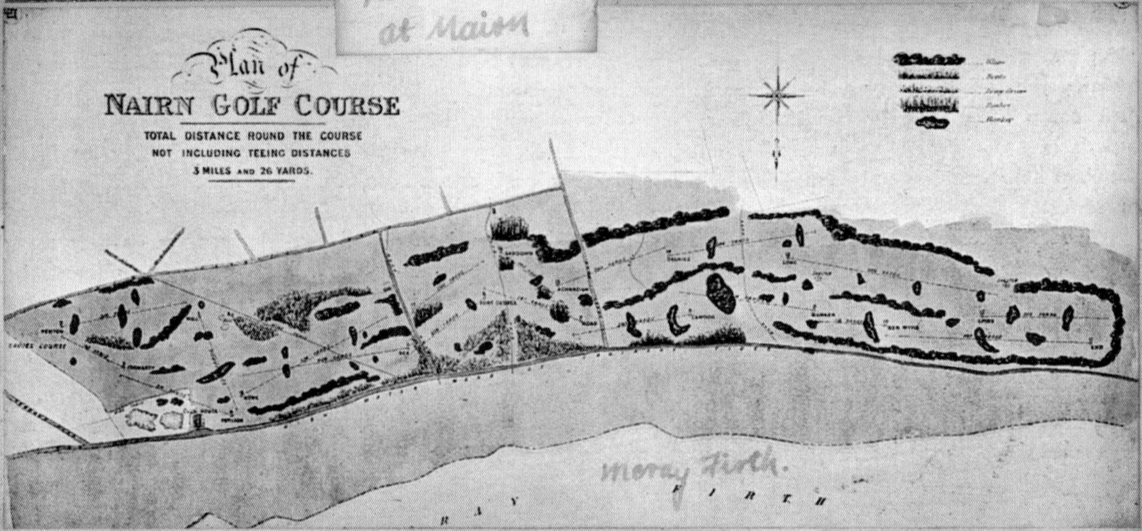

Nairn I laid out over six days in 1890

Below the 8th Hole

Above Mr Finlayson Secretary at Nairn and below - The Captain - Mr Newbigging in 1896

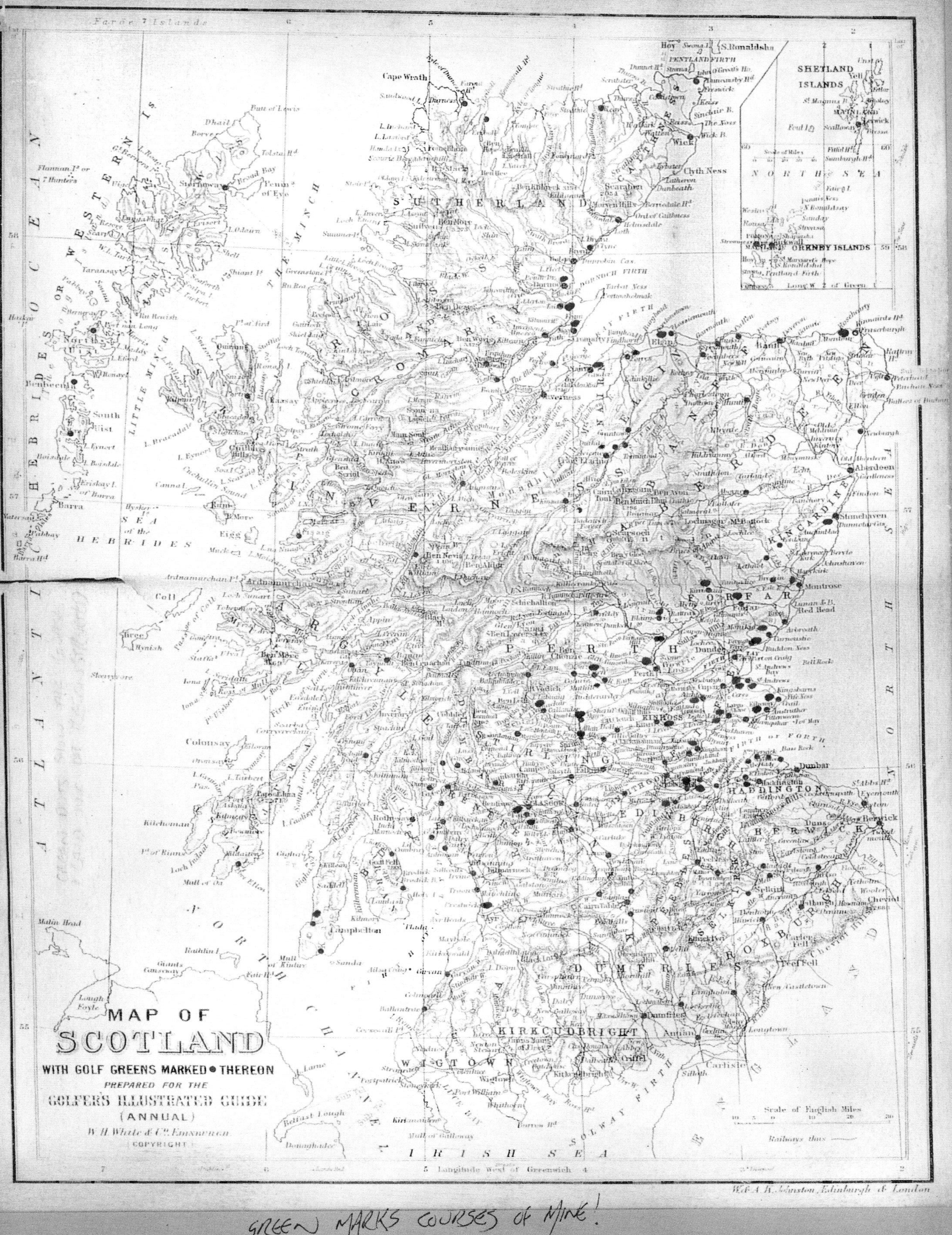

GREEN MARKS COURSES OF MINE!

It is pleasing to note that Dornoch is one of the driest spots known in the North—a fact which to every golfer, at all events, will give double meaning to the courtesy of the executive in calling their thirteenth hole after deservedly famous Morangie.

4TH GREEN, AND EMBO BAY

17TH HOLE.
D. J. Ross at "The Witch."

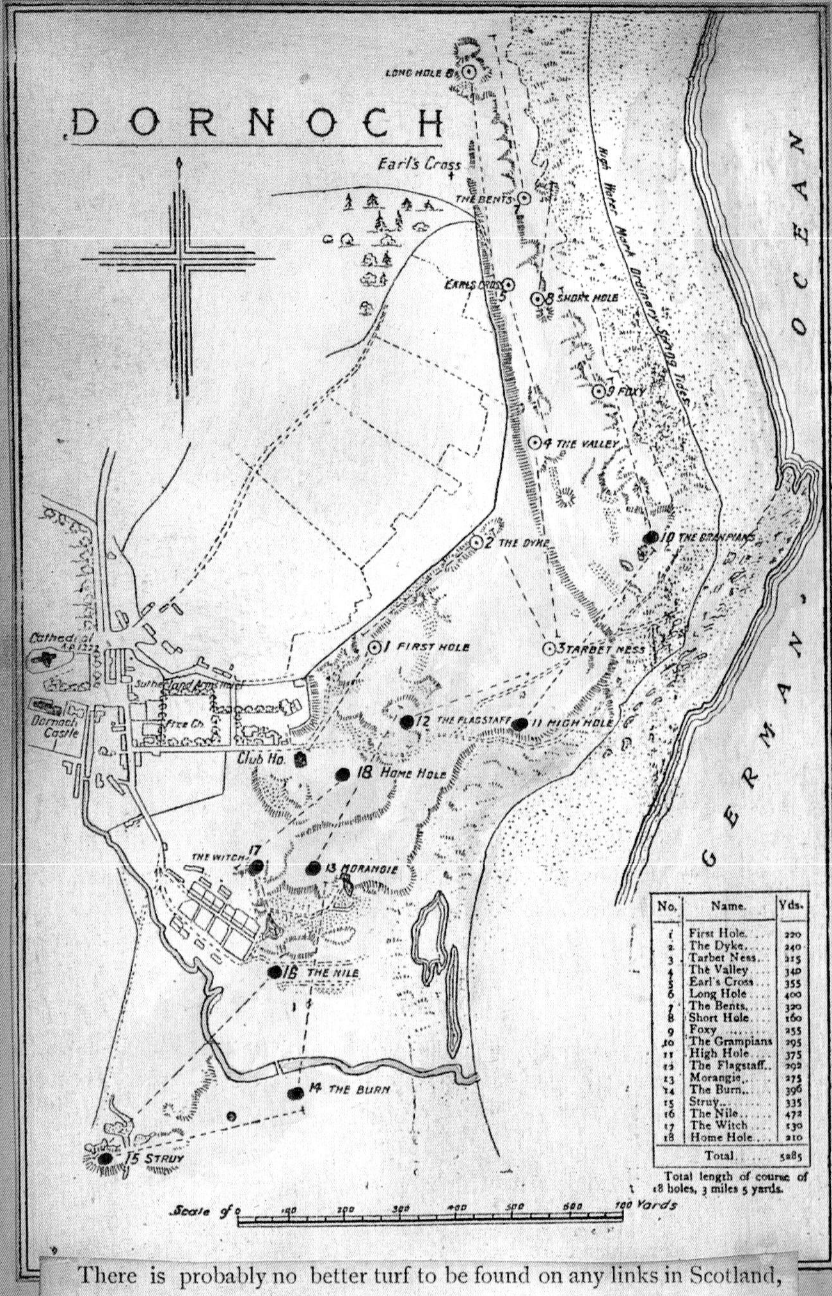

No.	Name.	Yds.
1	First Hole.	220
2	The Dyke.	240
3	Tarbet Ness.	215
4	The Valley	340
5	Earl's Cross	355
6	Long Hole	400
7	The Bents.	320
8	Short Hole.	160
9	Foxy	255
10	The Grampians	295
11	High Hole	375
12	The Flagstaff..	292
13	Morangie..	275
14	The Burn..	396
15	Struy...	335
16	The Nile	472
17	The Witch	130
18	Home Hole	210
	Total	5285

Total length of course of 18 holes, 3 miles 5 yards.

There is probably no better turf to be found on any links in Scotland, and well may Old Tom be proud of his handiwork in planning them. His reported remark runs: "There canna be better found for gowf"; and this seems to be the universal opinion of those who have tried them.

THESE links were laid out by Tom Morris in 1890, upon the Morich More, due south across the Firth from Dornoch Links and a mile or so east of Tain. The course is one of twelve holes, and is liberally supplied with whin, bent, and bunkers. "A curious feature of the course," says Mr. Cromb, "and one that shows its thoroughly sporting nature, is the fact that of the twelve holes only two can be seen from the tee as the player drives towards them, while in the case of six of them the flag remains invisible till the player comes well within iron reach of the disc." The hotel accommodation is first-class. Tain.

Golf and horse-racing used to be carried on by the inhabitants in old times upon the present links long before the present revival. About the centre of them is the "Gallows Hill," which exercised such a beneficial influence in the neighbourhood of old times. Of a like beneficial influence nowadays is, no doubt, the famous Glenmorangie distillery, which is also in the immediate vicinity, and dedicated to St. Duffus, the patron saint of the town and club.

MACHRIHANISH.

Gentlemen's Course.

No.	Name.	Yds.	No.	Name.	Yds.
1	Battery	422	11	Long Hole	486
2	Machrihanish	378	12	Kilkivan	344
3	Islay	170	13	Castlehill	368
4	Jura	359	14	Hut	161
5	Punch Bowl	266	15	Rorke's Drift	220
6	Balaclava	369	16	River	290
7	Bruach More	355	17	Trodigal	416
8	Craigs	268	18	Lossit	125
9	Clochkeil	208			
10	Straban	347		Total	5552

Ladies' Course.

No.	Distance, yards.
1	117
2	69
3	124
4	93
5	135
6	75
7	111
8	89
9	97
Total, 910	

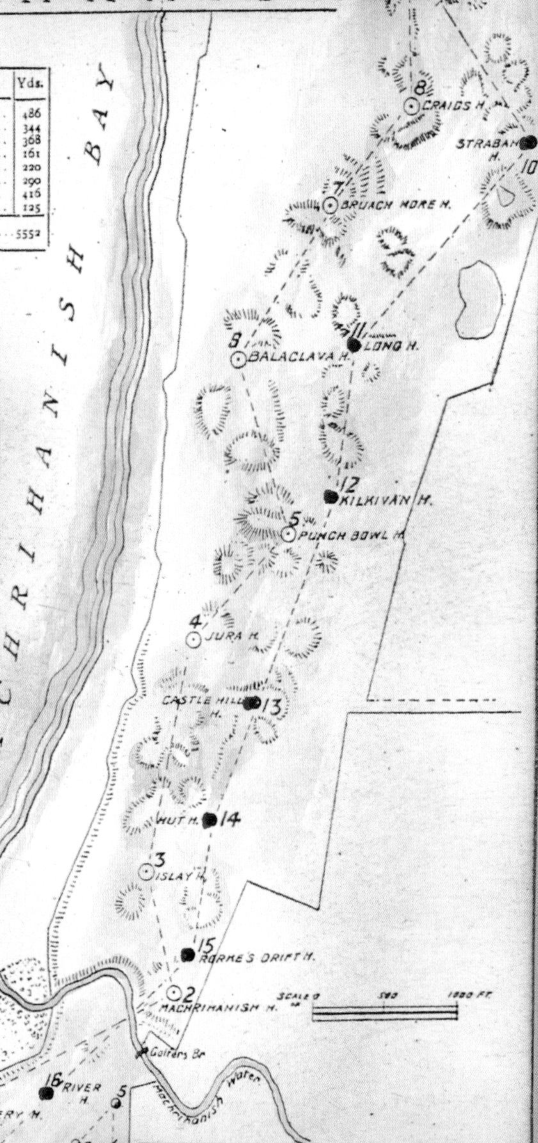

NOTICE.

At a Meeting of the Green Committee of St. Andrews Links held to-day, the following Resolution was unanimously come to, viz.: "That this Committee, learning that "the golf holes on the Old Course have been filled up by the "Custodian of the Links without authority, regret if any "inconvenience should have been caused to the Public, and "that such action should have been taken without notice "and general agreement among golfers, but recognising "that the Old Course is much in need of rest, resolve to "allow the holes to remain closed until 30th June.

ROBERT CATHCART, Convener.
JOHN M'GREGOR, Provost.

ST ANDREWS

181

Correspondence from J.O.F
about Jamie Anderson's clubs

TOM MORRIS

GOLF CLUB AND BALL MANUFACTURER

Links.

St Andrews Sep. 10th 1898

R. L. Harmsworth Esq

Dear Sir

I understand you wish some information as to the Clubs Mr Cameron handed you the other day. Well, there are 5 Clubs which belonged to Jamie Anderson and some of them he played with when he won the Championship in 1877-78 & 79. I think the Mid Spoon, Iron, and one of the Drivers would be the three he played with on these occasions. The two Philp Clubs, Putter & Driver are very old especially the Putter, which my father thinks must be between 70 and 100 years old.

Yours faithfully

J. O. F. Morris

The Links - the start and finish!

183

Sept 15 — 1899

An effort was made to get up a match this week for Vardon at Carnoustie, where last year he carried off first prize in an important professional tournament, after a particularly stiff game with J. H. Taylor. The arrangements for the Carnoustie fixture fell through. One of the suggestions was that Mr F. G. Tait should be Vardon's opponent on these links. Mr Tait, however, found himself unable to entertain the idea owing to his having another engagement for the contemplated date. At the same time he let it be known that he will not play any serious golf until the September meeting of the Royal and Ancient Club. Archie Simpson was also spoken of. Undoubtedly a match between the Champion and the old Carnoustie lad on this green would have aroused much interest in the district, and among golfers in Aberdeen, where Archie is now resident. Vardon was quite willing to stretch a point and add Carnoustie to the list. But Simpson was unable to accept the engagement, and the proposed date—the 18th—was given up to St Andrews.

Braid on the tee   Self seated   Herd Vardon Taylor

TOM MORRIS

(Ecce, Senex Andreanus)

[From the Latin, by A. Lang, not literally translated, and with apologies to the author of "John Peel."]

Dae ye ken an auld man,
  Wha's famous and so forth;
A part, tae, o' the shrine
  In a Mecca o' the North?
Dae ye ken an auld man
  Mair worshipped than the Saint
O' the grand auld city of St Andrews?

Dae ye ken an auld man,
  Wha's naething of a "toff,"
Wears ony sort o' jacket
  At the Royal game o' golf?
Dae ye ken the auld man,
  The *doyen* o' the craft,
In the golf-mad toon o' St Andrews?

Dae ye ken an auld man,
  The youthfu' golfer's frien',
Wha gi'es ye sage advice
  Wi' a sparkle in his een?
Dae ye ken the auld man,
  Wha says, "Tak' plenty san'"
His *open sesame* tae St Andrews?

Allan Robertson's Hand Hammered Gutty - used in his record breaking 79 on the Old in 1858

"THE PROFESSIONALS' BALL"

with the Triumvirate

2/-  **2/-**

LEADING PLAYERS EXPERIMENTING WITH NEW BALL.—BOGEY HANDICAP AT PARKWAY.

Golfers hereabouts are enthusiastic over a new ball. At Garden City on Saturday and Sunday, Walter J. Travis, Charles B. Macdonald, James G. Batterson and Robert G. Watson, Jr., were playing with an imported brand of rubber core. Batterson recently ordered 6 dozen from the other side, and when Macdonald finished playing on Saturday he was so impressed with the new idea that he immediately cabled to London for several dozen.—*"American Daily Paper."*

you can see me running into the picture here!

"WE MUST ALL HAVE IT."

Scotland v. England

Vardon and Taylor v. Herd and Braid over 2 Scottish greens and 2 English greens.

Harry Vardon about to hit through the ball.

The Triumvirate

Vardon Taylor Braid

Golf and Golfers of the Old School.

By Dr. J. G. McPHERSON.

Golf Illustrated April 1900

XVI.—TOM MORRIS.

IT was, I think, about 1862 that I got on speaking terms with Tom Morris. I had before that seen him play in foursomes, especially when Colonel Fairlie and he played against Mr. Erskine Wemyss and Allan during the medal weeks. But he had left Allan's workshop in 1851, three years after his glorious victory with Allan against the two Dunns. During these eleven years he was custodian of the links at Prestwick. For three years after Allan's death Auld Da' looked after St. Andrews links; but fortunately Tom was secured for the situation, which he now so honourably continues to hold.

On his arrival in St. Andrews, the city of his birth, for his new duties, he took the small shop (part of the site of Russack's Hotel now), when Jamie Wilson went up the "brae" to what was considered "nearer the lug o' the law." While here he made for me the most beautiful wooden niblick ever I saw; the head in imitation of Allan's, but the handle was thin and tapering, with a steely spring. I afterwards got a silver shield put on it for the work which it did. After that he went up to his present premises, and let the upper flat to the Thistle Golf Club, of which I was a member till the end of the sixties.

I am not going to give a monograph of the high priest of the hierarchy of Golf; it would take a volume to record his achievements and give a faithful account of his life and work. But what was he doing among the golfers of old?

First of all he began to put the links in thorough order. What would have been the state of things to-day if Tom had not brought his infallible cure of "saund" for all the diseases that the cut-up ground was heir to? It was a very important match indeed if he was not constantly seen taking up bits of cruelly cut turf and placing them in blank spaces with a press of his foot. What a boon it was, too, when he put in the tins into the holes on the putting green. Since his enthusiastic endeavours for the improvement and preservation of the green, the Royal and Ancient Golf Club have given him nearly *carte blanche* in the way of money. With a strong force he laid out the fine second course, which, but for the old associations of the first, would be considered as fine a green as exists.

"OLD TOM." Copyright, Golf Illustrated.

Tom had, in my college days, this very commendable trait of character; not only did he, like Allan, encourage a young player by his kindly words, but he would actually volunteer to waste his time playing with a real golfer without a fee. Many a single did I then play with him, to get my own hand in for my heavy matches, and when he and Bob Kirk were maintaining a most successful partnership against all comers, they played many a practising match against Major Boothby and myself. In 1865, Tom and Bob tackled and vanquished the brothers Park at St. Andrews; Willie Park and Andrew Strath, who had succeeded Tom at Prestwick, on Strath's adopted green; and on the same green, Willie Park and Dow. In the same year Tom and Strath challenged the world for £100, but nobody accepted the challenge. Until Tommy came forward to play against me I had many a match with Tom.

Twice had Tom won the champion belt at Prestwick before his return to St. Andrews; and in 1864 and 1867 he went back to Prestwick to win it again. During the four succeeding years the trophy was carried off by his illustrious son. The achievements of father and son have been unique in the golfing world.

I noticed Tom's remarkably methodical and temperate character at the four nights. He wisely looked after "number one" as to his dietary and baths; but "blackstrap" (stout) and his pipe were his only luxuries. Of course, Golf was our only subject of conversation, for golfers cannot be moderate in that respect. When they meet over a little sloe gin and a pipe they have Golf on the brain. The cracks were all there; but so much confidence had Tom in me that he challenged any two to play us. The two first men at the tournament, Bob Andrews of Perth and Andrew Strath (open champion the previous year) accepted the challenge. On the thirty-six holes we were dormy one; but by an unexplainable process, which Tom and I have never been able to clear up to satisfy both parties, we lost the hole after playing one off two, and halved the match. Still I shall ever esteem Tom for his confidence in the player whom he had so kindly trained.

Tom's matches against Willie Park are historical; perhaps no tougher struggle was ever experienced on so many occasions between two players at the top of the tree; yet, on the whole, honours were about evenly divided. And Park was a formidable rival, *the* most formidable, according to Tom himself, for Park also gained the open championship four times. I am not, however, going into these in detail.

The warrior who, in his seventy-eighth year, went round St. Andrews links in 87, has still to be reckoned with. His loose, "hunkered" swing is well suited for his years. But he will approach with anyone still where he knows every foot of the ground. He can now laugh at the missing of short putts, for he is always "there or thereaboot" with the longer ones, and it is long since he gave up placing his forefinger down the handle for the orthodox style, thereby completing the cure.

The first of the interesting "best-ball" matches was played by Messrs. Robert Clark and Gilbert Innes against Tom. I remember following the players; and I never thought at the time that Tom had so much to contend against. When they beat him by a single putt, I thought it strange. But only lately in Tom's sanctum we concluded that for one man to beat the two others with their choice of ball, he must be able to give each of them separately about a third.

Tom's sanctum is where the Thistle Club house was, the principal windows overlooking the green. From this Tom can detect any delinquents at the home putting green, or smooth down some dispute, when no one thought he was on the watch. Piles of Golf and Golf Illustrated give evidence of his literary turn of mind. Could he only write as he can speak he would out-Grace Grace in the literature of the game. As a very worthy Elder of the Kirk (according to A.K.H.B., "that great and good man"), he has the Bible on his side-table; and, if I am not mistaken, he has a capital copy of Burns beside it.

How can I condense my ideas of the genial and honest man himself? He is truly one of "Nature's gentlemen." He is "a' bodie's bodie"—all things to all men. He sends his tyro customers away as well pleased as the most affable tailor can please one careful in taste about his clothes. He is either playing or arranging matches. He has had Royalty among his pupils, and the ladies' putting green would be "dreich" without his courteous encouragement. Over the country he goes to lay out new greens, according to the Hoyle of the game. Artists have painted him, poets have sung him, lady amateurs have admired him. No one in the golfing world is so widely known, and, when known intimately, so beloved, as the grand old Nestor of Golf—Tom Morris.

"On Fame's triumphant wings Tom's name shall soar
Till Time shall end, or golfing be no more."

To a petulant member who was for ever complaining of the bad lies he got into and the disgraceful state of the course generally, auld Wullie used to rejoin, "Ay, sir, there's ower mony bad lies, nae doot; but there's ae thing caps me sir, an' that is hoo the deevil sic a graund player as yersel wull

TOM MORRIS CELEBRATES HIS EIGHTIETH BIRTHDAY

St Andrews Citizen June 1901

Tom Morris, who attained his 80th birthday on Sunday, celebrated the occasion on Monday by playing a round of St Andrews Links – a custom which he has followed annually for a number of years. His partner was Mr H. S. C. Everard. The couple started shortly after three o'clock, and throughout the round they were followed by a number of interested spectators, including four gentlemen whose ages, along with that of Old Tom himself, totalled 413 years. The weather during the match was cold and stormy, the latter stages being finished in heavy rain. Notwithstanding his advanced age, Tom played a remarkably good game, his driving being particularly steady, and his short game at times splendid. Mr Everard, who gave his opponent a third, turned one ahead. On the home journey the veteran won the first two holes, and was thus one up. He, however, lost his lead at the thirteenth, but again recovered at the fifteenth. After this Tom got into difficulties, and the match stood all square with one hole to play. The last hole was halved, and the match ended square. Although Tom has reached the advanced age of fourscore years, it is remarkable to see him moving about with much of the buoyancy of a man of half his years. He is wonderfully active, his spirit as bright and cheerful as ever, and his interest in all matters pertaining to golf has lost none of its keenness. He is still ever ready to give assistance in the way of advice when desired by Clubs, and it was only last week that he visited Crieff and gave his opinion regarding some alterations that are proposed to be made on the course there. His vitality is seen by his daily movements on the Links. If he is not strolling out on the course in company with his favourite collie Silver – a faithful companion – throwing his keen eye over the greens which are so dear to him, he will, in all probability, be found engaging in a round with one or other of his old friends connected with the Club.

Tom Morris 1901

ST MARY'S STUDIO ST ANDREWS

There seems to be an awful lot written about me these days!

Golf Illustrated Nov 1901

Old Tom Morris of St. Andrews.

BY THE REV. W. W. TULLOCH, D.D.

To my mind, not only the most famous, but the most lovable man, as well as the most attractive personality, in all St. Andrews, if not in all Scotland, is not any Principal or Professor, any priest or prophet, any philosopher or poet. It is the good man, the great golfer, and the friend of all true golfers, whom the whole world knows as Tom Morris, still more affectionately as Old Tom, less happily, yet truly, as the High Priest of the golfing Mecca—the G.O.M. of golf. Yet in certain circles of people, and those you would imagine from their special vocation to be well informed in regard to all celebrities, some six or seven years ago he was not known.

Having written "A. K. H. B."—and never was work more to my heart—as one of the series of "Celebrities at Home" in the *World*, and as, in addition to the true labour of love the article was well paid for, I was anxious to essay another paper of the same kind. So I wrote to the editor offering to make Tom Morris the subject of such another paper. I fancy the editor was not at home. Perhaps he, too, was ignorant. At any rate I got a letter from the sub-editor saying that in answer to my communication they would be glad to know who "Mr. Tom Morris" was, and what were his claims to a place in that particular series of articles. I replied stating that it might or it ought to be known to them that there was a not unpopular game called golf, and that "Mr. Morris" was the greatest exponent thereof.

My article in the *World* made a "pat" appearance. It came out on the very day of the great October meeting of the Royal and Ancient Golf Club, in the year that its captain was no less a personage than Mr. A. J. Balfour, M.P., politician, philosopher, and golfer. It attracted a great deal of attention at that "meeting," was highly commended, and, above all, I am glad to think it gave pleasure to its subject.

Tom Morris is a thorough Scot and Fifer, having been born in the North Street, St. Andrews, on the 16th of June, 1821, the son of John Morris, letter-carrier, and his wife, Jane Bruce. He was educated at St. Andrews, and began to play on its classic links as soon as he could toddle and his infant hand grasp a club. He can remember beginning to "gowf" when he was about six years of age, and as a lad of eight had few rivals of his age.

When fifteen he became apprentice to Allan Robertson, and learned his trade with that redoubtable veteran. He was four years an apprentice and five years a journeyman. Then he set up on his own account and prospered. He went to Prestwick in 1851, and was there making clubs, keeping the green, and playing grand gowf for fourteen years. He went to Prestwick through the persuasions of his life-long friend, Colonel Fairlie of Coodham. "No better gentleman ever lived than Colonel Fairlie; I'm perfectly certain of that." That is Tom's opinion of the Colonel, and one which all who had the privilege of his acquaintance will endorse.

OLD TOM MORRIS.

"The Most Attractive Personality in St. Andrews."

Tom Morris returned to St. Andrews in 1864. It was then he came into my life. I was at that time a lad of eighteen, and he won his place in my heart as he had done in that of many a better man. I can't remember when I first met him. He just grew into my daily life at St. Andrews, a part of which was almost always spent on the links.

For many years he occupied the very first position as a golfer. Of course, in these days the interest in great golf matches was confined more or less to Scotland, or at least to Scotch people. Perhaps the interest, if less diffuse, was more intense. And certainly the interest excited by any match in which Tom Morris figured was very great.

I followed all his important matches at St. Andrews, and espoused his cause to such an extent that his great rival of those days, Willie Park, I regarded as a sort of personal enemy. The idea of any one trying to wrest the supremacy of St. Andrews links from my hero was an offence to me. It was only, however, as Tom's rival that I disliked Willie Park. I knew and appreciated his good qualities, and none did so more than Tom Morris himself.

I used often to follow the big matches in which he took part in company with my old college friend, John MacPherson—Dr. J. Gordon MacPherson, to use the name by which he is now known in the clerical and golfing world—and many is the good blackstrap and smoke the three of us have had together as we discussed the golf of the day, and sometime between rounds that were famous. It was his friend Colonel Fairlie, he always alleges, who taught him to smoke. In these days they often took their luncheon on the green at Prestwick, and the Colonel would give him a cigar. Then he presented him with a pipe, and he adds—"I just *had* to buy tobacco." He never smoked till he was thirty, but he adds, with great delight, and one of those smiles which lights up his whole face—"I've made up for it since, and I have never felt it do me any harm." On one occasion, however, he gave it up for six weeks. This was when he went into training to play his great match over four greens with Willie Park. He played the same number of holes as the match consisted of, thirty-six, each day for six weeks. The match was played over Prestwick, Musselburgh, North Berwick, and St. Andrews links. Tom beat his opponent on each of the greens, and won the match at the second hole going out the St. Andrews links. It was then, as I related in the *World*, that he thinks he made the best record that he ever played in his life. At that time the "Rashies," near the old station, were a terror to the golfer. Tom's ball lay to the north of them from the tee. From there he took a tremendous swipe, and laid his ball within thirty yards of the hole—holing out in three. On that same occasion he did the third hole in three also.

One of his great matches was that in which he and his brother George played Willie and Davie Park thirty-six holes. Tom and his partner were not one hole up the whole way till they won the match at the last hole. Another of his great matches was that in which he and Allan Robertson played against the brothers Dunn. The Dunns carried everything before them at Musselburgh, but Tom and Allan won at North Berwick and St. Andrews. In these days matches were counted by greens, not holes, and though the Dunns were ahead by holes, Tom and Allan won the match on the greens. After this counting by holes was substituted for greens.

Talking of Willie Park, he says:—"He was a splendid driver and a splendid putter. I've been neither, yet I managed to beat him." Probably what he says is true, but as an all-round player he had few equals and no superiors. But it is as a man that he is loved as much as he is admired as a golfer. He was born in the purple, a gentleman all his life, and in all his feelings and actions—a simple, honest, guileless, God-fearing, brother-loving man.

Let us take a look at him in his home. His home is characteristic of him. The large window of his sitting-room looks out upon the home green—the teeing-ground for the start—the club-house, and the sea, of which he says he never tires. Above his mantelpiece there is a large frame containing photographs of his famous son and champion golfer, "Tommy," and his only surviving son "Jimmy." Between the two lads is a head of himself. Under the photograph of each son is a record of his best score out and in St. Andrews links. It tells that Tommy in 1869 went out in 37 strokes, and returned in 40, making a total of 77. Nineteen years later Jimmy (T.O.F.) went out in 38, and returned in 39, thus equalling his brother's magnificent record. The walls of Tom's sanctum are covered with photographs of famous golfers and great golf matches. His bedroom is similarly decked, and on his toilet-table and mantelpiece are heaps of golf balls. He always sleeps with his window open, and one morning he woke to find himself half-enveloped in snow. His habits are very simple, and on a Sunday night you will find him, after having seen him officiate as an elder in the Town Church, quietly reading his family Bible with the big print. And if you ask him, he will rise from its perusal to show you the famous trophy, the champion belt of red morocco, with rich silver ornamentations, bearing golfing devices. This became the property of young Tommy through three annual consecutive wins. It was won four times, though not consecutively, by Tom himself, and thrice by Willie Park.

Tom was a great friend and cronie of my father—"the Principal," as he always called him; and he had a great affection for "A. K. H. B.," his minister and friend, "the Doctor." Let me tell my readers a story of the three distinguished men never before published, and I am sure my dear friends, the Boyds, will forgive me for publishing it now. They will know and understand what my father meant. "I mind," says Tom one day, "it was a Monday, meeting your father, the Principal. It was at the second hole. I was coming in and he was going out. I says to him—'The Doctor was gey guid yesterday, Principal.' Your father just put his hand on my shoulder in the kindly way he has, and said, 'But, Tom, the Doctor's aye guid except when he havers.'"

Another and differently characteristic story of Tom's is one I heard just the other day. It was told me in the Manse of Stichel, a pretty Border village where golf is unfortunately not played. My informant was Mr. Young, the popular minister of Nenthorng, a cousin of Mr. Sloan, the excellent U.F. minister of St. Andrews. "I went into

184

the shop on the afternoon of the first day I had played golf to get a club. I was fortunate enough to find Tom himself in. I was carrying a straw hat. 'Have you been playing golf in that hat?' asked Tom. 'You'll never get the right swing with a thing like that on your head.' He took up a club, showed me the proper swing, in which the club just struck the back of my hat and knocked it off. So I eschewed that kind of headgear, and became a golfer."

There is a good story of my brother-in-law, Frank Tawer, and old Tom. Frank Tawer was a popular Eton master for many years. He is now retired, and plays golf at Walton-on-Thames, where he lives on the links. He got to know my people at Mr. Oliphant's, in Windsor, and came to St. Andrews for the long summer vacation. There he took the golf fever furiously, and did a great deal to make the game famous in England, even before the great boom came. He writes me:—"Old Tom always struck me as the only golf professional or club-maker whose hand it was an honour to shake. And in the old foursomes to which I was sometimes 'graciously' admitted with Whyte Melville, John Blackwood, etc., it was a great pleasure to talk and walk with him. I had been taking a part in rather a broad farce in the Town Hall, St. Andrews, at which he was present, and much amused. The next day he said to me—'Eh, Mr. Tawer, you could gi'e me more points (?) on the acting than I could gi'e on the gowf,' or some such words." "Odds" must, I think, have been the term used. "Points" is suggestive of whist, and that Tom does not play. So far as I know he never touched a card or handled a billiard cue in his life. Nor does he encourage Sunday golf. He was once asked his opinion of the much discussed question. His answer was very characteristic. "Well, gentlemen," he said, "all I can say is that if you do not need a rest on the Sabbath the links does."

No narrative of Tom Morris's career can be complete without mention of the great loss the good man received in the death of his son Tommy, on whom his affections were set as a father, and his golfing ambitions were more than justified by the great achievements. That death was closely connected with another sad event, well chronicled by his minister, Dr. Boyd, in his "Twenty-five Years of St. Andrews." "There was," wrote A.H.K.B., "a pathetic event here at the beginning of September in this year. The grand old Tom Morris (always so called in respect and affection, great golfer and best of men), had a son called, for distinction's sake, Tommy Morris, who was a greater golfer than himself. At an early age Tommy won the dignity of champion of the world, and bore it well and meekly. On Thursday, September 2nd, father and son went together to North Berwick to play a great match on the links there. Tommy left his wife perfectly well. She was a remarkably handsome and healthy young woman, most lovable in every way. Her brother was a great manager and speaker in the Trades Union world. But on Saturday afternoon that fine girl (she was no more) had her first child, and at once ran down and died. A telegram was sent to Tom, who told his son they must leave at once. A fine yacht was put at their disposal, and without the weary railway journey by Edinburgh they were brought across the Firth of Forth. Tom did not tell his son that all was over till they were walking up from the harbour. I was in the house when they arrived. What can one say in such an hour? I never forgot the young man's stony look—stricken was the word—and how all of a sudden he started up and cried—'It's not true!' I have seen many sorrowful things, but not many like that Saturday night. Poor Tommy went about for a little while, but his heart was broken."

Train passing the 16th green

Still playing the course in reverse about 1890 – one week clockwise – the next week – anti-clockwise.

191

CARNOUSTIE GOLF COURSE.

TWELVE miles north-east of Dundee, where the river Tay fairly reaches the sea, lie the Carnoustie Golf Links. The town of Carnoustie lies near the links, but as no town near a golf green is of the faintest interest to a golfer, the place may be summed up as "flat, stale, and unprofitable." With a fine contempt for the comfort of their best patrons, the railway company have placed their station a quarter of a mile past the golf green, and the wade back to the club house on a hot day through a perfect waste of sand more than ankle deep is a fine test for the temper, and a providential arrangement for putting a stout opponent off his game. The Dalhousie Club House, a fine two storey building, looks out on a broad triangle of fine turf laid out as a ladies' course of eighteen short holes, beyond which the German ocean comes rolling in grandly with a snowy surf, sometimes three feet high, just far enough off to be musical to the golfer's ear, without giving him an excuse for a scowl should he miss his shot. The brothers Bob and Archie Simpson, the well-known professional golfers, have their place of business inside the Dalhousie Club House ground, and are much esteemed for their obliging disposition, steadiness, and excellent workmanship. The Carnoustie Golf Links, as a whole, are not far behind any in Scotland, and before many in extent, in hazards, in fine putting greens, and in arrangement, as the out and in players never cross or collide. If St. Andrew's be considered the best green, and North Berwick the most dangerous, Carnoustie may fairly rank third, as it combines many of the good qualities of the first and the dangers of the second, with the expansiveness of both.

HOME HOLE.
Mr. H. S. C. Everard putting.

FISHING FOR BALLS IN THE BURN.

PLAN OF CARNOUSTIE GOLF COURSE 1888.

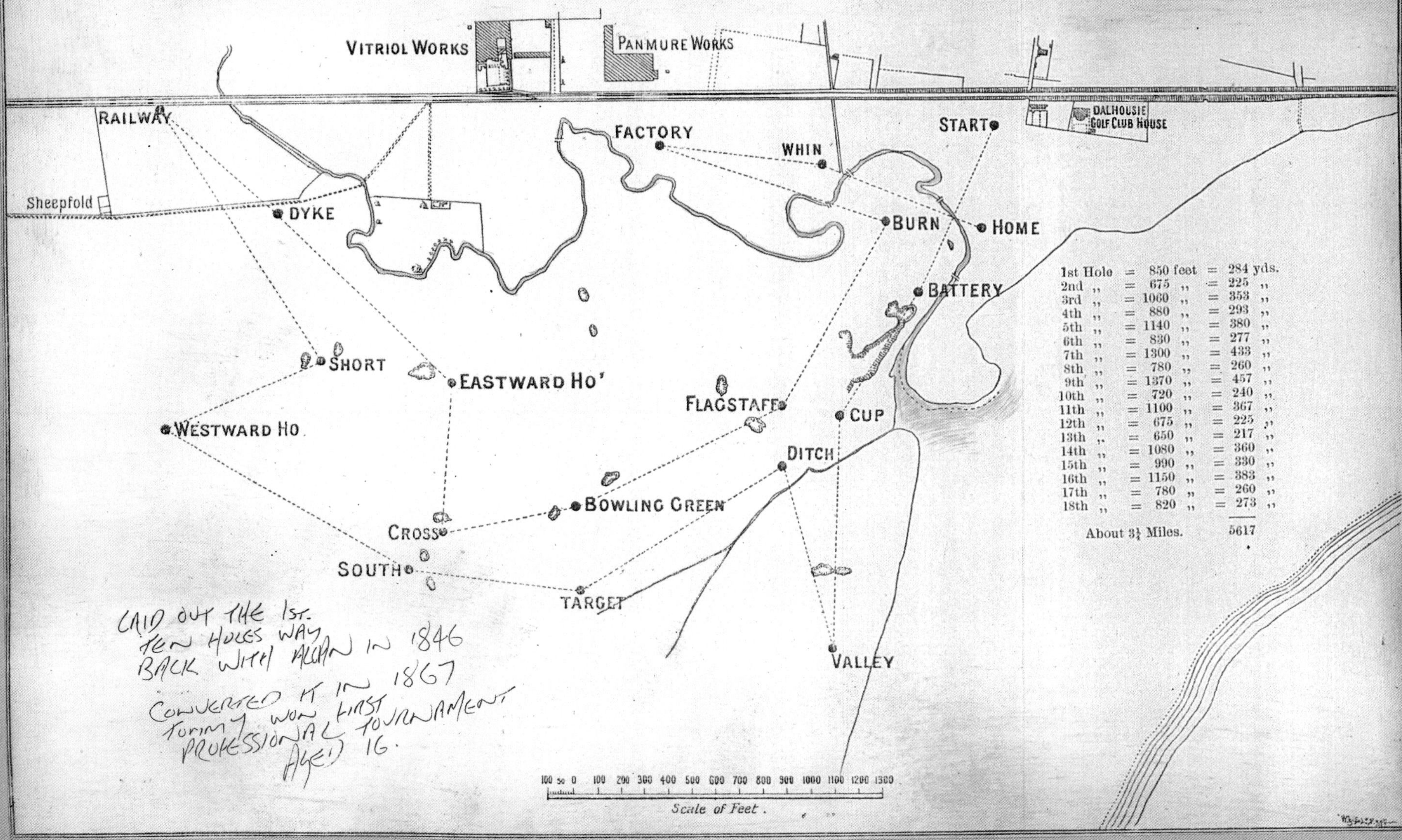

1st Hole	=	850	feet	=	284	yds.
2nd ,,	=	675	,,	=	225	,,
3rd ,,	=	1060	,,	=	353	,,
4th ,,	=	880	,,	=	293	,,
5th ,,	=	1140	,,	=	380	,,
6th ,,	=	830	,,	=	277	,,
7th ,,	=	1300	,,	=	433	,,
8th ,,	=	780	,,	=	260	,,
9th ,,	=	1370	,,	=	457	,,
10th ,,	=	720	,,	=	240	,,
11th ,,	=	1100	,,	=	367	,,
12th ,,	=	675	,,	=	225	,,
13th ,,	=	650	,,	=	217	,,
14th ,,	=	1080	,,	=	360	,,
15th ,,	=	990	,,	=	330	,,
16th ,,	=	1150	,,	=	383	,,
17th ,,	=	780	,,	=	260	,,
18th ,,	=	820	,,	=	273	,,
About 3¼ Miles.					5617	

Sea Shore
THREE MILES TO DEAL
Sea Shore
The Maiden
Hut
HADES
The Unknown Sahara
Swicran Barn
HILTON
TAIT
W.L.P. Inv.
1st ENGLISH OPEN CHAMPIONSHIP
J. H. TAYLOR WINNER 1894
HARRY VARDON 1899
PLAN OF
THE GOLFING COURSE
OF THE
ST GEORGE'S GOLF CLUB.
1888.
Holes I - 366 yards
II - 312
III - 267
IV - 405
V - 212
VI - 190
VII - 480
VIII - 180
IX - 338
X - 344
XI - 312
XII - 333
XIII - 480
XIV - 458
XV - 433
XVI - 272
XVII - 333
XVIII - 300
Total length 6,012 yards.
AMATUER CHAMPIONSHIP 1896
WON BY MR TAIT
Tall Red Flag showing line of Tee shot.
Tall Blue Flag shows the refuge.
Tall White Flag shows the far edge of putting green straight over hole.
Sandy Bunkers.
Grassy hollows.
Benty Ground.
TO SANDWICH ONE MILE
Clubhouse.
50 100 200 300 400 500 600 YARDS.

J. J. Hamilton. Geo. Nicol. J. E. Laidlay. Charles Hutchings. H. A. Richardson. John Gairdner. J. H. Graham. Hon. S. Finch-Hatton. Colonel Kennard.
John Taylor. James Cullen. Ernest Lehmann. E. Protheroe. G. P. Leach.

THE AMATEUR CHAMPIONSHIP MEETING OF 1896.

John Ball, jun. John Oswald. Lieutenant F. G. Tait. Capt. W. H. Burn. J. O. Fairlie. S. Muir Fergusson.
W. Rutherford. H. H. Hilton. H. F. de Paravicini.

The approximate distances are as follows :—

No. of Hole.	Distance, yards.	No. of Hole.	Distance, yards.
1	330	10	310
2	456	11	330
3	240	12	275
4	210	13	180
5	165	14	175
6	190	15	210
7	130	16	350
8	140	17	540
9	310	18	300

Total, 2 miles 1321 yards

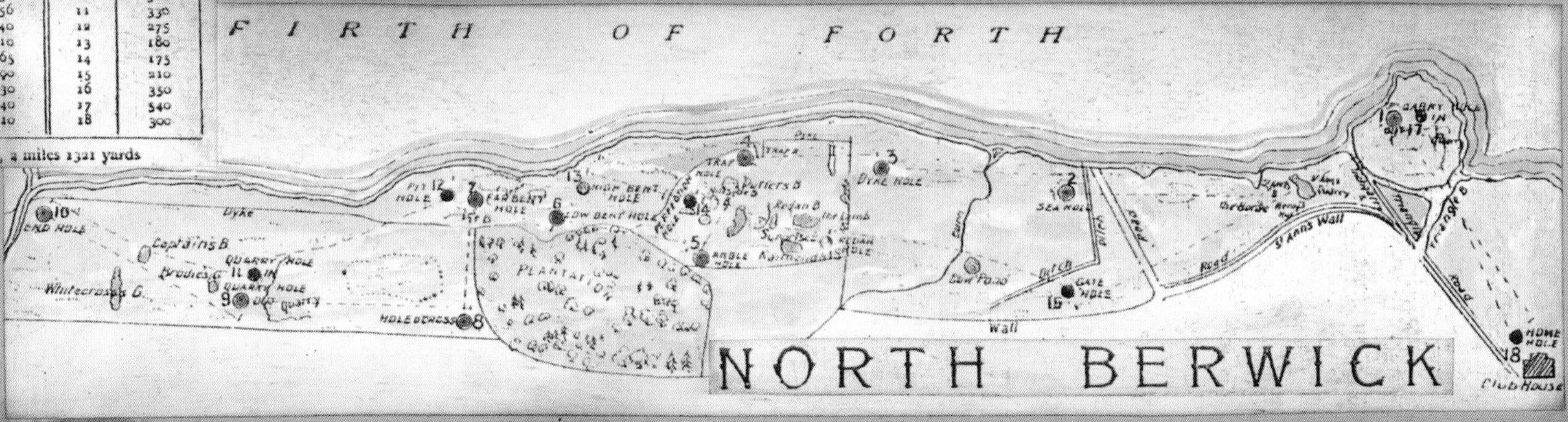

NORTH BERWICK

195

R. Walker.
C. R. Smith. J. Cuthbert. W. Smith R. Munro. T. Yeoman. T. Hood.
Peter Fernie. R. Kelly. A. Jackson. (Carnoustie). Peter Paxton. W. Aveston. R. Kirk. J. Sherlock. W. Mackie. J. S. Pearson. —— J. Ramsay.

J. White. T. Hogg. Alexander Herd. J. Rowe. J. H. Taylor, H. Vardon. James Braid.
Ben Sayers. *Open Champion,* *Open Champion,*
1894-5. 1896.

[*From a photo by C. Hussey, Harold Wood.*

GROUP OF PROFESSIONAL GOLFERS, 1896.

GOLF.

196

BY

HORACE G. HUTCHINSON
(Author of "Golf," "The Golfing Pilgrim," &c.

VI.

SOCIAL ASPECTS OF GOLF.

It is a sign of the times in golf that the team match is coming more and more into favour. One of the reproaches that the cricketer has delighted to hurl at the golfer is that he is the devotee of a gain entirely selfish and self-centred. There is none of that co-operation, he says, in golf, which makes cricket such a valuable education for youth, and so on. The golfer could always reply to this that if golf did not teach youth to help his fellow youth it taught him a sturdy self-reliance, and at that point you could leave the two quarrelling as to which was the more valuable quality for youth to acquire. The arguments on both sides were rather upset when some one came in with the observation that there is such a thing in golf as a foursome, but still, in the main the fact remained that golf was rather an unsociable, rather an individual game. It did not lead to gregariousness.

WHERE DIFFERENT CLASSES MIX.

Now that reproach is in a fair way of being removed, in great measure, by the habit of team matches which seems to have an increasing vogue. There are some golfers who do not have a good word to say for the team match at all. They say it lacks "finish," in the sense that it does not work up to a denouement, because, even if the match as a whole be close, the individual players do not know how close it is nor in what degree their individual efforts are contributing to gain a victory or avert a defeat, or to emphasise the one or diminish the other. This is a true saying, no doubt. No doubt the team matches would be better things than they are if one could have all the emotions that a close finish gives ; but because a thing might be conceivably better is not argument against its being good, and the spirit that makes team matches popular is certainly a sociable pleasant spirit, opposed to the curmudgeonly conception of the game. There is, in point of fact, not a little *esprit de corps* shown in many of these matches. The idea with which members of the team enter on the struggle is really not so much that they shall win their individual matches as that the team shall conquer, and we see this generous spirit of self-effacement for the good of the side shown not least conspicuously by teams of which the members are of the fairer sex. Teams of either sex travelling about the country to play matches with teams of other clubs are surely a means to sociability and general mutual knowledge and friendliness among golfers. Especially to be approved, in this respect, are the matches that so many clubs play with the working men's club it may be of their own district or may be of another to which they have journeyed. In the old days this mingling of the classes was certainly a good and pleasant feature of the game of golf, witness that historical match wherein a Scottish King took part with "one Patersone, a shoemaker," as his partner, with excellent results for the man of leather, for the king, having gained his match, was so pleased that he gave his gallant partner a house in the Canongate. What good old times were those !

But even as the world wags now, when houses in the Canongate are no longer the guerdon of meritorious golf, it is surely a right good thing to see the gentleman and working man meeting on their common ground and so acquiring that better understanding of each other which is all that is wanted for their mutual liking. And the writer is very sure that all who have taken part in those matches will abet him in bearing witness that no opponents that he can find in his own class can as a rule be more pleasant fellows to play nor more thorough sportsmen in its best sense than these working men golfers.

Among the many teams that go golfing about the country, perhaps the Oxford and Cambridge Golfing Society deserves a little notice to itself. It is composed of graduate members of the two Universities who have shown such a degree of proficiency as to be considered worthy of representing the society. The Society is able, naturally, from such recruits to put a very formidable army into the field. It has never yet probably played its full strength, and if it did it would need the strongest side of the strongest club to compete on equal terms with it. The Houses of Legislature are also pleased to occupy their august leisure in a few such team matches. The team match is very much a product, and one of the best products, of the modern spirit of golf. It is to be set against that inordinate rage for prize competitions which the golfer of the old school is apt to associate, with a certain justice, though less justly than he supposes, with the modern school.

197

CADDIES.

In very many places golf is played on public commons, where the first principles of good policy, as well as the less selfish considerations, demand a good understanding and friendliness with those who have the common rights. In no way is this arrived at more easily and satisfactorily than by the encouragement of those workmen's clubs whose membership is recruited from the young men who have acquired a taste of the game by carrying clubs in their youth. There is no doubt that the caddie receives an education in this service which is of value in proportion as his master realises that the service involves a certain responsibility on his part as well as on that of the juvenile henchman. Golf, as most of us have discovered, is a trying game for the temper, and under such trials the best of men occasionally make use of expressions that they would rather have left unspoken. The caddies, it is to be feared, now and again hear some rather evil language in the mouths of those whom they have been taught to consider their betters. Perhaps it is no less evil than that which they hear elsewhere, but still it is the duty of every golfer to strive that they shall hear as little of it on the links as possible. Setting these points aside as really a small factor in the general result, there can be no doubt that in every other particular the general tendency on the development of the caddie must be for good. He learns to do as he is told, he is told what to do, if his master be a reasonable man, in a way that is in itself a lesson in manners to him, and he sees the manners of his masters to each other, manners which though they may not be the perfection of courtesy, are yet rather nearer the ideal of perfection than he is likely to come into contact with in other places of his resort; and in point of fact it is observed that the club-carrying trade does exercise a good effect on the general behaviour of the youngsters, which is in itself witness to the good social influence from one point of view, of the game on whose good points we love to dwell. Nor do we know that from any point of view its social influence, such as it is, is other than good.

ing to gain a doubtful point, never playing in a grudging spirit. Such at least is how the writer has found them, and how therefore it behoves him to speak of them. It is to be piously hoped that their knowledge of the amateur as learned at the game of golf may not have lowered their conception of that fine if much abused term of "gentleman."

In a more general way golf has had a social influence in distributing over the land those who claim at least, we may hope with justice, the name of gentlemen. The house agents will tell you that the value of a small country place is increased by something like fifty pounds a year if it be near a decent golf links; and it is really hard, in these good times, to avoid the proximity of a decent golf-links even if one wished to do so. It is perhaps less a social than a financial view of the case that golf brings money, and all its incidental blessings, wherever it goes. The amount that a flourishing golf club expends in any locality even directly is by no means inappreciable; this direct expenditure is probably but a circumstance to the money changing of which it is indirectly the cause. For wherever there is a green, there is immediately an inducement, even in the absence of any other inducement, for a man to build a house. In point of fact, most golf greens are the occasion of many houses being built about them. The building of houses supposes (not always with justice) people to live in them. This is directly a social influence. Indirectly, and more financially, one of the results is that people suppose (always with justice) a demand for food. Consequently the butcher sells, and ought to buy (we believe he often does not) at an advanced rate. Dairy farming and market gardening produce go up in price. The money comes flying about where it was a luxury before, and so gives means to further luxuries of leisure and enjoyment, of humble hospitality and mutual intercourse. Great is golf.

Next Week:

"SOME AMERICAN VIEWS OF GOLF."

GOLF GOSSIP.

(By Cleekum.)

The Islay Tournament proved the unqualified success that the energy of the executive and the perfection of the green merited. The first prize was £100, and there were few absentees of weight among the professionals; but Mr Hilton was unfortunately unable to come. No one of importance fell in the first round; but in the second Fernie, Sayers, Yeoman, Tom Vardon, and Tingey were knocked out. The third was played in deplorable weather, with heavy rain and wind at times approaching a gale. Taylor beat Vardon at the 25th hole after a tie; Herd beat James Kinnell by two; Kirkaldy beat Ralph Smith by one; and Braid beat White at the 19th hole after a tie. The semi-final was played in rather better weather. Taylor beat Herd by 2 and 1; Braid beat Kirkaldy by 2 and 1. The final was played in ideal golfing weather. The first round ended square in 79. Taylor finally won by one, although Braid had been two to the good at the turn. Taylor richly deserved his victory; but Braid's defeat is described as having been mainly due to loose work through the green followed by indifferent putting.

On Saturday Braid, Taylor, Vardon, and Fernie played over the Irvine course at Bogside. The first three could not reach the course from Islay till after mid-day; not one had ever seen Bogside before, and though they had been travelling all night they started within a quarter of an hour of their arrival and gave a capital exposition of the game. In the forenoon Fernie, 77 (41, 36), beat Taylor, 79 (42, 37), by 2 and 1; Braid, 78 (38, 40), beat Vardon, 80 (40, 40), by 2 and 1. In the afternoon a four-ball match was played, the best balls being taken between the two countries. England won by 3 and 2. Vardon and Taylor, 70 (36, 34); Braid and Fernie, 72 (37, 35).

Many of your St Andrews readers, from Old Tom downwards, will read with pleasure of the veteran William Doleman's winning the Roger Jubilee Casquet, confined to members of Scottish Clubs who are fifty years or over. It was played on Thursday over the St Nicholas green in stormy weather. Thirty-three entered, representing 12 clubs. Doleman won from scratch with an excellent 84.

Donald Blue – Caddie – had postcards made up from this photograph to give out to the members

Drinking fountain in centre to commemorate the Jubilee

198

Scottish Professional Golfers

IN THE

Open Tournament at Leith, 1867.

Described by W. DALRYMPLE.

THIS group, for which we are indebted to the courtesy of Mr. D. W. Walker, S.S.S., Hon. Sec. of the Mortonhall G.C., is one of the most interesting ever reproduced in connection with the game, and we are fortunate in being able to give all the names. In the case of some of the players pretty careful enquiry leads to the belief that no other likeness is extant. The tournament was played at Leith on May 14th, 1867, under the auspices of the Thistle G.C., for prizes amounting to £25—a sum that to the professional of to-day would seem ludicrously inadequate, but at that date sufficed to attract nearly every one of the leading professionals, as will be seen from the following draw:—

1, David Park v. Jamie Anderson; 2, Tom Morris v. Willie Park, sen.; 3, Willie Dunn v. Willie Dow; 4, George Morris (Old Tom's brother) v. Bob Dow, Montrose; 5, Walter McDonald, Perth, v. Thos Hunter; 6, Bob Kirk v. Young Tom; 7, Tom Brown, Musselburgh, v. G. Paterson, Musselburgh; 8, Alexander Brown v. J. Campbell, Musselburgh; 9, Bob Fergusson v. James Hutchison; 10, Jamie Dunn v. Sandy Greig; 11, Bob Andrews, Perth, v. A. Smith, Prestwick.

The result was:—Bob Fergusson, 131; Hunter, 132; Jamie Anderson, 133; Bob Andrews, 133; Park, 134. In playing off the tie, Andrews beat Anderson by two—31 to 33.

GEORGE MORRIS.

If only out of compliment to Old Tom, let us take his brother George first. This is believed to be the only likeness of him extant. He was for long coachman with the Chambers' family. Rather oddly, "Rook" Andrews, lately dead, was for years in the service of another well-known golfing family, the Condies of Perth.

An old crony of the Morrises, whose likeness you lately reproduced, told me that George had a prettier style than his brother, but was never quite so steady; and this opinion is shared by Old Tom himself. George's name appears very frequently on the roll of honour of the St. Andrews Club—a very powerful townsmen's Society.

The finest and most interesting match that Old Tom considers he has ever played, was between George and himself against Willie and Davie Park, at St. Andrews in May, '58. The match was one of thirty-six holes, and the former were never ahead till they gained the last hole! Auld Willie remembers this match well, and gave me note of another. In '53, as a lad of 20, he played George a single over the St. Andrews green. It was during this match that Allan Robertson remarked:—"He frichtens us a' wi' his lang driving!" Park finally won by some 10 or 12; but it was after he had run away with the first eight holes that he distinctly remembers George exclaiming:—"For the love o' God, gi'e me a hawf!" Park corroborates that George Morris had a capital style.

OLD AND YOUNG TOM.

It would be sheer waste of space in any paper specially devoted to our game to linger over these well-known and loved names; but we may draw attention to the fact that both of the likenesses show marked differences from those with which we are most familiar. This is, perhaps, most noticeable in the case of Old Tom. That of his son is described to me by an old crony of him and Davie Strath, as undoubtedly an admirable likeness, but one that he had never seen before.

SANDY GREIG

Was a well-known player in his day, but never succeeded in getting into quite the front rank. Mr. Patrick remembers him quite well, but identifies him with Musselburgh rather than Leith.

WILLIE DOW,

On the other hand, was reputed one of the prettiest golfers of his time, and among the best; and in his case, too, this is believed to be the only likeness extant. A year or two ago Willie Park, jun., and Douglas McEwan, of Musselburgh, were kind enough to push some enquiry for me among their workmen; but, so far as they could learn, Dow's family is extinct in his old home.

Auld Willie remembers him well as "a very fine player—a rattling golfer and very long driver," whilst Old Tom describes him as "playing a great game," and gives rather an interesting yarn about him. Many a long year ago Major Bethune asked Tom if he thought he could tackle this formidable Musselburgh man. Tom cautiously replied that he could try anyway. He did and won.

The famous matches that Dow played, with varying fortune, are innumerable; but we have only space to note one or two. Thus, Park once allowed him three strokes on the three rounds of the home green. Dow was dormy one, but Park stymied and won in playing out. Again, at Prestwick in '62, he lost to Park by four out of twelve, but won next day by two. At the '64 September meeting, at Prestwick, he beat Park by a single over the two rounds; and so on.

The retirement of Tom Morris from the custodianship of St. Andrews Links is an event which may be said to mark the close of an epoch in the history of golf. "Old Tom" has been the tutelary genius of the classic green since most of us can remember and a good bit more, and he has been regarded by all golfers with an esteem and affection which falls to the lot of few men in any station of life.

BOB KIRK.

"I remember Bob Kirk very well," Old Tom told me. "He was a club-maker and a very fine player—none better—and used to keep the Blackheath green."

Small wonder that Old Tom remembers him! The two, away back in '65, inaugurated a satanic copartnery that pranced gaily over the length and breadth of Golf land—casually potting the Park brothers, Park and Strath, Park and Dow and so on! Auld Willie describes Kirk as "a good player and vicious hitter, but inclined to top."

The name of Kirk has, in fact, been associated with first-class Golf at St. Andrews for three generations. In the "sixties" no fewer than three appear on the roll of the St. Andrews Club; and our man is the son of yet another Bob, of whom Lockhart warbled :—

Swells like "Daw" or old Bob,
The apple-faced sage, with his nostrum for all,
"Dinna hurry the swing! Keep your e'e on the ball!"

He seems to have been at his best in '67. On the 3rd of May he won the first professional prize with 80 and—I have no pleasure in recording this—potted Old Tom by 12 in a thirty-six hole game! He also beat Young Tom by three; and in '68 by six and four in a thirty-six hole match!

But Kirk's memory should be kept green for yet another reason. He once extricated himself from an otherwise hopeless situation and won an important match, *thanks to his carrying a left-handed club!*

AUTUMN MEETING OF THE ROYAL AND ANCIENT GOLF CLUB

Intimation of my retirement 1902

The usual business meeting of the Club was held in the Club-House on Tuesday evening – Sir John Gilmour in the chair. Mr Cathcart, Chairman of the Green Committee, reported that Tom Morris had some time ago intimated his resignation of the position of greenkeeper, owing to his advancing years, and that the Green Committee were at present arranging for the appointment of a successor. It was unanimously agreed to record in the minutes the Club's appreciation of Tom Morris's long and faithful services, along with the hope he might be long spared to go about the Links. Mr Cathcart further reported that he might be long spared to go about the Links. Mr Cathcart further reported that the Green Committee thought Tom should continue to receive his present salary for the rest of his life, and be appointed honorary advising greenkeeper. He will accordingly continue to start the Club and Championship competitions......

TOM MORRIS'S CAREER

No figure is more familiar in the world of golf than that of Tom Morris. Born in North Street, St Andrews, in 1821, Tom at the age of 10 or 12 began to knock golf balls about on St Andrews Links, and soon afterwards became an apprentice to the famous Allan Robertson as a clubmaker. He quickly developed into a splendid player, and tried conclusions with even the great Allan Robertson himself. Allan was then *facile princeps* among golfers, yet on more than one occasion Tom played against him on equal terms and won. Allan and Tom were frequent partners in great golf matches. Mr H. S. C. Everard tells briefly in the Badminton book the story of the first match of importance in which Tom was a player – a foursome for £400, over Musselburgh, St Andrews, and North Berwick Links. Allan Robertson and Tom were opposed to Willie Dunn and James Dunn, of Musselburgh. The match system then in vogue was different from that now followed. The result did not depend on the aggregate number of holes won during the whole match. The play on each green stood by itself as a gain or a loss. Over their own green the Dunns were winners by 13 and 12 to play. Over St Andrews green Allan and Tom were winners by a narrow majority. The decisive battle was thus left to be tried on North Berwick Links. There the St Andrews couple halved the first round, lost the second by four, and halved the third. At the fourth hole of the last round they were five down. They were still four down when only eight holes remained to be played. "Odds of 20 to 1," says Mr Everard, "were freely laid on the Dunns, but here began a most extraordinary run of surprises, for Allan and Tom won the first hole, then the second, halved the third, won the fourth, halved the fifth, and won the sixth – all square and two to play. Amid breathless excitement Tom played a fine tee shot, which, however was not well followed up by his partner. The brothers, however, by pulling their second shot off the course, landed under a large boulder, and thus lost the hole, so Tom and his partner, retaining their advantage, pulled this remarkable match out of the fire." On the expiration of this time with Allan, Tom started a separate business on his own account; but in 1851, chiefly through the instrumentality of Colonel Fairlie of Coodham, for whom he carried clubs, Tom was appointed custodian of Prestwick Golf Links, just then established as a golf course. In this capacity he remained for 14 years, and in 1865 returned to the old grey city, which he has never since quitted. To record in detail Tom's famous matches would fill a volume. He has the credit of having won four Open Championships, namely, in 1861, 1862, 1864, and 1867. It is still to be one of his privileges though on the retired list, that Old Tom should superintend at the starting box on medal days, and on Wednesday he was out in good time, and in excellent health and spirits, to attend to his duty. Needless to say, he received from the members many expressions of their good wishes for pleasant years to be spent on his retirement.

From the *County Families Gazette*:—"H. Vardon and W. Fernie played an exhibition match on the new municipal links at Troon. . . . The course, which is 67,866 yards in length, is the longest in the United Kingdom." 38½ MILES!

The Beginning of My Golf.

V.—BY TOM MORRIS.

"THE beginning of my golf." Well, that is rather an old story now, because, you know, I have been playing golf off and on for the last seventy odd years, and that's a longer time, I'm thinking, than the most of folk now living can say. So you see it is a good bit to go back, and it is not so easy for me to mind just the very commencement of my playing, but I will try my best to tell you as much about it as I can remember.

There is one thing, at any rate, about which there cannot be any doubt at all, and that is *where* I began to play; for it was just on these same links as you can see before you now, although they were, of course, very different indeed, both in appearance and to play over, in these early days I am speaking of, from what they are like now. But I will, maybe, have something to say about what they were like at that time as I go on.

I began, then, to play golf down here, I am quite sure, as soon as ever I was able to handle or swing a club. Indeed, I must say that I don't remember when I didn't play, and I have been doing not much else ever since. My father and mother lived up in North Street, and it was there that I was born. My father was a weaver to his trade, and I am pretty sure I was intended to be a weaver too, but that never came off. For, somehow or other, both when I was at the school and after I had left it, and not very much of schooling did we get in these days—no, not very nearly so much as the young laddies get nowadays—I had always a very strong liking for the links and for playing at golf, and I can mind nicely how I and my companions used to go away down to the links, whenever we could get the chance, and with any kind of a club we could get a hold of, very funny-looking things some of them were, too, I can assure you, and I have often wondered what the golfers of the present day would have said about them; if they could only have seen them. And, as for balls, we had almost always to be contented with an old one, or, when we could not even manage that—and this was very often the case—we then had to be satisfied with only *a piece* of one. The balls were quite as dear in these old days as they are now, for the "featheries" cost half-a-crown apiece, and then, perhaps, too, we did not have so much money in our pockets.

I think I would be about right in saying that, whatever I may have done in the way of handling a club previously, I began to play golf in reality when I was about six or seven years of age, and I continued to do so, at every available opportunity, until, in due time, I went to work at making clubs and balls, principally the latter, with Allan Robertson. The feather ball, of course, it was at first, and I was still working there when the new guttas came in, and a fine how-do-you-do they caused between Allan and me.

I can remember the circumstances well. It all happened in this way. Allan could not reconcile himself to the new ball at first at all, just in the same way as Mr. John Low and many other golfers could not take to the Haskell when it first appeared. But the gutta became the fashion very quickly, as the rubber-cored ball has done, so what could we do? One day, and it is one that will always be clearly stamped upon my memory, I had been out playing golf with a Mr. Campbell, of Saddell, and I had the misfortune to lose all my supply of balls, which were, you can well understand, very much easier lost in those days, as the fairway of the course was ever so much narrower then than it is now, and with thick, bushy whins close in at the side. But to return to my story. I had, as I said, run short of balls, and Mr. Campbell kindly gave me a gutta one to try. I took to it at once, and, as we were playing in, it so happened that we met Allan Robertson coming out, and someone told him that I was playing a

THERE'S a notable Ancient named Tom
Whose fame is familiar from
Dunedin to Disko,
From Frankfort to 'Frisco,
And long may he flourish—Old Tom.

from the expression of his face, that he did not like it at all, and, when we met afterwards in his shop, we had some high words about the matter, and there and then we parted company, I leaving his employment. This minds me of something now. There are two big bushes out there in Allan's old garden. Well, one of them was planted by him and the other by me, just about that same time, so that they cannot be young bushes now.

But I must say that Allan had a great deal to do with the making of me, both as a golfer and otherwise. Because, although, before going to work with him at ball-making, I had always, as I have said, played golf almost from my very childhood, it was, in reality, only after I went into his workshop and had begun to play matches with him, that my game was drawn out, so to speak. He and I were the very best of good friends and quite inseparable partners then, and many and many a fine foursome did we play, all of which it would be perfectly impossible for me to relate here, for I am not able to remember the one half of them now. But these were really grand days, and he was, without a doubt, the best of partners. He was older than me by about some five or six years, having been born in 1815, the same year in which the battle of Waterloo was fought, and he died on the first day of September, 1859. His comparatively early death left me the master of the field here, for a while, at least, until some of the younger men, including my own son, Tommy, began to come to the front.

I don't know if you have ever heard how narrowly I escaped being made a Freemason in these early days. It was many, many years ago now, while Allan lived. Major Hay pleaded very hard indeed with the two of us to come and join the craft, and he was so keen about it that he even offered to pay all our expenses in connection with the interesting ceremony of taking "the word." Allan was, from the first, very doubtful of any benefits that might come from the concern, and he hesitated; on the other hand, I was quite willing to risk it, and had made great preparations. But, almost at the last minute, Allan backed out of it altogether, and so that was one match of ours at any rate which was never played, for I would not go into the thing at all without Allan, and "off" it has remained ever since that time.

I have said that the links here were very different in my young days from what they are like now, and I am sure I would be right, too, in saying that the golfers, playing over them today, would scarcely have recognised them as the same place. About 1835 or so, when Major Playfair, afterwards Sir Hugh, became the Provost of St. Andrews, he set about improving the links in real earnest; before that time they were very little more than an untrodden waste. And for a long time afterwards the old course—the only one then, because, you know, it is not so many years ago since the new one was made—consisted of but one single line of holes and putting greens, and both the outgoing and incoming golfers had to play at the same hole. I don't know, I am sure, if the people nowadays quite realise how much they are indebted to the late Provost Sir Hugh Playfair for the great and successful efforts he made for the betterment of our links. Up to Sir Hugh's time there was no club-house for the Royal and Ancient Golf Club, and it was mainly through his exertions rooms were rented for the accommodation of the members in a small, one-storey house, which was always after that called the Union Parlour, at that corner there where the Grand Hotel now stands. The present club-house was not begun to be built until about 1854.

In these times, you know, golfers were looked upon as men who had "mair siller than sense," and I've heard some folk say the same not so very long ago: but they're wrong.

ing company with Allan Robertson. After I left his workshop I began to work at ball-making on my own account. It was still the feather balls that I made. I am not sure if many people now will know how the old featheries were made, and, as it may be of interest, I will just tell you how we used to do it. You had a little bag or pocket composed of bull's hide, which had previously been cured with alum, and then you stuffed it as full as possible with feathers. You could put about a hatful of feathers into one ball, and the stuffing of them was no easy job, I can tell you. When that was done, you had just to sew up the opening in the side of the pocket and then your ball was made.

I did not begin to make the new gutta balls until I was about thirty years of age, and it would be just about the same time that I left St. Andrews to go to be the green-keeper and professional at Prestwick. It was Colonel J. O. Fairlie who got me the job and persuaded me to go there. He was one of the very best friends I think I have ever had, and I am sure no better and kinder-hearted gentleman than him ever lived.

There is one very funny thing about Colonel Fairlie which I must tell you, and it is this. That it was he who first taught me to smoke, and it happened in this way: In these early days, you know, there was no club-house at Prestwick, and the members of the club frequently had to resort to taking their luncheon, between the forenoon and afternoon rounds, on the green near the last hole, and it was at such times that the Colonel would often give me a cigar. Then one day, I well remember, he gave me a pipe, and I had just to buy some tobacco for myself, and after that I was a smoker for life. I had never smoked at all when I was a boy, and I would not now advise boys to smoke, young boys at least. But if I did not smoke until I was well on in life, I think I have made up for it by now, and to spare, for I have always done so regularly ever since that time, except upon one occasion, when I gave it up for about six weeks or so. You will maybe be saying, what has all this talk about smoking to do with the beginning of my golf? But I will say that it has to do with Colonel Fairlie, and he had a very great deal to do with both me and my golf.

These six weeks I speak of were just before I played my first big match for a money stake, which was with old Willie Park, of Musselburgh, and in which we played over four greens. Of course, from the time that I first went to Allan Robertson's workshop until this big match I had kept on playing golf regularly. But I went into real hard training for these six weeks, and practised very industriously, playing two rounds every day, without ever missing once. I then played him the match over the links of Prestwick, Musselburgh, North Berwick, and St. Andrews, and I succeeded in getting the better of him on each of those four greens, and was able finally to win the match at the second hole going out down there during the afternoon round.

It was at that hole, and on that day, that I played what was, I think, one of the very best shots that I have ever done, at least that I can remember of now. My ball was lying very badly, quite close beside what we called at that time "the Rashies"; they were to the right, and near the edge of the whins, but players nowadays won't know what I mean, I'm thinking. However, bad as the lie was, I managed to get my ball very well away, so well indeed, that it landed and lay nicely on the putting green; I then holed out the putt, doing the hole in three, and I can remember, too, that I also did the third hole in three strokes in the same match.

Big, important matches were oftener counted by greens than by holes at that time, and I believe it was the great £200 a-side foursome, which I took part in some time afterwards, that helped to bring about a change in that order of things. This was, of course, the match that Allan and I played against the two Dunns over Musselburgh, North Berwick, and St. Andrews, but I think I hardly need to repeat anything about the playing of it here, for I know it is all down in print already. But I can mind fine how Allan and I got our "licks" very badly at Musselburgh, but after that we managed to beat them at both North Berwick and St. Andrews. So you see that although the Dunns beat us counting by holes, we beat them counting by greens, and, as I have said, I think that matches were always reckoned by holes after that instead of by greens, just as the big foursome was the other week.

Then you know the Championship Belt was played for in these days. Willie Park won it on three different occasions, and I won it on four, but not year after year. Then my son Tommy was the winner of it for three years running, and having done so, it became his own property for good.

I have the belt in my house now, and it is the proudest possession that I have—in my eyes it is absolutely priceless. It is composed of a big, broad belt of dark red Morocco leather, with rich golfing designs in silver upon it as ornaments.

I could also show you two photographs—extremely interesting and valuable to me—of my two sons, Tommy and Jimmy. They are in one frame, and underneath the pictures are printed their best scores round St. Andrews Links, and curiously enough the totals are exactly the same—77. Tommy did it in 1869, going out in 37 strokes and returning in 40, and in 1887 Jimmy went out in 38 and came home in 39, both 77.

It was in 1864 that I left Prestwick to come back to St. Andrews again, as the greenkeeper of these links, and I have lived here ever since, and have always been playing golf, whenever I could get it, both at home and on other greens. But I have not lifted a club for a good while now—except my putter, in an occasional foursome with some of the ladies round their putting course—though I still take a great interest in the game, which I think, as I always have done, is the best that men—aye, and ladies, too—can play at.

I must say that I have never had the slightest cause to regret having returned to my dear native town, where everyone is my friend, and in which I don't think I have a single enemy.

Tom Morris

In my favourite chair
in the New Club
sketched for my 85th birthday

Sir George Reid, President of the Royal Scottish Academy, would, I feel sure, make a grand picture of the veteran, for he has such a head as Sir George especially delights in and excels at painting. Might not Old Tom be approached and a subscription list started for the picture? I am sure that golfers all the world over would gladly subscribe.

Golf Illustrated
1899

✠ ✠ ✠

and it was done just after my retirement in 1902

203

I've pasted in a full report of this Open as it may be the last I ever see again at St Andrews

June 1905

The Open Championship.

VICTORY OF JAMES BRAID.

THE classic links of St. Andrews had evidently been carefully prepared for the Open Championship with the intention of making it a severe test, even with the rubber ball in use. None but past-masters of the game had the slightest chance of returning a good score, and many of the most accomplished exponents of the game had to confess themselves beaten by the lengthened and profusely bunkered course. Complaints were freely made that the bunkers are too numerous and that in several instances they are unfair. Many an apparently excellent shot was found to be trapped, sometimes with disastrous results, and it was no unusual thing to hear a player declare while returning a bad score that he had played really a good game, and that golf on St. Andrews links was now largely a question of luck. These observations are given, of course, for what they are worth; but it is clear from the results that the course was found to be exceptionally trying.

THE CLUB-HOUSE AND EIGHTEENTH GREEN.

It is true that the strong cross-wind on the first day added considerably to the difficulty of making a low return, but on the second day the weather was by no means so bad, yet many scores handed in were higher than those for the first round. Much of the high scoring was due, by common consent, to the "glassy" condition of the greens, and consequently great credit must be given to those who succeeded, in spite of all the adverse conditions, in making good scores.

The greatest honour is, of course, due to James Braid, the ultimate winner, who played throughout—as he did in the recent tournament under similar conditions, at Bushey—like one who was winning all the time. His power on the tee is known to everybody, but it is not so well known, probably, that he has been making a scientific study of the delicate business of putting on hard greens. In the most systematic way at St. Andrews he would take his aluminium putter for his approach putts and then change to the putting cleek for holing out the short ones. His running-up shots, too, it was a treat to witness, and altogether his game and his style were admirable and deserved the substantial reward they earned for him.

This is, of course, his second lease of championship honours, his first being won at Muirfield in 1901. He was sixth in 1896, second in 1897 (only a stroke behind the winner), eleventh in 1898, fifth in 1899, third in 1900, he tied with Harry Vardon for second place (a stroke above A. Herd) in 1902, was fifth in 1903, and tied with J. H. Taylor (a stroke above Jack White) for second place last year. Truly, a wonderful record! in which the new champion may justifiably take pride. The winning score this year is nine strokes higher than that with which Braid won at Muirfield, when the gutty ball was in use. It is also nine strokes higher than that with which J. H. Taylor won with the same ball at St. Andrews in 1900. While, however, the fourteenth place in 1900 was won with a score of 337, there were twenty-three players who finished this year with a total of 336 or under. No more conclusive proof of the improvement in the general standard of play could be furnished.

First Day's Play.

The weather played a very important part in the first round of the great annual competition. For several days prior to June 6th the skies had been bright and the sea calm. What wind there had been came mainly from a northerly or southerly direction, and the professionals gathered together at St. Andrews from all parts of the kingdom had been reporting excellent scores as the result of their practice play. On the morning of June 6th, however, the crowd of aspirants for championship honours awoke to find that a strong wind was blowing and the biting nature of it was unpleasant but convincing proof that it came from that worst of all directions—the east. In the morning there was a little north in it. Instead of having a following or a head wind, therefore, the players were severely tried by a cross wind all the way round.

The record entry of 152 players had made a three days' meeting necessary, as at Sandwich last year. All the entrants except six put in an appearance at the first tee, and a large number of the early starters were sent on their first round

THE OLD BRIDGE OVER THE SWILCAN BURN.

by old Tom Morris, who, unfortunately, was looking somewhat feeble.

There had been during the preceding week much talk about the considerable increase which had been made in the bunkers on the classic course, and it is only recording facts to say that much of the criticism passed on the changes was far from favourable.

Certainly there were very few really good scores returned. On the last occasion on which the championship was decided at St. Andrews, in 1900, J. H. Taylor's winning score was 309, as compared with the same player's 322 in 1895, yielding averages of 77¼ and 80½ per round. Last year, at Sandwich, Jack White won with 296, or an average of 74.

Much speculation was indulged in on the question whether or no the tendency shown during the past few years for the winning scores to undergo steady, if not rapid, reduction, would be continued. This first round, unless followed by some decided improvement in the subsequent rounds, knocked on the head any hope of reduction this year. Of all the 146 starters not one was able to complete the course in less than 80 strokes, and only four were able to keep their total within that limit. Nine others came within a stroke of it, six more within two strokes, and three finished at 83. On the other hand there were 53 over 90. The much larger number of the higher scorers were returned by those who started after noon. Play began at 9 a.m., and an interval of five minutes being allowed between the couples, it was 3 o'clock in the afternoon before the last pair could be despatched on their journey.

HARRY VARDON'S BUNKER SHOT AT THE THIRTEENTH ON FRIDAY MORNING.

Amongst the early starters was J. H. Taylor, who naturally took away a big "gallery" with him. He made an auspicious start with three 4's, and continued steadily on his way up to the ninth, where he had a putt of about a yard in length for 37, but he failed to hole it. This was his first really serious mistake, and he finished the first half in 38, a score attained by extremely few of his competitors. In the inward half he was not quite so steady. At the long hole in he missed a putt and took 6. At the seventeenth his pitch on to the green was a shade too strong and he ran into the footpath. He required two more to get back, and eventually took 7. Another missed putt on the last green took his total to 80. It should have been three, if not four, strokes less, but as events proved it was not beaten by any competitor.

The only other players who equalled Taylor's score on the first day were Alex. Herd, Harry Vardon and Walter Toogood. Vardon, who had been unluckily struck in the back on the previous day from a tee shot by his fellow-Jerseyite, Edward Ray, was happily recovered from the blow. He played a good game on the whole and showed some improvement in his putting. A missed second at the fifth hole led to a 6 being ultimately recorded and to the half-round costing him a stroke more than his great rival, although he took the eighth and ninth in 3 and 4. He started homeward by pulling into the whins, and his card was spoiled by another 6. From this point he played a sterling game, except for a short putt missed on the last green. This, however, seemed to be the experience of about five out of six players who were not stoney dead from the approach putt or run up. Herd's 80 was the result of good steady play under trying conditions. He had a yard putt on the eighteenth green for 79, but, like others before and after, he failed to hole it. Walter Toogood, after starting with 4 and 6, had a remarkable run of 4's, securing nine holes in succession in that figure. Afterwards he had a considerable run of 5's. Having gone out in 38, his 42 home still enabled him to equal the best score for the day. Toogood was driving splendidly.

Another player who had an excellent chance to beat this score was T. G. Renouf, who, while taking 40 for his first half, was still only four over 4's with four holes to play. He found the bunkers at the fifteenth and seventeenth, however, and took 6 for each hole. He yet had a 4 at the last for 80, but required 5, and thus his total was 81. This gave him a tie with Braid, who had made a very unsteady start and was six over 4's at the seventh hole and at the turn. He was a little wild in his driving occasionally, and he, like everybody else, found putting extremely ticklish work on the glassy, wind-swept greens. Others who finished in 81 were Wilfrid E. Reid (Versailles), Arnaud Massy, J. Sherlock, Alec Smith (Nassau County), R. Thomson and R. Hunt. E. Ray spoilt his card with three 7's, mainly the result of strokes lost on the greens. It may in short be said that this was the main cause of the bulk of the high scores. Alfred Toogood was not in good health, and had the tall score, for him, of 89.

The only player amongst the amateurs to make a really good score was Mr. John Graham, jun., who finished in 83. He started steadily with two 4's, but he occasionally dropped a stroke and at the fifteenth he was bunkered, and a 6 was recorded. Otherwise he played a strong game. The Amateur Champion (Mr. A. G. Barry) reached the turn in a good score of 40, but he went off his wooden club play on the return journey. At the last hole he got a great slice on to his second shot and the ball almost went into an upper window of one of the houses off the roadside. The next best amateur score to that of Mr. Graham was Mr. W. H. Fowler's 86. Mr. Jas. G. Craik, of St. Andrews, Mr. Norman Hunter, Mr. H. H. Hilton and Mr. Edward Blackwell all finished at 87. The Hon. Osmund Scott took 88, and Mr. R. Maxwell and Mr. G. S. Lyon (the Canadian Champion), 89.

Second Day's Play.

A considerable improvement in the weather was experienced on the second day. The sun once more shone through an unclouded sky, and although the wind was still blowing from the east it was much less strong, and a great improvement in the scoring was anticipated. Strangely enough, this expectation was not realised for a considerable period. A large proportion of the scores of the early starters were even higher than those returned by the same players on the preceding day. The first good one was that handed in by James Sherlock, the Oxford professional, and winner of the Ranfurly tournament, but his round of 84 was three strokes higher than his first. J. H. Taylor shared in the misfortunes of the "early birds." A start of 4, 5 and 6 was far from satisfactory. The 6 was the result of a visit to the bunker at the left hand edge of the third green and of the necessity of playing two shots to get out. Three 5's and three 4's followed, and his total for the half round ran up to 42. He started homeward well by taking the first four holes in an average of 4's, but he afterwards found the putting rather treacherous. At the sixteenth he was trapped, and at the seventeenth, as on the first day, he ran over the narrow green into the foot-road. Two 6's at the sixteenth and seventeenth may have unnerved him: anyway, he failed with his drive on the last tee and struck the old stone footbridge over the Eden. Eventually holing out in 5, he had a total of 85, five strokes greater than his first round.

BRAID'S RAILWAY SHOT AT THE SIXTEENTH IN THE FINAL ROUND.

Andrew Kirkaldy exactly equalled his first round of 83, and Alex. Herd was unable to equal his 80 of the first day, but he gained three strokes on Taylor by returning an 82. He was out in 38, but his game in the return half was somewhat unsteady. It should be remembered, however, that the incoming was the more difficult half, not only by reason of the length but of the wind. At this point Herd was the leader, but he was soon afterwards displaced by Arnaud Massy, who came in with an excellent score of 80, only marred by a 7 at the Road hole. He had a 5 and a 4 for 76, but he sliced his drive on the seventeenth tee and paid a visit to the station-master's garden. Before succeeding in holing out he had taken seven shots, and he lost a stroke by over-approaching the last green.

Quickly following Massy came James Braid, who was the first to return a score under 80. He gave no promise of doing this when he started for he found the greens very slippery, and in consequence of the difficulty in holing out he registered three 5's. Subsequently he gauged the strength better, and, playing a powerful and steady game, he reached the turn in 40. He gave a pretty exposition of perfect golf on the way home, securing the nine sporting and difficult holes in 38. His total was thus 78, and he accordingly in turn displaced Massy from the leadership. The details of his round were:—

Out	..	5	5	4	5	4	5	3	4=40	
Home	..	3	4	4	5	5	4	5	4=38	=78

Some sensation was caused when, a little later, Braid was himself relegated to second position by Rowland Jones, who, in spite of several brilliant performances in recent times, was scarcely looked upon as a likely man to outdo the "Elie giant." Nevertheless he succeeded in beating Braid's score by a stroke and returning the best round of the day, made up as follows:—

Out	..	3	5	6	5	5	4	4	3	4=39
In	..	4	4	4	5	4	3	5	5=38	=77

Jones was almost the only player who managed to squeeze three 3's into one round. Those for the first and sixteenth were particularly brilliant efforts. From the sixth hole onwards his game was practically perfect, his 4 at the eleventh and 5 at the last hole being the only scores that could well have been bettered.

The only other player who succeeded in getting below 80 was James Kinnell, of Purley Downs. His score of 79 was the outcome of sterling golf and especially of putting that was above the average attainments of the crowd of professionals competing.

A score of 81 was achieved by Tom Williamson (Notts), R. Thomson (Romford), J. Johnston (Glasgow), E. Gray (Littlehampton), Laurence Gourlay (Kettering), Willie Park (Huntercombe) and Jack Rowe (Ashdown Forest). One stroke higher came, in addition to Alex. Herd, E. Ray (Ganton), who was putting better; A. W. Brown (Worsley), who had taken ten strokes more on the previous day; J. Parr (Bromborough), J. B. Batley (Bushey), and last, but not least, Harry Vardon.

The game shown by Harry Vardon was a little variable. As on the first round, he reached the turn in 39, and for the first four holes in he was two strokes better. At the twelfth he was bunkered from the tee but reached the green with a pretty third, and holed out in a very fair 5. At the thirteenth a beautiful brassie shot was trapped by a pot bunker near the edge of the green. He got well out, and on to the green, and, holing an 18-yard putt, got a 4. By this time a great gallery had assembled, and at times the progress and freedom of the players were considerably hampered. In one instance, indeed, a ball driven by Vardon's partner, Mr. C. A. Palmer, fell in the midst of the crowd, and one gentleman had cause to remember the occurrence for the rest of the day. At the long hole Vardon just failed to get down a three-yard putt for a 5, and at the fifteenth he had a similar experience with a two-yarder for 4. A 16-yard putt at the sixteenth hit the back of the hole but failed to drop in. The seventeenth even Vardon, going strongly, found very difficult to play, and it was necessary to write down a 6 on his card. A very curious thing happened at the last hole. In playing his second shot Vardon got the ball up to a great height and there was so much slice on that the ball curled right round to the houses overlooking the home hole and bounced off the top of the bay window of an upper room on to the roof of the four-storey building. Dropping another ball, Vardon this time got away a perfect shot and holed out in 5.

Walter Toogood, who was amongst the four players who tied for the best score on the first day, took 83. His cousin, Alfred Toogood, who was now in better health again, also returned an 83.

Jack White, the holder of the title, also finished in 83, and thus took three strokes off his first round, but his aggregate of 169 left him eleven strokes behind the leader and ten strokes worse than Braid. Other players who returned 83 were James Kay (Seaton Carew), J. Taylor (Aldeburgh) and A. H. Scott (Earlsferry). The last-named took ten strokes more for the first round.

The amateurs were again, with the solitary exception of Mr. John Graham, out of the running. He again played a powerful long game, and, while many others were adding a considerable number of strokes to their previous score, he kept his second round within a stroke of his first. Thus he finished with an aggregate of 167, or nine strokes behind the leading return. No other amateur, not even Mr. Maxwell or Mr. Hilton, succeeded in qualifying for the final day's play. Mr. Barry was driving a very long ball, and he managed to get round in six strokes less than on the first attempt; but Mr. Maxwell, losing many strokes on the fiery greens, could do no better than 88, one stroke less.

The leader's score being 158, all players with scores over 172 were excluded by the new rule from participating in the final day's play. It will be remembered that whereas 20 strokes was formerly the excluding limit it had been resolved since the championship was last held that in future competitors who came fifteen strokes or more behind the leader at the end of the second round should be compulsorily retired. By the operation of this rule only 45 players, or considerably less than one-third of the starters, were entitled to take part in the third and fourth rounds. Last year a score of 168 qualified, and in the previous year the figure was 169.

First and Second Round Scores.

The scores for the first and second rounds were as follow:—

	1st rd.	2nd rd.	Total.
Rowland Jones (Wimbledon)	81	77	158
James Braid (Walton Heath)	81	78	159
Arnaud Massy (North Berwick)	81	80	161
Jas. Kinnell (Purley Downs)	82	79	161
A. Herd (Huddersfield)	80	82	162
H. Vardon (Totteridge)	80	82	162
R. Thomson (Romford)	81	81	162
Walter Toogood (Ilkley)	80	83	163
Ernest Gray (Littlehampton)	82	81	163
J. Sherlock (Oxford)	81	84	165
J. H. Taylor (Richmond)	80	85	165
Tom Williamson (Nottingham)	84	81	165
W. Park (Huntercombe)	84	81	165
Andrew Kirkaldy (St. Andrews)	83	83	166
T. G. Renouf (Silloth)	81	85	166
E. Ray (Ganton)	85	82	167
Mr. J. Graham, jun. (Royal Liverpool) ..	83	84	167
A. Matthews (Rhyl)	84	84	168
James Hepburn (Surbiton)	84	84	168
J. Johnston (Glasgow)	87	81	168
J. Parr (Bromborough)	86	82	168
James Kay (Seaton Carew)	85	83	168
John Rowe (Royal Ashdown Forest) ..	87	81	168
W. Hunter (Richmond)	84	85	169
A. Smith (Nassau County)	81	88	169
Wilfred Reid (Versailles)	81	88	169
H. Cawsey (Ashford)	82	87	169
Willie Fernie (Troon)	83	86	169
Jack White (Sunningdale)	86	83	169
D. Stephenson (Huntercombe)	84	86	170
Tom Vardon (Sandwich)	84	86	170
T. Simpson (St. Anne's-on-Sea)	82	88	170
H. Hunt (Reigate Heath)	81	89	170
James B. Batley (Bushey)	88	82	170
Percy Hills (Manchester)	87	84	171
Ernest Foord (Burnham)	85	86	171
John Johnstone (North Berwick) ..	85	86	171
Tom Watt (Southport)	86	85	171
Archie Simpson (Aberdeen)	87	84	171
Charles Gibson (Royal North Devon) ..	87	85	172
Ben Sayers (North Berwick)	84	88	172
A. H. Toogood (West Essex)	89	83	172
Fred Collins (Llandudno)	86	86	172
J. Taylor (Aldeburgh)	89	83	172
Robert Simpson (Carnoustie)	87	85	172

The foregoing qualified for the final rounds. Other returns were:—

	1st rd.	2nd rd.	Total.
C. R. Smith (West Middlesex)	87	86	173
J. Forrester (Earlsferry)	84	89	173
P. G. Wyatt (Herne Bay)	88	85	173
P. J. Gaudin (Manchester)	86	87	173
Mr. A. G. Barry (St. Andrews University)	90	84	174
L. Gourlay (Kettering)	93	81	174
P. Wynne (Tooting Bec)	87	87	174
A. W. Brown (Worsley)	92	82	174
G. Cawkwell (Sheffield)	87	87	174
Willie Anderson (New York)	86	88	174
J. D. Edgar (Newcastle-on-Tyne) ..	90	85	175
Mr. H. H. Hilton (Royal Liverpool) ..	87	88	17
G. Pannell (Littlehampton)	90	86	176
G. Coburn (Erskine)	89	87	176
A. Denholm (Brighton and Hove) ..	88	88	176
John Hughes (Hunstanton)	85	91	176
Mr. T. M. Hunter (Honourable Company)	91	85	176
A. H. Scott (Earlsferry)	93	83	176
Mr. C. A. Palmer (Handsworth) ..	91	85	176
Hon. Osmund Scott (Royal North Devon)	88	89	177
T. G. Renouf (Manchester)	91	86	177
W. Auchterlonie (St. Andrews) ..	90	87	177
Davie Grant (North Berwick)	92	85	177
J. Kirkaldy (St. Andrews)	89	88	177
G. Duncan (Timperley)	88	89	177
Jas. Nelson (Peebles)	89	88	177
A. Tingey (West Herts)	91	86	177
Mr. R. Maxwell (Tantallon)	89	88	177
G. H. Cawsey (Malvern)	85	92	177
Mr. A. Gallacher (St. Andrews Thistle) ..	92	85	177
W. P. Lewis (King's Norton)	90	87	177
Arthur Catlin (Mid-Herts)	93	85	178
A. Guthrie (Portmarnock)	93	85	178
T. Yeoman (Seaford)	91	87	178
G. Pulford (Northwich)	82	96	178
E. Sinclair (Leith)	8[illegible]	[illegible]	[illegible]

	1st rd.	2nd rd.	Total.
W. Hambleton (Romiley)	87	92	179
Mr. J. Walker (Barton-on-Sea)	89	90	179
A. F. Kettley (Shoreham)	86	93	179
A. Beck (Filey)	87	92	179
J. L. Cassidy (Harrogate)	92	87	179
F. Coltart (Perth)	88	91	179
Mr. G. S. Lyon (Lambton, America)	89	90	179
E. H. Risebro (Norwich)	88	91	179
W. Hutchings (Derby)	89	90	179
Mr. J. G. Craik (New Club, St. Andrews) ..	87	93	180
H. Hamill (Portrush)	94	86	180
Mr. T. A. Kennedy (Edinburgh University) ..	91	89	180
T. Jamieson (St. Michael's)	94	86	180
W. L. Mackie (Barnehurst)	91	89	180
D. Kenny (Kirkcudbright)	89	91	180

Mr Norman Hunter, Mr. Edward Blackwell and Mr. W. H. Fowler retired after the first round.

The Concluding Day's Play.

The weather on the concluding day was delightful. The warmth was pleasantly tempered by a cool breeze, and everything was favourable to a good finish. There was only a difference of seven strokes in the scores of fifteen competitors, and of the 45 players who had qualified to take part in the third and fourth rounds the great bulk no doubt had some hopes of getting into the severely-restricted list of prize-winners. James Braid, although not at the head of the list at the conclusion of the second round, was only one stroke behind Rowland Jones, who occupied that honourable position with a score of 158. Next followed Massy and James Kinnell with 161, while at 162 there was a tie between Harry Vardon, Alex. Herd and R. Thomson, the last-named being Braid's successor at Romford. Walter Toogood and Ernest Gray tied at 163, while J. H. Taylor had only been able to come within seven strokes of the leading score, in which position he was joined by J. Sherlock, Willie Park, and Tom Williamson. Here was a nice opportunity for one or two of the players a little down the list to come away with a strong game and displace the leaders.

Attention was devoted very largely to J. H. Taylor, who won at St. Andrews both in 1895 and 1900. Unfortunately for him the weather and the condition of the course was against his special kind of play. Pitching up to the hole was altogether out of the question and running up was the order of the day. Rowland Jones failed to maintain the high character of his play in the second round, as he took 87. A crowd of spectators followed the fortunes of J. H. Taylor.

He began well with a 4, but a hooked drive led to a 5 at the next. At the fifth he had the misfortune to see his ball roll into a bunker after striking one of the numerous hillocks. Exercising to excellent effect his powers of recovery he holed out in the par score of 5. Under all the circumstances his score of 38 out was very good, but it might have been a couple of strokes better. One or two slips in the return journey led to a score of 40 for that half, his total being thus 78. This gave him an aggregate of 243 for the three rounds. Massy and James Kinnell, with steady scores of 82, had the same aggregate.

Braid took away with him a great "gallery," for he was already looked upon as an almost certain winner. He began with a 4, which was nearly a 3. Over-approaching at the second led to a 5, but thereafter his play was perfect. After two terrific wooden club shots at the long hole out he got a brilliant 4, and he all but got the next in 3. At the turn his total was only 36. At the short hole in he was bunkered, and took 5. The long hole in cost him 6 in consequence of misjudgment in putting. When seven holes in had been played Braid had a 5 and a 4 to equal Taylor's 78 and thus to retain his lead of six strokes over that dangerous

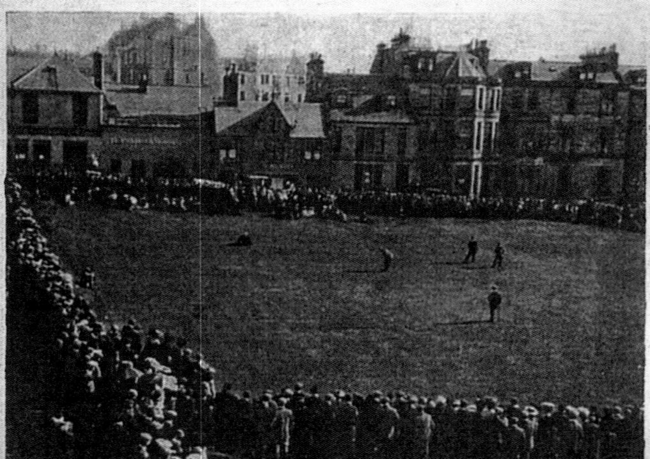

THE CROWD AT THE LAST GREEN.

BRAID STARTING FOR THE LAST ROUND.

rival. He succeeded in this object, but not without a great effort. At the "death-trap" he narrowly escaped running into the road with his second shot. Then he had an awkward "shoulder" to play over and he carefully inspected the ground. There was just one level spot, about a yard or so square, and he pitched dexterously on to it, but the ball very nearly kicked into the road or among the feet of the spectators. Then he was rather short with his approach putt but got down the next and so secured his 5. At the last hole he also got his 4 all right, but he was somewhat assisted by a fortunate accident. His second shot was pulled and seemed to be going well towards the club-house steps when it was stopped by the crowd congregated there to witness the play on the last green. Braid now assumed the lead with an aggregate of 237, and no score was attained nearer to this than the 243 of Taylor, Massy and Kinnell.

The aggregate of Rowland Jones, Herd and Sherlock was 245. Tom Williamson, with an excellent round of 79, and R. Thomson, with 82, managed to beat this trio by a stroke. Tom Watt, a Scotsman engaged at Southport, in spite of a 7 at the seventh hole, also had a score of 79 for the third round, but his aggregate of 250 was beaten by E. Gray (247), E. Ray and T. Simpson (248) and A. Kirkaldy (249). Harry Vardon played at times almost as brilliantly as ever but lacked his old consistency, and seemed as much troubled as anyone on the glassy greens. For the third round he took 84, which left him with an aggregate of 246, no fewer than nine strokes behind Braid.

Final Round.

When the last round was commenced, therefore, Braid was a prime favourite, and some 4,000 spectators attended him on his journey round the course. He commenced this time with a 5, in consequence of pitching his second too strongly over the Swilcan Burn. He took the same number for the second, where his run up was rather short. He very nearly got a 3 at the third with a five-yard putt, and he secured another 4 at the fourth amidst encouraging applause. Again at the long hole he had a long putt for a 4, but did not succeed in holing it. He nevertheless reached the turn in 38, and only wanted a score of 40 in to make him absolutely safe.

He started homewards auspiciously with a 4, and followed this with another 4 at the Eden hole in. Then came a 5 at the twelfth, consequent on a misjudged approach and a long putt that failed by an inch of its goal. With two long shots Braid was on the edge of the big thirteenth green, and he was down in two more. At the long hole in he had a possible putt for a 4, after three perfect shots, but just missed it. In playing his second to the fifteenth Braid visited the railway. He got well off the permanent way but the ball pitched among the spectators and was stopped from running. After these vexations he almost secured a 5, the actual score being 6. Disaster seemed to be impending at the sixteenth. Braid's partner, Robert Simpson, found one of the pot bunkers—"spitoons," they have been irreverently named—and Braid himself was caught in one 20 yards further down the course. The latter played a long shot out, but the ball ran on to the railway line once more near to the green and was found in the four-foot, about six inches from the right-hand rail and close up to the sleeper. Braid failed to get the ball away at the first attempt and the crowd held their breath. The score, so good at the turn, was now beginning to mount up, and a few more mistakes and accidents might mean the loss of the cup and medal. The next stroke, however, sent the ball over the railway fence and across the green at the end. A well-played approach left the ball within six inches of the hole and, in spite of two shots lost on the railway, a 6 was recorded. Taylor had already returned with an 80, giving him a grand aggregate of 323. Braid was now 72 for sixteen, and thus had an advantage of 14 strokes over Taylor with only two holes to play. Massy was two strokes higher than Taylor, and Kinnell was one stroke more. Herd and

Vardon were both playing only a moderate sort of game, and Braid had little to fear, therefore, from anybody. Two powerful shots took him within 30 yards of the "death-trap" green, and a nice run up left him with a four-yard putt for a 4. This he missed, but scored a par 5, and he was still ten strokes the better of any return already made. The last hole was safely taken in a fair 5, and immediately the stalwart Scotsman had holed out his last putt he was surrounded by a surging crowd and lifted shoulder high, while hundreds of hands were held out to grasp his enthusiastically while he was congratulated warmly on what was felt to be a certain victory.

No one really challenged his supremacy, and the only player who disputed with Taylor for the honour of retaining the second place was Rowland Jones, who completed the fourth round in the fine score of 78. He was only 3 over 4's with three holes to play, but each of these last three holes cost him five strokes. Even so his grand total was the highly meritorious one of 323, exactly Taylor's figure. The next best proved to be James Kinnell, who, after being off his putting for a long time, had come back to it, with happy results. The extreme steadiness of his game is revealed by his four returns of 82, 79, 82 and 81. The remaining couple who secured places in the short prize list were A. Massy and E. Gray.

The scores of the former—81, 80, 82 and 82—showed that he, too, had played very consistent golf; but Gray was variable, his returns being 82, 81, 84 and 78. Every one of the six prize-winners did very good work.

It was quite a new experience for Harry Vardon not to be included in the prize list. His brother Tom, who had qualified for the concluding rounds, failed to put in an appearance, and Mr. John Graham, jun., after taking 85 for the third round, retired. Alfred Toogood, who had made a bad start on the first day, when he was far from well, also retired, as did H. Cawsey (Ashford).

The prizes were presented to the winners by Mr. Stuart Forthringham, ex-captain of the Royal and Ancient Golf Club.

Appended is a list of the prizes won and of the scores returned :—

	1st rd.	2nd rd	3rd rd	4th rd	Total
J. Braid, Championship Cup, gold medal, and £50	81	78	78	81	318
J. H. Taylor, £20	80	85	78	80	323
R. Jones, £20	81	77	87	78	323
J. Kinnell, £10	82	79	82	81	324
A. Massy, £7 10s.	81	80	82	82	325
E. Gray, £7 10s.	82	81	84	78	325
R. Thomson	81	81	82	83	327
J. Sherlock	81	84	80	83	328
H. Vardon	80	82	84	83	329
T. Simpson	82	88	78	81	329
E. Ray	85	82	81	82	330
J. Rowe	87	81	80	82	330
Tom Williamson	84	81	79	87	331
W. Park	84	81	85	81	331
A. Herd	80	82	83	87	332
T. G. Renouf	81	85	84	83	333
A. Smith	81	88	86	78	333
T. Watt	86	85	79	85	335
A. Simpson	87	84	81	83	335
J. White	86	83	83	83	335
J. Johnstone	85	86	84	80	335
P. Hills	87	84	84	81	336
F. Collins	86	86	83	81	336
A. Kirkaldy	83	83	83	89	338
W. Hunter	84	85	88	81	338
J. Hepburn	84	84	87	83	338
E. Foord	85	86	84	83	338
W. Toogood	80	83	87	89	339
D. Stephenson	84	86	83	86	339
J. Kay	85	83	85	87	340
J. B. Batley	88	82	80	91	341
W. Fernie	83	86	82	90	341
H. Hunt	81	89	84	89	343
J. Parr	86	82	86	89	343
B. Sayers	84	88	85	87	344
A. Matthews	84	84	87	92	347
W. E. Reid	81	88	85	94	348
C. Gibson	87	85	85	91	348
J. Taylor	89	83	91	88	351
R. Simpson	87	85	90	90	352
J. Johnstone	87	81	94	91	353

The detailed scores of the competitors at the head of the list were as follow :—

James Braid.—First Round.

4 4 6 4 5 6 5 4 4=42 ; 4 4 4 4 4 5 4 5 5=39=81

Second Round.

5 5 5 4 5 4 5 3 4=40 ; 3 4 4 4 5 5 4 5 4=38=78

Third Round.

4 5 4 4 4 4 4 3 4=36 ; 4 5 5 4 6 5 4 5 4=42=78

Fourth Round.

5 5 4 4 5 4 4 3 4=38 ; 4 4 5 4 5 6 6 5 4=43=81

J. H. Taylor.—First Round.

4 4 4 5 5 4 4 3 5=38 ; 4 3 4 5 6 4 4 7 5—42=80

Second Round.

4 5 6 5 5 5 4 4 4=42 ; 4 3 4 5 6 4 6 6 5=43=85

Third Round.

4 5 4 5 5 4 4 3 4—38 ; 5 3 5 4 5 5 4 5 4—40=78

Fourth Round.

4 4 5 5 5 5 4 3 4=39 ; 4 3 4 5 5 5 5 5 5=41=80

Rowland Jones.—First Round.

5 5 4 5 5 4 4 4 5=41 ; 5 4 4 5 7 3 4 4 4=40=81

Second Round.

3 5 6 5 5 4 4 3 4=39 ; 4 4 4 4 5 4 3 5 5=38=77

Third Round.

4 4 5 5 8 6 4 3 4—43 ; 5 4 4 4 6 6 4 6 5=44=87

Fourth Round.

5 4 4 3 5 3 5 3 5=37 ; 4 4 5 4 5 4 5 5 5=41=78

The arrangements for the meeting were smoothly carried out by Mr. C. S. Grace, secretary of the Royal and Ancient Club, acting under the directions of the Council.

BRAID DRIVING AT THE FOURTEENTH TEE.

209

THE LATEST IMPROVEMENTS AT ST. ANDREWS,

Hugh Hamilton replaced me two years ago and has already made his mark !

He had experience as Keeper at North Berwick before going to Portrush where I met him when laying out four fine courses in Ireland – Rosapenna, Lahinch County Down and holes at Portrush

Past Open Champions up to 1905

Back – Jamie Anderson Bob Martin

Hugh Kirkaldy Willie Fernie

Seated Willie Park Jnr.

Jack Simpson

J H Taylor, Jack White, John Ball, Harold Hilton, James Braid, Self, Bob Ferguson, Willie Auchterlonie

Seated front Sandy Herd

Harry Vardon

211

DEATH OF MR JAMES MORRIS

Mr James Morris, the only surviving son of Old Tom Morris, died at his father's house on Sunday last. In his early manhood Jamie, as he was familiarly known, was one of the prettiest golfers in the country, and he took part in many important matches. On one or two occasions championship honours seemed to be within his grasp, but notably in the year 1876 a fatal penultimate hole, the crucial 17th, at St Andrews in the second round shattered his hopes and robbed him of victory. On this occasion he had two sixes to win, but bad luck necessitated a 9 and a 6 being recorded. At the Championship meeting at Prestwick in 1878 Jamie was among the early arrivals, and his score was so good that he was congratulated on being the probable winner. Bob Kirk, however, came in with one less, and then Jamie Anderson followed with two less which won him the championship. On two consecutive occasions he played his own ball against the best of two and the best of three amateurs' balls respectively, accomplishing the round at St Andrews in the very fine totals of 78 and 77, a remarkable feature of the case being that every single half round was below 40 – viz., 39 and 39, 38 and 39. He excelled in putting, and unlike his famous brother Tommy, he could putt indifferently well with any sort of instrument which the wit of man has devised for the purpose. His splendid pluck also enabled him to pull off many stiff matches. About 20 years ago Jamie played Willie Campbell of Musselburgh in a home – and – home match for £25 a – side. Jamie pulled the match out of the fire and won after an exciting finish, by one hole. Campbell feeling the stigma of defeat, a few months later, played a return match with Jamie and had the satisfaction of defeating him. It was Jamie Morris and Jamie Anderson who organised many of the great golf matches at St Andrews in their heyday. The St Andrews Golf Club was at its strongest 20 years ago, and a challenge match was arranged between 7 of their best players and 7 of the local professionals. Jamie Morris was chiefly responsible for the arrangements on this occasion, and he played for the professionals who proved the victors.

In 1887 Jamie equalled his brother Tommy's score of 77 for St Andrews Links, which had been the record of the Old Course since 1869. This record was further reduced by Hugh Kirkcaldy in 1888 by a score of 74. The details of Jamie Morris's score were:-

Out, 4 4 4 4 5 5 5 3 4 – 38
In, 4 3 3 5 5 5 5 5 4 – 39 - 77

He was proud of this feat, and nothing pleased him better when showing off his own and his brother's trophies than to point to a photograph of the two brothers, the subscription on which was the mystic number "77." An attack of rheumatism many years ago laid him aside, and from that time till his death the only connection he had with the game was the managing of his father's clubmaking business. He had been ill for some time, and his death was not expected. He was 52 years of age, and unmarried. The funeral which took place on Wednesday was largely attended, many members of the Royal and Ancient, New, and other Golf Clubs being present. Impressive services were conducted by the Rev. James Wallace, Town Church. The pall-bearers included deceased's father (Old Tom Morris). Out of respect for deceased the flags for the various Clubhouses, &c., were half-mast, and the blinds of the shops and houses *en route* to the burying ground were drawn.

The last photograph I have of J.O.F.
and the shop. me hanging out the window
-- and Bob twice winner of the Open here
still working in the shop (second left).

213

Tommy

J.O.F.

In last week's issue of *The World* we have some interesting remarks on "the Nestor of Golf," from which we give the following :—

"Tom Morris' home is characteristic of him. A large window looks out upon the first hole, the club house, and the sea, of which he says, he "never wearies." Above his mantel-piece hangs a large frame containing full-length photographs of his famous son and champion golfer, "Tommy," and of his other son, "Jimmy" (J.O.F.) Between the two lads is a portrait head of himself. Under the photograph of each son is a record of his best score in and out the St. Andrews' links. From it you see that Tommy, in 1869, went out in 37 strokes and returned in 40, making a total of 77. In 1887 Jimmy went out in 38 and returned in 39, making the same magnificent total as his brother. The walls of Tom's sanctum are covered with photographs of great golf-matches and famous golfers, professional and amateur; Allan Robertson's occuring most frequently among the former, and Colonel Fairlie's of Coodham, among the latter. His bedroom is similarly decked, and on his toilet table there are heaps of golf-balls; if he does not dream of his favourite game, it is not the fault of his surroundings. In his sitting-room, is preserved the famous trophy, which became his son's property through three consecutive wins. The champion belt is of red morocco, with rich silver ornamentations bearing golfing devices. It was won thrice by Willie Park, once by Andrew Strath, four times by Tom himself, before it was finally won by young Tommy his son. Sitting in his easy chair, in deliberate tones he will tell you all about this and other golfing feats. You hear that he was born in St. Andrews, and that he was seventy-three years of age last June; that he began to play Golf when he was six or seven, 'maybe younger.' so you may say he has played for sixty seven-years. He was apprenticed when quite a laddie to Allan Robertson, the famous golfer and ball-maker. Balls were then made by compressing a hatful of feathers into a little pocket of bull's hide cured with alum. The operation involved pretty hard work. "Ye were just like a kind o' shoemaker; for after ye had filled them ye had to sew them." They were shaped more like an egg than the perfect round gutta now in use. There was a prejudice against the guttas when they first came in, and especially upon the part of the makers of feather balls. Allan Robertson was particularly sore at the innovation, and his prejudice led to a rupture in the business relations of Tom and himself, though it never interfered with their friendship."

I think it's time
to stop this
scrapbook again
I'm on my own - but
I still have my faith
I've been a Kirk
elder for years,
and surrounded by
some fine folk.

written 13 years ago

T. MORRIS
7
T. MORRIS

On Sunday the 24th of May 1908

Tom Morris died.

It was just three weeks before his 87th birthday

I, Agnes Bayne Hunter (granddaughter) complete

this scrapbook on his behalf. 30-9-1910.

I am the oldest of four grandchildren of Tom Morris. My parents first son was born three months after the death of "Young Tom", and was named Tommy Morris Hunter, but died two months later

I was born 21-6-1877
My brother William - 13-6-1879.
Sister Elizabeth - 24-7-1883
And Jamesina - 25-6-1886
(She was born here five months after our fathers tragic death at Mobile - Alabama - in 1886.)

As far as I can ascertain, Grandpa had three sisters, and three brothers - sisters were - Janet - 11-7-1809: Margaret - 14-1-1816 Jean - 24-8-1823.

Tom was born - 16-6-1821. I know one of his brothers, George, was a prominent golfer who was professional at Carnoustie for a while. George laid down the first holes at Hoylake, which his son Jack has run since 1869. Jack, and his brother George were among the pall bearers at the funeral alongside my brother William Bruce Hunter and my husband - William Rusack. — PHOTOGRAPH — myself in foreground, "Old Tom" in first automobile - 1902, purchased by my husband

Inscription on my mothers family bible

"From Tom Morris, St Andrews
To -
His only daughter
(Lizzie (Elizabeth)
Married to James Hunter
25th February - 1875.

GOLF ILLUSTRATED.

Death of Tom Morris.

IT is with the deepest regret that we record the tragic death, on Monday afternoon, of Old Tom Morris, the veteran St. Andrews golfer. The circumstances were that Tom, who was in his usual health, had gone down to the New Golf Club, of which he was a member, and, after staying in the club-room there for a time, had got up, intending, it is thought, to go to the lavatory; but, mistaking the door, he opened one immediately next to it, leading, with a long stair, to a cellar, and down this, fully eight feet,

Tom fell. When found he was still alive, and was taken in an ambulance to the Cottage Hospital, but he died soon afterwards.

The news of the well-known golfer's death cast a gloom over the city.

Tom Morris and "Silver."

Death of Old Tom Morris
"The Grand Old Man of Golf"

The closing days of the Grand Old Man of Golf were abruptly terminated in his native city last Sunday under sad circumstances. As was his wont, he had "daundered" along to the New Club, (of which he was an honorary member), about four o'clock in the afternoon to have a chat with some of his friends. A few minutes after his arrival he left the Club-room, and almost immediately the noise of someone falling was heard from the vicinity of the passage. Investigation was at once made, and Old Tom was found in an unconscious condition at the foot of the cellar stair, which leads from the passage. He was removed immediately to the dining-room where he was examined by Doctor Paton, who found that the base of the skull had been severely injured. The doctor held out little hope of recovery, but in order to ensure the best treatment, Old Tom was removed in an ambulance van to the Cottage Hospital. There he passed away a few minutes after being admitted. Almost a nonagenarian, Old Tom's faculties were fast going, and he was becoming very absent-minded. The cellar door and the lavatory door of the New Club are in the same passage, and it is quite evident that Tom had mistaken the cellar door for the lavatory.

THE LATE GRAND OLD MAN OF GOLF.

Tom Morris, of St Andrews, met his death accidentally on Sunday, May 24th, 1908. He was born in North Street, St Andrews, in June 1821, and was thus close on his 87th birthday. The sad news came as a shock to his fellow-citizens, for as Tom had been going about as usual, his end was not expected. Not only in St Andrews was the profoundest regret expressed at the loss of so unique a personality, but throughout the whole golfing world. Under Tom's fostering care St Andrews Links maintained their premier position, and his services were frequently in request when new greens were to be laid out in different parts of the country. Tom was devoted to the care of the Links, and the utmost confidence was reposed in him. His word was law on most matters relating to the control of the Links. During his career at St Andrews Tom came in contact with representatives of all grades of Society from Royalty downwards, and his fine personality impressed everyone. Tom was always natural. He never assumed any airs, and stuck faithfully to his native "Doric." Many writers on golf have expressed their appreciation of Old Tom as a man. Mr Everard sums him up admirably in the following sentence :—" Never could there be met with a more perfect specimen of what is called Nature's gentleman than Old Tom " ; and this has been an opinion which has been universally assented to. Mr Horace Hutchinson wrote of Old Tom— " Most remarkable of all is the unvarying sweetness of his temper and courtesy, which have won him the hearts of all who ever played or came in contact with him, and doubtless gone very far to win him many of his matches."

Scotsman
25. V. 08

like many of grandpa's early scraps
this one has faded a bit already.

ACCIDENTAL DEATH OF A FAMOUS GOLFER.

TOM MORRIS'S CAREER.

Tom Morris, of St Andrews, met his death yesterday afternoon under circumstances of a tragic character. Old Tom, as he was familiarly called, had been spending an hour in the New Club, of which he was an honorary member, and between three and four o'clock he was found lying in an unconscious condition on the floor of the wine cellar. In the lobby of the ground floor there are two doors—one leading to the lavatory accommodation, which is on the floor level, whilst the other door opens directly on to a flight of eleven steps leading to the wine cellar, the floor of which is constructed of concrete. No one witnessed the accident, and it is conjectured that the veteran golfer had taken the wrong door and fell to the bottom of the stairs. When picked up he was unconscious. The ambulance van was at once called for, and he was removed shortly after five o'clock to the Cottage Hospital. He had not, however, been many minutes in the institution when he expired. An examination was made of the body by Dr Hunter Paton, and he found two contusions at the base of the skull sufficient to account for death.

Last week Tom Morris was in his usual cheery condition on the links, taking great interest in the Ladies' Golf Championship, and was looking remarkably fit and well for one of his advanced age, he being within a month of completing his 88th year. Deep regret was expressed in St Andrews at his tragic end. The funeral will take place on Wednesday afternoon at two o'clock.

The death of Tom Morris, of St Andrews, removes one of whom it might be said that he was known in almost every part of the civilised world. Several generations of golfers have arisen since first he drove a ball on the old course, and there are few playing golf to-day to whom his name was not familiar. His death snaps the main link connecting the past with the present. He had seen golf progress from the time when it was the pursuit only of a small section of the population until now, when few, in Scotland at least, may be said to be outside the ranks of the great army of golfers; and though in recent years the club had been laid aside for the

to mature old age. "Born and bred at St Andrews, and a gowffer a' ma days," was how Tom Morris summed up his connection with the Royal and Ancient game.

The son of a letter-carrier, Tom Morris was born in St Andrews on 16th June 1821, and as far back as he could remember he carried a club in his hand. Even at the age of eight he had few rivals in the Royal and Ancient game. His introduction to a professional career dated from the time when at fifteen he was apprenticed to the renowned Allan Robertson, then the greatest living master of the game. Bred in the home of the game, and instructed under such a tutor, it was not surprising that Morris soon began to acquire great proficiency in the game and to earn distinction on the links. His first public appearance, so to speak, was in 1849, when, as partner with Allan Robertson, he played in a match for £400 against the brothers William and James Dunn, of Musselburgh, and it was mainly due to the efforts of Morris that he and his partner succeeded on the last day of the match, after being four down with eighteen to play, in winning the stake. In 1851, at the age of thirty, he left the employment of Robertson under rather peculiar circumstances. Up to that time the feather balls had been used almost exclusively, but now the gutta ball was beginning to make headway. Fearing the new invention would damage their business, ball-makers resolved to discourage its use in every possible way, and it was well known that Robertson was one of those who would not tolerate it within his premises. In an evil moment Tom was tempted to play with the new ball, and the offence having come to the knowledge of Robertson, a dispute arose between the two men, the result of which was that they parted company. Shortly afterwards Tom left St Andrews for Prestwick, having been persuaded in this course by his old friend, Colonel Fairlie, of Goodham, and there for twelve years he played possibly the finest golf of his life, for it was while he was at Prestwick that he won the first and second of his four championships. In the first championship contest in 1860 Morris was only one stroke behind the winner, but next year he succeeded in carrying off the championship belt, and after repeating his brilliant performance in 1862 he was champion again in 1864 and 1867. Had it not been that about the last-mentioned date there arose a new star in the golfing firmament in the person of his son—"Young Tom"—the championship belt would in all probability have again been his.

His first public appearance, so to speak, was in 1849, when, as partner with Allan Robertson, he played in a match for £400 against the brothers William and James Dunn, of Musselburgh, and it was mainly due to the efforts of Morris that he and his partner succeeded on the last day of the match, after being four down with eighteen to play, in winning the stake. In 1851, at the age of thirty, he left the employment of Robertson under rather peculiar circumstances. Up to that time the feather balls had been used almost exclusively, but now the gutta ball was beginning to make headway. Fearing the new invention would damage their business, ball-makers resolved to discourage its use in every possible way, and it was well known that Robertson was one of those who would not tolerate it within his premises. In an evil moment Tom was tempted to play with the new ball, and the offence having come to the knowledge of Robertson, a dispute arose between the two men, the result of which was that they parted company. Shortly afterwards Tom left St Andrews for Prestwick, having been persuaded in this course by his old friend, Colonel Fairlie, of Goodham, and there for twelve years he played possibly the finest golf of his life, for it was while he was at Prestwick that he won the first and second of his four championships. In the first championship contest in 1860 Morris was only one stroke behind the winner, but next year he succeeded in carrying off the championship belt, and after repeating his brilliant performance in 1862 he was champion again in 1864 and 1867. Had it not been that about the last-mentioned date there arose a new star in the golfing firmament in the person of his son—"Young Tom"—the championship belt would in all probability have again been his. Between them the father and son held the golfing championship for eight years, and though three others have equalled Old Tom's achievement of winning the Championship on four occasions, it has never been excelled. Apart from his championship successes and the match above referred to, Morris was of course engaged in many memorable encounters on the links, far too numerous to be treated here. In connec-

was much sought after, and when the boom in golf took place some years ago he planned many courses in different parts of England and Scotland.

The memory of Morris will be cherished not only on account of the high position which he occupied among the golfers of his day, but as the devoted and much-esteemed servant of the Royal and Ancient Club, a position which brought him into close touch with many of the leading

recreations. "Courteous to all alike," writes one who knew him intimately, "he was as much at ease in the presence of royalty as when playing a match with his own particular crony." By all classes from message boy to millionaire, from caddie to club captain, Tom was regarded with a peculiarly intimate feeling of esteem. By his deeds on the golf links he no doubt exercised a great influence, but above all it was his life-long association with the city and his gentlemanly bearing and genial disposition that secured for Tom Morris the high place he occupied in the estimation of all in St Andrews. He never presumed. If he knew he had earned the respect and confidence of the members of the club, he did not forget what was due of a servant to his master. At the same time his word was law unto all on the links, and carried with it an authority probably greater even than that of the Convener of the Green Committee. An incident in the final round of one of the St Andrews tournaments may be recalled in illustration. Before the players started the late Mr Cathcart of Pitcairlie suggested to those around the first tee that they should be careful to see that the competitors got fair play, and that there should be no unseemly scrambling and crushing around the greens. But no sooner had the balls been played over the Swilcan Burn than there was a general stampede for the Bridges. "Stop, stop," shouted Tom at the top of his voice; "did ye no hear what Mr Cathcart said?" Instantly all within hearing drew up. Tom had spoken. And no better example of his fine character could possibly be found than that which was furnished on one occasion when he was playing the late Captain Broughton. At the High Hole Tom's ball was lying in bents, and when he had played "three more" he was advised by the Captain to give up the hole. "Na, na," said Tom, "I'll maybe hole this." "I'll give you £50 if you do." "Done with you, Captain," said Tom. He holed at the next attempt! The following morning the Captain arrived at Tom's shop with the £50. "What is this?" said Tom. "What you won yesterday," was the reply. "Take it away," retorted the old man; "we were just in fun." His respect for the Sunday and his aversion to Sunday golf were well known, and he has left behind him a dictum which will find supporters whenever and wherever the question of Sunday play is raised—"If the players dinna want a rest on Sunday, the green needs it." "A great and good man" was how A. K. H. B. spoke of him, and one who knew him when at the height of his fame has left it on record that with his genial countenance, penetrating eye, imperturbable temper, unflinching courage, and indomitable self-control under circumstances the most exasperating, he was an honour to himself.

GOLF ILLUSTRATED.
JUNE 5, 1908

St. Andrews Gossip

FUNERAL OF OLD TOM MORRIS.

LE roi est mort, such has been the feeling in St. Andrews since that fatal Sunday, May 24th, when our Grand Old Man passed away from us; *le roi est mort, vive le roi,* it is said, but alas ! St. Andrews knows that a place has been left vacant in her life, in her associations, and in her affections, which will not be filled again in a like manner for many a long day, if ever. To those who had never seen him at all, or even but rarely, he was but a name, a revered and respected one, no doubt, but to us who have lived alongside of him, have seen him every day and chatted with him, he was a personal friend, and the wrench is a severe one. Even now it is hard to realise that we shall never see him more in his accustomed place ; and one can almost imagine one sees him sitting at his shop door yet, beside one or other of his old friends, as was his wont in the warm summer days ; but no, it is a memory only. In the "Beginning of My Golf", by Tom Morris, which appeared some time in these columns, and afterwards, along with others, in book form, he concluded his reminiscences by saying : "I have never had the slightest cause to regret having returned to my dear native town, where everyone is my friend, and in which I don't think I have a single enemy": and that was most true, for he was revered, respected and beloved of all, and St. Andrews is immeasurably the poorer, and the attractions of the environment of her links lessened by the death of our Grand Old Man. His achievements in the golfing world were great, and will be handed down from time to time ; but the great moral of his life was that, no matter in what sphere, it is character that achieves the greatest victories. Old Tom was great as a golfer, but greater still as a man.

On Wednesday, all St Andrews turned out to pay their last respects to their departed hero. It was a glorious summer day, and the links looked beautiful and tempting, but, save a few players in the very early morning, there were no golfers on the course at all during the day. An unusual stillness had settled over the links, it was a stillness and quiet which, despite the glory of the day, told of the sadness of the ceremony that was to be carried out, for he who had played over and carefully tended to these links for well nigh forty years, was to be laid to rest that day in the Old Cathedral burying ground. Up town there were also many signs of mourning ; the places of business were all closed, and over the Town Hall buildings and other public places the flags were flying at half-mast high ; and no doubt at the funeral hour the thoughts of many in all quarters of the globe would be turned towards St. Andrews and the sad ceremony that was being reverently enacted there.

The coffin had been removed from his house at the links to St. Mary's Church in the early morning, and placed, covered with beautiful wreaths, in front of the pulpit. There was a large congregation present at the funeral service, which was conducted by the Rev. P. M. Playfair and the Rev. W. H. Leatham. When the service was over a long procession was formed outside, including a great many members of the Royal and Ancient, St. Andrews, and other local golf clubs. The members of the Royal and Ancient were preceded by Mr. Nicholas Robb, the club officer, and Mr. Hugh Hamilton, the greenkeeper, carrying the club's silver clubs and balls draped in crape ; and the St Andrews Club also had their emblems thus ; behind them came the Parish Kirk Session, the local professional golfers and caddies, and the general public. As the procession wended its way through the streets it was witnessed by thousands of people, the footways being thronged. On arrival at the cemetery gate, the coffin was carried shoulder-high down the Old Cathedral aisle to the grave marked by the monument in memory of Young Tommy, and after a short service, the remains of Old Tom were laid to rest beside those of his famous son. The pall-bearers were Mr. W. Bruce Hunter (grandson), Mr. Jack and Mr. George Morris (nephews), Mr. James Black, Mr Charles Hunter, Prestwick, Mr william Rusack, Jnr. (grand-daughter's husband), the Rt. Hon. the Earl of Stair, Captain of the Royal and Ancient Club, and Mr C. S. Grace, W. S. A very large number of wreaths were sent from all parts of the country. The accompanying photo shows the funeral procession passing along South Street on its way to the cemetery.

The cortége passing
allan Robertsons tombstone

Order of Service.

The Sentences.

"I am the Resurrection and the Life, saith the Lord: he that believeth in Me, though he were dead, yet shall he live; and whosoever liveth and believeth in Me shall never die."

"I know that my Redeemer liveth, and that He shall stand at the latter day upon the earth. And though after my skin worms destroy this body, yet in my flesh shall I see God: whom I shall see for myself, and mine eyes shall behold, and not another."

"We brought nothing into this world, and it is certain we can carry nothing out. The Lord gave, and the Lord hath taken away; blessed be the name of the Lord."

Paraphrase 2.

Genesis xxviii, 20-22.

O God of Bethel! by Whose hand
Thy people still are fed;
Who through this weary pilgrimage
Hast all our fathers led.

Our vows, our pray'rs, we now present
Before Thy throne of grace:
God of our fathers! be the God
Of their succeeding race.

Through each perplexing path of life
Our wand'ring footsteps guide;
Give us each day our daily bread
And raiment fit provide.

O spread Thy cov'ring wings around,
Till all our wand'rings cease,
And at our Father's lov'd abode
Our souls arrive in peace.

Such blessings from Thy gracious hand
Our humble prayers implore;
And Thou shalt be our chosen God,
And portion evermore.

AMEN.

Lesson

1st Cor., xv., 20

Hymn 255

"We have not an high priest which cannot be touched with the feeling of our infirmities."

When our heads are bowed with woe,
When our bitter tears o'erflow,
When we mourn the lost, the dear,
Jesus Son of Mary, hear!

Thou our throbbing flesh hast worn,
Thou our mortal griefs hast borne,
Thou hast shed the human tear;
Jesus, Son of Mary, hear!

When the solemn death-bell tolls
For our own departing souls,
When our final doom is near,
Jesus, Son of Mary, hear!

Thou hast bowed the dying head,
Thou the blood of life hast shed,
Thou hast filled a mortal bier;
Jesus, Son of Mary, hear!

When the heart is sad within,
With the thought of all its sin;
When the spirit shrinks with fear;
Jesus, Son of Mary, hear!

Thou the shame, the grief, hast known
Though the sins were not Thine own,
Thou hast deigned their load to bear;
Jesus, Son of Mary, hear!

AMEN.

Prayers

St. Mary's Church,

St. Andrews.

27th MAY 1908.

TOM MORRIS.

BORN 16th JUNE 1821. DIED 24th MAY 1908.

OLD TOM'S LATTER DAYS.

SOME PERSONAL REMINISCENCES BY A LIFELONG FRIEND.

IN GOLF ILLUSTRATED for September 29th, 1905, in an article entitled "The Beginning of my Golf, by Tom Morris," it is stated that he returned to St. Andrews from Prestwick in 1864. The Rev. Dr. J. G. McPherson, of Ruthven, is of opinion it was in 1862. Numerous controversies have been waged over the point. To ascertain the real facts of the case, I consulted Mr. C. S. Grace, Hon. Treasurer to the Royal and Ancient Club, and he obligingly made reference to their minutes to clear the knotty point. "Old Tom" was appointed greenkeeper in May, 1864.

In my notebook, under date May 5th, 1906, appears the following:—"Tom has been confined to the house all the week from another severe attack of lumbago, and our accustomed stroll has been abandoned. To-day his back was so painful I had literally to drag him, gently yet firmly, from his easy-chair to allow him to sit at the window for a little to rest it. He seemed loth to part from me to-day, and expressed the hope that next week would be a better one after the rain had ceased."

May 2nd, 1906. Medal Day:—"This is the first occasion since his appointment that he has been unable to attend to the starting and finish of the play for the medal competitions, and he felt the disappointment very keenly. No man had the interests of golfers more at heart than he. From his easy-chair he cannot see the players, and he harped away, wondering 'how mony times I have acted as starter on such occasions. Could ye no find oot?'—hence my appeal to Mr. Grace to learn the true state of matters and gratify his by no means unnatural desire."

Although "Old Tom" was unable even for a short time to leave his easy-chair, his interest in the proceedings never flagged. "Wha's at the flag at the end hole the day?" was his first query, as I entered his room at 11.30 a.m. "Nobody, Tom, just like an ordinary day," was my reply. He heaved a heavy sigh as if something serious had happened. Had he been as good a classic scholar as he was a golfer he would have relieved his pent-up feelings by exclaiming *Ichabod*!

As each couple started, I read out their names from the programme, and he made suitable and often pithy and characteristic remarks on many of them, *e.g.*, when Messrs. Fairlie and Balfour-Melville were announced, he said: "*That* should be a close an gude mautch, at ony rate." Pretty similar was his remark on Mr. John L. Low and his partner. When it came to Mr. Robert Maxwell and Mr. D. J. Lamb, it was somewhat like this: "Mr. Lamb has heavy metal against him the day, an'll need a' his pluck to mak' a gude feenish." On the arrival of the last couple—Mr. Edward B. H. Blackwell and partner—accompanied by a considerable "gallery," I said: "That is the last couple now, Tom, and from the clapping of hands I jalouse one of them is the winner." "Oh! that'll be Maister Blackwell, nae doot," said he. The piece of artillery used on such occasions then went bang, and shook the chair on which I sat. "Did you feel your chair shake, Tom?" "No! but that gun has made very loud reports the day. Surely Sergeant-Major McGhie has put in a dooble chairge!" and he laughed heartily. Then came the same query with which he started our conversation: "Is there naebody at the flag yet?" "No, Tom, nobody has been there to-day." Another sigh, and "Weel, that's awfu'!" The worthy old man then grew pensive, and "the light of other days" seemed to have dawned upon him, so I quietly bid him "Good afternoon" and slipped away.

THE LAST PHOTO OF OLD TOM MORRIS.
On the right of the picture is his lifelong friend, Mr. David Louden, who contributes some personal reminiscences of Old Tom on this page. The photo was taken by W. Patrick, St. Andrews, on Thursday, May 21.

Ever since I settled down in our native city—nearly five years ago—it has been my custom to finish my morning "constitutional" by resting in "Old Tom's" workshop during the winter months, or to meet him at the ladies' pavilion in summer, and chat about old times and current topics. Many a quiet pipe (and occasionally snuff) have we enjoyed together on such occasions.

In September, 1905, when he was seriously ill and unable to be about as usual, his granddaughter, Agnes Hunter, asked me, as a special favour, to walk out with him after his slow but gradual recovery, and this practice was most rigidly adhered to every forenoon from 11.30 to 12.45—Sundays excepted.

A carriage was provided for another old chum and myself to accompany him to his son's "J.O.F." funeral on April 11th, 1906, and I had also the pleasure of seeing him safely seated in the brougham of Dr. John Moir (his medical attendant), when he went to record his vote for Major Anstruther-Gray at the last General Election.

As has already been said, "Old Tom" left Prestwick in May 1864, to become custodian of St. Andrews links, and there he remained till his death, becoming every year more popular, and every year making new friends; for no one of consequence who ever visited St. Andrews, whether golfer or not, ever left without being introduced to the high priest of golf.

There have been many professional and famous men in St Andrews, but none such a general favourite as he—none whose reputation and fame are so world-wide as his. He was associated with all classes, from the late Prince Leopold to the humblest caddie, and equally reverenced by all. When Lord Roberts visited the ancient city in the autumn of 1903, what was it that chiefly engaged the attention of our Field-Marshal? Not the chapel of the Culdees, the relics of our once noble and stately cathedral, the classic colleges the "Bottle Dungeon," or the Kirk of "A. K. H. B." His lordship was taken to the links and was intensely interested in the game of golf and the worthy man who for so many long years adorned it *Requiescat in pace!*

Transcript of grandpa's dialect during a conversation with the Right Hon. Balfour.

↓

'An it had na been for gowff, I'm no sure that at this day, sir, I wad hae been a leevin' man. I've had ma troubles an' ma trials, like the lave; an', whiles, I thocht they wad hae clean wauved me, sae that to "lay me doun an' dee"—as the song says—lookit aboot a' that was left in life for puir Tam. It was like as if ma vera sowle was a' thegither gane oot o' me. But there's naething like a ticht gude-gowing mautch to soop yer brain clear o' that kin' o' thing; and wi' the help o' ma God an' o' gowff, I've aye gotten warsled through somehow or ither. The tae thing ta'en wi' the tither, I hae na had an ill time o't. I dinna mind that iver I had an unpleasant ward frae ony o' the many gentlemen I've played wi'. I've aye tried —as ma business was, sir—to mak masel' pleesant to them; an' they've aye been awfu' pleesant to me.

'An' noo, sir, to end a long and, maybe, a silly crack—bein' maistly about masel'—ye'll jist come wi' me, an ye'll hae a glass o' gude brandy, and I'll have ma pint o' black strap, an' we'll drink a gude New Year to ane anither, an' the like to a' gude gowffers.'

RECOLLECTIONS OF OLD TOM.

SUTHERLAND, who gave his name to one of the bunkers on St. Andrews course, because of the frequency with which he visited it, said of Alan Robertson, on the day of that famous golfer's funeral, "They may toll the bell, and shut up their shops in St. Andrews, for their greatest is gone."

Once more the cortége passes from the links; this time, after half a century, the city mourns Alan's friend and compeer, for "there is a prince and a great man fallen this day" in St. Andrews.

The bronzed face, with full brown-grey beard, laughing eyes, and briar-wood pipe of the veteran golfer have long seemed part and parcel, not only of the links, but of St. Andrews itself. Looking back, the most lasting impression an old player has of Tom Morris is of him either sitting in his workshop, turning out balls from Orchar's machine, or standing, flag in hand, showing the hole on the plateau in front.

As a golfer, and at his best, there was only one man to whom he would yield the palm—his own son Tommy, cut off in his prime, and who in his time was *facile princeps* on the links. He was his father's pride, and shared the joys of his many victories with him, even though the youth was at times inclined to "craw a little crouse." "My faither," he once said, "would be a fine putter, if the hole was a yaird nearer him!" But he was the only one in those days who could afford to make disparaging remarks about Old Tom's golf.

Not as a golfer alone, however, was Tom esteemed. It was to other and more valued qualities that he was indebted for his promotion to memberhip of the Kirk-Session of the Parish Church. It was during the pastorate of "A. K. H. B." that Morris was so honoured of his fellows, and the genial essayist and cultured divine used to speak of his elder with playful affection as "that great and good man, Tom Morris"; and the latter reciprocated the feeling, for while others sometimes cavilled, he was loyal to his chief to the last.

Latterly Morris became a striking example of the possibilities of golf for old age. He played as long as he could walk, and even as an octogenarian could give a good account of himself against players of a high class. Up till a year or two ago he occasionally compiled scores that would not have disfigured the record of the "Royal and Ancient" competitors. His play was always distinguished by good temper and steadiness; and if there was one counsel addressed either to pupil or partner, on which he put more stress than even on that to "tak' tent to be up on the green," it was "dinna press."

Tom's genial nature and courteous bearing made him a very desirable partner, and he was much in demand for foursome play; so that Premiers and Principals became his everyday associates. This gave him a knowledge of men, and an insight into character not otherwise easily obtainable. He was accordingly sometimes disillusionised. Playing one day with the head of a college, one whom we used to regard as a modern Chrysostom, and whom Tom partnered many a time, the couple found themselves in the happy position of dormy three. The next two holes, however, went to their opponents, and, when playing to the last hole, the Principal exhibited what ever after appeared to Tom as an extraordinary want of ordinary intelligence, for he bent down and whispered in his partner's ear: "Oh, do be careful, Tom, or we will lose it yet."

Among the many great things done by Old Tom, there was none he recounted with greater pride than the round played, more than fifty years ago, by Alan Robertson and him, when the pair eclipsed all previous records with a 79. Though the links were a bit shorter then than now, for there was no heather hole, in other respects they were more difficult. He used to say that when that round was played there had never been upon any of the putting greens either roller, mower, scythe or broom. There were no billiard-table greens then.

Old Tom lived a full-rounded life; a long and remarkably healthy one, chequered no doubt like that of others, with light and shade. He stood at the very top of his profession, and goes hence beloved and lamented by all who knew him, and it is by common consent that the lines have been applied to him:—

> "Surely never did there live on earth
> A man of kindlier nature."

* * *

The late Tom Morris was probably photographed oftener than any other golfing celebrity, but with the exception of the fine picture of him by Sir George Reid, which hangs in the Royal and Ancient clubhouse, we were not aware that his portrait was ever painted. It appears, however, that in 1891 Mr. Charles A. Sellar, R.S.W., obtained sittings from the old man when Mr. Sellar had a studio at Leuchars. We give a reproduction of the picture, which it will be seen is an excellent likeness of the famous player shown in a characteristic attitude on the links he loved so well. We understand that the portrait is now on view at Messrs. Fletcher Melville and Sons' gallery in South Street, St. Andrews, and that it is for sale. The size of the picture is four feet by three feet. Anyone wishing to make a presentation to his golf club could not wish for a more handsome and appropriate gift.

Now in the Glasgow Golf Club

PROPOSED MEMORIAL TO THE LATE TOM MORRIS

The proposal that a permanent memorial should be raised to the late Tom Morris is one that will be heartily supported in all parts of the world where golf is played. At a meeting of the St Andrews Green Committee last Saturday a movement was inaugurated to give effect to the proposal, and the Rev. P. M. Playfair on Sunday, in his appreciation of Old Tom, also supported it. As to the form the memorial should take, the idea that first suggests itself is that a statue of Old Tom should be erected at some prominent and convenient place at the Links. The natural poses Old Tom often assumed were just what would inspire a sculptor. Few men have been photographed oftener than Old Tom was, so that there should be no want of material for a sculptor to select from. But this only a suggestion on our part, and the R. and A. Committee may have a better scheme in view.

St Andrews Citizen 6th June 1908

Golf Illustrated. ←

FRIDAY, JUNE 5th, 1908.

THE TOM MORRIS MEMORIAL AT ST. ANDREWS.

The Bronze Relief in memory of the late Tom Morris was last week placed in its position underneath the clock on the West wall of the Royal and Ancient Clubhouse at St. Andrews. The Memorial is the work of Mr. Hubert Paton, Edinburgh, and on it is represented a life-size bust of Old Tom, and, as the accompanying photograph shows, the artist has succeeded in securing a very good likeness indeed; and, although many would have preferred to see the great golfer wearing his cap, as he was more familiar thus—satisfaction is generally felt at the result of the artist's work. The Memorial, which is set in a frame of grey granite, bears the following inscription: "Tom Morris, 1821-1908"; the dates of his birth and death; and so for years to come the face of our departed hero will look down on the first tee of the St. Andrews Old Course, where during his lifetime he was so familiar a figure.

This Memorial has been subscribed for by Golfers and Golf Clubs over the whole world, and besides this a bed is to be endowed in the Memorial Cottage Hospital at St. Andrews—to which St. Andrews clubmakers and caddies are to have a prior claim—to perpetuate Old Tom's memory.—J. B.

Photo by J. Patrick.

The Bronze Memorial to the late Tom Morris which has been placed on the wall of the Royal and Ancient Club house at St. Andrews.

September 1910

To TOM MORRIS

Dear Old Tom,

Will you accept for your eighty-seventh birthday this account of your long and honourable life, and of the many great matches in which you have taken part and been interested? I trust it may recall to you many happy days and many memorable triumphs in the game with which your name and that of your distinguished son will always be associated. It will also, I hope, help to preserve to new generations of golfers the charm of your personality and the memory of the "brave days of old."

With all good wishes,

Ever yours,

W. W. TULLOCH.

TOM MORRIS.

A SALUTE.

TOM MORRIS has finished his round,
He leaves us with a hand-wave;
We also signal to him that he is still our comrade,
We look to him that he will continue to watch our ways.

Not by great adventures is he acclaimed hero,
These he met on his pathway, but they were not of his seeking;
Only as friend do we see him, quietly mingling with golfers,
Gaining his triumphs almost unconsciously.

In life often stricken, but in play seldom conquered;
With equal mind Tom Morris makes no change in his faith or his fortunes;
Quietly he takes by the hand all good men,
And together they walk forward strengthened.

Most single was the love of Tom Morris for the old links of St. Andrews—
Great gift of nature to a world full of golfers
Nothing he recked of its value to city or stranger,
But the old course, for the love of itself, he nurtured most tenderly.

Loved of all golfers, Tom Morris leaves the links which lie 'tween the Swilcan and Eden;
Loving all golfers, Tom Morris still walks and plays with them, and partakes in their pleasures,
Or standing by the last hole makes the round end gladly by his converse,
Victory becoming more happy, and misfortune forgotten in cheerfulness.

. . . . . .

Patriarch and High Priest, Father and dearly-loved Friend of Golf,
At the end of your long round we salute you!
We see you make an indicative motion with your hand towards us,
We hurry forward to grasp it, hoping never to relinquish our hold.

J. L. LOW.

HISTORICAL NOTE

In 1988, I was seeking information on the 1864 Open Championship (the Belt competition), having in my possession Old Tom Morris' winning scorecard, the oldest winner's scorecard extant.

A fellow collector, Brian Hanson of Penrith, Cumbria, rang to say that several years before he had bought from a dealer in the Lake District (who specialized in railway items) a collection of early newspaper cuttings covering golf. These were pasted onto both sides of large sheets printed on what appeared to be railway ledgers. Many of the newspaper cuttings, Brian told me, were dated by hand and one had considerably more writing on it. He sent me photocopies of some of the sheets. The book dealer Norman Kerr, of Grange-over-sands, had told Brian that a few years earlier he had bought a considerable quantity of railway ephemera, including these cuttings, from a Mr. Stirling Everard, an old man at the time, who had been connected with the Gaslight and Coke Company of London.

I was immediately quite excited by the Everard connection and it occurred to me that these cuttings could have been Harry Stirling Crawford Everard's, who wrote extensively on golf for the newspapers and other publications between 1880 and 1908. I assumed that the writing was his, and that he had made use of them for information in his writings.

I therefore told Brian that I would very much like to add them to my collection, but was at a complete loss as to their value. We agreed to let Bob Grant of Grant Books, Droitwich, a specialist golf book dealer of considerable reputation, put a value on the sheets. When Bob decided on a value of a few hundred pounds, I bought them at that figure.

Two or three months went by before I made the journey to Brian's home in Penrith to collect them, and apart from a cursory glance at them, they lay in my "pending" category for several more months at home. At last, in late November/December of 1988, I finally got round to looking at the charts in some detail and to reading several sides containing the cuttings. The cuttings were almost exclusively about matches at St. Andrews and Prestwick between the great players of the day, both amateurs and "professionals," as well as reports of the spring and autumn meetings of the R & A. As I progressed with my reading, it struck me that there was a virtual total absence of materials about Leith, Musselburgh, North Berwick and the Edinburgh clubs. The cuttings were overwhelmingly about Old and Young Tom Morris, Allan Robertson, the Dunns, the Fairlies, and the spring and autumn meetings. These were H.S.C. Everard's cuttings, so why virtually no mention of the southern shores of the Firth of Forth? This, I thought, was odd, as was the fact that the Morrises and Robertson were featured so prominently. For the first time, I began to doubt that these were Everard's cuttings.

The red lights started flashing when I came across a cutting concerning a testimonial and dinner for Old Tom that was given by the Prestwick St. Nicholas Club, which had been marked by crosses in ink on all four sides. I then started to look more closely at the ink-written dates at the head of many of the cuttings. "Aug" and "1864" looked very familiar to me, arising from the fact that I had in my collection Old Tom's resignation letter "To the Committee of the Prestwick Golf Club," which was dated August 1864. Comparing the cuttings with the letter, they looked to be in the same hand—the "A," "8" and "4" being very distinctive in style.

With mounting excitement, I then looked more closely at the "railway ledgers" to which the cuttings were pasted. These were printed, "Glasgow, Paisley, Kilmarnock and Ayr Railway. Return of Daily Traffic—Passenger Department, Prestwick Station...1848." These "ledgers" had been used and they carried hand-written details of traffic carried, with a separate sheet for each day. The number of such charts is 15, giving 29 pages of cuttings (one side has no cuttings pasted to it). In addition, there is a detached end board. The significance of the fact that they were returns from "Prestwick Station" was not lost on me.

Was this, then, the personal scrapbook of Old Tom? I was fully aware of Allan Robertson's scrapbook, also randomly put together and out of chronological order. When Old Tom went to work at Prestwick, did he start his own scrapbook? And was this it? The adrenaline was flowing, but I knew that full and conclusive authentication of the handwriting was essential if it was to be shown that what I had was Old Tom's scrapbook. While I was aware that it had been said that Old Tom could neither read nor write, there was no doubt that he could sign his name (in 1904, the R & A published *signed* prints of the Reid portrait of Old Tom). Furthermore, Prestwick GC had many receipts in his hand, signed by him. I did, however, keep an open mind as to whether he could write (other than his name), in spite of me having the 1864 resignation letter to Prestwick that is signed by him. He could read, however, as it was reported that in his latter years he read the Bible every night, "the one with the big print" (now in possession of his descendant Sir Ian Morrow).

I contacted Dr. J. Day of London, a handwriting expert. The first thing I wanted to do was authenticate the 1864 signature on the resignation letter against 1896, 1904 and a proven 1906 signature in my collection. Secondly, I wanted to match the resignation letter signature to the contents of the letter and then to match the hand of the letter to the hand of the writings on the newspaper cuttings.

Dr. Day confirmed that the 1864 signature was by the same person as the 1896, 1904 and 1906 signatures, that the body of the letter was in the same hand as the signature and that the writing on the newspaper cuttings was in the same hand as the letter. Interestingly, Dr. Day reported that Old Tom's "writings show a sharp, active mentality, intuitive, creative and obsessive, almost a compulsive personality—he may have suffered some nephritic disorder in later life."

Obviously, I was elated to have the cuttings authenticated.

In 1989, while David Joy was preparing for his one-man show on Old Tom and a commercial video called "Keeper of the Green," he asked me for access to Old Tom's "scraps." This, I gladly granted. And it was the prelude to the interesting, informative and historical book that you now hold in your hands.

PETER CRABTREE